MORAL DEVELOPMENT AND POLITICS

Moral
Development
and
Politics

Edited by
Richard W. Wilson
Gordon J. Schochet

CALIFORNIA SCHOOL OF PROFESSIONAL PSYCHOLOGY
LOS ANGELES

PRAEGER

PRAEGER SPECIAL STUDIES • PRAEGER SCIENTIFIC

Library of Congress Cataloging in Publication Data

Main entry under title:

Moral development and politics.

   Includes bibliographies and index.
   1. Moral development. 2. Political psychology.
3. Political ethics. I. Wilson, Richard W., 1933-
II. Schochet, Gordon J., 1937-
BF723.M54M67   320'.01'9   79-15922
ISBN 0-03-044231-1

Published in 1980 by Praeger Publishers
CBS Educational and Professional Publishing
A Division of CBS, Inc.
521 Fifth Avenue, New York, New York 10017 U.S.A.

© 1980 by Praeger Publishers

0123456789   038   987654321

Printed in the United States of America

To

Deborah and Michael
Peter and Anne

PREFACE

The relationship of moral development to politics has attracted a large and growing interest in the disciplines of political science, philosophy, psychology, and sociology. As a modern field of inquiry, moral development first matured within psychology and is still best known by those who work in this discipline and by educators who have attempted to implement in school curricula some of the findings that have emerged from the more theoretical literature. Moral development, however, has for centuries been of deep concern to political philosophers, and more recently has attracted the attention of social scientists who work in the areas of political socialization and political leadership as well as those whose special interests concern the relationship between social structure and personality. In fact, scholars in many diverse fields have long felt that their work relating to moral development ought to be better known by their colleagues in other disciplines. This book is an initial attempt to bring the work of such scholars together and, more specifically, to address the question of the relevance of moral development studies for an understanding of politics. In keeping with this goal of convergence, the authors of the individual chapters of this book are drawn from a variety of disciplines, and they address the general topic from the distinct perspectives of their disciplines.

This collaborative volume has grown directly out of a Conference on Moral Development and Politics organized by the editors and held at the Eagleton Institute of Rutgers University April 13–15, 1978. The conference was attended by nearly all those whose work appears in this volume. Others who did not contribute papers to the publication but whose participation made notable impacts on the proceedings include Carol Amatangelo, Jerry Bailey, Harry Bredemeie, Steve Chilton, Don Cochrane, Sebastian DeGrazia, Sidney Greenblatt, David Haber, Roberta Sigel, Shanti Tangri, Amy A. Wilson, and John P. Wilson.

Most recent conferences in the social sciences have been structured around a set of previously articulated interlocking hypotheses. Given the newness of the field of moral development and politics, it was felt that such a limitation was premature and that it might well hinder rather than stimulate future work. In the initial stages of exploration of a new field, a set of a priori hypotheses or guidelines places restrictions upon data and inhibits the capacity of subsequent scholars to develop more fruitful hypotheses. For those persons who were invited to the conference, however, definitions and alternate approaches in the field of moral development were set forth at length. These definitions and approaches emerged from a flow of correspondence that preceded the conference. The authors were asked to prepare their papers quite self-consciously from the perspectives of the fields they individually knew best. Many of the papers were circulated in advance to all the participants and the conference was organzied in such a way as to maximize fruitful and critical involvement. At the conference itself efforts were made to evaluate and examine different approaches and to make these efforts themselves subjects of debate. As a result, the conference was exceptionally lively.

The material in this volume is presented in a manner that the editors hope will most clearly reveal their goals as they were initially formulated. Clearly, it is not possible for one publication to cover all aspects of this broad subject. It is hoped, however, that this volume will stimulate others to further research and that it will make apparent why the joining of moral development and politics is an exciting new field of inquiry.

The editors wish to give special thanks to the National Endowment for the Humanities for funding for the conference and for the editorial costs in preparing this volume. They are also happy to acknowledge their debt to the Rutgers University International Center for graciously providing organizational assistance both for the conference and for the preparation of the manuscript. Special thanks in this regard are due to Catherine Tranfo as well as to Grace Kurkowski and Phyllis Telleri.

CONTENTS

LIST OF TABLES

LIST OF FIGURES

INTRODUCTION

Richard W. Wilson
Gordon J. Schochet

Moral development research has been undertaken by educational psychologists and scholars in related areas for a number of years, but it is only recently that this work has attracted wider academic attention. One reason for this increasing interest is that many of the general issues raised by moral development studies have always been investigated by scholars of other disciplines. The theory of moral development, however, suggests for many the prospect of a reorientation of their traditional concerns and the possibility of new and exciting progress. Political science is certainly no exception to this generalization. Yet while political scientists have dealt with morals and moral development, their work has been done in relative isolation from one another and, in general, is unrelated to systematic efforts to evaluate the fruitfulness of this approach for the field.

Even cursory examinations of bibliographies in political science reveal a paucity of materials that directly address the relationship between moral development studies and politics. The relative absence of scholarship in this area is especially noteworthy when it is set against the background of a growing volume of literature on moral development in fields such as child development, value change, and educational and social psychology. This absence is perhaps even more remarkable when it is contrasted with the huge quantity of literature in political philosophy that addresses the question of morality in politics.

The infrequency of attempts to link moral development studies and politics suggests both the significance of and the opportunities for research in this area — opportunities that with a few notable exceptions have not yet been fully grasped. One reason for the slowness of political scientists to utilize moral development perspectives in their research may be the inherent difficulties of applying such techniques as content analysis, psycho- and sociolinguistic analysis, and systematic interviewing. However, a growing awareness in political science, and in the other social sciences generally, of the importance of this topic and of the possibilities for fruitful research suggests that this methodological obstacle can be overcome. Another and perhaps even greater hindrance is the fact that scholars who have worked on some aspect of moral development and politics and who represent a variety of disciplines have had few chances to interact with one another in terms of this common intellectual interest and research problem. These conditions have ramifications for college and graduate school pedagogy as well; students of the social sciences do not perceive moral development as an easily accessible area of research and remain relatively indifferent toward it as a perspective that has a bearing on other issues addressed by their disciplines.

The articles in this volume bridge several academic areas that have had weak interrelationships. To take only three examples at this point, the moral evaluation of political systems and recommendations about individual capacities for moral judgment and virtuous conduct are among the central concerns of political philosophers; students of political behavior and socialization are interested in the cognitive development and learning aspects of moral development theories; and educators have devised curricula for moral and civic education and for testing various moral education strategies. The relations among these various concerns are obvious enough, but they have coexisted and developed largely within their separate fields and without reference to mutual and supporting work in the other areas.

Among political scientists it is almost a point of pride for philosophers and students of behavior to ignore one another. Part of the reason for the gap between the philosophical and behavioral wings of political science is that their methodologies have diverged; moreover, theories that are germane to specific subfields have also tended to develop relatively independently. The question of morality in politics, however, is common to all areas of political science and is a unifying issue that holds out the promise of drawing scholars from various subfields into mutual dialogue. As Thomas Lickona has stated with regard to the value of moral development as an integrating concept,

[It represents] the viewpoints of cognitive-development, psychology, psychoanalysis, psychobiology, social learning theory, social psychology, education, clinical psychology, political psychology, and social ecology. Morality emerges from this multiplicity of perspectives as one of the major interdisciplinary crossroads. It offers a broad integrative framework for dealing with a wide range of theoretical and empirical concerns in the study of both child development and adult behavior; violence, altruism, criminality, cooperation, honesty, child-rearing, self-control, situational variations in behavior, modeling, the influence of heredity versus experience, bystander response to emergencies, social and political attitudes, personality functioning, and the impact of culture on socialization, to name just a few.[1]

The study of political behavior is a venerable field in both the philosophical and behavioral areas of political science. To date, however, there have been no persistent efforts to apply the growing body of theories and findings from moral development to the analysis of political behavior in either of these areas. The manner in which the development of particular moral value stances affects political behavior and the ways that certain moral behavior patterns become manifest within a given political culture are only two of the issues that could be studied with profit from the general perspective of moral development. The point is that moral development studies have matured to the extent that findings from this field can be directed to the study of political behavior, and findings from political behavior to an understanding of the operation of political systems. Conversely, the effect that particular types of political systems have on forms of individual-level moral development is also an issue of exceptional importance.

Most of the scholars interested in moral development reject the pervading pessimism of the times but recognize a need for a public ethic. The progress of modernization is accompanied by — and perhaps contributes to — a climate of aimless violence at the individual level and of warfare, even genocide, at the societal level, which, when combined with the increase in public "corruption," are more than enough to make people dubious about prospects for the future. Yet fresh findings in such fields as anthropology and sociobiology have stimulated the belief that desires to create a genuinely ethical society are neither pointless nor foredoomed to failure. There can be no question that a major and concerted effort will be needed to eliminate the present dismay, but students of moral development have not turned to the radical restructuring of society as a source for ethical conduct. Instead of adopting the Marxist and communitarian stance that has become so popular, they have opted for the liberal, individualist belief in the moral primacy of the autonomous but responsible will. How one achieves an autonomous, moral will is the root question guiding the study of moral development. Much of the interest in moral development can be seen as part of the demand for a normative dimension to the analysis of human behavior. This demand, which has been growing for some time, rejects the purely descriptive realms of psychology and insists instead that the study of both social institutions and individual behavior should be infused with the belief that ethical conduct is possible and with the knowledge that new tools for understanding how such conduct may develop are at hand.

Emphasis upon moral development as an explanatory factor has the exciting potential of leading to a deeper understanding of the relationships among political socialization, political philosophy, and the structure of political systems. Such a focus unites the behavioral and normative dimensions of the study of politics through analysis of the interaction between the environments in which people live and the dynamics of individual development. Moral development theories, which address the ethical dimensions of social behavior, provide a means for dealing with such disparate issues as human capacities, the nature of desirable social institutions, and the achievement of justice and fairness in peoples' dealings with each other.

BACKGROUND ISSUES

Moral Development

In its more narrow sociopsychological framework, the field of moral development has experienced vigorous debate and inputs from scholars of diverse backgrounds and theoretical interests. The current state of the field — at the risk of oversimplification — reflects a division, generally, between those scholars who favor a social learning approach and those whose allegiance is to the cognitive development school. The basic difference between the two approaches concerns what is regarded as the more important factor in the development of mature moral judgment — the autonomous reorganization of cognitive processes during growth, or the social inputs that affect individuals during childhood and beyond.

Social learning theorists believe that such influences as models or punishment schedules are critically important for the internalization of cultural rules. From this perspective a characteristic moral orientation for any given person is said to arise from behavioral conformity and affective adherence to social norms; these orientations themselves will presumably differ within the population of a given society due to the fact that individuals respond to stimuli during learning in a differential manner. In the sense that the norms governing behavior are different for different societies, modal moral development outcomes noted at the level of the social system are presumed to be culturally relative.

Cognitive development theorists, on the contrary, assume a correspondence or reflection between moral and cognitive development which, while not necessarily direct, is presumed to follow from an internal age-related construction and consequent reorganization of cognitive structures. Stages of moral development are said to occur in a sequential order in which each stage is a qualitatively different reintegration of previous stages deriving from a process of cognitive development that is a common human attribute. The overriding importance of social-learning influences is disputed, and the proposition is advanced that any individual in any society can achieve a specific nonrelative form of moral judgment and behavior. Since it is possible for every human being to manifest judgment patterns characteristic of any of the stages, the existence of any stage is presumed to be possible for every society; thus moral development, as a process, is conceived as essentially culture-free.

This description of the two dominant schools of thought in current moral development studies does some injustice to both. Social learning theorists, for instance, do not ignore internal needs and drives or the mediating effects in learning of previously acquired dispositions. Rather, their special emphasis is on external social influences as major causal antecedents to the development of particular moral stances, and they tend to give pre-eminance to these factors. In like manner, cognitive development theorists, with their emphasis on the internal construction and reorganization of cognitive structures as the basis for the development of particular types of moral orientations, are not unmindful of external influences and, indeed, believe these to be of profound importance. Yet, while recognizing the role of the external environment in the development of moral judgment and behavior, these theorists are oriented primarily toward understanding how mental judgmental capabilities develop, and this orientation leads them to place primary emphasis on cognitive processes.

These issues in the current literature on moral development have profound implications for the study of politics. Both schools are concerned with the means of enhancing and developing more mature moral judgment faculties that can inform the behavior of citizens and leaders. The relative importance given to external influences, conceived as the general political environment or socialization input, is significantly different, however, and suggests that the conclusions formulated by adherents of one or the other approach embody widely differing options.

Morals and Political Philosophy

Political philosophy has always had at its core the relationship of social and political structures and practices to human capacities and to moral standards. From Plato and Aristotle through Thomas Hobbes, John Locke, Jean-Jacques Rousseau, Karl Marx, and John Stuart Mill, to such modern political philosophers as Herbert Marcuse and John Rawls, conflicting and speculative presumptions about peoples' moral capabilities and the nature and validity of their ethical values have formed the bases of political thought.

Theories of moral development provide a dramatic and contemporary contribution to this historical debate. Equally important, moral development theory offers a means of reuniting political philosophy with psychology proper, areas that have become increasingly separated during the last century despite their obvious relationship. Unlike behavioral psychology and its learning-theory account of values that political philosophy rejected many years ago, moral development theories take seriously and deal with those very normative issues that are vital to political philosophy. Consequently, another benefit of the introduction of moral development theories to political philosophy should be the reintegration of political philosophy with the more empirical social science disciplines, to the benefit of both areas.

It has become increasingly evident that political philosophy has suffered because of its separation from the social sciences and that the social sciences themselves have lost an important normative and critical perspective because of their divorce from political philosophy. If it is fair to say that political behavioralists have not adequately addressed the normative dimensions of politics, it is equally fair to say that political philosophers, who have addressed such issues, have done so in a speculative manner. Classical political philosophers, after all, examined the psychological bases of political morality without regard to, or knowledge of, contemporary social psychological theories. Yet both philosophical and behavioral forms of inquiry are concerned with questions such as the disposition to obey, the acceptance of the legitimate claims of others, and the ability of individuals to make reasoned judgments about right and wrong. Such questions are all integral to a proper understanding of politics and suggest, in short, that with the appropriate bridge, political philosophy and the behavioral sciences can inform each other.

Legal Codes, Formal Institutions and Moral Development

Issues concerning genocide, political repression, revolution, war, and endemic intrasocietal violence or antisocial behavior have been raised by a number of scholars.[2] Analysis generally centers on the legal, psychological and/or social antecedents to asocial, socially dysfunctional, or uncooperative and even violent behavior. Implicitly the question is asked: what social conditions and/or psychological predispositions exist to impel or motivate individuals to disrupt intra- or intersocietal life? While there is no wish to imply that every socially disruptive act is "immoral," it is asserted that analyses in this general area implicitly address the question of what patterns of moral development characterize both those who engage in disruptive behavior and those who oppose them.

CONCLUSION

The editors' own interests and intellectual antecedents mirror the problems and possibilities that have been noted above. As political behavioralist and political philosopher, respectively, their jointly held belief that the emerging field of moral development is of critical importance for the discipline of political science brought them together in mutually instructive interaction. From these initial fruitful exchanges there developed a common conviction that while moral development and politics are indeed closely linked, yet at the same time they are components of a field that is still to be defined. This search for definition, therefore, is central to the purpose and form of this volume. The articles are written by scholars with different intellectual viewpoints and no attempt has been made to impose upon them a uniformity of perspective. (Indeed, some contributors forthrightly evidence skepticism concerning the conjunction of moral development and politics.) The volume, then, accurately reflects the current stance of those with an interest in moral development and politics; different perspectives abound, and varying pathways for future research are proposed. The thread that unites this endeavor is the self-conscious belief on the part of all contributors that the ethical dimensions of political life demand scrutiny and that moral development theories may be critically relevant in this regard.

NOTES

1. Thomas Lickona, "Preface," in *Moral Development and Behavior: Theory, Research, and Social Issues,* ed. Thomas Lickona (New York: Holt, Rinehart and Winston, 1976) p. x.

2. Hannah Arendt, *On Violence* (New York: Harcourt, Brace & World, 1969); Ted R. Gurr, *Why Men Rebel* (Princeton: Princeton University Press, 1970); Irving Louis Horowitz, *Genocide: State Power and Mass Murder* (Edison, N.J.: Transaction Books, 1976); David C. Schwartz, *Political Alienation and Political Behavior* (Chicago: Aldine, 1973); and Neil J. Smelser, *Theory of Collective Behavior* (New York: Free Press, 1962).

THEORY AND CONTEXT

EDITORS' COMMENTS

The articles in this introductory part have been developed against the background of social philosophy and thus differ considerably from those of more conventional introductions. Moral development as a concept is discussed, but from the perspective of its relationship to politics. Indeed, the mutual interaction between moral development and politics is the central issue of this introductory section. The explicit debate among the cognitive development school of moral development, social learning theorists, and advocates of psychoanalytic explanations is muted here, but it is certainly to be noted in many of the later papers in this volume.

In the first chapter Irving Louis Horowitz reviews a number of important works in social philosophy that have addressed the relationship between development and politics. He points out that there are profoundly different social implications depending upon whether one is speaking of moral development or of the development of morals. A moral development process imposed upon citizens by authoritarian rulers has, in his opinion, been the general human experience. In conclusions that depart dramatically from these earlier, pessimistic comments, he suggests that the development of morals presupposes a society with a plethora of moral standards and that such a plurality and diversity of standards offers the best possibility for the genuine development of ethical citizens.

Richard W. Wilson's paper develops ideas within a sociobiological framework. Wilson argues that social cooperation is a universal quality of humans, derived from their particular development pattern. His conclusions are pessimistic, for he contends that the social and political frameworks that support forms of social cooperation have historically tended to be rigid and closed. What is more, these political inducements to cooperation have been intimately linked with patterns of individual-level moral development that foster closed and rigid moral orientations.

In the final chapter in this introductory part, Elizabeth Lane Beardsley, like Wilson, notes the negative aspects of paternalistic forms of social order. Her conclusions, however, are essentially optimistic, for she suggests that the state can genuinely foster mature moral behavior in its citizens without lapsing into paternalism. In essence, Beardsley provides a set of propositions that show how nonpaternalistic and nonauthoritarian governments may facilitate the moral development of citizens.

MORAL DEVELOPMENT, AUTHORITARIAN DISTEMPER, AND THE DEMOCRATIC PERSUASION

Irving Louis Horowitz

As a prolegomena to this paper let it be said that it is based on the premise that the development of morals is diametrically opposed to and categorically distinct from moral development. Moreover, the pluralism inherent in the study of how morals develop over time and environments is at the opposite pole from the monism inherent in the study of how a particular form of moral development is to be imposed on the human race. It has become fashionable to decry open-ended notions of human variations, and equally in vogue to identify surviving political systems with moral purpose. Moral education, the parent of moral development, has become the rage from Peking to Cambridge. The fact that different forms of morals are being taught has seemingly been downgraded in the rush to judgment, in the widely held belief that the very instruction into the moral order is some sort of cultural universal that transcends what is specifically being taught.

One's intellectual life is privy to such a barrage of rhetoric concerning a crisis in morals, breakdown in discipline, collapse of purpose, that there is a tendency to forget the dangerous consequences of living in a society in which there is no crisis in morals — only moral certitude — and in which moral purpose is imposed by a political regime with a tenacity and ferocity that makes moral doubt, even ethical confusion, a dangerous posture. The short and long of this discussion is that those who believe in democracy must have a corresponding faith in the evolution of moral choice, and individuals who, to the contrary, believe that only instruction in moral order through a preset notion of moral development will ensure the survival of civilization, have already denied the essential premises and practices of a democratic system.

RELATIVISTS AND NORMATIVISTS

The problem of moral development, then, is inherent in the coupling of the two words. Few would dispute that there is such a thing as morals, and fewer still that there is another entity called development. Whether they fit together conceptually in a neat, two-tiered package becomes a large question. The present disarray of moral philosophy has contributed to the puzzle. Ethicists are as polarized as can be. One sense of moral development is that it is historical, evolutionary, and sociological concept of expanding rights. Relativists like Richard Brandt[1] and Abraham Edel[2] have argued this thesis. There is a diametrically opposite view of moral development, advocated by people such as Leo Strauss[3] and Richard Flathman,[4] claiming a normative, natural-law foundation to human behavior, the assumption being that social obligations, like mathematical axioms can be deduced from a set of first principles.

Underlying this debate between relativists and normativists is an assumption about the degree to which options and choices in the world exist. For the relativists, choices are limited only by circumstances, and hence decision making about political issues is a series of historically conditioned searches for rights. For normativists, the world is far less permissive, sometimes even predetermined, and hence the real search ought to be for the foundations of obligations. At stake are a series of choices people make on the basis of fundamental, underlying premises of the rights and wrongs of behavior. For relativists, morals are constantly evolving in a wide-open universe, whereas for normativists, choices are made within well-understood, or at least well-defined, social structures. At the risk of turning a drastic oversimplification into caricature, what is good and what is evil for relativists constantly shifts, often according to community norms and changing external pressures. What is good and what is evil for normativists stays the same, for people do the shifting, achieving higher levels of ethical purification in the process.

Reconciliation of these two long-standing positions is in order, and many efforts in this direction are under way. The rise of both the social sciences and policy research may offer some clues to these new directions. The author proposes a retention of the normativist framework: what is good and what is evil remain essentially the same now as they were in the world of ancient Athens. To this should be added the relativistic perspective: what change drastically are the consequences of choices. Both political sociology and political psychology can shed light on the subject of moral development.

In the past, people tended to think of homocide as an evil under most circumstances, but the arbitrary termination of life has also been viewed as basically a one-to-one relationship: one person destroying another person. In the twentieth century, however, the situation is more that of one nation destroying another nation. The magnitudes, technically conditioned and depersonalized, so profoundly alter the consequences of behavior, that the same moral choices have hugely differing outcomes. There are qualitative leaps in technology that make decisions about life and death critical for large numbers.

Several caveats are in order. First, if by moral development one means that a set of goals for society determined and defined by political leadership is good and that departures from those pretested, preset norms are evil, then the phrase is simply a clever disguise for totalitarian temptations; for moral development in this sense means nothing short of the total unification of a society along a certain path, road, or in conformity with a particular model. So conceived, moral development is but an Orwellian device disguising political repression. Second, and contrariwise, if moral development is viewed in a pluralistic context, as expanding possibilities for making meaningful choices, serving both personal, particular, general, and universal goods, the phrase — moral development — can be infused with democratic meaning if the prospect of the development of a moral sensibility as an attribute of individuals is introduced. The ability to place oneself in another's position, rather than moral development as an attribute of a social system as a whole, becomes the touchstone of moral education. At such a level, moral development is related to cognitive prerequisites rather than collective demands.

Both collective and individual standpoints must be reckoned with. Those societies that have put forth eugenic theories of moral development, such as the Nazi view of the biologically healthy individual, are clearly willing to sacrifice the individual self to the organic whole. Such moral development leads to uncritical supporting of systems and ultimately outlaws all choices and decisions as attributes of unsponsored individuals. On the other hand, if the development of morals represents a statement of how each individual is ultimately responsible for, and is a repository of, both personal and general goods, the spirit of the democratic interpretation is preserved. Whether we appeal to John Locke in the British constitutional tradition or to Mahatma Gandhi in the Hindu tradition of nonviolent resistance to tyranny, such a view of a morally centered polity — in which individuals determine their own fates — has been of great significance in the evolution of societies in both the East and West.

MORAL STRATEGIES AND STRATEGIES ABOUT MORALS

Moral development can be viewed epistemologically. The process of cognition by which citizens learn to distinguish what constitutes right from wrong or good from evil is a learning situation. Moral development is a process of socialization. The literature on political socialization is by and large concerned with describing how such concepts are acquired and subsequently applied to the body politic. Studies of children's reactions to the assassination of Martin Luther King, Jr., or the late President John F. Kennedy, represent empirical studies of the process of becoming socialized into things political. The works of political scientists like Richard Dawson[5] and L. Harmon Zeigler[6] typify such orientations, and can properly be said to constitute a special sort of theory of moral development, one based on experiential adaptation, rather than a didactic set of commitments to ritualist or rote learning.

From the standpoint of political sociology, moral development can be considered moral postures that result from class, ethnic, or racial factors. Within such a social framework, moral development refers to the growth of isomorphism between human consciousness and socioeconomic interests. Specifically, moral development is viewed as representing a coalition of factors between a stake in a social order and perceived political and ideological responses. This aspect of moral development is considerably different from political socialization, for political sociology assumes a correlation between interests and behavior. The work of Karl Marx,[7] Karl Mannheim,[8] and Max Scheler,[9] among many others, suggests a special vision of moral development: the development of a set of moral postures based on class positioning and the effect of this on such ascriptive "superstructural" features as religion, culture, or race, among others.

A third notion of moral development, evolving from the Kantian tradition of transcendental apriorism, and perhaps Platonic sources as well, considers the question of moral development axiomatically, as a process of learning to distinguish truth from falsity. In this way it is assumed that individuals come closer to identifying with the true nature of a political system as they appreciate the structure of such a system. Politics in this sense represents an exiomatic vision of the moral order. Becoming political is like becoming mathematically adroit, that is, learning about those axiomatic foundations determines the logical structure of the state (in the case of Plato) or world order (in the case of Kant).

The psychoanalytic tradition has contributed a fourth perspective on moral development. Even if the obvious "moralistic" biases of Freudian psychoanalytic theory are ignored,[10] Freud — at the conscious level at least — eschewed a moral grounding for mental health or illness. This is not the case with some of the New Freudians. For instance, Erik Erikson's views on the "ages of man" provide a clear-cut prolegomena to a psychoanalytic theory of moral development.[11] The ages (or better, states) are oral, anal, phallic, oedipal, latency, and puberty. Without arguing about the presumed "intuitive righteousness" of Erikson's ages, as some have, it can be seen that the position of Erikson on theological or political figures like Luther and Gandhi[12] indicates that the post-puberty stage — extending from roughly fourteen to death — involves a powerful moral component of responsibility for behavior not carried or anticipated in the earlier adolescent period.[13]

This notion of anticipatory development, or more inclusive identities, implies a fusion of rational prognosis and moral rightness (or at least the absence of dogmatism) and a sensitivity to the diversity and complexity of the human personality. Whether such broad categories can be operationalized or, if realized, can prevent an arbitrary and capricious rendering of moral behavior is a problem faced not only by Erikson, the veritable father of the theory of human development, but by the psychoanalytic tradition as a whole. While the stages of development in adolescents are essentially behavioral, and by implication not easily subject to adult criteria of morals, just how that moral self eventually penetrates human behavior remains cloudy. Freud saw in morality a transliteration of superego and censor mechanisms, but he did not say clearly how good works become a moral good. *Civilization and its Discontents* describes the antagonistic mechanisms of work and sexuality but not how moral components infuse such broad ranging, biosocial categories.[14]

There is, in fact, a commonsensical definition of moral development that is all too easily overlooked among sophisticated analysts, that is, the notion of moral development as rendering instruction for those in need of it, a sort of gerontological vision of advice from the elderly or established to the youthful or ill advised. More than one group of those who are responsible for the current revival of interest in this subject of moral development have as their hidden agenda instruction in right morals.[15] In contrast to this is a briefer, but probably equally honorable tradition in which moral education has to do with the ability of an individual to absorb new information without those hierarchical or traditional impediments otherwise known as learning.[16] The learning concept is less taken up with status considerations of who does or does not have the right to offer instruction. Learning is a process far more difficult than teaching, since it involves the far more complex art of listening rather than speaking.

If these strategies of moral development could be kept clear of each other, many problems would dissolve, along with the linguistic ambiguity and confusions created by overlapping conceptual frameworks. However, not only are these standpoints on moral development not properly distinguished, they are further saddled by the conceptual map of social psychology in which phrases like "human development" are viewed as isomorphic with moral development and, more pertinently, in which correlated concepts of cognition and judgment, description and prescription, are muddled beyond belief. As if this situation inherited from the past is not a severe enough handicap, educators have thrown in an additional phrase for good measure — "moral education" in contrast to "affective education".[17] Here one turns full circle, with a strong tendency to equate "fundamental" with normative. Hence, pedagogical conservatives speak of moral education and the political order as an intertwined behavioral process summed up in the restoration of civics and civil behavior.[18] Deficiencies in education rather than inequalities in society are held to strict account for the current breakdown and malaise presumably characteristic of the times.

The language of breakdown and fragmentation replaces that of social structure and political system as crucial explanatory devices. As a consequence, and without too much elaboration, one can see that the ebb and flow of interest in moral development, far from being self-explanatory and transparent, is actually comprised of a series of distinctive policy frameworks — some of which offer the potential for new linkages between events and ethics, whereas others offer little more than further intellectual disputation, or worse, an end to disputation in order to disguise the paucity of naturalistic solutions to long-standing human problems.

MORAL PRINCIPLES AND PRINCIPLES ABOUT MORALS

Getting beyond strategies and addressing principles becomes the next and by far the most difficult step in evolving a meaningful statement about moral development. To take this giant step one must return to the classical statements on democratic political theory from John Locke to John Rawls, for the essence of that classic tradition is, in fact, the linkage of politics to ethics. The fundamental debate over the relationship of personal rights to social obligations is what moral development is about, and the highest form of such development is to maintain the balance, the tension, between rights and obligations. This tension — the antithesis rather than the synthesis — is precisely what justice is about, and moral development is the wisdom to engage in the conduct of justice. To resolve in some arbitrary, ultimate way the argument over rights and obligations, is to surrender the society either to the Anarch or, at the other extreme, to the Behemoth.[19] And such a resolution can be bought only at the price of democratic community. Theories that account for political obligation in terms of the consent of the governed are highly ambiguous and confusing. It is rarely clear whether laws are justified by the fact that they are "willed" by those subject to them or by the justice of what is enacted. In Locke two quite different arguments are inextricably interwoven. His aims were to defend the obligation to obey legitimate authority (that is, authority based on consent) and to defend the right to resist coercive force in the absence of legitimate authority. He based authority on contractual consent, but behind the contract are the laws of nature, and ultimately the standard is the "good of the community."[20] Since man in the state of nature has only as much power over others as he needs to preserve his own life, liberty, and security of possessions, this degree of power is all he can properly be asked to surrender to the state.

> Men being . . . by Nature, all free, equal, and independent, no one can be put out of this Estate, and subjected to the Political Power of another, without his own *Consent*. The only way whereby any one devests himself of his Natural Liberty, and *puts on the bonds of Civil Society*, is by agreeing with other Men to join and unite into a Community. . . . When any number of Men have so *consented to make one Community* or Government, they are thereby presently incorporated, and make *one Body Politick*, wherein the *majority* have a Right to act and conclude the rest.[21]

Locke used the term "consent" broadly. At first he insisted that it was consent only in the sense of voluntary agreement undertaken by people who knew what they were committing themselves to, that made authority legitimate, but later he argued that when a man inherits property, he gives consent to the state recognized by his father. In fact, consent is given tacitly whenever a man travels on the roads, takes lodging for a week, and so on. Locke's argument, that by remaining within the state and accepting its benefits one tacitly consents to its legitimacy and acknowledges an obligation of obedience to its laws, is fraught with difficulties.[22] For one thing, it removes any distinction between legitimacy and coercion. Lock could be accused of forgetting one of his primary tasks, the moral justification of the right of revolution. He avoided this dilemma by making obligation dependent on the nature of government. Men enter society with the intention of better preserving themselves, their liberties, and their properties, and the power of the government they establish can never extend further than the preservation of the common good.

It is one thing to show that people have a right not to have a government thrust upon them before a government has been founded, and quite another to argue that no one is required to obey an established government unless he or she has agreed to do so. S. I. Benn and R. S. Peters suggest that "if consent is a necessary condition for political obligation, it would deny a government any rightful authority over anyone who dissented from the basic principles of the constitution."[23] People who reject the basic assumptions of the goals of government cannot be morally obliged to obey laws, for the laws would not be their laws. On the other hand, if consent is taken as a sufficient condition for obligation, it implies that, having once submitted, one is bound to accept the consequences thereafter. This argument is not very appealing to the person who conceives of moral development as accepting postulated goals and ideals of government but disapproving of the practices of a particular government in straying from one's perception of these goals.

In order to overcome these difficulties between rights and obligations, Locke was forced to find ways to prove that men have agreed to obey, even when they have not in fact done so. In the end he virtually makes obedience imply consent. Locke failed to distinguish between how political authority arises and what makes it legitimate. As John Plamenatz correctly notes, "Political authority is always limited by the ends it ought to serve, so that, where those who have this authority do not serve those ends, their subjects have a right to resist them or get rid of them."[24] Obligation depends, therefore, not on moral development but on whether the government is such that one ought to consent, whether its actions are in accord with the authority a hypothetical group of rational men in a state of nature would give to any government they were founding.

If it could be established that a given set of political arrangements deserved one's consent, would this not make moral development irrelevant to political obligation? A distinguished line of political philosophers have taken this position. T. H. Green, for example, stated that his purpose was "to consider the moral function or object served by law . . . and in so doing to discover the true ground or justification for obedience to law." Society's claim to exercise powers over the individual rested on the fact that "these powers are necessary to the fulfillment of man's vocation as a moral being, to an effectual self-devotion to the work of developing the perfect character in himself and others."[25] Thus, laws are morally justified only to the extent that they promote the self-realization of the individual, but moral development is meaningful only if it obeys laws. This circular reasoning was no monopoly of the conservatives; liberals and socialists have developed their own variations on this theme.

Harold Laski followed Green in arguing that politics is an activity in which men work through the state as an instrument of social organization to achieve personal and social fulfillment. Laski defined the state as "an organization for enabling the mass of men to realize social good on the largest possible scale." The social good becomes "an ordering of our personalities," so that people are driven "to search for things it is worthwhile to obtain, that, thereby, we may enrich the great fellowship we serve."[26] Accordingly, it must be recognized that the moral development of individuals cannot be abstracted from the general good of other people. In this way, fabian socialism incorporated utilitarian doctrine with startling simplicity.

Explanations that suggest that the grounds of political obligation inhere in the nature and purposes of government can be criticized on the ground that it is impossible, and not necessarily desirable, to find general criteria to justify political obligation. Necessary and sufficient conditions of good government and political obligation can never be known. Only in totalitarian regimes can the aims of the state be reduced ·to one overriding purpose. Concepts such as the social good or the general welfare should not be conceived as something determinate. Nor should it be assumed that moral development means agreement about ultimate ends. In a sphere of activity such as politics, there can never be complete agreement about what counts as right, as there can be in other spheres or rule-governed activity. What reasons can be given for believing that a given state represents the "rational will" or the "common good," and by what criteria is one to be guided in deciding whether particular states or institutions conform to these requirements?

Rawls's vision of justice contains a doctrine of moral development that overcomes some weaknesses of the classical arguments, but not others. Obligations are defined by the principle of fairness. They are related to institutions or practices that can be judged by principles of justice for institutions. Obligations are thus tied to the nature and ends of government. This construct is based on a variant of contract theory, which, according to Rawls, overcomes the pitfalls of the classical theories of Locke and Rousseau. This is so because the principles of justice are those that would be chosen by rational men, acting in their own self-interest, in an initial position of equality. However, the actual adoption of these principles is purely hypothetical; all that is needed for the purposes of the theory is that the principles be adopted by fully moral persons. Confusion over the questions of how authority arises and what makes it legitimate is conveniently avoided.

Rawls maintains that "a person's obligations and duties presuppose a moral conception of institutions and therefore that the content of just institutions must be defined before the requirements for individuals can be set out." The choice of principles for individuals is simplified by the fact that the principles of justice for institutions have already been adopted. Rawls uses what he calls "the principle of fairness" to account for all requirements that are obligations as distinct from natural duties.

> A person is required to do his part as defined by the rules of an institution when two conditions are met: first, the institution is just (or fair), that is, it satisfies the two principles of justice; and second, one has voluntarily accepted the benefits of the arrangement or taken advantage of the opportunities it offers to further one's interests.[27]

There are no political obligations for people generally, since obligations arise as a result either of voluntary moral acts, which are express or tacit undertakings, or of simply accepting benefits. The first part of the principle of fairness formulates the conditions necessary for these voluntary acts that give rise to obligations, since the content of obligations is defined by Rawls as an obedience to rules of justice that specify requirements for voluntary actions. Rawls's theory also implies that it is not possible to be bound to unjust institutions or to institutions that exceed the limits of "natural duties" of individuals to one another.

The principle of fairness is related to what H. L. A. Hart calls mutuality of restrictions. In this version, moral development is defined as follows:

> When a number of persons engage in a mutually advantageous cooperative venture according to rules, and thus restrict their liberty in ways necessary to yield advantages for all, those who have submitted to these restrictions have a right to a similar acquiescence on the part of those who have benefited from their submission.[28]

The moral obligation to obey rules is a function of cooperation; people who accept legislative enactments consecrate standards of behavior. This moral reason for obeying the law is distinct from other moral reasons in terms of good consequences or the principle of fairness. Further, acceptance of the law does not imply that there will be no circumstances where disobedience is justified. The obligation to obey the law on these grounds is based on rights. The law arises between members of a particular political society, out of their mutual relationships. Again, for Hart as for Rawls, moral development is a societal balancing act preventing either the Anarch or the Behemoth from triumphing.

The principle of fairness binds only those who assume public office or state power. The implication behind Rawls's theory is that those individuals who possess the most advantages in society are those likely to accept the obligations of the state. There is a difference between institutions that apply to individuals because of ascriptive factors of birth and those that apply because individuals have done certain things as a way of advancing the ends of achievement. Thus there is a natural duty to comply with the constitution and an obligation to carry out the duties of an office. Obligation is therefore a term reserved by Rawls for moral requirements that derive from the principle of fairness, while other requirements are called natural duties.

Rawls implies that one is bound to obey the law simply because it exists. He insists that "as citizens our legal duties and obligations are settled by what the law is."[29] This is certainly true as a statement of fact. However, to fall back upon the obligatory character of law is surely to avoid the problem of moral consent. It does not solve the problem of why the presence of legitimate authority provides a ground for acting in the manner required by this authority. What the law demands and what justice requires are distinct questions, even if the two principles of justice are used by the courts to interpret and apply the law. There are two principal ways in which injustice may arise: first, current arrangements may depart from the publicly accepted standard of justice; and second, arrangements may conform to a state's conception of justice, but this conception itself may be unjust. Rawls maintains however that "when the basic structure of society is reasonably just, we are to recognize unjust laws as binding provided that they do not exceed certain limits of injustice." This is so because when one submits to democratic authority, one submits to the extent necessary to share equitably in the inevitable imperfections of a constitutional system.

This argument is also beyond democracy. It was made earlier in sociology by Robert MacIver. The notion was that traditions of loyalty include the assumption that one should extend law-abidingness beyond the limits of immediate approbation.[30] There is a danger that this line of reasoning could be carried to such an extreme that virtually no right of resistance would remain, and moral development would be restricted to blatant violations rather than to ethical decision making as a whole.

It is just too dangerous and limiting to reduce moral development to how one defines "equal liberty" and "fair equality of opportunity." There may be numerous occasions when resistance is justified, despite the duty "not to invoke too readily the faults of social arrangements." Civil disobedience is an appeal to the conscience of the larger society, and may be justified if the established authority is acting inconsistently with its own established standards. In this sense, moral development is equivalent to a careful weighting of individual desires and social goods, including a constant sifting of legal statutes and their impingement upon personal standards or principles. Resistance is justified by reference to social principles, that is, the two principles of justice, but not by appeals to conscience. On the other hand, some element of individualism is critical if moral development is not to be reduced simply to reasons of state or appeals to the people.

> In morals every man must be his own legislator and rely in the end on his own judgment. . . . A duty can be a moral duty, then, only if it can be shown to serve a greater good or avert a greater wrong. It is therefore a conditional, not an absolute duty, and must depend on the use to which authority is put. And this implies that though we may have an obligation to act on someone else's judgment, we have no duty to suspend judgment.[31]

That individuals cannot be deprived of the right to form their own judgments is part of any adequate definition of moral development. As Hannah Pitkin has said, "the capacity for awareness and intention is a precondition for being fully obligated."[32] It follows that one is not really obligated unless one empirically recognizes and morally acquiesces in that obligation.[33] However, obligation does not consist only of inner awareness and intentions; it also has a long-range aspect. It is concerned with the social consequences of action. In the public realm, one is confronted with official interpreters and institutions who judge actions. At times of resistance or revolution these authorities are called into question. The question then arises: Who is to decide what times are normal and which are not, or whether resistance is justified or even obligatory? If one says that each individual must decide for himself, then one denies the morally binding character of law and authority; if one says the majority must decide, one is unable to cope with a situation where the majority is being challenged. Herein lie the limits of moral development.

There is no final answer to the problem of moral development, since one cannot hope to specify a set of necessary and sufficient conditions of political obligations for all eternity. If society is faced with an indefinite set of vaguely shifting criteria, differing for different times and circumstances, then it may often, if not nearly always, be necessary to scrutinize political relations to see whether individuals are on particular occasions justified in giving support to a measure or a government or withholding it. But in doing so, a theory of political rights apart from a corresponding theory of political obligations is resurrected. Again, moral development is the decision-making process whereby the balance wheel of rights and obligations is maintained. If such a balance wheel becomes impossible, then the problem of moral development becomes moot, since the choice is made on the basis of raw power — and for decision making in the absence of choice one needs counterpower, not moral standards.

DEMOCRATIC PERSUASIONS AND AUTHORITARIAN DISTEMPERS

The fusion of moral development, political style, and democratic persuasion takes one from Deweyan to Meadian premises, from pragmatism as a theory of education to symbolic interaction as a theory of politics. George Mead understood democracy to mean the ability to absorb information from others — to listen before forming judgments, to take the role of the "generalized other" as a precondition to action.[34] In this sense, moral education for democracy entails the ability to learn how to absorb information about people with different sentiments, values, and interests. This naturalistic vision is the opposite of a notion that moral education is a matter of "our" teaching "them" right values. Democracy always has had, and will continue to be plagued by, a certain ambiguity, an indecisiveness. Admitting to not knowing everything a priori is characteristic of the democratic polity.[35] The tentativeness that permits breakdown also makes possible a theory of moral development based on learning new information rather than instruction others about the virtues of old information.

A democratic theory of politics must make a clear differentiation between moral development and the development of morals. Such a distinction takes on distinctive practical meaning, because it is primarily in the context of statist repression (or permission) that either notion (moral development or the development of morals) has ultimate significance. Moral development as a brute fact, derived from commonsense attitudes toward order and civility, is handmaiden to a panoply of authoritarian ideologies. The forms of such an ideology may be thoroughly benign, even genteel. Ultimately, however, the notion of moral development rests on the imposition of behavior through methods of authority or divinity. At the same time, the notion of the development of morals, in its nature, assumes a plurality and even a plethora of moral standards and standpoints; hence, the development of any one set of morals signifies the sorts of codifications that are essential for a society's growth and survival.

The democratic persuasion is not an argument claiming the unlimited nature of moral possibilities or the impossibility of assessing relative advantages or disadvantages of one ethical framework against another. It is an assertion that moral choices are not ultimate or revealed verities that deductively or cosmologically flow from the nature of the state. Ethics can be measured by the consequences they yield to the person and society, rather than by initial goals set for the person or society. Contrariwise, activities of a routine sort are often measured by ethical standards deemed operationally satisfactory, even necessary, in specific societal contexts. The democratic position is now back in a world of discourse where the quest is for certitude rather than experience. Certitude blocks out possible lines of inquiry, and hence limits the range of experiences, while experiences tend to produce yet newer experiences and thus create the grounds for ever-increasing doubt and uncertainty. The choice is by no means an easy one to make, but the consequences have a great bearing on what citizens in a republic may expect from their polity.

Quite apart from the need to disaggregate normative and empirical frameworks to examine issues of moral development, it has become evident that the situation in theory basically mirrors conditions in world affairs. It can be said without much fear of contradiction that the twentieth century bears witness to powerful demands for life-giving egalitarianism, in both intimate and international relations, while at the same time it has exposed an underbelly of genocide and impersonal mass murder that has transformed moral issues into engineering issues; that is, questions of punishment, execution, burial and so on are reduced to matters of cost efficiency and double-entry accountancy.[36] In European nations where deeply rooted tendencies toward egalitarianism were formerly manifest — for example, in Socialist Germany and Communist Russia — one often found forms of genocide raised to the highest levels of science. Of course, traditional forms of genocide can be found where one might expect, in places such as Paraguay and Uganda. In these latter instances, genocide serves to prevent contact with the developing world. But one must be cautious about offering general theories; forms of democracy are found in unanticipated places, just as genocide takes place in equally unexpected nations.

Moral propositions about political systems are suspect, those about democratic systems doubly so; inherent in the concept of democracy is a sufficient latitude regarding moral ambiguity to make principles no less than strategies subject to alteration over time. From their reluctance to correct inherited forms of inequality, to a vague tolerance for all sorts of waste, democratic societies invite criticism for being morally obtuse, not to mention insulated from the needs of wide sectors of those disenfranchised from the democratic process. The search for moral first principles, based on absolute convictions as to where we come from and hence where we must go, is an inevitable offshoot of democratic society. All decry the waste inherent in interest-group politics and single-issue organizations, but few are brave enough to state which interest groups they would abolish or what particular interest group's issues they feel are frivolous and deserving of being suppressed. The potency of democratic systems only partially derives from its own first principles; more pointedly, its strength derives from the dangerously limited options awaiting those who would abandon a democratic notion of moral choice.

Too often ideas of the perfect have led to intense fanaticism, to what Hannah Arendt[37] and Jacob Talmon[38] in different ways have described in terms of totalitarian democracy and political messianism. The process of perfecting is admittedly infuriatingly vague, but it provides the intellectual space that permits free people to operate effectively, if inefficiently. Holding firmly to the inefficiencies of such an open-end notion of moral development is a costly affair in economic terms, inviting a certain amount of waste; but to achieve moral development at the price of political democracy is an unholy trade-off that assures only bureaucratic efficiency.

Several years ago, Harold Lasswell shrewdly observed that there is a linkage between personality systems and demands for severity. By extension, there is a relationship between demands for moral development as some sort of methaphysical given and the extensive network of international punishment in the form of global warfare and genocidal conflict. It is worthwhile to appreciate the degree to which concepts such as moral development are little else than disguised decisions for sanctioning norms. The warrant for such behavior deserves to be explained by social and behavioral scientists but not necessarily rationalized.

The claims of a society to impose suffering as an end in itself usually carries within itself a further compounded belief that such suffering is warranted for the maintenance of order and the establishment of first principles. But claims of this sort involve beliefs in political goals more nearly than statements of cultural universals. Comparative studies between cultures reveal the relative nature of most, if not all, universal claims. This does not imply that a society should avoid choices or that some moral systems are not superior to others against alien factors and forces. Rather, the danger inheres in the belief that somehow social ideologues can properly sanction what thousands of years of theological edicts and constraints have failed to achieve — a finely tuned theory of moral development. Again, one can scarcely find a better mentor than Lasswell in determining the limits of social science as an agenda-setting network for moral development.

> We cannot look to the behavioral scientists in their professional capacity to shoulder our individual responsibility for deciding what manner of individuality to seek in ourselves or to permit in our children, or in others whom we influence. But the growth of knowledge will expose the total consequences of conformity as well as of originality of deviation. The crude initial studies of the costs of difference will be supplemented — as indeed they are being supplemented by studies of the costs of stereotyping and conformity. Already there are indications of the latent problems that arise when talents and propensities are suppressed or repressed out of deference to the steamroller of conformity. These are the issues that rise to plague and embitter the later years of life with a sense of estrangement from experience and a haunting sense of chagrin and guilt for a lifetime of timidity and cowardice. We are engaged in a vast reconstruction of our cultural inheritance in the light of the behavioral sciences. Our conclusion is that the impact upon primary and sanctioning norms has been to bring the practices of our civilization into somewhat closer harmony with the basic ideals of human dignity.[39]

If the democratic persuasion involves choices, then a notion of moral developments needs to be enlarged. Helen Merrell Lynd, paraphrasing Guyau, writes: "Not 'I must, therefore I can,' but 'I can, therefore I must.' " Lynd amplifies her view by noting that the scientific temper of discovery poses issues not in terms of morality and immorality, but among conflicting moralities. Writing in the maelstrom of McCarthyism, she put forward the notion that the fusion of the democratic temper and scientific credo offers a solution to the dangerous quest for certainty on the one hand and the complete relativizing of values on the other. "Entering fully into the nature of contemporary conflicts calls upon one to make choices beyond coping with difficulties to gain security: beyond the polarity of good on one side, evil on the other. Acting in the faith that there may be ranges of individual and social development as yet unknown requires ability to live with ambiguity and varied probabilities and possibilities."[40] It would be difficult to find a superior foundation for democratic policy making and, at the same time, a wiser grounding for core principles from which can be derived a democratic vision of morals in development.

NOTES

1. Richard B. Brandt, *Freedom and Morality* (Lawrence: University of Kansas Press, 1976); and *Ethical Theory: The problems of Normative and Critical Ethics* (Englewood Cliffs, N.J.: Prentice-Hall, 1959).

2. Abraham Edel, *Ethical Judgment: The Use of Science in Ethics* (Glencoe, Ill.: Free Press, 1955); and *Method in Ethical Theory* (Indianapolis, Ind.: Bobbs-Merrill, 1963).

3. Leo Strauss, *Natural Right and History* (Chicago: University of Chicago Press, 1953); and *What is Political Philosophy?* (Glencoe, Ill.: Free Press, 1959).

4. Richard E. Flathman, *Political Obligation* (New York: Atheneum, 1972).

5. Richard E. Dawson and Kenneth Prewitt, *Political Socialization: An Analytic Study*, 2d ed. (Boston: Little, Brown, 1977).

6. L. Harmon Zeigler, *Interest Groups in American Society* (Englewood Cliffs, N. J.: Prentice-Hall, 1964); and *The Political Life of American Teachers* (Englewood Cliffs, N.J.: Prentice-Hall, 1967).

7. Karl Marx and Frederick Engels, *The German Ideology* (London: Lawrence and Wishart, 1970).

8. Karl Mannheim, *Ideology and Utopia: An Introduction to the Sociology of Knowledge* (New York: Harcourt, Brace & World, 1968).

9. Max F. Scheler, *Formalism in Ethics and Non-Formal Ethics of Values: A New Attempt Toward the Foundation of an Ethical Personality*, 5th rev. ed. (Evanston, Ill.: Northwestern University Press, 1973).

10. Philip Rieff, *Freud: The Mind of the Moralist* (Garden City, N.Y.: Doubleday, 1961).

11. David Elkind, "Erik Erikson's Eight Ages of Man," in *Readings in Human Development: Contemporary Perspectives*, ed. David Elkind and Donna C. Metzel (New York: Harper & Row, 1977), pp.3–11.

12. Erik H. Erikson, *Young Man Luther: A Study of Psychoanalysis and History* (New York: Norton, 1958); and *Gandhi's Truth: On the Origins of Militant Nonviolence* (New York: Norton, 1969).

13. Erik H. Erikson, *Childhood and Society*, 2d ed. (New York: Norton, 1963).

14. Sigmund Freud, *Civilization and its Discontents*, trans. James Strachey (New York: Norton, 1962).

15. Robert L. Ebel, "What are Schools For?", in *Readings in Human Development: Contemporary Perspectives*, ed. David Elkind and Donna C. Metzel (New York: Harper & Row, 1977), pp. 12–16.

16. John Dewey, *Democracy and Education: An Introduction to the Philosophy of Education* (New York: Macmillan, 1917).

17. Lawrence Kohlbert, "Development of Moral Character and Moral Ideology," in *Review of Child Development Research*, ed. Martin and Lois Hoffman (New York: Russell Sage Foundation, 1964), pp. 398–401.

18. For a behavioristic summary of the "cognitive" standpoint on moral development, see Lawrence A. Kurdek, "Perspective Taking As the Cognitive Basis of Children's Moral Development," *Merrill-Palmer Quarterly* 24 (January 1978): 3–28.

19. Irving Louis Horowitz, *Foundations of Political Sociology* (New York and London: Harper & Row, 1972).

20. John Locke, *Two Treatises of Government*, ed. Peter Laslett, "Second Treatise" (Cambridge: Cambridge University Press, 1960), Section 163, p. 394.

21. Ibid., Section 95, p. 348. See also Section 119, p. 366.

22. David Hume, "Of the Original Contract," in *The Social Contract*, ed. Ernest Barker (New York and London: Oxford University Press, 1946), pp. 221–22.

23. S. I. Benn and R. S. Peters, *Social Principles and the Democratic State* (London: George Allen & Unwin, 1959), p. 322.

24. John Plamenatz, *Consent, Freedom and Political Obligation*, 2nd ed. (New York and London: Oxford University Press, 1968), pp. 230–31.

25. T. H. Green, *Lectures on the Principles of Political Obligation* (London: Longmans, 1895), pp. 29–41.

26. Harold Laski, *A Grammar of Politics* (London: George Allen & Unwin, 1970), p. 25.

27. John Rawls, *A Theory of Justice* (Cambridge, Mass.: Harvard University Press, 1972), pp. 110–12, 114–117.

28. H. L. A. Hart, "Are There Any Natural Rights?" in *Political Philosophy*, ed. Anthony Quinton (New York and London: Oxford University Press, 1968), pp. 61–62.

29. Rawls, Theory of Justice, pp. 349, 351.

30. Robert M. MacIver, *The Modern State* (New York and London: Oxford University Press, 1926), p. 154.

31. Benn and Peters, *Social Principles,* pp. 326–27.

32. Hannah Pitkin, "Obligation and Consent," in *Obligation and Dissent*, ed. Donald W. Hanson and Robert B. Fowler (Boston: Little, Brown, 1971), pp. 41–44.

33. Burton Zwiebach, *Civility and Disobedience* (New York: Cambridge University Press, 1975), pp. 169–200.

34. George Herbert Mead, *Mind, Self and Society: From the Standpoint of a Social Behaviorist*, ed. Charles W. Morris, et al. (Chicago: University of Chicago Press, 1934); see also, Anselm Strauss, ed., *On Social Psychology:* Selected Papers (Chicago: University of Chicago Press, 1964).

35. Ralph Barton Perry, *General Theory of Value* (Cambridge: Harvard University Press, 1926); and *Puritanism and Democracy* (New York: Vanguard Press, 1944), pp. 589–609.

36. Irving Louis Horowitz, *Genocide: State Power and Mass Murder*, 2d ed. (New Brunswick, N.J.: Transaction Books, 1977).

37. Hannah Arendt, *The Origins of Totalitarianism*, rev. ed. (New York: Harcourt, Brace & World, 1966).

38. Jacob L. Talmon, *The Origins of Totalitarian Democracy* (London: Secker & Warburg, 1952); and *Political Messianism* (New York: Praeger, 1960).

39. Harold D. Lasswell, "The Choice of Sanctioning Norms," in *On Political Sociology*, ed. Dwaine Marvick (Chicago: The University of Chicago Press, 1977) pp. 348–65.

40. Helen Merrell Lynd, *On Shame and the Search for Identity* (New York: Science Editions, 1961).

2

A MORAL COMMUNITY OF STRANGERS

Richard W. Wilson

Enough recent work has now been produced on the subject of moral development to allow an investigation of the relationship of individual-level moral development to macro-social-level characteristics. It will be the purpose of this chapter, therefore, to examine moral development at the individual level in relation to social structure and general social behavior. The aim will be to show that the potential for cooperative behavior involving reciprocity, which ultimately includes political activity, need not be conceptualized as the consequence of some metaphorical social contract, nor even derived as the product of compelling logic, but as an inherent, in fact partially defining, characteristic of human beings. Since the capacity for social cooperation is considered to be a necessary but not sufficient condition for individual moral behavior, the discussion will begin by setting forth an explanatory framework for the assumption that the potential for cooperative behavior derives from patterns of social relationships that are inherent to the species. However, cooperative social behavior does not in and of itself insure mature moral behavior. An understanding of the ways in which forms of cooperation relate to types of morality involves awareness of influences both at the individual level, in terms of moral development, and at the group level, in terms of social patterns, that may strengthen or impede alternate outcomes. It should be clear that this overall effort is not one of hypothesis testing but is rather an exercise in hypothesis formation. Should the ideas presented here prove persuasive, the next step will be to develop tests of the propositions that have been generated.

MAKING CONTACT WITH STRANGERS

Avoidance of incestuous sexual relationships is not a uniquely human characteristic. Such avoidance has been observed among a number of social animals, although the regulation of this type of sexual activity is for them essentially innate rather than partially governed by the taboos of a normative code. Among red deer, for instance, the life pattern of the species involves segregation of the sexes for most of the time so that the probability of an incestuous relationship is greatly minimized. Among zebras, Patas monkeys, and Hamadryas baboons, a harem organization of females headed by a dominant male effectively relegates most other mature males to bachelor bands. While such an organization does not prevent father-daughter incest, it does effectively control mother-son and sibling forms of incestuous relationships. Among Rhesus monkeys, on the other hand, there are frequent promiscuous relationships and paternity is usually an unknown factor. However, Rhesus monkeys avoid mother-son and sibling incest; young males tend to move away while those that remain rarely mate with their mothers, and even sibling pairing is far less common than between unrelated animals. The same holds true for chimpanzees.[1] Observations of these close animal relatives of mankind bear out these assertions. Jane Goodall, for instance, has found that in chimpanzee bands sexual interaction among siblings occurs very rarely. Male offspring do not mate with their mothers despite the fact that every other mature male in the band may do so.[2] Observations such as these, of course, cannot show how incest is regulated in human groups. They do, however, suggest that sexual behavior and group relationships are intimately related and that this may be as true for humans as it is for other species.

Noting that incest prohibition occurs among mammalian social groups of primitive intelligence suggests a biological explanation for incest prohibition that may be related to the advantages of gene dispersal.[3] For humans, however, there are also social aspects to incest prohibition that appear to be particularly characteristic of this species. A focus on human social regulations permits concentration not on the danger of inbreeding, which may govern animal sexual behavior, but on the benefits that accrue to the species from outbreeding. Analysis in this area allows one to transcend the influence of innate characteristics on incest prohibition, which to a degree hold true for mankind, and instead examine the importance of human patterns of aspirations, learning, and social organization as molders of sexual and social behavior.

It is known statistically that incest occurs in human social systems and even that it has been sanctioned for some groups in certain societies (for instance, among the members of the royal families of ancient Egypt, Inca America, and Hawaii). Such anomolies notwithstanding, sexual relations between parents and those members of the social group who are considered to be their children, or between those who are considered to be siblings, has rarely, if ever, been permitted in any society.[4] The incest taboo, as Talcott Parsons reminds us, is universal among human societies although the specific cultural rules regulating sexual and marital relationships are certainly different among societies and different, depending upon the historical period, within the same society.[5]

The size of most prehistoric human groups is somewhat difficult to estimate. Many primate groups number 100 or fewer and there are also estimates that prehuman Australopithecine groups numbered between 10 and 200 individuals, or about the range of size observed for modern baboon troops.[6] Australopithecines, of course, were plains dwellers, as are baboons, and this may have had an effect on group size.[7] Actual prehistoric groups of truly modern men, which evolved some 50,000 years ago, may have been considerably smaller than the largest sizes noted above, averaging perhaps five or six family units. Such a size corresponds relatively well with what is known about the few extant modern hunter-gatherer societies. Groups of this size would thus have been comprised of approximately 25 persons who, in addition to membership in a particular band, would also have been members of a larger dialect group that might have included as many as 500 people. Five hundred has been estimated as the probable size for the dialect group, since such a number would insure a balance of boy and girl babies and provide the optimal opportunity for pairing for any given age cohort.[8] In the small group of about 25 people there might be approximately 14 children, one-quarter of whom would reach sexual maturity at any one time. Considering just the small group, this fact in itself suggests a severe lack of choice in terms of finding an appropriate mate, so that exogamy may partially have been a necessity rather than something that had to be normatively required.

It is perhaps of some interest that in contemporary small hunter-gatherer groups incest taboos are observed without exception and marriages are almost always arranged between separate bands. Initially the male may leave and join the band of the bride until he has demonstrated an ability to support her or to produce children. In fact, the longest journey the young man may ever make is the one that he takes in order to find a spouse. But why, it may be asked, do young males tend to leave the group at all in order to find their brides? Why should they not remain and vie among themselves for the available young females or dispute with the older males for all the females? After all, one knows from Freud about the cross-sexual impulses that motivate most children with regard to their parents and other members of the family, and one might infer from this that in-group competition for sexual favors might be the expected pattern.[9] One contrary explanation that has been offered is that from a biological standpoint a male seems to be sexually most successful with a female who is lower in dominance than himself and this, of course, is particularly not true of the relationship of a young male with his mother. Siblings also appear to be somehow "too familiar" for it has been observed in primitive societies that there is a general dampening of sexual inclination toward childhood intimates, a factor also noted, incidentally, in Israeli kibbutzim.[10]

The importance of males going outside the group for brides, however, transcends questions of in-group social dominance patterns or of lack of sexual curiosity toward childhood friends. More crucial seems to have been the importance of developing a broader network of blood relationships, an importance related to the fact that any factor binding larger numbers of individuals together cooperatively appears to have contributed to the success of the human species.[11] While life in primitive times in hunter-gatherer societies probably had more amenities than most modern people believe, it is also true that people were at the mercy of the elements to a degree not common today and that the environment contained many threatening factors, not least of all from dangerous carnivores and from other people. Lions and humans, after all, are the only mammals who deliberately devour their own species and while exocannibalism appears more characteristic of later settled agricultural societies than nomadic hunter-gatherer groups, the fact alone tells us something about the environment of predation among which earlier humans lived.[12]

The formation of habits of sharing, particularly with regard to food, appears to be strongly characteristic of mankind. Hunting meat, in fact, seems to be a prerequisite for altruism, in which the distribution of meat puts the distributor (almost always a male) at the center of a network of reciprocal relationships.[13] The development of cooperative relationships for joint hunting expeditions and defense was clearly of tremendous importance for human survival, and the finding of brides outside the small group appears to have been one major way in which larger group solidarities were created. Of course, other factors such as language helped to maximize the possibilities for cooperation and to minimize the naked dominance patterns so characteristic, for instance, of baboon societies. But beyond such factors, the incest taboo appears to have been a major social mechanism fostering awareness of other groups and leading, when brides moved, to the development of a shared sense of identity with others whom they might not have previously known in any real sense. In fact, of course, marital arrangements for mutual advantage are still observable in historical times in political marriages between powerful families. Once a bond between groups had been made on the basis of a sexual pairing, powerful social regulations contributed to preventing aggressive behavior among members of the two groups. No father, after all, presumably wished to be the killer of his daughter's husband or vice versa. Slowly, through use of a variety of kinship terms and other special terminology relating to common group identification, an awareness of the link between the two groups was forged; individuals became aware that they were members of a social grouping larger than just the small band.

DEVELOPING IDENTIFICATION WITH STRANGERS

Although a number of scholars have tried to isolate a single characteristic that presumably sets human beings apart from other species, it is probable that the explosive development of mankind was due to the interaction of a number of factors and that positive feedback among these factors accelerated development in general. The increase in the size and capacity of the brain, for instance, and the ability to hunt appear to have been positively related and both to have had a relationship to a developing capacity for tool making. Uniquely constructed hands freed for the use of tools appear to have favorably interacted with the growing ability for upright walking, and upright walking, in turn, with hunting in which success was undoubtedly facilitated by the capacity to vocalize a high number of sounds for speech communication, and so on. A number of such interaction patterns can be postulated and each is no doubt an important link in understanding the evolution of the human species. This evolution itself has been likened to the climbing of a ladder by steps, from simple to complex, each step being stable in itself, so that the process metaphorically resembles a climber who consolidates each new gain before proceeding to the next task.

Recent work suggests that cognitive ability itself may be an attribute that is genetically controlled. Edward Wilson, for instance, has said, "The capacity to learn certain behaviors is itself a genetically controlled and therefore evolved trait."[14] At the same time humans as a species were evolving, the cultures within which they lived were also becoming more complex. Two kinds of evolution, therefore, closely interwoven, were going on at the same time. Both involved a selective adaptation to an environment and both helped individuals to obtain what they needed, to avoid what was dangerous, and to transmit the lessons learned to newer generations. This interaction pattern has been characterized as follows: "The capacity to undergo changes in behavior which make a culture possible was acquired in the evolution of the species, and, reciprocally, the culture determines many of the biological characteristics transmitted."[15] Moreover, just as the evolution of human genetic characteristics is not isolated in one group, so is there also no strict isolation of cultures; for while the process may seem agonizingly slow, increasing contact among the world's cultures has gradually become a pronounced historical feature.

Should the human species survive for several more millenia, it is interesting to speculate concerning what future historians may observe as some of the main patterns and trends of this present transition period. Certainly they will note an enormous increase in technological capability. They may also note that participation by common people in political processes has become far more prevalent. Another less obvious feature, but one that in the author's opinion is just as important, is what is called here the raising of identity levels, the capacity to be aware of and to empathize with other human beings who are toally unknown and with whom one has no personal affective ties, to see these people as having some relationship to oneself and to perceive a commonality underlying human existence. However, if the development of a self-perspective that includes identification and empathy with strangers should become known in the future as a marked feature of the age, the trend at this time is certainly by no means universal or even, in most places, well developed. It remains, rather, a process that is in the act of becoming. The potential exists from the propensity of humans to contact others for mutual advantage. However, while such contacts historically brought strangers together, the groups involved were small in size and their memberships mutually recognizable and associated through common kinship terms. Such ties are inherently particularistic; in the vast number of nonmodernized societies that exist today people still make family considerations the major determinants of decisions that govern their lives.[16]

The previous discussion concerning incest and exogamy is of value only because it posits a reasonably justifiable basis, conforming with currently available data, for explaining the human propensity to seek out and engage in cooperative behavior with strangers and to include these strangers in a definition of what constitutes humanity. Mankind, after all, did not begin with any absolute instinctive aversion to incest. For if instinct by itself were sufficient to prohibit certain forms of sexual behavior, there would clearly be no need for a cultural taboo to prevent the formation of such relationships. The known facts suggest that incest prohibition and accompanying rules of exogamy had a strong practical basis in that they gave the small, hunter-gatherer, "mutual aid" group a great boost in its struggle for survival by fostering the formation of cooperative alliances with others who were not members of the basic primary group.[17]

Norms relating to incest and exogamy require a prior ability to recognize one's kin. This ability, in itself, assumes the capability to understand a self-other orientation, the ability to go beyond pure self awareness and be aware of broader patterns of relationships. If rules regarding incest and exogamy augment survival by fostering the forging of links with unknown others, these links are clearly precarious without complementary rules and standards that establish the rights, privileges, obligations, and so on among people who have previously been unknown, or virtually unknown, to each other. One cannot, therefore, think of incest taboos apart from corollary developments in the general area of social bonding.

The norms governing group social relations soon take on a vastly more multifaceted and self-sustaining quality, once patterns of intergroup relationship go beyond the simple matter of mate selection and involve maintaining stability among people now related through kinship ties. There is, in fact, even a kind of rough pattern that characterizes the development of identification with strangers. In hunter-gatherer societies, the relationships were usually legitimized by the use of elaborate kinship terms, a pattern that even today is recognizable in the special words that are applied to people who have previously been unrelated. While the U.S. society is not as terminologically elaborate as some in this regard, and is perhaps becoming less so, the words mother-in-law, sister-in-law, brother-in-law, and so on are still accepted as terms for describing kinship relationships formed only through marriage.

Approximately 10,000 years ago, as human beings began to settle into more populous and sedentary agricultural conglomerations, there seems also to have been a slow but concomitant rise in the development of elaborate normative codes that prescribed relationships in nonkinship terms. For instance, geographically bounded religions arose in which the relationship of strangers to each other was based on a common tie to a deity. There were, of course, competing religious groupings and even within any single religious group there was often further fragmentation in terms of language affiliation and local political orientation, each of which defined membership in a smaller secondary group that was, as far as the individual was concerned, usually of paramount importance. In present times the universalizing of identity has frequently appeared in political form, the best examples of which are the nationalisms so readily observable around the globe. Another broader example, although one that is suffering extraordinary strain (partly as a result of competition with nationalism), is the worldwide Communist movement with identification based on class and shared political commitment. It is also noteworthy that people find it difficult to identify with membership in a worldwide community. The term "world citizen" has no meaning for most people and is, for them, a difficult concept toward which to direct affective attachment. Before the advent of the nation-state, the notion of national citizenship must have seemed equally foreign.

SOME MORAL DEVELOPMENT FACTORS AFFECTING THE DEVELOPMENT OF MORAL RELATIONS WITH STRANGERS

Preceding sections have suggested that developing cooperative bonds with strangers was an important element in human survival and that this ability partially defines the human species. At this point, therefore, it is appropriate to examine the learning process and the environment within social units, which facilitate the possibility of admitting strangers into the realm where moral codes govern behavior.

Milton Rokeach, who is possibly the leading scholar on the subject of values in general, defines moral values as those which have an interpersonal focus and which, when violated, arouse guilt or shame in the individual.[18] There is a presumption that what an individual states his moral values to be will tend, in the long run, toward convergence with actual behavior, though at any given time the relationship may be problematical.[19] A further and corollary assumption states that an individual's moral values will roughly reflect the normative standards of the culture within which that individual lives.

Strong emotional feelings about certain kinds of behavior do not, in themselves, define morality. If that were the case, one would have to say that an animal trained to behave in a certain way had moral values; but this, obviously, is not the case. Rather, following Lawrence Kohlberg, mature moral behavior consists of acts that would be acceptable to any individual within a given context where every individual who is involved in the situation must play one of the roles related to that context, but does not know in advance which role.[20] For such acts to occur, feelings about behavior must mesh with a capability for abstract thought with regard to certain kinds of role behavior and self-other relationships. It can, therefore, be very generally stated that mature moral behavior is most crucially a function of strong affective responses with regard to values that refer to reciprocity and empathy, to an ability to perceive abstractly how the self and others must behave in order to realize these values, and to an awareness of who the others are with whom one is interacting.

In a recent work, a model of moral development was presented that attempted to integrate findings from both the social learning and cognitive development schools of moral development.[21] A series of necessary but insufficient variables were posited as influencing the development of moral judgment capability. While it would be out of place here to recapitulate the entire argument presented in this earlier work, it may be appropriate to summarize certain of the major ideas.

Individuals, it was posited, have an innate capability both for cognitive development and for affective response. These capabilities are acted upon during learning by several interrelated external socialization influences that were defined as affective manipulation, morals training, and secondary-level role training. Each influence, in turn, may be further subdefined in terms of its component characteristics. For instance, with regard to affective manipulation, such punishments as physical pain, love-oriented techniques of discipline, or induction training are all associated with different forms of anxiety and are related to different types of behavioral response.

It was postulated that these three socialization influences will occur serially and cumulatively with age. As an example, affective manipulation begins at birth, whereas formal morals training, with its heavy dependence on the acquisition of verbal skills for the learning of cultural rules, will usually not begin (and be linked with affective manipulation) until the rudiments of language have been acquired. Secondary-level role training, which occurs even later, refers to the acquisition of internalized motivations for behavior where the affective component of motivation is self-generated and is not dependent on cues from others with whom one has affective ties. This influence is called secondary-level since the author believes that acquiring this particular kind of role behavior requires the development of an awareness of and a sense of belonging to the secondary groups of which one is a member. Without this awareness situational cues will, to a great extent, dominate interpersonal relations. Even in modern societies such awareness will not really begin until middle childhood and for many it may occur even later in life, sometimes not until adulthood; for some individuals, especially those in primitive societies for whom secondary-level affiliations may be extremely weak or nonexistent, it may not occur at all. In addition to socialization influences per se, the model also postulated the importance of informational and emotional feedback from actual situational contexts to one's moral judgment capability, and from this developing capability to the ways that socialization influences affect the moral development of others. The effectiveness of feedback on the development of a mature moral judgment capability is presumed to vary according to the nature of the social milieu. It was postulated that variations in socialization influences and feedback conditions will occur from culture to culture and that these variations account for some of the empirical differences in the development of moral judgment capability that have been noted in the literature on moral development.[22] These ideas, which are most certainly not entirely unique, are set forth in Figure 2.1.[23]

With reference to Figure 2.1, there is particular (but not sole) concern with four factors that influence the development of mature morality and a consequent ability to relate to strangers. The first of these involves the kind of feelings that underlie an ability to identify with strangers, the second and third involve abstract thought and secondary-level role training, and the fourth, the nature of the social environment within which feedback takes place. The remainder of this chapter, therefore, will primarily address these issues.

EMPATHY, ABSTRACT THOUGHT, AND SECONDARY-LEVEL ROLE TRAINING

Robert Hogan has stated that the development of moral character can be measured in terms of five concepts or dimensions, which he defines as moral knowledge (knowing moral rules), socialization (regarding rules as

FIGURE 2.1

Moral Development Model

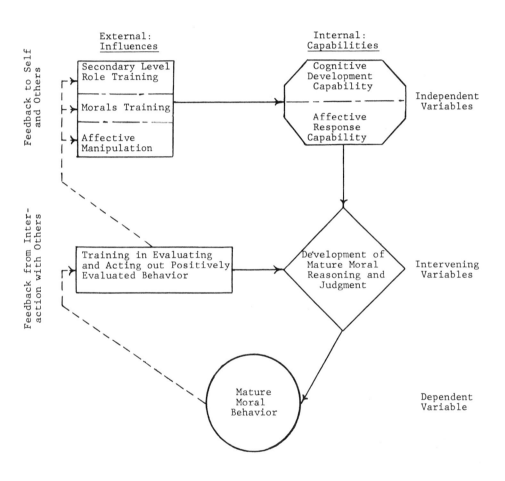

personally mandatory), empathy (consideration of one's actions for the welfare of others), autonomy (self-esteem unrelated to the judgments of others), and an ethic of conscience and responsibility.[24] The acquisition of socialization and empathy appear to be especially critical for mature moral development;[25] in fact, Hogan states that the morally mature person is someone who is both high in socialization and high in empathy (see Figure 2.2).[26] These two dimensions are related to the external influences that were enumerated in Figure 2.1 in that moral knowledge is a result of morals training, while empathy is related to an interaction between morals training and affective manipulation. Empathy, especially, is the product of induction training which focuses on the consequences of an act for others.[27] As can be noted from Figure 2.2, persons low in empathy, that is low in an ability to relate affectively to other people, are either delinquent or rigid in terms of their application of moral standards. However, the process of acquiring emotional sensitivity toward others, and particularly toward strangers, is neither easy nor foreordained. William McGuire has noted that short-term contact with strangers, in fact, intensifies hostility, while only long-term contact produces a trend toward overall positive and favorable responses.[28] Paradoxically such hostility may even be greater toward proximate strangers than toward more distal ones whose very complete strangeness may cloak them in an unthreatening aura.

Interest is also focused on abstract thought as a component of moral development and on social influences that may further the ability to think abstractly. Vocabulary, to some extent, is dependent on the speech practices of important other people, a factor of considerable comparative importance in studies of childhood socialization where differences may exist among societies in the concepts to which the child is introduced. In learning, the introduction to, followed by the acquisition of, a language for an abstract concept then allows one to make more concrete differentiations within a particular conception.[29] As Helen Keller is reported to have said on her first experience of knowing that words for phenomena exist, "Everything had a name and each name gave birth to a new thought."[30] The author believes that the development of awareness of secondary-level associations and of groups that are important at that level of abstraction will follow for each individual "a natural progression whose sequence and content will be indicated by the experience that his interpersonal world provides him as this experience is organized by his evolving cognitive capacities."[31]

It is the contention here that the ability to be aware of a secondary group of which one may be a member and to identify with others in this group requires the capability to conceive of that group and its members. This is so since other members of that group will be almost entirely unknown to the individual, and knowledge of the group and other members must be

FIGURE 2.2

Moral Type as a Function of Socialization and Empathy

	Socialization (Regarding rules as personally mandatory)	
Empathy (Consideration of one's actions for the welfare of others)	Low	High
High	Le Chic Type	Morally Mature
Low	Delinquent	Moral Realist

through learning about and adherence to sets of values and symbols (often of political significance, such as a flag) upon which affective sentiment can be attached. There is a suspicion that there is a feedback loop involved, where a developing capability to think abstractly permits one to become aware of membership in a secondary group and where awareness of one's membership triggers a reverse ability to further deal with abstractions in general.

The major point with regard to awareness of secondary-level membership is not, however, that it furthers the ability to think abstractly, for there are many other learning influences that may be equally valid in this regard (formal morals training, as one example). Awareness of secondary-level membership and identification with others at that level is important in the sense that these attributes, once acquired, "pull" the use of abstract concepts for the governance of interpersonal relations in place of the continuation of behavior that is largely governed by situational ethics. Awareness thus makes possible the likelihood of principled behavior in all types of interpersonal contexts, both with individuals who are known and with strangers. Identification with others at the secondary level does not, of course, mean that one has lost all sense of identity with and feeling about less inclusive groups of which one may be a member, such as one's family, one's religious group, and so on. But by having transcended exclusive particular affiliations, by developing a concomitant affinity toward those who were previously strangers, one has stepped on the path toward an ability to transcend, where appropriate, all particularistic behavior patterns.

The assumption is that the ability to see oneself in terms of membership in a secondary-level group is related to the development of mature moral orientations in the sense that the possibility of interactions involving reciprocity with people who are unknown and with whom one has no affective ties presumes a prior internalization of norms — in effect an orientation to the principles governing behavior rather than an orientation to social rules per se or to cues from others who are known and with whom one has a specific and affectively charged relationship. A truly principled response goes beyond patterned reactions to situational cues, or rigid and unbending adherence to normative prescriptions whatever the consequences may be for others, and involves the ability flexibly to mold behavior in adherence to principles of reciprocity in formulating behavioral responses that are appropriate for anyone.

THE FEEDBACK ENVIRONMENT AND SOME POLITICAL IMPLICATIONS

In terms of Figure 2.1, the development of mature morality seems to be critically related to the social environment of the feedback process. In social systems where questions about the validity of certain beliefs are discouraged, where what is true is what some authority figure says is true, where the worth of people is set by a priori criteria rather than by generalized empathy, and where the capacity of the individual to explore freely a variety of group attachments is hindered, it appears that behavior solely in terms of some particular group's norms and group authority structure is a likely outcome.[32] Of course, the morally rigid person who is the frequent product of such influences has internalized moral values just as has the morally mature person, and the behavior of both types will be similar in many contexts. What distinguishes them is the inability of the morally rigid individual to transcend the rules of his own social order, to stand genuinely outside the bounds of his particular world and admit strangers into the realm of reciprocity.

In the learning process the sense of belonging to a particular secondary-level grouping is at first confused by the child with membership in a particular family. However, with the slow overcoming of egocentricity and the ability to apply reciprocity behavior at progressively higher levels of social generalization, there begins the process of "attaining to a scale of values culminating in relatively abstract values and, at the same time, . . . [success] in integrating spacio-temporal and logical relationships into the invisible whole formed by the nation or the country."[33] The major problem that may occur during this process, however, is the reemergence of egocentrism in the form of sociocentricity rather than the genuine conquest of egocentricism leading to reciprocity.[34] What this means, in effect, is that egocentricism is simply disguised by a similar type of identification, only now with groups that are progressively farther removed from the child's initial self-centered interests.[35] It is assumed that the more manifest aspects of sociocentricism relate to an inability to see events in any terms that do not directly relate to one's self or one's group, a failure to develop the ability to identify with unfamiliar others, and a failure to have real empathy. The result is a rigid moralism, à kind of law-and-order outlook manifested by conventional and authoritative behavior patterns. Strangers are dealt with in a number of ways: by acceptance and politeness up to a point, by reserved behavior, by rejection or worse. Admitting strangers into the realm of acceptability is done only by including the stranger within some existing group definition (family, religion, club, and so on), rather than by expanding one's own conception of the social boundaries within which one lives.

These hypothesized relationships have enormous political implications. They suggest that the greatest possibility for the development of the largest number of mature, moral individuals is interrelated with a social and political environment where the individual has maximum opportunity to develop an identification that includes all others, and where learning that only one group and that group's set of values are important is muted.

Needless to say, no such system currently exists and, in a pure form, probably never can, although tendencies toward such an environment are discernable in some societies. The greatest impediments in many countries are concerned with social boundaries determined by race, religion, sex, ascriptive class and caste designations, and by values of human worth based on wealth or the ownership of property.

Figure 2.3 presents a summary of two hypothesized ideal relationships among types of socialization influence, types of social and political environment, and types of moral orientation. No assumption is made that the two overall sets of relationships differ in a statistically significant sense.they may, of course, but at this stage considerable overlap and ambiguity are perceived. Each is termed an affinity relationship in which there is an hypothesized internal interaction among the component variables. The nature of the socialization influence variables has been noted previously as has the difference, with regard to types of moral orientation, between a rigid closed moral orientation and a flexible open moral orientation. With regard to social and political environment, closed means that moral behavior has a social boundary that excludes certain others, whereas open refers to a highly permeable or nonexistent boundary.

Although no statistical difference between the two overall sets of relationships has been predicted, the great divergence between them must be noted. Both, of course, are compatible with mankind's basic drive to establish broader cooperative relationships and as such, both are culminations of a long historical process, although the closed environment/rigid closed moral orientation type has been overwhelmingly more common and persistent. In one sense the two types stand in a stage relationship to each other. In another sense, however, they are also related in a contradictory fashion with a highly unstable possibility for joint existence. This, the author believes, holds as true for social systems as for the moral development of individuals. How the contradiction can be resolved, however, is beyond the scope of this study.

CONCLUSION

McGuire has said that it is entirely possible that xenophobia is a partially innate attitude in humans.[36] Perhaps this is so, but in this chapter the attempt has been made to suggest — without, however, any strict causal proof — that the types of cooperative bonds that people have with others are related to the nature of social systems.

Attention was focused initially on human mating patterns in primitive societies in order to reveal tendencies in the species to enlarge sets of cooperative relationships. This tendency, in the author's opinion, is a cru-

FIGURE 2.3

Affinity Relationships among Socialization Influence, Moral Orientation, and Social and Political Environment

	Closed Social and Political Environment	Open Social and Political Environment
Rigid Closed Moral Orientation	Secondary Level Role Training Identification Training is Sociocentric (Outcome: Ethnocentricism)	Secondary Level Role Training Identification Training Transcends Sociocentricism (Outcome: Cosmopolitanism)
	Morals Training Moral Indoctrination (Outcome: Inadmissability of alternative value orientations)	Morals Training Exposure to Moral Contradictions (Outcome: admissibility of alternate value orientations)
	Affective Manipulation Physical and Love-oriented Discipline (Outcome: fear, shame or guilt)	Affective Manipulation Induction Training (Outcome: empathy)
	Feedback Only one Socially Approved Channel (Outcome: strict adherence to normative prescriptions)	Feedback Channel not Socially Determined (Outcome: experimentation concerning modes of reciprocity)

The right-hand column is labeled **Flexible Open Moral Orientation**.

cial aspect of the development and survival of humankind and a major defining characteristic of humanity itself. An attempt was also made to show that the degree to which one expands one's capacity to include others as recipients of moral behavior is related to the development of mature morality. In this sense, the development of a notion of membership in a larger community and the quality of a group's political and social life may both depend on and be formative of the moral development process of individuals. Yet, as suggested, there are many impediments that limit the development of this mature morality, which in turn lead to forms of social interaction that block the development of mature morality. An inability to transcend personal or national interests may lead to forms of sociocentricism, manifested, in some cases, by a rigid moral outlook, where only the norms of one's own group are assumed to have validity. Where social interaction patterns emphasize strict identification with only one particular group and strict adherence to only one set of norms, such that feedback from one's behavior provides little allowance for others who are not members of one's own clan, class, caste, religion, profession, sex, race, nationality, and so on, then the probability of some form of sociocentricity would seem to be enhanced. In such ways, the environment of a social system may adversely affect the moral development of that society's citizens, even though the mature moral development of some citizens may act slowly to change forms of social and political interaction.

In most situations it is no doubt true that people tend to preserve the existing integration of their values. This tendency keeps them from transcending their own insularity, and when reinforced by social and political influences, too often leads to the jealous assertion of particular values as having an exclusive primacy, thus denying the claims of alternate ideals and the possibility for an awareness of the potential validity of other values. Conversely, open social and political systems foster the development of conditions that will generate greater concern for reciprocity, promote justice and fairness with regard to the claims of others, encourage individuals to explore alternate avenues to enhance relations with others, and reduce pressures for conformity to only one set of social and political values.

NOTES

1. Richard E. Leakey and Roger Lewin, *Origins* (New York: Dutton, 1977).

2. Jane van Lawick-Goodall, *In the Shadow of Man* (Boston: Houghton Mifflin, 1971).

3. Stephen Jay Gould, "Evolution: Explosion, Not Ascent," New York *Times*, January 22, 1978, p. 6E.

4. Alvin A. Rosenfeld, Carol C. Nadelson, Maralyn Krieger, and John H. Backman, "Incest and Sexual Abuse of Children," *Journal of the American Academy of Child Psychiatry* 16 (1977): 327–39.

5. Talcott Parsons, "The Incest Taboo in Relation to Social Structure and the Socialization of the Child," *British Journal of Sociology* 5 (1954): 101–17.

6. Leakey, *Origins*.

7. A. Irving Hallowell, "Personality, Culture, and Society in Behavioral Evolution," in *Psychology: A Study of a Science*, ed. Sigmund Koch (Study II, Empirical Substructures and Relations with Other Sciences. Volume 6. Investigations of Man as Socius: Their Place in Psychology and the Social Sciences) (New York: McGraw-Hill, 1963).

8. Leakey, *Origins*.

9. Sigmund Freud, *The Interpretation of Dreams* (New York: Basic Books, 1955).

10. Leakey, *Origins*.

11. Ibid.

12. Ibid.

13. Ibid.

14. Edward O. Wilson, *Sociobiology: The New Synthesis* (Cambridge, Mass.: Harvard University Press, 1975), p. 255.

15. B. F. Skinner, *Beyond Freedom and Dignity* (New York: Knopf, 1971), p. 129.

16. Marion J. Levy, Jr., *Modernization and the Structure of Societies: A Setting for International Affairs* (Princeton, N.J.: Princeton University Press, 1966).

17. R. E. L. Masters, *Patterns of Incest: A Psycho-Social Study of Incest Based on Clinical and Historical Data*, (New York: Julian Press, 1963).

18. Milton Rokeach, *The Nature of Human Values* (New York: Free Press, 1973).

19. F. E. Trainer, "A Critical Analysis of Kohlberg's Contribution to the Study of Moral Thought," *Journal for the Study of Social Behavior* 7 (1977): 41–63; Stephen M. Pittel and Gerald A. Mendelsohn, "Measurement of Moral Values: A Review and Critique," *Psychological Bulletin* 66 (1966): 22–35; William A. Scott, *Values and Organizations: A Study of Fraternities and Sororities* (Chicago: Rand McNally, 1965).

20. Lawrence Kohlberg, "From Is to Ought: How to Commit the Naturalistic Fallacy and Get Away with It in the Study of Moral Development," in *Cognitive Development and Epistemology*, ed. Theodore Mischel (New York: Academic Press, 1971), p. 213.

21. Richard W. Wilson, "A New Direction for the Study of Moral Behavior," *Journal of Moral Education* 7 (1978): 122–31.

22. Lawrence Kohlberg, "Stage and Sequence: The Cognitive Developmental Approach to Socialization," in *Handbook of Socialization Theory and Research*, ed., David A. Goslin (Chicago: Rand McNally, 1969), pp. 382, 384–85; and "Development of Children's Orientations toward a Moral Order," in *Educational Psychology*, ed. Richard C. Sprinthall and Norman A. Sprinthall (New York: Van Nostrand-Reinhold, 1969), pp. 84–85; and with Carol Gilligan, "The Adolescent as a Philosopher: The Discovery of the Self in a Postconventional World," *Daedalus* (Fall 1971): 1070.

23. Wilson, "New Direction," p. 127.

24. Robert Hogan, "Moral Conduct and Moral Character: A Psychological Perspective," *Psychological Bulletin* 79 (1973): pp. 217–32.

25. Ibid.

26. Ibid., p. 223.

27. Martin L. Hoffman and Herbert D. Saltzstein, "Parent Discipline and the Child's Moral Development" *Journal of Personality and Social Psychology* 5 (1967): 45–57.

28. William J. McGuire, "The Nature of Attitudes and Attitude Change" in *The Handbook of Social Psychology*, 2d ed., vol. 3, ed. Gardner Lindzey and Eliot Aronson (Reading, Mass.: Addison-Wesley, 1959 and 1969), pp. 225–26.

29. Richard M. Merelman, "The Development of Political Ideology: A Framework for the Analysis of Political Socialization," *American Political Science Review* 63 (1969): 750–67.

30. Quoted in Carl Sagan, *The Dragons of Eden: Speculations on the Evolution of Human Intelligence* (New York: Random House, 1977), p. 122.

31. Norah Rosenau, "The Sources of Children's Political Concepts: An Application of Piaget's Theory," in *New Directions in Political Socialization*, ed. David C. Schwartz and Sandra Kenyon Schwartz (New York: Free Press, 1975), p. 174.

32. James Fishkin, Kenneth Kenniston, and Catherine MacKinnon, "Moral Reasoning and Political Ideology,' *Journal of Personality and Social Psychology* 27 (1973): 109–19; R. S. Peters, "Moral Development and Moral Learning," *Moralist* 58 (1974): 541–67.

33. Jean Piaget assisted by Anne-Marie Weil, "The Development in Children of the Idea of the Homeland and of Relations with Other Countries," *International Social Science Bulletin* 3 (1951): p. 567.

34. Ibid.

35. Ibid.

36. McGuire, "Nature of Attitudes."

3

MORAL DEVELOPMENT AS AN OBJECTIVE OF GOVERNMENT

Elizabeth Lane Beardsley

For a philosopher, the topic of this study invites two principal lines of inquiry. The first is to ask whether it is conceptually possible for a government agency to foster the moral development of an individual. The second is to ask whether, if it is conceptually possible, it is morally justifiable for a government agency to do so. The question of conceptual possibility will be discussed in the first two sections of this chapter, and the question of moral justifiability in the third section.

A preliminary task, however, is to explicate the concept of moral development that will be used here. It will be assumed that the general term "development" refers to a process of change in the direction of "some end-state which is the culmination of the process."[1] Such a process of directional change involves an essential reference to degrees of approximation to the end-state. It follows that a developing entity can be characterized as manifesting to a high or low degree the qualities constituting the end-state for its development.*

It is assumed that the term "moral development" refers to change in the direction of a morally good character, that is, in the direction of possessing traits that are morally good (moral virtues). The fundamental moral virtues include at least those that are required for participating in the moral life or for having a morality. To explicate what it is to "have a morality," W. K. Frankena's account is adopted:

> X has a morality, or a moral AG (Action Guide), only if it includes judgments, rules, principles, ideals, etc., which concern the relations of an individual

---

*The thesis that development is scalar does not entail that it proceeds by identifiable "stages."

(e.g., X) to others . . . (and) involve or call for consideration of the effects
of his actions on others (not necessarily all others), not from the point of view
of his own interests or aesthetic enjoyments, but from their own point of
view.[2]

Frankena's account is not framed in terms of moral goodness or virtues,
but it readily yields a specification of the fundamental moral virtues: first,
a disposition to consider the interests of others, which will be called the
virtue of benevolence; second, a disposition to try to understand the points
of view of others, which will be termed the virtue of empathy. These two
virtues — benevolence and empathy — must be present in individuals if
they are to have a morality at all. Two additional virtues need to be added.
The first is a disposition to give to the interests of others equal consideration — the virtue of fairness.[3] The final virtue central to a morally good
character is respect for the autonomy of another, to be discussed later.

It is stipulated here that each of the moral virtues concerned with the
treatment of others is a disposition to treat other persons in a certain way
for the sake of the others.[4] This feature of the moral virtues discussed here
will be called their other-regarding motivation.

It can be said, that the end-state for moral development is a person who
is to a high degree benevolent, empathic, and fair, and who also has to
a high degree the disposition to respect the autonomy of another. The
question of whether there is anything in the concept of moral development
as here explicated that makes it impossible for the moral development of
an individual (say, X or Y or Z) to be fostered by a govenment agency
(say, GA_1 or GA_2 or GA_3) will now be considered.

CONCEPTUAL POSSIBILTY

Some will contend that it is indeed impossible for GA_1 to foster the
moral development of X, for the reason that it is conceptually impossible
for any other person to foster one's moral development.[5] This claim will
be referred to as the thesis of other-exclusion. Though false, this thesis
may enjoy a spurious plausibility through its being confused with a claim
that is true. The true claim is that X himself must play a significant part
in fostering any change in himself that can count as moral development.
This latter claim will be called the thesis of self-involvement.

That the self-involvement thesis is true can be seen if one considers
whether moral development should be regarded as subject to moral praise.
It seems clear that it should. But this assertion makes moral sense only
if one regards moral development as, at least in part, an achievement by
the developing individual X. In this connection it is helpful to recall a

passage from John Dewey's *Reconstruction in Philosophy*. Here Dewey maintains that, after a necessary reconstruction in moral conceptions has been made,

> No individual or group will be judged by whether they come up to or fall short of some fixed result, but by the direction in which they are moving. The bad man is the man who, no matter how good he has been, is beginning to deteriorate, to grow less good. The good man is the man who, no matter how good he *has* been, is moving to become better.[6]

One need not subscribe to Dewey's claim in quite so strong a form to feel that it represents a valuable moral insight. It is enough to assert that the direction of moral change should count heavily (not necessarily most heavily) in any overall assessment of the moral character of X. But even to assert this much requires that moral development be construed as something X *does*, and not as something that X *undergoes*. In the Dewey passage, the man who is "moving to become better" must be seen as climbing a moral staircase, not as riding a moral escalator. The self-involvement thesis, in other words, is true.

But the self-involvement thesis does not entail the other-exclusion thesis. For Y to foster the moral development of X, Y must foster the involvement of X in his own moral growth. Y must, that is, bring it about that X voluntarily seeks to attain a higher degree of moral goodness. But there is no conceptual impossibility here. The voluntary acts of an agent can be caused by others, as Joel Feinberg has convincingly argued.[7] X's voluntary steps to attain a higher moral level can be caused by Y.

The conclusion is that the mere fact that an individual or agency is other than X does not support the claim that he or it cannot foster the moral development of X.

There are, however, certain approaches to the project of fostering X's moral development that are ruled out on conceptual grounds. If the virtues of benevolence, empathy, and fairness are construed as involving other-regarding motivation, in the way stipulated above, then the use of coercion by Y or GA_1 seems to be precluded; for if X decides to try to become morally better from a desire to avoid coercive penalties, the decision is incoherent.

A point less obvious, but still undeniable, is that the lure of popularity, power, or prestige cannot be held out to persuade X to become morally better.[8] In general, any appeal to a self-regarding motive is ruled out unless it can be used only to induce X to begin progress toward moral goodness.[9]

MORALLY ACCEPTABLE METHODS

If the argument of the preceding section is correct, a government agency can foster the moral development of X by any method that does not appeal exclusively to the self-interest of X. One must now ask what methods typically used by government agencies meet the test of other-regarding motivation. The most important methods to consider here are those employed by the legal system.

It may seem at first sight that the legal system does not meet the test of other-regarding motivation. An argument that might be offered for this conclusion, at least with respect to the criminal law, runs as follows: first, the criminal law involves the use of coercive sanctions; second, coercive sanctions deter acts harmful to others exclusively by appealing to the self-interest of potential agents (to their desire to avoid sanctions, that is); third, conduct so motivated may be morally right, but with regard to moral goodness and badness it is neutral;[10] therefore, the criminal law cannot foster moral development.

Of the three premises in the above argument, the first and third are true; but the second is false. To assume that legal punishment shapes conduct and character traits only by appealing to self-interest is to disregard what has been aptly called "the expressive function of punishment."[11] In punishing certain acts committed from certain motives, a government makes a statement that ranges in its scope beyond considerations of the self-interest of its citizens.

This is acknowledged by some legal writers, as well as by philosophers. For example, Justice Macklin Fleming, having defined crimes as "intentional invasions of primary personal rights," asserts: "By imposing sanctions on the criminal we seek to teach potential criminals the lesson that this particular crime did not pay, that crime is poor policy, and that *crime is morally wrong*" (emphasis added).[12] Fleming here captures the multifaceted nature of a system of criminal law and recognizes the ability of this governmental institution to meet the test of other-regarding motivation, which rules out only an *exclusive* appeal to self-regarding considerations. The argument discussed above therefore fails to establish its conclusion, since the second premise is false.

Consider a little more closely how the use of coercive sanctions is a form of rational persuasion, but not exclusively through its appeal to self-interest. The criminal law vividly shows how strongly society reprobates certain harms to others. By bringing to bear on certain conduct the entire apparatus of the criminal law (formidable if not majestic), society expresses in the strongest possible terms the judgment that such conduct is wrong. But if X learns from all this only that his community regards harming others as wrong, without going on to see that it *is* wrong, in that it violates the rights of others, he has not progressed far toward becoming morally good.[13] Still, he has taken an initial step.

It seems clear, then, that the legal system affords one means by which a government agency can foster the moral development of individuals.

Understood in the way just described, the legal system becomes a mechanism that fosters the moral development of X by teaching him something, by a kind of rational persuasion.[14]

Rational persuasion may also be attempted in the pronouncements of government officials. Examples of success here are certainly not numerous, but they can be found. One such example was afforded by statements made by Governor Brown and others in persuading California voters to vote against installing a certain nuclear power plant. At a conference sponsored by the Atomic Industrial Forum, the director of the TVA asked the following question: "Does this generation have the moral right to enjoy the benefits of nuclear power before it has built a reasonably safe nuclear trash can to safeguard future generations?"[15]

The appeal in this question is to the rights of others, in this instance others not yet born. Here a government agency may have succeeded in fostering the moral development — specifically the benevolence and the fairness — of a large number of voters and state legislators. It is a heartening demonstration that for GA_1 to foster the moral development of X, Y, Z, et al. is not only conceptually possible, but, on occasion, empirically possible as well.*

The discussion so far has been on methods available to government agencies for fostering moral development through rational persuasion. There are other methods belonging to another approach, which will be called "causal facilitation." This term is used as an umbrella phrase for methods of fostering moral development by increasing either the readiness of X to respond to rational persuasion, or his ability to make moral progress, once he decides to try.

It is natural to think first here of removing major sources of anxiety for X and his fellow citizens. Insecurity with respect to economic well-being and health constitute obvious obstacles to moral development. Government agencies may take measures to reduce anxiety about poverty and illness, and such procedures may foster moral development through causal facilitation, as a school breakfast program may foster intellectual development.

In the case of moral development, the removal of insecurity is not open to the objection of appealing to self-interest, since the goods and services distributed are not treated as rewards for merit, but only as meeting minimal needs.

Some may, however, object that to meet the minimal needs of X and

---

*The author is grateful to those members of the Rutgers Conference who emphasized the need for empirical data to show whether or not rational persuasion was causally effective in the situation mentioned.

Y, and thereby foster their moral development by a form of causal facilitation, risks arousing resentment in Z and W (who perceive their own needs as being unmet), and thereby impeding their moral development by a form of what may be called "causal retardation." For a government agency to fail to meet the minimal needs of X and Y because of a possible regression in moral development in Z and W is morally unacceptable, a case of treating X and Y as means only. But note that this is so, not because the moral development of X and Y is preferred to that of Z and W, but because all citizens are entitled to have their minimal needs met.* It is this principle that justifies special government help for X and Y.

A further objection may now be raised by those who regard the account of fostering moral development by causal facilitation through the distribution of goods and services as much too limited. Individuals may be seen as entitled to goods and services beyond what they need for mere subsistence. David Norton, for example, argues forcefully that a human being "is entitled to what he needs and can effectively use in his work of self-actualization."[16] Norton is willing to follow this line of thought to its logical conclusion: "A good sculptor is entitled to Carrara marble in the amounts he can use, a beginning sculptor to less."[17]

Since Norton conflates moral and nonmoral worth in his concept of a "worthy individual," it is difficult to see his "actualization entitlements" as a necessary element in any account of fostering moral development through a distribution of goods and services. Indeed, the counterintuitive features of Norton's social program underline the importance of distinguishing moral value from nonmoral value. In any case, this study deals only with specifically moral development.

Possible methods of fostering moral development through causal facilitation include maintaining patterns of social organization as well as distributing goods and services. For example, it may be argued that family life and community life or both are highly conducive to moral development in children and others. Government measures taken to strengthen families or communities may seem warranted on the ground that they will foster by causal facilitation the moral development of a large number. Here it is important to bear in mind that a higher degree of benevolence, empathy, and fairness toward an in-group may be secured at the expense of a markedly lower degree of these attitudes toward an out-group. That this risk is genuine and potentially very grave is chillingly shown in Hannah Arendt's description of the "good family-man" in Nazi Germany.[18]

---

*If this principle is deemed to require justification, the Rawlsian defense (of the "maximin" principle) may be used.

Moral development may be fostered by distribution of goods and services, and by patterns of social organization. Other social arrangements may also play a part in fostering or impeding moral development. Here certain insights of the social and moral critic Henry Fairlie are particularly penetrating. The sin of envy is one with which this writer deals incisively, and it becomes clear that an individual consumed by envy cannot become fair, benevolent, or empathic. Fairlie indicts contemporary society for fostering envy through its commercialism: "One of the most uncomfortable facts about our economic system is that it is bound to incite Envy in those to whom it must sell. It must persuade everyone to want what everyone else has."[19]

Fairlie also charges our society with fostering envy through its meritocracy:

A system of elites that are, or are supposed to be, chosen on merit must rest on two assumptions: that everyone begins with an equal chance from the same starting-line, and that the rules of the competition are fair at every stage. . . . What matters here is that the idea of merit is rooted in the idea of equality. . . . It [the idea of merit] therefore has to meet the leveling spirit of Envy, when someone asks why he did not make it to the top, instead of someone else who is "just like him."[20]

Even if the role of society in fostering or impeding moral development through such phenomena as commercialism and meritocracy is substantial, the question remains as to whether government can or should take steps to control or influence these phenomena. This question is too complex to be addressed here. It may be noted briefly, however, that government support for affirmative action programs of certain sorts may do much to meet Fairlie's criticism of meritocracy; that is, it may foster the moral development not only of those who are the direct beneficiaries of those programs but also of those who are not.

SHOULD GOVERNMENT FOSTER MORAL DEVELOPMENT?

An attempt has been made to show that GA_1 can foster the moral development of X. With regard to the question of whether it is morally justified in doing so, one answer that might be given here is that since an affirmative answer to this question is so clearly warranted, the question itself is otiose.

In the *Politics*, according to a leading expositor, Aristotle recognizes that "the good life of the state exists only in the good lives of its citizens" and "speaks as if the state were merely ancillary to the moral life of the individual."[21] Centuries later, a political theorist is said to defend the thesis that "the goal of politics is autonomy or moral agency."[22] If the purpose of government is to produce individuals of high moral calibre, then it is obvious that GA_1 should foster the moral development of X. But such a theory of the purpose of government is far from persuasive. If it appears to invite instituting a certain treatment of Y and Z on the ground that this would foster the moral development of X, this must be for either of two reasons: first, that such activity is in the interest of X; second, that it is in the interest of others. The question of whether either justification meets critical scrutiny needs to be asked.

First, with regard to the claim that GA_1 should foster the moral development of X in the interest of X, much depends on whether it is assumed that moral development is instrumentally valuable for X (as enabling him to secure other goods) or as intrinsically valuable for X. Consider first the assumption that X's moral development is instrumentally valuable to him; that is, that to reach a higher level of moral goodness will help him to further his own (nonmoral) interests. To use this rationale in seeking to persuade X himself to undertake moral growth is, as has been seen, conceptually impossible. The present question is whether GA_1 can have in its own rationale a reason that it must keep secret from X himself. Such a situation is familiar to us: parents often have reasons *for* persuading children to do or be something, which are not the reasons they use *in* persuading the children. There is nothing contradictory or even hypocritical in the parents' behavior, but there is something very patronizing. At least, it would be called patronizing in a relation between adults, of which the relation of GA_1 to X is presumably an instance.

The justification that GA_1 should foster the moral development of X is therefore rejected on the ground that his own moral development is instrumentally good for X. Consider now the other assumption — that his own moral development is intrinsically good for X.

Here those who have, as does the author, a strong tendency to oppose paternalism will be on their guard. Paternalism has been defined as the restriction of X's liberty for his own good.[23] Since the coercion of X himself was ruled out above as a possible means of fostering his moral development, paternalism in this sense is not a threat. Under consideration here is the justifiability of GA_1's fostering the moral development of X only by rational persuasion or causal facilitation. Such procedures may not be paternalistic, but they are patronizing.

This is because it is one thing for Y to try to help X secure a good for X at X's request, and quite another thing for Y to try to secure a good for X without X's request, however good the good may be. The latter procedure is initiated by a significant decision concerning X's life not taken by X. This way of treating X, if X is an adult, is patronizing. It is a mild form of a failure to respect autonomy. There is a moral spectrum here, with the treatment of X as a mere means at one end of the spectrum, paternalistic treatment next, and patronizing treatment next. These are morally objectionable in very different degrees, but it is important to recognize the common thread running through them*

The justification of fostering the moral development of X on the ground that this will be valuable for X, either instrumentally or intrinsically, is open to serious question. This justification is, it has been argued, either conceptually impossible or patronizing. What can be said then about the thesis that GA_1 is justified in fostering the moral development of X on the ground that this will be valuable for others?

This justification rests on a much stronger moral foundation. The thesis that Y and Z have rights (justified claims) to security in their persons and property is relatively unproblematic, as is the thesis that government agencies have an obligation to protect these rights. Since moral development in X will assist in this protection, it is reasonable to argue that GA_1 should foster the moral development of X.

However, this justification needs to be clarified in certain respects. First, it does not imply that other methods of protecting the rights of Y and Z are ruled out for GA_1.† Second, it must not be understood as failing to respect the autonomy of X. Those who would argue that to foster the moral development of X on the ground that this will be in the interest of Y and Z is to treat X as a means only, have failed to grasp what is involved in fostering someone's moral development. If this project is conceptualized in the way proposed in the section on conceptual possibility one may say that GA_1 is morally justified in carrying it out.

Thus, whereas GA_1 is not justified in treating Y and Z in a certain fashion on the ground that this would foster the moral development of X, for GA_1 to foster the moral development of X on the ground that this protects certain interests of Y and Z is justified. To put the matter in another way, one may say that Y and Z have a right to security, but that X does not have a right to the fostering of his moral development. The latter formulation itself calls for further philosophic examination, but this cannot be undertaken here.

In this chapter an attempt has been made to show that it is both conceptually possible and morally justifiable for government to adopt as an objective the moral development of its citizens. In answering both the

---

*The author attempts to analyze this common threat in "Paternalism and Benevolence," in progress.

†In thinking about this point the author has profited from Paul Tong's discussion of some of his unpublished work on Chinese legal concepts.

original questions affirmatively, however, an effort has been made to show some of the qualifications that must form part of an acceptable affirmative answer.

NOTES

1. P. H. Hirst and R. S. Peters, *The Logic of Education* (New York: Humanities Press, 1971), p. 43. The authors are summarizing an account of development given by Ernest Nagel; see his essay in *The Concept of Development*, ed. D. B. Harris (Minneapolis: University of Minnesota Press, 1957), pp. 15–24.

2. W. K. Frankena, "The Concept of Morality," in *The Definition of Morality*, ed. G. Wallace and A. B. M. Walker (London: Methuen, 1970), p. 156.

3. See W. K. Frankena, "Some Beliefs About Justice," in *Freedom and Morality*, ed. John Brick (Lawrence: University of Kansas Press, 1976), pp. 53–70.

4. This concept has been clarified by recent philosophic examination. See especially J. A. Brook, "How to Treat Persons as Persons," in *Philosophy and Personal Relations*, ed. A. Montefiore (Montreal: McGill-Queens University Press, 1973), pp. 62–82.

5. Mary J. Gregor, *Kant's Doctrine of Virtue* (New York: Harper, 1964).

6. John Dewey, *Reconstruction in Philosophy* (Boston: Beacon, 1957), p. 176.

7. J. Feinberg, "Causing Voluntary Acts," in *Doing and Deserving* (Princeton: Princeton University Press, 1970), pp. 152–86.

8. For an argument that the desire for fame serves just this purpose, see David Hume, *An Enquiry Concerning the Principles of Morals* (Indianapolis: Bobbs-Merrill, 1957).

9. This is a particular form of the general line of thought termed the "paradox of moral education." See James McClellan, *Philosophy of Education* (Englewood Cliffs, N. J.: Prentice-Hall, 1976).

10. See W. D. Ross, *The Right and the Good* (Oxford: Oxford University Press, 1930).

11. Joel Feinberg, *Doing and Deserving*, pp. 95–118.

12. Macklin Fleming, *Of Crime and Rights* (New York: Norton, 1978), p. 126.

13. In a general form, this point is clearly stated by Kurt Baier, "Ethical Pluralism and Moral Education," in *Moral Education*, ed. C. M. Beck et al. (Toronto: Newman, 1971).

14. Constitutionalism can exert a notable moral force in fostering moral development. In this connection, the discussions of the U.S. Bill of Rights by David A. J. Richards are especially illuminating; see *The Moral Criticism of Law* (Encino, Calif.: Dickensen, 1977).

15. Tom Wicker, "Reacting Against Reactors," in New York *Times*, March 10, 1978, p. A29.

16. David L. Norton, "Individualism and Productive Justice," *Ethics* 87 (1977): 119.

17. Ibid., p. 118.

18. Hannah Arendt, "Collective Guilt," in *Guilt, Man and Society*, ed. R. W. Smith (New York: Doubleday Anchor, 1971), pp. 255–68.

19. Henry Fairlie, *The Seven Deadly Sins Today* (Washington: New Republic Books, 1978), p. 69.

20. Ibid., pp. 74–75.

21. W. D. Ross, *Aristotle* (London: Methuen, 1956), p. 187.

22. This view is attributed to A. Levine by S. G. Salkever; see Salkever's review of Levine, "The Politics of Autonomy," *Political Theory* 5 (1977): 539.

23. G. Dworkin "Paternalism," in *Morality and the Law*, ed. R. Wasserstrom (Belmont, Calif.: Wadsworth, 1971), pp. 107–26.

PART II

MORAL DEVELOPMENT AS LIBERAL IDEOLOGY

EDITORS' COMMENTS

The connection between moral development theory and Western liberal ideology is directly addressed in this section of the book. While most modern, social psychological theories of moral development have originated in the West, they have purported to be universally applicable. This assertion has been put forth most strongly by Lawrence Kohlberg who is perhaps the leading contemporary theorist of moral development. His initial paper in this part points out how his own theory of moral development substantiates the notion that liberalism will persist. He suggests that findings from his research cut against claims made by others that liberalism as a philosophical force in the West is exhausted.

The remaining chapters in this section question the assumption of universality. In the first of these, Alan M. Cohen questions whether moral development theories, especially those of Kohlberg and his followers, can genuinely reveal people's political behavior, political choices, and political allegiances. Insisting that knowledge of a person's moral judgment level does not permit inferences about that person's actions, Cohen finds that moral development theory leaves critically important gaps in the area of politics.

James Fishkin is concerned with empirical data from Kohlberg's work, which show that some individuals, who are termed relativists, have apparently regressed in moral stage level in a manner that is contrary to the invariant progressive developmental notions of the theory itself. Fishkin's critique is that an erroneous conceptual framework has led to a misinterpretation by Kohlberg of his own findings. Relativistic behavior, according to Fishkin, can be seen as consistent and coherent, but the assumptions behind it are "incompatible with the possibility of liberalism as a coherent moral ideology."

The final chapter in this part by Herbert G. Reid and Ernest J. Yanarella directly confronts Kohlberg's theories as a species of liberal ideology. Arguing from a modern, critical theory perspective, they conclude that Kohlberg's theory cannot be regarded as universal precisely because it is an ideological reflection of the Anglo-American liberal tradition.

4

THE FUTURE OF LIBERALISM AS THE DOMINANT IDEOLOGY OF THE WEST

Lawrence Kohlberg

This chapter will focus on the moral dimension of ideology. Ideology refers to a very general pattern or structure of belief that defines evaluation and choice. One part of an ideology is its pattern of assumptions about factual matters, about the nature of man, society, and the cosmos. Of even more significance are the assumed moral principles, which, together with assumptions about facts, determine choice for that ideology.

The approach to ideology here comes from a structural developmental perspective. Structuralism, as popularized for instance by Leo Strauss, attempts to identify the invariants under transformation of a set of ideas or symbols. As structure, an ideology is a recurring system of logically interrelated general assumptions about facts and includes a set of general moral principles.

As examples of a structure liberalism, which the author believes has been the dominant ideology of the past two centuries in the West, John Dewey's *Liberalism and Social Action* and Roberto Unger's recent critique of liberalism, *Knowledge and Politics,* are particularly useful writings on the subject.[1] Dewey traces liberalism from John Locke's doctrine of the social contract and of natural rights to Jeremy Bentham's and John Stuart Mill's utilitarian philosophy of social reform and then to his own less individualistic and more organic philosophy of social reform.

Behind these historically varying doctrines is a structure. According to Unger, liberalism is a way of thinking. To grasp a way of thinking we have to understand the problems it is concerned with and the methods it uses to solve them in the context of an experience of the world. Problems, methods, and experience constitute the "deep structure" of the thought. This "deep structure" allows for a variety of philosophic positions, depending on which part of the underlying experience is illuminated. . . . It cannot be demonstrated that the different premises of the libral doctrine follow from one another by a strict logical necessity. But one can analogize the relationships among the doctrines of liberal thought to logical entailments and the conflicts among them to logical contradictions.[2]

From a structural point of view, liberalism is first of all a doctrine of social reform, of progressive or constitutional social change. Central to it are moral principles of justice, where justice is defined in terms of individual rights, all of which revolve around liberty. These principles of justice are usually defined and justified through a social-contract theory. The theory of a social contract may be viewed as a set of premises about fact; notions that law and society did emerge from a contract of men living in a state of nature. But the theory of a social contract is actually neither history nor sociology; it is a way of specifying the moral principles adhered to by the liberal.

This view of the social contract has been elaborated best in one of the newest great books of the liberal tradition, John Rawls's *Theory of Justice*.[3] In Rawls's version, the state of nature — "the original position" — is arrived at by rational men contracting about the principles of justice or the moral principles that should govern a society. The original position imagined is that in which each man is under a "veil of ignorance" as to the position he will have in the society. Thus he must choose principles of justice that he is willing to live with, whether he is rich or poor, black or white, male or female, whatever. Rawls contends that under these conditions, the first principle chosen would be the right to maximum individual liberty compatible with the liberty of others; the second principle would be that there is no justification of inequalities unless they are to the benefit of the least advantaged. Rawls claims that his principles of liberty and equality are not just the principles of Western liberalism, but would be those chosen by rational men in any society, acting under a veil of ignorance, as they worked toward development of a contract that would maximize their individual values.

Rawls explicated the structure of liberalism in the direction in which liberalism is still evolving or developing as a dominant ideology of the West. The death of liberalism as an ideology and its replacement by a new ideology has been the theme of many books, the most popular of which has been Charles Reich's *The Greening of America*,[4] and one of the most scholarly, Unger's book previously discussed. It will be the contention here that Rawls's book is one example of a new structural development of liberal ideology, more radical than its predecessors, but still operating as a new stage in the development of liberal thought. In that sense, liberalism will probably not be replaced by a new ideology of the West but will continue to be its dominant ideology for the next century.

To develop this theme, the author proposes to review his own empirical work on the development of stages of moral judgment in the individual, on generational differences in moral judgment stages, and on the relation of the modal moral stage of a society to its sociostructural complexity. In so doing, empirical work following up a neglected sociological classic of the early twentieth century, L. T. Hobhouse's *Morals in Evolution,* will also be reported on.[5]

RESEARCH ON MORAL DEVELOPMENT

Central to the work is the problem of relativity of values. Are there universal values that children do or should develop? The solution to this problem rests on recent findings of psychological research that show culturally universal stages of moral development.

The cognitive developmental theory of moral psychology used in presenting the facts here is basically that of John Dewey, more recently elaborated by Jean Piaget and this author. This theory proposes that moral development passes through invariant qualitative stages, and that the stimulation of moral development, like other forms of development, rests on the stimulation of thinking and problem solving by the child.

The cognitive developmental or progressive approach starts from a different view of morality than either common sense or most psychology. It claims that morality represents a set of rational principles of judgment and decision valid for every culture: the principles of human welfare and justice. The lists of rules and commandments drawn up by cultures and schools are more or less arbitrary, but as a matter of both psychology and philosophy it is maintained here that there are, in fact, only a few ethical principles and these are culturally universal. A moral principle is not the same as a rule. "Thou shalt not commit adultery" is a rule for specific behavior in specific situations, in a monogamous society.

By contrast, the categorical imperative (act only as you would be willing that everyone should act in the same situation) is a principle — not a prescription for behavior, but a guide for choosing among behaviors. As such it is free from culturally defined content; it both transcends and subsumes particular social laws and hence has universal applicability.

Related to Kant's principles of the categorical imperative and central to the development of moral judgment is the principle of justice. Justice, the primary regard for the value and equality of all human beings and for reciprocity in human relations, is a basic and universal standard. As social psychologists, the author and his colleagues have gathered considerable evidence to indicate that the concepts of justice inhere in human experience and are not the product of a particular cultural world view. This follows Jean Piaget who says: "In contrast to a given rule imposed upon the child from outside, the rule of justice is an imminent condition of social relationships or a law governing their equilibrium."

Related to the principle of justice is the principle of role taking, the Golden Rule. All social life necessarily entails the assumption of a variety of roles, taking other people's perspectives and participating in reciprocal relationships, so that arriving at mature principles of justice is the result of reworking one's experiences of role taking in successively more complex and functional forms.

Individuals acquire and refine a sense of justice through a sequence of invariant developmental stages. In 1957, a start was made in testing the moral judgment of a group of 72 boys aged 10 through 16 by asking them questions involving moral dilemmas. A typical question raises the issue of stealing a drug to save a dying woman. The inventor of the drug is selling it for ten times what it costs him to make. The woman's husband cannot raise the money and the seller refuses to lower the price or wait for payment. What should the husband do? From the answers given by the group to such dilemmas, six basic types of moral judgments were distinguished that correspond to developmental stages. Subsequent retesting of the group at three-year intervals has shown growth proceeding through the same stages in the same order. The stages are defined below.

1. *Preconventional level*

At this level the child is responsive to cultural rules and labels of good and bad, right or wrong, but interprets these labels either in terms of the physical or the hedonistic consequences of action (punishment, reward, exchange of favors) or in terms of the physical power of those who enunciate the rules and labels. The level is divided into the following two stages:

Stage 1: The punishment-and-obedience orientation. The physical consequences of action determine its goodness or badness regardless of the human meaning or value of these consequences. Avoidance of punishment and unquestioning deference to power are valued in their own right, not in terms of respect for an underlying moral order supported by punishment and authority (the latter being Stage 4.).

Stage 2: The instrumental-relativist orientation. Right action consists of that which instrumentally satisfies one's own needs and occasionally the needs of others. Human relations are viewed in terms like those of the marketplace. Elements of fairness, of reciprocity, and of equal sharing are present, but they are always interpreted in a physical, pragmatic way. Reciprocity is a matter of "you scratch my back and I'll scratch yours," not of loyalty, gratitude, or justice.

2. Conventional level

At this level, maintaining the expectations of the individual's family, group, or nation is perceived as valuable in its own right, regardless of immediate and obvious consequences. The attitude is not only one of conformity to personal expectations and social order, but of loyalty to it, of actively maintaining, supporting, and justifying the order, and of identifying with persons or groups involved in it. At this level, there are the following two stages:

Stage 3: The interpersonal concordance or "good boy — nice girl" orientation. Good behavior is that which pleases or helps others and is approved by them. There is much conformity to stereotypical images or what is majority or "natural" behavior. Behavior is frequently judged by intention — "he means well" becomes important for the first time. One earns approval by being "nice."

Stage 4: The "law-and-order" orientation. There is orientation toward authority, fixed rules, and the maintenance of the social order. Right behavior consists of doing one's duty, showing respect for authority, and maintaining the given social order for its own sake.

3. Postconventional, autonomous, or principled level

At this level, there is a clear effort to define moral values and principles that have validity and application apart from the authority of the groups or persons holding these principles and apart from the individuals' own identification with these groups. This level again has two stages:

Stage 5: The social-contract legalistic orientation, generally with utilitarian overtones. Right action tends to be defined in terms of general individual rights, and standards that have been critically examined and agreed upon by the whole society. There is a clear awareness of the relativism of personal values and opinions and a corresponding emphasis upon procedural rules for reaching consensus. Aside from what is constitutionally and democratically agreed upon, the rights are a matter of personal "values" and "opinion." The result is an emphasis upon the "legal point of view," but with an emphasis upon the possibility of changing law in terms of rational considerations of social utility (rather than freezing it in terms of Stage 4 "law and order"). Outside the legal realm, free agreement and contract is the binding element of obligation. This is the "official" morality of the American government and constitution.

Stage 6: The Universal-Ethical Principle Orientation. Right is defined by the decision of conscience in accord with self-chosen *ethical principles* appealing to logical comprehensiveness, universality, and consistency. These principles are abstract and ethical (the Golden Rule, the categorical imperative); they are not concrete moral rules like the Ten Commandments. At heart, these are universal principles of justice, of the reciprocity and equality of human rights, and of respect for the dignity of human beings as individual persons.[6]

The stages are not defined by particular opinions or judgments, but by ways of thinking about moral matters and bases for choice. Stages 1 and 2, which are typical of young children and delinquents, are described as preconventional since decisions are made largely on the basis of self-interest and material considerations. The group-oriented Stages 3 and 4 are the conventional ones at which most of the adult population operates. The final principled Stages 5 and 6 are characteristic of about 10 percent to 20 percent of the adult population, but only about 5 percent of the adult population arrives at Stage 6.

The same stages of development are found in various cultures, although average progress is faster and farther in some than in others. Youngsters in the United States, Great Britain, Mexico, Turkey, Taiwan, and Malaysia have been tested and the same patterns of thought occurring in the same developmental sequence have been discovered. It is interesting to observe that the stages occur in a fixed sequence because each successive stage orders a more intricately perceived social world in terms of a logic of role taking and justice more capable of dealing with its complexity.

At the first or preconventional level, the individual sees moral dilemmas in terms of the individual needs of the people involved. Situations of moral conflict are seen as situations in which needs collide and are resolved, either in terms of who has the most power in the situation (Stage 1) or in terms of simple individual responsibility for one's own welfare (Stage 2), with the exception of situations in which marketplace notions of reciprocity are operable.

The next two stages of moral development are termed conventional because moral conflicts are now seen and resolved in group or social rather than in individual terms. Right or justice is seen to reside in interpersonal social relationships (Stage 3) or in the community (Stage 4) rather than in the individual.

However, if one society defines the right and the good, what is one to think when one recognizes that different societies label and define good and bad or right and wrong quite differently? When abortions were illegal in this country, they were legal in Sweden. With increasing exposure to how others live, there is a greater recognition of the fact that a given way is only one among many.

If one cannot simply equate the "right" with the "societal" and the "legal," then what is one to do? Adolescents may go through a period of ethical relativism during which they question the premises of any moral system. If there are many ways to live, who can presume to say which is best? Perhaps everyone should do his own thing.

The way out of this moral relativism or moral nihilism lies in the perception that underneath the rules of any given society lie moral principles and universal moral rights, and the validity of any moral choice rests on the principles that choice embodies. Such moral principles are universal in their application and constitute a viable standard against which the particular laws or conventions of any society can and should be judged. When obedience to laws violates moral principles or rights, one is justified in violating such laws.

At the last two stages, then, choice is based on the principles that supersede convention, just as previously the claims of society or convention were seen as the grounds for adjudicating differences between individuals.

There are intrinsically two constraints on this developmental process. The first is the cognitive capacity of the individual. The second has to do with the nature of the child's social experience. To the extent that social experience is perfectly consonant with the child's stage of reasoning, no conflict or disequilibrium of development will occur. If there is no coherent society or group of which the child sees himself as a member, then he cannot understand the basis for conventional moral thought. If his society is the only one he knows, there is no basis in experience for postconventional or principled thinking.

It follows, then, that social institutions influence the moral development of the child insofar as they inevitably affect both the cognitive development and the social experiences that are its necessary preconditions. Social institutions also directly impede or foster moral development by the conception of justice they embody, which either creates a stimulus for growth or acts to fixate the individual at his current level. Research indicates traditional prisons are Stages 1 and 2 justice structures and inmates respond (and partially regress) accordingly. The author experimentally helped create a democratic prison community with a Stage 3 or 4 justice structure and moral atmosphere that resulted in development of the individual moral stage in participating inmates. Larger societies, as well as small institutions, may have modal levels of institutional complexity and of justice structures. Following Hobhouse, developing social complexity may lead to, or accompany, changes in modal moral level.

APPLICATION TO THE SPECIAL PROBLEMS
OF THE PRESENT:
THE DIRECTION OF MORAL CHANGE IN THE 1970s

The "liberal" position just reviewed holds that there is a tendency for both individuals and societies to move in a positive direction under normal conditions. A faith in progress is a core of the liberal tradition. The liberal faith is not a faith in the inevitability of progress by some iron law of social history or by some biological unfolding in the child. The liberal faith is, rather, that under conditions of open exposure to information and communication and of a degree of control by the individual over his actions and the ensuing consequences, basic changes in both individuals and societies tend to be in a forward direction in a series of steps or stages moving toward greater justice in terms of equity or recognition of universal human rights. This seems a proper point at which to provide some documentation for the liberal faith in progress at a time in which such faith has come to seem naive or obsolete.

Historical and cross-cultural evidence supports the notion of a long-range moral evolutionary trend on the societal level. Do societies go through stages of moral evolution? Acceptance of the existence of these stages was popular in the nineteenth century and then supposedly disproved by early twentieth-century anthropology and sociology. The best early work on societal stages of moral evolution was done by Hobhouse in 1906 as cited above. Hobhouse pooled cross-cultural ethnographic data with the limited data of written history to define cultural stages that roughly parallel the psychological stages defined above. He found a strong correlation between these moral stages and the level of sociotechnological complexity of a society. Donald Elfenbein replicated Hobhouse's findings, using newer methods for scaling social complexity and using more precise definitions based on moral stages to classify ethnographic descriptions or institutions and beliefs. Sample descriptions of stages in cultural development of legal-judicial structures are presented below.

Stage 1
Disputes are settled by physical retaliation by the victim (or his kinsmen). Retaliation typically takes the form of talion — doing back to the offender what he did. Settlement is dependent on strength in that retribution is unfeasible unless the victim can muster sufficient strength. Sanctions are physical and are intended to harm the offender, who deserves to be harmed, and to expurgate bad acts or bad people.

Stage 2
Disputes are settled through negotiations in which the disputants attempt to press their claims to their own advantage. Negotiations entail bargaining and reciprocal exchange (e.g., restitution for the offense) with each side trying to maximize the instrumental satisfaction of its needs. A compromise settlement is typically arranged. The outcome of the negotiations is partly dependent upon strength, insofar as strength improves a disputant's bargaining position. The sanctions ultimately agreed upon serve as appeasements of the victim and typically take the form of reciprocal, quantitative compensation, or damages.

Stage 3

Disputants abide by the expectations of a mediator who intervenes in the dispute or by conventional social expectations or standards. In mediation a third party who, by virtue of personal qualities, commands the respect of the disputants, intervenes in the dispute and persuades them to accept a settlement. The disputants abide by the mediator's recommendations in order to win his approval or to conform to conventional standards which he espouses. Alternatively, the disputants are induced or compelled to abide by the informal, shared expectations of society as to the kind of settlement which should be imposed. A consensus regarding how the dispute should be settled is typically arrived at during collective deliberations of the community. The purpose of the sanctions imposed is to reconcile the disputants and to reform the offender.

Stage 4

Disputes are adjudicated by an individual (or agency) delegated by society to fill the role of judicial authority. The authority is a representative of the social order. Fixed, general rules define adjudicative procedures which are consistently followed when disputes arise. Typically these procedures are conducted within a system of courts. The scope of the authority's powers is delimited by rules. Decisions of the authority are enforced uniformly, regardless of persons or circumstances, on a societywide basis. Sanctions are administered in order to communicate society's outrage at the offense, to serve as a deterrent, and to require the offender to expiate his crime, to "pay his debt to society."[7]

Why should there be a cultural as well as an individual progression through stages of justice? Justice is both a sociological and a psychological concept. A just solution of a social conflict is a better equilibrated resolution of a conflict. By definition, justice is a resolution of conflicting claims in light of principles and procedures that appear fair to the parties involved in the conflict. When a society has arrived at a relatively just solution to a conflict, that solution tends to be maintained, whereas a situation of injustice is always a situation in disequilibrium, particularly in a society whose sociopolitical institutions have a constitutional democratic (Stage 5) or "open" basic structure so that authority and force do not maintain arbitrary, unjust solutions. Qualifications regarding an evolutionary trend toward justice in an open society, however, must be made first.

The concept of justice is relative; justice perceived as being at one stage of development cannot be at another. The American conventional majority perceived racial discrimination and prejudice as compatible with justice. There was always a certain tension between justice and discrimination for the Stage 4 individual, but not in the sense that there was for the individual with a principled sense of justice. Second, the progress of a sociopolitical system formally at a certain stage or level is contingent on the moral level of the majority of members of the system.

To classify an institution or a society at a certain moral stage does not mean that all or even the majority of members of the society are at that stage. The American constitutional system is a Stage 5 social system. It is founded on the premises of liberalism (whether of a Stage 5 or Stage 6 variety). While the American social system is a Stage 5 system, the majority of Americans and sometimes their leaders are conventional (Stage 4 law and order) in their moral reasoning. The American constitutional system, of course, was never assumed to require that most members of society think and act in terms of liberal moral principles. Rather, the system was designed to ensure that political and legal decisions compatible with liberal principles would emerge from the constitutional democratic process itself. The Constitution was an integration of liberal moral principles with a carefully suspicious sociology and psychology that attempted to consider all the abuses of power to which Stage 2 instrumental egoistic human nature was liable.

The agonizingly slow but relatively consistent trend toward greater justice, civil rights, and racial equality is one of many historical indicators of the directionality of a democratic system toward carrying its original premises of justice beyond the boundaries accepted by the founders of the system. Indeed, the major moral crises of the past 20 years have represented conflicts between universal justice and the boundary-maintaining demands of society-sustaining morality. From a liberal or morally principled view, the agony of Vietnam can be recognized as the first time a war engaged in for national security has been massively questioned in terms of universal human rights to life. On the whole, American history has supported not only the sheer viability of a Stage 5 sociopolitical system, but the fact that a sociopolitical system based on Stage 5 premises can move in a direction of moral progress even though the bulk of the members of the system and even sometimes its leaders may be Stage 4, or conventional. Such sociomoral progress, however, will always be accompanied by temporary waves of reaction as long as the majority of the members of the society are conventional.

The notion that there is a trend toward moral advance in our society is supported by generational findings. Interviews conducted (keeping education controlled) with men in their 20s and with their parents found a higher proportion of the younger generation to be principled than of their mothers and fathers. These results can be explained largely in terms of increased awareness at an earlier age of value conflicts within conventional morality and of conflict between conventional morality and more universal value principles. Awareness of value conflict is not enough to stimulate movement toward principled morality. Even now, a relatively small percentage of persons in their 20s reach principled thought.

PROBLEMS OF MORAL CHANGE IN THE 1970s

The above exposition presents a liberal evolutional view of current moral change. From this perspective, the older generation's distress about the decline of the work ethic, the rise of the new sexual morality, the indifference to patriotism, and the decline of authority at first seem to be merely a reactionary or a conventional (Stage 4) law-and-order response to progress toward postconventional or principled morality. This is not, however, entirely true. The decline of conventional morality in the youth is more than the expression of movement toward a more principled stand. While the movement toward principled morality starts with a questioning of conventional morality, such relativistic questioning can also occur without movement to principles. Here are two college student examples:

> *Elliot:* I think one individuals' set of moral values is as good as the next individual's. . . . I think you have a right to believe in what you believe in, but I don't think you have a right to enforce it on other people.

> *John:* I don't think anybody should be swayed by the dictates of society. It's probably very much up to the individual all the time and there's no general principle except when the views of society seem to conflict with your views and your opportunities at the moment and it seems that the views of society don't really have any basis as being right. In this case most people, I think, would tend to say, "Forget it and I'll do what I want."

The college students just quoted are, from the point of view of moral-stage theory, in a transitional zone, Stage $4\frac{1}{2}$. They understand and can use conventional moral thinking, but they view it as arbitrary and relative. They do not yet have any clear understanding of, or commitment to Stage 5 moral principles that are universal and have a claim to some nonrelative validity. Insofar as they see any principles as nonrelative or generally applicable, it is the principle of "Do your own thing and let others do theirs." This principle has a close resemblance to the principles characteristic of younger children's Stage 2 instrumental egoistic thinking.

In this decade, the extreme doubt and relativism that earlier characterized only a minority of college students has appeared both earlier in individuals' lives and much more pervasively. It is now often found toward the end of high school. A majority rather than a minority of adolescents now seem to be aware of relativism and of postconventional questioning, though it is still a minority who really attempt postconventional or principled solutions to these questions.

From the point of view of the contemporary middle-class adolescent, then, a questioning of conventional morality leads less to systematic rebellion or a search for ideal or universal values than it does to only partial acceptance of and commitment to the basic social institutions in which they participate. Adolescents, as well as adult liberals, currently question a faith in human institutions as agencies of human progress, human rationality, and human ethics. Part of this questioning is attributable to a basic distrust of technology (in which institutions have invested so heavily) because of the potential it offers for ecological and nuclear destruction. In addition, there is a postindustrial taking for granted of freedom from basic want, together with a questioning of whether technological progress will ever eliminate poverty, which today's youth views as an inherent aspect of injustice in society.

There is also in both adults and adolescents a widespread questioning of democracy, or of the fundamental political structure, as an agency of social progress. The form of government, and the nation itself, are seen not only as the preservers of human rights but also as a system in conflict with the rights and needs of minorities within the country, of others abroad, and of the natural environment.

This is a questioning, it is believed, of the inadequacies of the dominant Stage 5 liberal ideology of the constitutional democracy to resolve world moral problems, not a questioning of its inadequacies as an institutional system compared to some other possible system. To overcome these inadequacies requires reformulation of the liberal ideology in the more morally principled terms of Stage 6, along the lines of Rawls's effort, as opposed to the more utilitarian or more laissez faire individualistic views of social-contract liberalism found at Stage 5.

One specific example will clarify the need to find an ideological rationale for a constitutional guarantee of the right to human dignity. Compulsory desegregation and abolition of capital punishment are two issues that have faced the Supreme Court and been uncertainly decided on grounds of formal procedural justice and related notions of "equal opportunity." Both issues, however, represent a concern for a Stage 6 Kantian principle of equal respect for all humans as persons, only tenuously supportable by a utilitarian or laissez faire consideration of justice or equal opportunity.

The Supreme Court, in *Furman,* rejected capital punishment as cruel and unusual punishment, but did so primarily on Stage 5 grounds: that as presently administered it violated procedural justice, and that a large part of democratic public opinion rejected it.

When legislation for fixed mandatory capital punishment was enacted in some states, the Court then decided that capital punishment was constitutional since it did not violate procedural justice. The argument of some justices in *Furman* held that capital punishment was cruel and unusual by "evolving standards of justice." Against this argument were public poll data showing majority support for capital punishment. The notion of a sociomoral evolution supports Justice Brennan's and others' contention that capital punishment is cruel and unusual by evolving standards of justice. While the majority of the adult research subjects (mainly conventional or "law and order") supported capital punishment, almost all at the fifth and all at the sixth stage rejected it.

At the fifth stage, opposition to capital punishment, however, is contingent on the factual view that it fails to deter murder, that it is not utilitarian, or that it is procedurally unfair. At the sixth stage, subjects reject capital punishment for the same reasons articulated by Justice Brennan, that capital punishment is cruel and unusual "because it treats members of the human race as non-human. It is inconsistent with the fundamental premise that even the vilest criminal remains a human being, possessed of 'common dignity.' "

Justice Brennan invokes what was earlier termed the fundamental universal principle of justice of Stage 6, formulated by Kant as the categorical imperative: to treat human beings always as ends, not as means. Kant himself believed in capital punishment, holding that treating a criminal as an end, not a means, meant a retributive rather than a utilitarian view of punishment, a rather farfetched interpretation of the principle.

In contrast, Rawls's reworking of Kant's moral philosophy leads to a different solution. Would a rational man contract into capital punishment for his society if he did not know who he was to be in the society, murderer or victim? Even by hard rational standards, no one does know whether he or his child might become a murderer. Given this ignorance, the additional protection of the deterrence of capital punishment over life imprisonment in the role of victim would hardly nullify the certain death through capital punishment in the role of the murderer. Neither Kant nor the constitutional founding fathers and early justices rejected capital punishment, just as the founding fathers failed to reject slavery. The movement from Kant to Rawls, or from Justice Marshall to Justice Brennan, is seen as part of an ideological movement of the liberal social contract from Stage 5 to more consistently Stage 6 premises. Meanwhile, Watergate is a reminder that the Stage 5 social contract still waits for the majority to evolve.

NOTES

1. John Dewey, *Liberalism and Social Action* (New York: Putnam's Sons, 1935); and Roberto Unger, *Knowledge and Politics* (New York: Free Press, 1975).

2. Unger, *Knowledge and Politics*, pp. 8, 15.

3. John Rawls, *Theory of Justice* (Cambridge: Harvard University Press, 1971).

4. Charles A. Reich, *The Greening of America* (New York: Random House, 1970).

5. L. T. Hobhouse, *Morals in Evolution* (New York: Henry Holt, 1906).

6. Lawrence Kohlberg, "From Is to Ought: How to Commit the Naturalistic Fallacy and Get Away With It in The Study of Moral Development," in *Cognitive Development and Epistemology*, ed. T. Mischel (New York: Academic Press, 1971), pp. 164 – 65.

7. Adapted from Donald Elfenbein, "Moral Stages in Societal Evolution," Unpublished A.B. thesis, Harvard Unversity, 1973.

5

STAGES AND STABILITY: THE MORAL DEVELOPMENT APPROACH TO POLITICAL ORDER

Alan M. Cohen

POLITICAL ORDER

Why individuals become the loyal soldiers or restless revolutionaries of their ages has puzzled those who study political order. Reflecting a desire to isolate those variables that contribute to the formation of political allegiance, social scientists have examined the school, the church, the peer group, and the media in search of the wellhead of political ideology. The ancients knew what modern social scientists have only recently come to accept — that psychology and politics are aspects of the same subject: the study of the human in its many states and patterns of interaction. To say with Plato that to study the politics of a man you must know his appetites, his propensity to love and to hate, and how he has acquired these habits of mind, is only to suggest the significance of the term "moral development" for the study of politics.

In spite of the current revival of interest in cognitive moral development theories, most notably the stage theories of Jean Piaget and Lawrence Kohlberg, for the reasons advanced below such theories cannot account for or inform one about the stability or instability of the legal or political order.* Put another way, questions of political behavior, of political

The author wishes to acknowledge his indebtedness and thanks to Professor Richard Wilson and Professor Gordon Schochet of Rutgers University for their careful editorial assistance and, more importantly, for their critical commentaries aimed at sharpening the ideas presented in this chapter. Special thanks must be extended to Professor David Haber of the Rutgers University School of Law for the hours of conversation devoted to strengthening the analysis contained herein.

*Since this chapter focuses on the works of Jean Piaget and Lawrence Kohlberg, the term "moral development theory" will be used to denote the cognitive development approach to moral development.

choices, of political allegiance cannot be answered with reference to moral development theories. The attractiveness or lure of moral development theories is attributable to two functions that such theories purport to perform. First, such theories provide a descriptive framework detailing the "culturally universal and sequentially invariant" stages in the development of moral reasoning.[1] Stages are characterized by their differing orientations toward questions of reciprocity, equality, justice and punishment. Second, beyond this essentially descriptive function, stage theories of development contain a prescriptive component. Rather than regarding the stage theory of development as a description of the judgmental capacity that is attendant to cognitive advance, cognitive moral development theorists assert that movement through the stages is a progression from morally inferior to morally superior forms of reasoning.[2] In line with this, for example, is Kohlberg's contention that his highest stage, Stage 6, is morally more adequate than the earlier, lower stages, that it is an ethically superior level of moral judgment.[3] Detailed below are the reasons for concluding that in neither the descriptive nor the prescriptive sense are such cognitive moral development theories useful in describing or assessing political behavior.

Assuming that the moral development theorists have accurately described the stages in the development of moral reasoning, it is not at all clear that this fact in itself should be of interest to someone studying political behavior. Insofar as knowing and doing diverge in what would be considered normatively significant ways, the proposition that moral reasoning develops in a stage-like sequence is of limited predictive value. In their classic study of the relationship between moral knowledge and action, H. Hartshorne and M. A. May concluded that students who acknowledged that cheating was wrong were just as likely to cheat as those who did not accept the foregoing principle. Perhaps of greater significance, conduct (cheating) was found to vary not with the attainment of moral knowledge, but with situational factors such as the likelihood of being caught.[4] Such a finding lends support to the approach to moral development advanced by social learning theories which acknowledge the significance of environmental factors, for example, fear, guilt, or shame, in the assessment of moral attitudes and actions. Moreover, with specific reference to his own research, Kohlberg observes that levels of moral judgment are not much more reliable than were the levels of moral knowledge tested by Hartshorne and May in predicting "conforming" principled behavior.[5] Thus, knowing that Johnny is capable of moral reasoning at Stage X cannot tell us with any certainty that he will act accordingly in any given situation. It is unclear in what sense individuals possessing the capacity to engage in more advanced levels of moral reasoning, that is, those employing more complex and abstract reason, should be considered morally superior. Perhaps it is only within an individual's own cognitive framework that more advanced levels of moral reasoning are to be preferred. However, at least to the extent that the stages are not behaviorally predictive — that is, where moral thought and action diverge at successive stages — cognitive moral development theory does not address problems of political behavior.

The difficulty with employing Kohlberg's stage theory in analyzing po-·litical behavior is further complicated by the fact that political acts are not readily classifiable, that is, characteristic of one or another stage. For example, students operating at Kohlberg's Stages 5 and 6, (denominated "post-conventional" or "principled" moral reasoning) exhibit behavior that is identical to that of individuals at lower stages. In a test of his stage theory often cited approvingly by Kohlberg, Haan, Smith, and Block characterized participation in the Berkeley free-speech movement as indicative of principled moral conduct. However, while they found that 75 percent of those students characterized as operating at Stage 6 (principled orientation) participated in the protest, more than 60 percent of those students operating at Stage 2 (egoistic orientation) followed the same course.[6] Two groups of students, whose levels of moral reasoning are presumably worlds apart, act in an identical, principled way. Whatever such statistics say for the convergence of thought and action at Stage 6, these results confirm the predictive limitations of the theory as applied to political behavior. Knowing that certain individuals are capable of principled moral thought will not inform one as to whether their principled thought (or some baser motives) will guide their actions. Further, knowing that A, B, and C have engaged in particular conduct does not, without more evidence, provide a means for discerning the moral reasoning process that contributed to their acting in that fashion.

Yet another factor urges caution in the use of Kohlberg's moral development theory to explain or to account for political behavior. Both Kohlberg and Piaget regard their developmental schemes as hierarchal cognitive sequences of natural structures that provide for the organizing, filtering, ordering, and accommodating of human experience.[7] Moral development, in structural terms, refers to irreversible, qualitative changes in the subject's organizational and response capacity, with each cognitive stage representing an integration and differentiation of earlier stages. Stages are structural wholes; that is, reasoning that is characteristic of prior stages disappears with the emergence of subsequent stages. So, for example, the moral reasoning that is characteristic of earlier stages — for example, Stage 2 (self-interested orientation) — should be replaced in subsequent stages by more principled moral reasoning. It is these structural features of moral development theory, coupled with the culturally universal and sequentially invariant nature of the stages, that account for the theoretical attractiveness of these theories to philosophers, psychologists, and other social scientists. However, the stages or structures lack the discreteness that the notion of structural wholes conveys. As Kohlberg reports, approximately 20 percent of his middle-class sample exhibited what was described as "functional regression" in development, that is, a shift from moral reasoning at Stage 4 (conventional orientation) and/or Stage 5 (principled orientation) to reasoning characteristic of Stage 2 (egoistic orientation).[8]

Kohlberg tâkes comfort in the fact that whatever "mysterious forces" (his language) caused this regression, these same forces permitted the subjects to regain their higher moral ground in later life. Yet behind this functional retrogression may be a clue to the functional nature of moral reasoning. Kohlberg advances two theories that he says may partially explain why the retrogressors suffered their setbacks. First, their retrogression may have stemmed from the fact that they were confronted with the relativity of moral expectations and opinions, that is, moral relativism. Second, what individuals perceived as the gap between moral expectations and moral behavior, that is, moral inconsistency, may partially account for the observed retrogression. Since everyone possesses the capacity to comprehend or to draw upon lower levels of moral reasoning without losing the capacity to reason at one's highest level of comprehension, it is especially significant that these regressions were triggered by confrontations with moral crisis in their lives, as opposed to ones revealed in responses to hypothetical dilemmas posed by researchers. Such slippage argues for a functional view of moral reasoning. Perhaps Kohlberg has tacitly acknowledged this point when he observes that a "legitimate regression" — structural or functional? — occurs in the sense that "no one uses Stage 6 thinking in bargaining in an oriental market-place. . . ."[9] One might properly respond by asking whether such legitimate regressions occur in moral judgements in the context of other market situations or other instances where questions of economic well-being are concerned. Finally, Kohlberg engages in question begging, when he characterizes the above regressions as functional regressions within a structural cognitive development framework. His explanation assumes the validity of the very development framework that this contradictory evidence was designed to demonstrate.

Perhaps it is Piaget who sounds the clearest warning to those interested in examining political and legal ·systems through the telescope of moral development theory. In putting to rest the notion that the language of moral development is appropriate to characterize the social or political realm, Piaget writes:

> From the point of view of equilibrium, it seems to us that nothing stabilizes a legal system, whether it is held together from the standpoint of its form or its powers of control and self-preservation, if contradictions with other values

and other norms in play in a society lead to conflict and revolution. It seems then that the equilibrium of the system of legal norms does not derive from us, but from its content, that is to say, from the role played by legal rules insofar as they are instruments or obstacles in the distribution of values (translation by Alan M. Cohen).[10]

Piaget's caution here suggests that social scientists should resist the temptation to apply concepts such as equilibration, that is, a stabilization in the developmental process, to the social and political order in which conflicting values and norms are controlling factors. An analysis of the dynamics of legal or political order that employs language descriptive of the development of moral reasoning is thus likely to result in a distorted view of political reality.

MORAL ORDER

The author suggests that a serious conceptual difficulty rests in Kohlberg's prescriptive use of his stages of moral development. In what sense can one regard moral reasoning at one stage — Stage 6, for example — as being morally more adequate or superior to that of lower stages? At the very least, such an assertion demands that Kohlberg defend the adequacy of his judgment of what is adequate. Several lines of defense are offered on this case, none of which seems to meet with objection. First, Kohlberg argues that philosophers from Kant to Hare have found Stage 5 and Stage 6 types of thinking constitutive of "moral" thought.[11] Second, Kohlberg notes that individuals in fact prefer the more advanced stages of thinking to the lower ones. Neither of these assertions is convincing. Producing evidence of the intuitive appeal of higher stages to individuals at lower stages only demonstrates that some individuals find these higher stages desirable. It does not demonstrate that the later stages are superior, that is, morally more adequate, than any others. To sustain this prescriptive feature of his theory, that people ought to prefer to achieve a Stage 6 level of moral reasoning, Kohlberg is required to show why these stages are desirable. His psychological theory lacks an ethical foundation in a theory of good or right that its prescriptive nature demands. Put another way, to say that people are as they are — assuming they are at Stage 6 — is not to state why one should esteem them as they are.

For his theory of the good or the right, Kohlberg turns to the coincidence of psychological and philosophical views of the nature of moral judgments. The fact that Kant, Hare, and Ross come close to agreeing with the contents of Kohlberg's stages is interesting, but it does not go very far toward persuading even Kohlberg of the validity of his claims. He concedes the need to supplement their formalist view of moral reasoning in making his stage assignments.[12] This is not surprising, given the detailed moral hierarchy suggested by this stage theory of development. Without articulating his own theory of the good, Kohlberg cannot demonstrate that the liberal democratic principles that surface in his Stage 6 morality are superior to philosophical principles found in the works of Kant, Hare, Ross or anyone else. Instead, Kohlberg is content to rely on his empirical observations about people's preferences, and the similarities between his views and those of traditional philosophers. His own argument for the adequacy of the higher stages of moral reasoning rests on a Stage 3 or 4 kind of reasoning, in that the appeal to the respect and authority due philosophers such as Kant or Hare seems consistent with the Stage 4 morality of authority, while the observation that most men, in fact, prefer the higher stages is characteristic of the Stage 3 practice of adhering to the expectations and actions of others. In short, Kohlberg's defense of the higher stages would have profited from a thorough-going Stage 6 principled argument.

One suspects that it is Kohlberg's philosophical and moral development that explain pinning of the moral-adequacy label onto the higher stages. For example, as noted earlier, Kohlberg cites approvingly the denomination of participation in the Berkely free-speech movement as principled conduct engaged in by Stage 6 individuals. Reliance on participation, that is, conduct, as the measure of principled behavior seems to contradict one of the major premises of the theory. Recall that Kohlberg's stages are stages of moral reasoning and that one of the essential features of these stages is that at any given stage one can reason for or against a particular course of action employing the moral reasoning appropriate for that stage. This claim is especially strong in the material on moral education. This may be explained by the desire to show that "moral education" — in Kohlberg's sense of it — does not consist of learning particular rules or norms.[13] An interesting contrast to this evaluation of "principled" behavior is found in the fact that Kohlberg, in another situation, describes participation in a demonstration blocking Dow Chemical recruiters from coming on campus as being morally less adequate, that is, indicative of a lower stage of moral reasoning. The distinction between these two protest activities, without a detailed knowledge of the moral reasoning of the participants would not seem to be indicated by the activities themselves. One might wish to make political or tactical commentary on these activities, but it is not at all clear in what sense the conduct itself is readily susceptible to stage classification. While Kohlberg may approve or disapprove of one or another form of political protest, judgments about the morality of particular actions call for a justification of the ethical systems behind those evaluations and not a mere slotting of the actions into stages prelabeled as morally adequate or inadequate.

According to Kohlberg, stages or structures of moral development are the natural, sequential result of the processing of moral experience[14] and are not reflective of particular moral teachings or moral ideology. In structural terms, an equilibrium is said to be achieved when the moral reasoning employed at a given stage does not result in unresolved moral conflict; that is, moral dilemmas not soluble with reference to the reasoning appropriate at that stage. A stable moral structure at Stage 6 (where rights and duties are recognized as being correlative) is characterized as follows:

Universalizability and consistency are fully attained by the reversibility of prescriptions of actions. Reversibility of moral judgment is what is ultimately meant by the criterion of the fairness of a moral decision. Procedurally, fairness as impartiality means reversibility in the sense of a decision on which all interested parties could agree insofar as they can consider their own claim impartially, as the just decider would. If we have a reversible solution, we have one that could be reached as right starting from anyone's perspective in the situation, given each person's intent to put himself in the shoes of the other.[15]

What is suggested below is that the concepts of universalizability and reversibility do not, in themselves, demonstrate the moral adequacy of Kohlberg's stages. It is further argued that Kohlberg does not specify what is intended by the inclusion of the terms "universal principles" of "justice," "reciprocity," "equality of human right," and the "dignity of individual persons" in his definition of Stage 6 morality. Moreover, the content of these terms is nowhere explicated in his work.

In determining whether Kohlberg has met the burden of proof as to the moral adequacy of his highest stage, it is necessary to take seriously the contention that mature moral structures should inform those who hold them on how to resolve competing claims in difficult situations.[16] What follows is not meant to deny the proposition that there is a sense in which the contents of any ethical or normative system, including Kohlberg's higher stages, may guide or inform judgments or choices made with reference to particular moral dilemmas. All that is suggested below is that Kohlberg offers an inadequate defense of his claim that the reasoning employed at Stage 6 should be regarded as morally superior. Consider, for example, whether the notions of reversability or universalizability are useful in identifying a morally adequate solution to the following dilemma.

Imagine a hospital ward occupied by ten patients, each of whom is suffering from terminal kidney disease. The hospital possesses only one life-saving kidney machine, and turns to the patients to decide among themselves on a decision-making criterion. According to Kohlberg's formulation of Stage 6, any course of action that all of the victims could agree to follow must meet the conditions for universality and prescriptivity. In circumstances in which self-preservation is factored into the moral equation, the requirements of reversibility and universalizability merely contribute a vehicle for advancing a minimal risk solution. Assuming that an admissible fact is a common desire for longevity, then, the only solution likely to meet with everyone's agreement is one that equally distributes the risks — for example, a lottery. However, even when the language describing the lottery is in the Stage 6 language of rights and duties, the words will not disguise the instrumental, Stage 2-like reasoning of each individual. The point here is simply that imposing requirements of universalizability and reversibility in no way guarantees that the resolution will be more principled than those reached at other stages. As is evident from the example, the principled solution to this dilemma makes no reference to the equal moral worth of the individuals, but only to their equal capacity to act to the detriment of others.

Lest someone suggest that this example is faulty, a look at Kohlberg's bona fide Stage 6 philosopher's conception of justice will reveal the self-interested underpinnings of his principled moral judgments. When Kohlberg contends that a "just solution to a moral dilemma is a solution acceptable to all parties, considering each as free and equal, and assuming none of them knew which role they would occupy in the situation,"[17] he is echoing John Rawls, who has turned the minimal risk strategy into the foundation of his conception of justice as fairness.[18] Even in Rawls's original position, a hypothetical construct designed to attain a universalizable and reversible result, the selection of the principle of justice focuses on securing one's maximal well-being while suffering minimal risk — a rather Stage 2-like intention. Conversely, one could take Rawls's acknowledgement that individuals adhere to the principles of justice because they promote "our good and that of those with whom we are affiliates" as indicative of a Stage 5 rule utilitarian orientation. In either event, that the principles of justice are derived in a fashion calculated to meet the requirement that all men would agree in no way guarantees that the solution will be motivated by more principled reasoning than is characteristic of other lower stages of reasoning. As suggested in the above example, attempting to resolve questions of the moral distribution of scarce human resources through the formal requirements of universalizability may not generate universal agreement. Note that Rawls's formulation of distributive principles to which all men would agree, besides being fraught with prudential and utilitarian calculations uncharacteristic of Stage 6 moral reasoning, has met with less than unanimous acceptance. Insofar as Kohlberg regards questions of distributive justice as moral conflicts that are susceptible to Stage 6 analysis, the difficulty is that those distributive principles that individuals may be willing to subscribe to as universalizable will run the gamut of political and economic theory. Perhaps more importantly, some of the principles to which all men might agree, rather than reflecting the Stage 6 respect for rights and duties, may spring from baser, self-interested motives, while other principles may stray far from the liberal democratic ideals presently reflected in the higher stages.

The requirement that Stage 6 moral principles be universal prescriptive principles — another way of saying that they should be universalizable — leads to still another problem. Consider two warring tribes, each of which engages in the practice of devouring its enemies upon victory. Now assuming that this ancient practice conforms with the unanimous consent of all the members of both tribes — that is, all would agree either because it is a great honor to meet this fate or because such a practice conforms with their view of justice — there appears to be no other sense in which their practice fails to meet the requirement of reversibility and universalizability of Stage 6. It is suspected that Kohlberg would respond here, as he did to Alston's suggestion that racial destiny was susceptible to a Stage 6 formulation, by noting that such a universal prescriptive principle is counterintuitive.[19] However, Kohlberg's theory of moral adequacy of Stage 6 reasoning is not, at least overtly, based on intuitionism, although Kohlberg's "Philosopher 3," whom he regards as a Stage 6 type, speaks in terms of "interesting" rights and duties.[20] Thus, consistent with the culturally universal nature of the theory, it should embrace as being morally superior those principles that the relevant individuals would accept as moral even though Kohlberg does not. This is not to lapse into some form of cultural relativism, but only to hold Kohlberg to the notion that the stages or structures of moral development apply to moral reasoning per se.* Unless Kohlberg insists on his own definition of what would qualify as universally prescriptive or reversible, he is bound to accept as principled those solutions that incorporate views of what constitutes persons, rights,

---

*This is not an argument for a Stage 3, cultural relativism position. It is only to recognize that insofar as the terms "justice," "rights," and "duties" are to be supplied their constant Stage 6-type reasoning, the results of that reasoning may not be coincident with what Kohlberg has in mind when he uses these terms. It is possible that by "universal prescriptive norms" Kohlberg means to preclude certain views of what constitute rights or justice. Yet, insofar as this is his view, how one goes about finding or discovering a universal norm is left unstated.

human dignity, individuals, and so on, which do not coincide with his decidedly Anglo-U.S. view of these concepts.

Nor does Kohlberg remedy this problem by his efforts to make Kant's notion of universalizability workable through the introduction of substantive principles of justice, equality, and respect for persons.[21] While no attempt is made by Kohlberg to detail the content of these phrases, their meaning can be known through the equation of universalizability and reversibility. These, Kohlberg asserts, should be understood to require that rights and duties be regarded as correlatives. What Kohlberg means by this statement is explicated only by reference to the rights and duties that emerge in the "Heinz steals the drug" dilemma.[22] There Kohlberg informs us that — at least in the Stage 6 resolution of the problem — the woman in need of the drug possesses a right to life that gives rise to a corresponding duty to save a life (assuming an ability to do so). Although it should be evident that the same solution could be reached through resort to either act or rule utilitarianism* or by reference to the nature of the relationship between the individuals involved,[23] it is unlikely that the correlativity of rights and duties is sufficient to explain the response that Kohlberg denominates as the Stage 6 result.

First, there are at least two senses in which A's right to do X entails a corresponding duty on B's part. Now, as in the Heinz example, A may have a right to life, but is it so clear that B's corresponding duty is to save A's life? B may have merely a duty that can be called a negative duty, not to take A's life without justification (assuming that under appropriate circumstances B's failure to save A's life could be justified). On the other hand, and this is the sense of affirmative duties that Kohlberg seeks to validate, B may have a duty to do X in order to save A's life. However, not all rights entail affirmative duties. For example, the right to free speech may give rise to a duty that unspecified others refrain from abridging or infringing upon that right (a debate of no small magnitude rages over just this point among constitutional lawyers), but there is no corresponding duty on the part of others to listen or to provide a forum or a printing press.

Moreover, this view of rights and duties is too simplistic, for it ignores those rights possessed by third parties, for example, the druggist. Certainly the druggist can be characterized as having the right to his property with a corresponding duty belonging to others (presumably including Heinz) either to abstain from infringing on his property rights (forbearance) or

---

*In fact, the "philosopher 3" response to the Heinz dilemma and Kohlberg's discussion of that response invokes language of "moral calculus" and "weighting" of interests. These are decidedly utilitarian-sounding concepts.

to protect others' property from theft (affirmative). Even assuming a duty to save a life — that is, to take affirmative steps to save a life — it is not the absence of correlative rights and duties between Heinz and the druggist that make for the Stage 6 solution. Rather, it is the weighing or balancing (a term that Kohlberg conspicuously avoids using, perhaps due to its utilitarian sound) of the merits of these competing duties that dictates the principled result. Kohlberg's Stage 6 philosopher acknowledges as much and more, when he begins his response by suggesting a moral calculus in which "the legal duty not to steal is clearly outweighed by the moral duty to save a life."[24] To some who do not recognize this duty, the philosopher explains that "he is not viewing the situation from the role of the person whose life is being saved as well as the person who can save the life, or from the possibility of anyone filling these two roles. . . . [I]t would be irrational to act in such a manner as to make human life — or the loss of it — a means to the preservation of property rights."[25] The point here is that the solution to this problem is not based on the existence of correlative rights and duties, but rather on an appeal to what Hume would have recognized as sympathy. It is an appeal that can be neatly encapsulated in the interrogatory, What would you want done if you were drowning? The only solution that universalizability forecloses, and this only for the individual whose sense of self-preservation does not call forth the universal prescriptive norm of saving drowning persons where possible, is the self-interested or egocentric response, "But *I* am not drowning."

By changing the facts of the Heinz dilemma, one can see that something other than a recognition of the correspondence of rights and duties is involved in reaching a solution. Assume in the Heinz example that the druggist has already sold the drug (still in his possession) to another person in equal need of it. While the same right to life exists, the introduction of a legitimate competing right to life alters one's view of what, if any, duty to steal the drug exists. Similarly, the Stage 6 response to the kidney-machine hypothetical would not be that the right to life of A entails a corresponding duty to B to provide A with a means of survival without regard to C, D, and E. In addition, in either the Heinz variation or the kidney-machine example, one would need to evaluate the validity or legitimacy of the claim to superior rights on the part of individuals with the requisite economic resources to purchase the drug or machine (as opposed to those lacking such resources). In either event, Kohlberg's view of the correlativity of rights and duties is of no assistance in evaluating competing claims to scarce human resources. The language of rights and duties assumes the answers to prior questions of the validation of and ordering of competing claims (as opposed to rights). It is this unarticulated valuation of competing claims to scarce human resources — for example, land, wealth, property, power — that occupies much of political and legal discourse, and on which Kohlberg, for all his writings about moral adequacy, is silent.

LEGAL ORDER

In several articles Kohlberg and his colleagues have advanced the argument that their research has revealed the basic structure and developmental sequence of moral reasoning.[26] The strength of this claim lies in the empirically demonstrable fact that moral development is "culturally universal and sequentially invariant." From the existence of this genetic or developmental fact, moral development theorists have assumed the capacity to diagnose moral disorder in the same sense that the psychiatrist speaks of mental disorder.[27] However, what one chooses to consider normal, appropriate, acceptable standards for moral reasoning is a question quite independent of the fact that the development of a capacity to reason in increasingly abstract ways, including moral ways, occurs in a particular manner. The legal significance of this distinction can be brought into focus by reference to the role of the concept of mental disorder in assessing criminal responsibility. The Model Penal Code §4.01(1) sets forth the following standard for establishing an insanity defense: "A person is not responsible for criminal conduct if at the time of such conduct as a result of mental disease or defect he lacks substantial capacity either to appreciate the criminality of his conduct or to conform his conduct to the requirements of the law."[28] This standard highlights the fundamental difference between a moral and a mental disorder. Of all of the possible psychological facts to be accorded legal significance in a criminal proceeding, only the defendant's ability (or inability) to distinguish right from wrong has been selected as a basis for defining what will be viewed as disorder. Certainly in the legal context described above, and arguably in all other relevant contexts, the use of "facts" in identifying those in need of treatment — that is, moral education to achieve moral advance — presupposes a view of normal moral functioning. Yet it is the absence of consensus as to what are relevant facts that, from a philosophical perspective, plagues Kohlberg's work.

Related conceptual problems arise with the attempt to translate moral development theory and research into treatment programs to be used in correctional facilities. Kohlberg's "Just Community Approach to Corrections: A Theory," advances a rehabilitation plan designed to foster moral growth in inmates through the establishment of democratically organized prison units in which inmates and prison staff hold sessions designed to expose and resolve moral conflict.[29] The aims of such programs include reconciling "the inherent conflicts between rehabilitation and control" and "promoting moral development rehabilitation."[30] There is no quarrel here over the assertion that a democratically organized prison unit is more desirable than an authoritarian one (leaving open the question of the extent to which a prison can be democratized): the concern is over the implicit assumption that prison inmates, as a class, are in need of moral character reformation.

Consider two different prisoners. Prisoner A is a draft resister whose objection to war and to killing is firmly rooted in his moral and philosophical beliefs. It is precisely this set of beliefs that led him to engage in the acts of civil disobedience that resulted in his imprisonment. Presumably capable of Stage 6 reasoning, in what sense is Prisoner A in need of moral rehabilitation? Implicit in the moral development approach to corrections is the notion that violations of the law are indicative of stunted moral growth. Yet this is clearly not universally true. To carry this example further, let us assume in the Heinz dilemma that he confessed an intent to steal the drug. Is there any question that he would be guilty — as a legal matter — of the crime of larceny?[31] At the time of sentencing one might want to advance arguments about the difference between moral and legal responsibility,* but in terms of having committed a statutory crime, being a Stage 6 person is no defense (although it may provide justification). At a minimum, laws are codifications of what legislatures have identified as "bad acts": there is no necessary relationship between criminal liability and moral culpability.

Prisoner B is a convicted check forger. This inmate willingly acknowledges that the conventional morality (Stage 4) or the social contract (Stage 5) approach to resolving hypothetical dilemmas is to be preferred, but objects to abiding by such norms because "that's not the way the rest of the world really operates." This individual in practice operates according to Kohlberg's oriental-marketplace approach to morality by negotiating with a world perceived to be unfair or unjust on its own terms. Perhaps this orientation is more appropriately described as a functional regression. Evidence for the operation of just such an approach to moral decision making is provided by Kohlberg when he observes that "it has been found that inmates, when given a dilemma set in the outside world — use higher stage reasoning than they do in similar dilemmas set in the prison."[32] Thus, a functional explanation of moral reasoning would account for an inmate's

---

*It is at this juncture that, assuming sentencing discretion exists, one might want to know the judge's level of moral reasoning before making an appeal to the moral responsibility of the defendant. However, it is just such knowledge — not cast in terms of moral stages — on the basis of which courthouse-wise lawyers "shop" for a sentencing judge.

willingness to accomodate himself to the reality of the prison setting. Kohlberg tacitly acknowledges that the inmate's approach to moral reasoning is contextual or situational through his desire to manipulate that environment, that is, through the introduction of the "just community," in order to achieve moral advance. Returning to Prisoner B, insofar as he has tailored his conduct to fit his perception of social reality, the fact that he is capable of abstract moral reasoning is, per se, of diminished importance.

While the rehabilitation of a prisoner's perception of social institutions so that he may appreciate the extent to which social arrangements advance individual and common good may be appropriate to correctional facilities, it is not at all clear that such programs should go under the title of moral development.

CONCLUSION

The current revival of interest in cognitive moral development theory is animated by articles in professional journals searching for the applicability of such theories to a wide variety of disciplines. The purpose of this study has been to urge caution on those scholars looking to embrace the new naturalism embodied in Kohlberg's stage theory of development. Two reasons commend this conclusion. First, from the behavioral perspective, even assuming the validity of Kohlberg's construct, the relationship between one's capacity for sophisticated moral reasonings and one's being (and acting as) a moral person is far from perfect. For example, in the political context, knowing that an individual's moral reasoning corresponds to Stage X or Y may tell very little about whether that person will become the loyal soldier or restless revolutionary, or even how that particular decision will be made. Second, from the philosophical perspective, the professed moral superiority of higher or later stages of development is grounded only in Kohlberg's observation that some philosophers prefer higher to lower levels of reasoning. Without some derivation of and defense of the universal prescriptive norms embodied in Kohlberg's highest stage, there is no reason to accept this conclusion that such principles are morally superior. Finally, as the earlier discussion of the just-community approach to corrections suggests, the use of Kohlberg's moral development theory as the foundation for a program in moral therapeutics runs the risk of ignoring the true causes of criminal or deviant behavior by assuming that such conduct is precipitated by a moral disorder suffered by the actor.

NOTES

1. See Jean Piaget, *The Moral Judgment of the Child*, trans. Marjorie Wardin (Totowa, N.J.: Littlefield Adams, 1972); and Lawrence Kohlberg, "Moral Development," in *International Encyclopedia of the Social Sciences* (New York: MacMillan and Free Press, 1968), pp. 483–93; Lawrence Kohlberg, "Development of Moral Character and Moral Ideology," in *Review of Child Development Research*, vol. 1, ed. Martin Hoffman and Lois Hoffman (New York: Russell Sage Foundation, 1964), pp. 383–431. See generally, Martin Hoffman, "Moral Development," in *Carmichel's Guide to Child Psychology*, 3rd ed., ed. Paul Mussen (New York: Wiley, 1970), pp. 261–81.

2. Lawrence Kohlberg, "The Development of Children's Orientation Toward a Moral Order: 1 Sequence in The Development of Moral Thought," *Vita Humana* 6 (1963): 11–33; and L. Kohlberg and R. Kramer, "Continuities and Discontinuities in Childhood and Adult Moral Development," *Human Development* 12 (1969): 93–120.

3. Lawrence Kohlberg, "From Is to Ought: How to Commit the Naturalistic Fallacy and Get Away With It in The Study of Moral Development," in *Cognitive Development and Epistemology*, ed. Theodore Mischel (New York: Academic Press, 1971), pp. 151–235; and "The Claim to Moral Adequacy of a Highest Stage of Moral Development," *Journal of Philosophy* 70 (1975): 631–47.

4. H. Hartshorne and M. A. May, *Studies in the Nature of Character*, vol. 1: *Studies in Deceit*, vol. 2; *Studies in Self-Control*, vol. 3; *Studies in the Organization of Character* (New York: MacMillan, 1929–30). See especially their discussion of "The Relation of Moral Knowledge to Conduct," vol. 3, Pt. 2, Chapter 10, pp. 153–57, and "The Contribution to the Theory of Character Education," vol. 3, Pt. 5, Chapter 26, pp. 377–79.

5. Kohlberg, "Development of Moral Character and Moral Ideology," p. 409. For a discussion of this point, ee W. Kurtines and E. B. Greif, "The Development of Moral Thought, Review and Evaluation of Kohlberg's Approach," *Psychological Bulletin* 81 (1974):453–70; and S. Schwartz et al., "Some Personality Correlates of Conduct in Two Situations of Moral Conflict," *Journal of Psychology* 37 (1969):41–47.

6. N. Haan, M. B. Smith, and J. Block, "Moral Reasoning of Young Adults: Political-Social Behavior, Family Background and Personality Correlates," *Journal of Social Psychology* 10 (1968):183–201.

7. Jean Piaget, *Structuralism*, trans. Chaninah Maschler (New York: Harper and Row, 1970); and *Genetic Epistemology*, trans. Eleanor Duckworth (New York: Norton, 1970); Kohlberg and Kramer, "Continuities and Discontinuities," pp. 98–99, echoes Piaget's definition of stages as structures. For a comparison of Piaget and Kohlberg, see Helen Weinreich, "Kohlberg: Aspect of their Relationship in the Field of Moral Development," *Journal of Moral Education* 4 (1975): 201–13.

8. Kohlberg and Kramer, "Continuities and Discontinuities," p. 113. The authors refer to these regressions as being caused by "mysterious forces." Ibid., p. 111.

9. Ibid., p. 113, note 4.

10. Jean Piaget, *Introduction a L'Epistemologie Génétique: La Pensée Biologique, La Pensée Psychologique, et La Pensée Sociologique*, Tome 3 (Paris: Presses Universitaire de France, 1950), pp. 229–30.

11. Kohlberg, "The Claim to Moral Adequacy," p. 635.

12. Kohlberg, "From Is to Ought."

13. Lawrence Kohlberg, "Stages of Moral Development as a Basis for Moral Education," in *Moral Education: Interdisciplinary Approaches*, ed. C. N. Beck, B. S. Crittenden, and E. V. Sullivan (New York: Newman Press, 1971), pp. 23–92; see Appendix 4, p. 92 where

Kohlberg sets forth the differing views of a moral dilemma possible at any given stage. See also Lawrence Kohlberg, "Education for Justice," in *Moral Education*, ed. Nancy F. and Theodore R. Sizer (Cambridge: Harvard University Press, 1970), pp. 79–82.

14. Kohlberg, "The Claim to Moral Adequacy."

15. Ibid., p. 641.

16. Kohlberg, "From Is to Ought."

17. Ibid., p. 213. See John Rawls, *A Theory of Justice* (Cambridge: Harvard University Press, 1971). In Rawls' formulation of his theory of moral development, one linked to his conception of justice as fairness, he acknowledges his indebtedness to the cognitive moral developmental themes of Kohlberg and Piaget.

18. For a critical review of this aspect of Rawls' theory, see Brian Barry, *The Liberal Theory of Justice*, (London: Oxford University Press, 1973); John Rawls, "Theory of Justice," *Political Studies* 19 (1972): 63–80; and David Lyons, "Rawls Versus Utilitarianism," *Journal of Philosophy* 69 (1972): 535–42.

19. Kohlberg, "From Is to Ought." Alston's criticisms of Kohlberg's article appear in his "Comments on Kohlberg's 'From Is to Ought,' " in *Cognitive Development and Epistemology*, ed. Theodore Mischel (New York: Academic Press, 1971).

20. Kohlberg, "From Is to Ought," p. 219.

21. Kohlberg, "From Is to Ought." The difficulty with the addition of these substantive principles is that their meaning and/or content is apparently to be determined through just that procedure, that is, universalizability, that Kohlberg felt the need to supplement in the first place.

22. Ibid. Hereinafter referred to as the "Heinz dilemma."

23. See Joel Feinberg, "The Nature and Value of Rights," *Journal of Value Inquiry* 4 (1971): 243–257.

24. Kohlberg, "From Is to Ought," pp. 208–9.

25. Ibid.

26. Lawrence Kohlberg, "Moral Stages and Moralization: The Cognitive Developmental Approach," in *Moral Development and Behavior: Theory, Research, and Social Issues*, ed. T. Lickona (New York: Holt, Rinehart and Winston, 1976), pp. 31–53.

27. Lawrence Kohlberg et al., "The Just Community Approach to Corrections," *Journal of Moral Education* 4 (1975), 243–60.

28. Kadish and Paulsen, *Criminal Law and Its Processes: Cases and Materials* (Boston: Little, Brown, 1969), p. 591. A discussion of the traditional formulation of the insanity or mental defect test is found in the authors' discussion of the M'Naughton Rules, ibid., p. 584.

29. Kohlberg, "Just Community Approach to Corrections." See, generally, Roy Feldman, "The Promotion of Moral Development in Prisons and Schools" in this volume.

30. Kohlberg, "Just Community Approach to Corrections," p. 247.

31. N.Y.P.L. §155.05 (1976–77). While the definition of larceny in the penal code makes reference to the "wrongful" taking of property, this term refers to legal entitlements, rather than to moral claims.

32. Kohlberg, "Just Community Approach to Correction," p. 249.

6

RELATIVISM, LIBERALISM, AND MORAL DEVELOPMENT

James Fishkin

Some moral reasoners respond to moral questions by questioning the very possibility of answering those questions. In the literature on moral development derived from Lawrence Kohlberg, these reasoners have been classified as relativists. Because there is no clearly appropriate place for these relativists within the Kohlberg scheme of six stages, they have been variously interpreted as a regression back to the preconventional reasoning of the most primitive moral stages, or as a transitional phenomenon in the movement beyond conventional moral reasoning to stages of moral principle. In either interpretation relativism is thought to be a transitory and inconsistent phase of confusion.

A different interpretation will be offered here. Rather than viewing relativism as necessarily inconsistent and confused, it will be claimed that it may be consistent and coherent. Indeed, it is a position that is not only logically coherent, but that is also logically required by certain assumptions that seem to have an important place in moral culture in the present. Far from being confused and obviously wrong, these relativistic reasoners who have puzzled the Kohlberg researchers are facing up to conclusions that are logically required — given certain assumptions.

However, those assumptions are themselves open to serious question. An attempt will be made here to identify them and argue against them. While the author shares with Kohlberg the view that the arguments for

Portions of this essay are excerpted from the author's forthcoming book, *Cynicism: A Study of Moral Reasoning*. The author would like to thank Richard Wilson and Gordon Schochet for many helpful editorial comments.

relativism offered by ordinary reasoners are mistaken, they are not obviously so. Indeed, the grounds for quarreling with the relativistic arguments of ordinary reasoners will also bring into question Kohlberg's own
account of Stage 6 and his criteria for moral adequacy at that stage.

This chapter will have four parts. First, it will examine the problem
relativism has posed in the literature on moral development. Second, it
will examine some relativistic interviews drawn from a larger study —
interviews that support the contention that relativism may be coherent
and logically consistent. Third, it will be argued that the assumptions
employed by these relativistic reasoners are incompatible with the possibility of liberalism as a coherent moral ideology. This means that if one
is willing to grant the possibility of liberalism as a moral position, then
these arguments are mistaken. Fourth, it will be argued that the critique
of relativism offered here undermines the claims for moral adequacy offered by Kohlberg and the moral development researchers. While the
arguments of relativistic reasoners do not actually imply relativism, they
do raise some important questions about the particular notion of moral
development employed by the Kohlberg researchers.

RELATIVISM AND MORAL DEVELOPMENT

It is useful to begin by examining the problem of relativism in the
psychological literature on moral stages. In his pioneering work on moral
development, Kohlberg asks reasoners to respond in interviews to hypothetical moral dilemmas such as the following:

> In Europe, a woman was near death from a special kind of cancer. There
> was one drug that the doctors thought might save her. It was a form of radium
> that a druggist in the same town had recently discovered. The drug was
> expensive to make, but the druggist was charging ten times what the drug
> cost him to make it. He paid $200 for the radium and charged $2000 for a
> small dose of the drug. The sick woman's husband, Heinz, went to everyone
> he knew to borrow the money, but he could only get together about $1000,
> which is half of what it cost. He told the druggist that his wife was dying, and
> asked him to sell it cheaper or let him pay later. But the druggist said, "No,
> I discovered the drug and I'm going to make money from it." So Heinz got
> desperate and broke into the man's store to steal the drug for his wife. Should
> Heinz have done that? Was it actually wrong or right? Why?

Because this dilemma (which was developed originally for interviews
with children) appears to pose so straightforward a moral problem, the
responses of sophisticated relativist reasoners may appear all the more

surprising. One of Kohlberg's relativists is Roger, aged 20, a veteran of the 1964 Berkeley free-speech movement. Roger has trouble judging Heinz's action; he asserts the purely subjective nature of any judgment he might make. Heinz, he says, "was a victim of circumstances and can only be judged by other men whose varying values and interest frameworks produce subjective decisions which are neither permanent nor absolute."

Was it Heinz's duty to save his wife's life? It is not up to Roger to determine. "A husband's duty is up to the husband to decide," he says, "and anybody can judge him, and he can judge anybody's judgment. If he values her life over the consequences of theft," Roger concludes, "he should do it."

Does the druggist have a right to charge as much as he wants? Roger is equally adept at avoiding this question. "One can talk about rights until doomsday and never say anything." He asks, "Does the lion have a right to the zebra's life when he starves? When he wants sport? Or when he will take it at will? Does he consider rights? Is man so different?"[1]

Another relativist cited by Kohlberg was willing to excuse Heinz, but implied that he was also willing to excuse the druggist, provided that the latter was conforming to his own "capitalist morality":

> There's a million ways to look at it. Heinz had a moral decision to make. Was it worse to steal or let his wife die? In my mind I can either condemn him or condone him. In this case I think it was fine. But possibly the druggist was working on a capitalist morality of supply and demand.[2]

Another of Kohlberg's dilemmas asks "whether it was right to break the law and aid slaves to escape before the Civil War." A medical student cited by Kohlberg reveals his subjective position in his hesitations about whether he can make the judgment that slavery was wrong at all:

> All I can say is that it is my opinion [that slavery is wrong]. I can't speak for anyone else. I think it was wrong, but I think you would have to take it back to the framework of the people of that time. Many people sincerely felt they were not dealing with human beings, maybe in that framework it was morally right from their point of view.[3]

The Kohlberg researchers have attempted to fit these relativistic responses within the framework of their proposed moral stages in two ways. First, relativists were interpretated as constituting a regression from Stages 4 or 5 back to the preconventional level. More recently, relativists have been interpreted as a phenomenon of transition in the development of postconventional reasoning. According to the first interpretation, relativists were assigned a particular stage (they had regressed back to 2). According to the second, relativists are thought to be in movement between two stages (for example, 4 and 5). According to both of these interpretations, as the inconsistencies in the position are worked through, a new equilibrium of moral principle (typically Stage 5) is eventually reached.

To examine the regression hypothesis first, Kohlberg describes the appearance of retrogressed subjects as follows:

> That paradigm of the psychological study of the normal, the college sophomore, turns out to be the oddest and most interesting moral fish of all. Between late high school and the second or third year of college, 20% of our middle class sample dropped or retrogressed in moral maturity scores.[4]

This retrogression was substantial enough for them to be reclassified at Stage 2 the "pre-moral" stage of "instrumental hedonism," even though they had earlier been classified at Stages 4 or 5 in high school.[5] However, unlike the variety of Stage 2 encountered in the normal process or development (a stage whose incidence decreases substantially from age 10 onwards), these Stage 2 reasoners had "not lost their earlier capacity to use stage 4 and stage 5 thinking."[6]

This regression hypothesis would thus violate two of the central assumptions of the theory: the assumption that the stages represent an invariant sequence, and the assumption that the stages represent a hierarchy of perceived adequacy such that subjects will adopt the highest stage they understand.[7] The first assumption would be disconfirmed, obviously, because these reasoners have moved from Stages 4 or 5 back to 2. The second assumption would be disconfirmed because these reasoners continue to understand Stage 4 or 5 reasoning but reject it in favor of 2.

A more recent interpretation, intended to avoid these difficulties, has been put forth by both Kohlberg and Elliot Turiel. This is the transitional hypothesis:

> The apparent stage 2 thinking of the longitudinal subjects was not actually a return to an earlier pattern of stage 2 thought used when they were younger, but was actually a pattern of thought used in the *transition from* conventional to principled reasoning. The thinking of the transitional relativists in our sample could best be characterized as stage 4 ½, i.e., as a way of thinking which equated morality with stage 4 thought and then questioned the validity of morality, conceived in stage 4 terms [italics in the original].[8]

Relativism in this view is a symptom of the "deformation" of conventional morality prior to the "formation" of post conventional morality.[9] Such an experience of disequilibrium is merely "part of stage transition." It "may be seen as a state in which the inconsistencies of an existing stage are perceived."[10] In these terms, movement to the next stage results as these confusions are sorted out and overcome.

But whether or not these reasoners should be classified at Stage 4½, it is now admitted that this phase between stages is not necessarily brief. For example, Kohlberg and Carol Gilligan cite unpublished data collected by M. H. Podd which leads them to the conclusion that relativism in the counter-cultural atmosphere of the late 1960s commonly proved to be a stable rather than a transitory phenomenon. "Podd's findings from the *late* sixties differed from those of Kohlberg and Kramer in the early sixties" [italics in original] in that "extreme relativism no longer appeared to be a temporary ego-developmental maneuver of a small group of subjects in crisis, but rather to represent a more *stable,* less crisis-like pattern of low commitment" [italics added].[11] Kohlberg and Gilligan explain this new stability by citing the fact that "the relativistic rejection of convention . . . is now manufactured as a cultural industry called the 'counterculture.' " It has been "transform[ed] . . . into yet another conventional system."[12]

In another article Kohlberg has similarly qualified the Kohlberg and Kramer conclusions about the instability of relativism:

> . . . there is no doubt that under some social conditions such ideologies become stabilized orientations. At their moral worst, these ideologies declare themselves "beyond good and evil," and the examples of Hitler and Stalin force us to take this amorality seriously; at their best, they celebrate a moral conscience little distinguishable in its principles from the stage 3 or 4 moral sense.[13]

Thus, depending on the rest of a reasoner's ideological assumptions, relativism may or may not stabilize. Kohlberg has admitted that a distinctive fact about relativists, which distinguishes them from genuine Stage 2 hedonistic reasoners, is that their egoism was "jazzed up with some philosophic and sociopolitical jargon."[14]

It can be argued that once this jargon is analyzed, relativism will be seen not as inconsistent and confused but as a position that subjects reach because it is more logically consistent and less confused than its alternatives, given the assumptions from which they are reasoning.

In this sense, the relativism that Kohlberg interprets as transitory and inconsistent will be interpreted here as consistent and possibly stable, although misguided. However, to understand both the consistency and the misguided character of relativism one must distinguish between the kind of classifications employed by Kohlberg and the assumptions to be examined here.

The classifications in Kohlberg's theory are normative ethical — that is, they concern "what should one do?" or "what would be right?" in particular situations of moral choice. The arguments to be examined here, on the other hand, are metaethical — that is, they concern "how does one judge?" or "how does one justify a moral judgment?" The focus will not be on specific moral judgments but rather on the general nature of moral judgments — their basis, their structure, their limitations, their legitimacy.

Once the metaethical arguments used to support relativism are examined, they can be seen as constituting a resolution to perplexities rather than a source of them. In other words, the same motivation for consistency and equilibrium which, according to Kohlberg, drives reasoners through his sequence of stages, also drives some of them, instead, to relativism. These reasoners are deflected in this way because of assumptions they hold that render relativism uniquely attractive as an alternative position.

Of course, normative ethical and metaethical reasoning are commonly intermixed. In fact, the metaethical arguments discussed here were uncovered simply by posing some normative ethical questions, such as Kohlberg's moral dilemmas. But the distinction is important to the claim that relativism has been misunderstood, for what may appear in normative ethical terms as sheer confusion may be, in metaethical terms, an attempt to arrive at a consistent and intellectually defensible position.

THE LOGIC OF RELATIVISM

This section will examine in detail the reasoning of some relativistic students. The cases are drawn from a larger study of moral reasoning among U.S. and English university students. The quotations cited come from tape-recorded interviews in which relativistic responses were offered to Kohlberg dilemmas. When these reasoners were asked to support or clarify their positions, arguments of the kind cited below were offered. While the discussion here is limited to three of them, there are additional arguments that conform to the same pattern and are subject to the same critique applied to these three.*

In this chapter the practice in the Kohlberg literature of treating relativism as a single position will be followed. However, it is worth noting that these relativists differ in important ways. For example, some of them believe that they can apply their (admittedly subjective) values universally to everyone; others believe that they should judge others by *their* respective values; others believe that their (admittedly subjective) values apply, in

---

*In *Cynicism* six arguments of this kind are discussed.

some sense, only to themselves; still others attempt to avoid any moral judgements at all. In other words, the various positions treated together as relativism can plausibly be subdivided, but these refinements in classification need not be of concern here.* All of the various claims that morality is subjective, relative, or arbitrary will be treated as instances of relativism..

Hence, for purposes of this analysis, ethical positions can be divided into two broad categories: relativism in its various versions, and non relative or objective moral positions. These latter positions attribute objective validity to moral judgments. They claim that morality is not subjective, relative, or arbitrary because one is (in some sense to be specified) justified in adopting one moral position rather than another.

The arguments for relativism discussed here share a common structure. Each argument posits some characteristic of morality (x) as a necessary condition for an objective (or nonrelative) morality. The argument then proceeds from the failure to satisfy that necessary condition as follows: (1) the objective character of a moral position requires that it have characteristic x; (2) it does not have characteristic x; (3) therefore, it cannot be objective.

In each version of the argument discussed below, x will be different. Each argument is based on a different expectation, in other words, about the character of an objective morality.

The critique of these arguments will depend on showin that there is a coherent possible position which lacks each of these x characteristics — and which is, nevertheless, an objective position. This ethical position turns out to be a characteristically liberal one, for it links the tentativeness and incompleteness of moral judgment to a defense of liberty. If this liberal ethical position is a possible nonrelative position, then these relativistic arguments must be mistaken. Each version of step 1 in the argument must then be rejected because the possibility of an objective position lacking each of the supposed necessary conditions (each version of x) will have been admitted.

The First Argument

Brian, an Ivy League undergraduate, responds to the Heinz dilemma as follows: "I've got a whole problem: I'm not quite sure what moral criteria are. I would do it. I'm not quite sure what it means to say that it's right."

---

*Discussed at length in *Cynicism*.

He decides that he cannot say that stealing the drug would be justified. "Because to me, justification means that there is something *back there* that we have all agreed on . . . and then you show me logically how those justifying elements agree with your actions."

"And I simply don't understand what is back there," he continues, "how anything has the power of justification other than the revelation of God — which you can't deny, by definition. Otherwise, I don't see how any phrase you happen to drop carries with it the power of justification."

He tries to spell out the difficulty more precisely. "I assume when you say 'justify,' you're talking about 'justify' using logic and using reason and using certain definitions. My problem is reason can't deal with that."

The attempt to use reason is overwhelmed, he believes, by a kind of "infinite regress"; for, he responded, "If you say, 'Justify Z in terms of Y,' and I say, 'Well, explain Y or defend Y,' and you end up using X, and so forth and so on. At no point can you *stop*."

"At the point where you stop," Brian explains, "you have to say 'just because.' And once you get to that point, that's not open to reason."

At that point, the rationales are merely "because I think that's right" or "I feel that's right." Brian agrees that "you need something more than that to stop." His problem is that "reason does not allow anything. I don't think there is anything. . . . I don't even think anyone's been able to define for me God, or the stopping point or whatever — the procedure to find the stopping point."

While "everything else is liable to reason *after* that point — assuming you find consistency the mark of moral reasoning," his problem is that he sees no basis for his most fundamental assumptions.

But what kind of basis is he searching for? Brian mentions that many cultures probably share some fundamental values such as "certain conditions in which you do not kill somebody else," (although "that in no way says that they all agree on any given set of conditions"). But even if there were agreement on the conditions for not killing, Brian says, "In order to make it meaningful to me, you would have to show that that was somehow *inherent* in the structure of the animal — the human animal almost had to agree not to kill under these circumstances for whatever reasons."

What Brian is seeking are basic moral assumptions that are, in some way, beyond reasonable question. In fact, as he considers the question, he concludes that even if conditions for not killing were "somehow inherent in the structure of the animal," he would *still* not have found a sufficient basis. Even if men somehow found it necessary to agree, he would conclude, "That's no moral basis, that's not moral revelation. That's a genetic determination."

Without an undeniable basis in, for example, "moral revelation," he feels driven to the conclusion that his ultimate premises can be no better — and no worse — than anyone else's. Brian points out, "How can one say 'I don't have the revealed word of God, I don't know what is truth, I realize that my resources are exactly symmetrical with the other guy who I'm condemning, but somehow he's wrong and I'm right'? I would like to see some argument for that, some consistent argument for that. And I don't see how one can even devise such an argument, just because of the nature of reason."

In this way Brian reaches the conclusion that others' values are as valid as his own. Even in the case of Hitler, he feels forced to admit, "I imagine he has as good a grounds for acting as I do." In fact, Brian concludes that, in general, "My view would be the other guy has a perfectly, as sound a ground as I do for acting, and I can't make any value judgment of him other than the fact that I don't *like* what he's doing."

Stephen, an Oxbridge medical student, is led to a subjective position by a similar search for assumptions that are beyond reasonable question. It is his unsuccessful quest for a rationally unquestionable "ultimate framework" that leads him to conclude "that I wouldn't be in a state to judge for anybody else."

As in Brian's case, the arbitrariness of his basic assumptions is revealed by a seemingly infinite regress of questions. In describing his Catholic upbringing he says, "God was a belief, and if you believed in it, that was cool. And you followed those rules, if that's what you believed He wanted you to do. And if you didn't believe in God, well, you had to go away and find something else."

Stephen's skepticism arises from the fact that "whenever you got to an impasse (which is the sort of thing you get to when you analyze everything), you suddenly come to a great big *abyss*, and you know there's nothing that's going to fill it to enable you to get to the other side — if there is another side. And whenever that came, it would always end up being filled in by your belief in God." He finds this way of resolving questions unconvincing. "Doesn't it sound unreasonable whenever you're stuck, to go and appeal to God?" he asks. "And it does, it really does."

"But everything else," Stephen says, "proved to be the same, to the touch if you like. I would take something up as possibly leading to a sort of ultimate framework and would come to exactly the same emotional disillusionments with it." Each assumption, in turn, appears open to question: "Like I'd climb up a ladder and at a certain point you'd say 'Am I ever going to get to the end?' And the answer was always — 'Doesn't look like it.'"

The end of the questioning seems unreachable to Stephen because he could never "come to the point that you got to the question that was self-answering or something like that — some point where there would obviously be a terminus."

"And it never looked like coming," Stephen says of this stopping point. "Whenever there was a question, you'd provide an answer, and then, more or less by definition, you'd have to explain the answer, and then you have to explain the explanation. And so on. So I ended up not believing in anything."

Harvey, a student of mathematics and logic, similarly connects his subjective position to the lack of undeniable basic assumptions. He is attracted to logic because "things are either true or false. It's decidable. You can decide whether a proof is correct or incorrect."

The situation is quite different in ethics and philosophy. "It's endless arguments because you can never say *for sure* that yours is a better argument than somebody else's. It's a matter of personal choice, isn't it?"

Harvey proposes an analogy. "It's sort of like choosing the axioms for a system," he says, "whereas the laws of logic — the deduction laws — are always absolute, you see? Choosing those axioms is a personalistic affair, but once you choose them, then the laws are absolute."

While implications can always be rigorously deduced once the axioms are chosen, there are no criteria for the basic choices, which must be arbitrary. "You feel something is important and you feel something is not important. I mean you don't know what the criterion is, ever. . . . Your feelings change from moment to moment, so you don't know what you're going to feel is important later on either."

As a result, controversies are never settled. "In subjects like sociology and ethics . . . and philosophy it's more a matter of personal taste, and we don't really have good analytical criteria; we don't have anything that's unarguable. You'll always have different schools fighting. That's what the history of the subject will be."

Any criteria that may seem absolute are really based, at bottom, on choices that are no more than personal taste. As Harvey notes, "trying to present foundations for morals and ethics on a broad enough level — unless it's tautology and unless it depends on formal rules of deduction . . . it won't go to the a priori axioms or the a priori statements. I don't think you can get any for morals — any a priori foundation before any fact. It's all empty from that point of view. You can only have implicational or tautological statements about such things — just like in any system."

Because there is no a priori foundation, Harvey concludes that one cannot give reasons in ethics at all. He explains that "by 'reason' I mean some kind of rationale derived from some kind of principle." In this sense, he believes, "You really can't give reasons. It's an infinite regress; you say 'I did this because of this.' And why is that? 'Because of this.' You can never get back to something fundamental — for me, I mean, I can't get back to something fundamental. It's all very amorphous."

Without reasons based on something fundamental, he concludes, "there's not really any question of right or wrong."

These cases all offer variants of the same argument. Because their judgments lack a basis that is beyond reasonable question, they must be relative or subjective. Brian, for example, is looking for assumptions that have "the power of justification" — assumptions that "you can't deny, by definition." Without such assumptions, he views his values as having no justification whatsoever. Stephen, similarly, is searching for an ultimate framework that is undeniable: "the question that was self-answering or something like that." For Harvey, without an "a priori foundation before any fact," there is no room for reasons in ethics at all.

In each case, these reasoners assume that a necessary condition for nonrelative values is that they be beyond reasonable question. The difficulty of identifying values that would conform to this expectation leads them to the conclusion that values must be relative. It is in this way that they feel logically impelled to relativism as the only apparent alternative.

Their argument would be refuted, however, if the possibility were admitted of a position that was neither relative, on the one hand, nor beyond reasonable question, on the other. Such a liberal middle ground defines a position that will be discussed later.

The Second Argument

Doug, an Ivy League undergraduate, asserts, "I do not believe that there is or can be any small, or even very large, set of fundamental principles from which you can deduce moral theorems or moral laws which people or society 'should' guide themselves by."

He explains, "The first meaning of my statement that there are no such sets of principles is this, that no reasonably small set of principles could possibly capture unambiguously and to everyone's agreement in every situation the astronomically complex, and for the most part, astronomically ambiguous situations that people are required to make decisions on every day."

With some hyperbole, he continues, "There is no small set of principles, in no set of volumes, in no five books of principles, in no five libraries of principles, in no five libraries of single sentences, or single paragraph sets of independent principles — viewed as rigid laws — could there be enough information to adequately describe or take account of the tremendous complexity."

The difficulty of designing moral principles that could adequately apply as rigid laws is such that "even if you believed that some God could set down a set of principles which would unambiguously and completely determine the proper moral decision in any situation . . . such a set of principles would not be small and no human or set of humans could possibly hold it all in his mind at once. And if he could, he couldn't possibly spend the time to make such a decision. It would take him a trillion years to evaluate the moral principles properly."

But without such an adequate set of rigid laws he is left only with rules of thumb which he chooses "for convenience only" and which, he believes, reflect nothing more than "the arbitrariness of the construction of my own psychology." Because principles, if applied *rigidly,* must be inadequate to the complexity of the human situation, he believes that there are no "fundamental principles . . . moral theorems or moral laws which people or society 'should' guide themselves by."

Another Ivy League undergraduate, Jonathan, makes a similar argument. Because there are no "absolute" values that are "inviolable" (his terms), he has no basis, he believes, for making moral judgments at all. The main philosophical alternative he sees to his own position is this possibility: "I would imagine that in many religions there are absolute values which are more important than self-interest — which are inviolable." He offers the Ten Commandments as an example.

However, he does not believe in such absolute values because "there are times when any two values can conflict." He explains, "When you have to make a decision between conflicting principles and you decide that one principle always survives the conflict, then that principle is the inviolable one and that's the one which you have to build your system on."

For example, Jonathan says, "Certainly it's not logical to believe that you can never steal under any circumstances. . . . If human life were at stake . . . then you'd say, well you can never steal unless you save a human life. And then if you're talking about human life, I think there are some times when you could, perhaps, kill a person justly, maybe in saving other human lives."

He continues to envision possible exceptions. "So the value 'Never kill anyone at all' wouldn't be good, and perhaps 'maximize the total number of lives' might be one which you might want to abide by, which would have no exceptions." Even this last postition must be overridden, he believes, because "the number of lives, in itself, is not necessarily the most important point. It's the value of those individual human lives." For example, "Two great men" might be more important than "six rotten men," he speculates.

However, he offers these values only as examples, for he believes the only principle that might be inviolable is self-interest, and he does not regard that as a moral principle at all. In explaining that the inviolable principle is "the one which you have to build your system on," he adds, "And so if I had a moral system, I would build it upon self-interest." Yet he believes that to regard such a system as moral would be "absurd and redundant." It is in this way that he takes his rejection of inviolable principles as an argument for having no moral principles at all.

Nick is an Ivy League college senior planning to go to medical school. Nick views his values as relative because he cannot view them as absolute. They are not absolute, he says, because "a dilimma can be set up where two values are supposedly held highly, and cannot be chosen between."

An absolute system, however, "should not involve any contradictions." He says of such conflicting values that pose dilemmas, "In terms of the absolute system, supposedly those shouldn't come up. The decision between them should be resolvable, the idea being that you shouldn't be able to create dilemmas."

In such an absolute system, he explains, "Supposedly, there would be no dilemmas, as such. All the values should be readily ranked so that as soon as you identify the salient points, then you can decide which way to go."

But dilemmas seem unavoidable. And "in the lack of such an ideal system" (which would not be subject to dilemmas) "the difference between all such systems that are in use does not really permit much of a moral judgment — I guess, in the strong sense of the word — to be placed on anybody."

In this way, he moves from the claim that his values conflict (in dilemmas) to the claim that his values, as a result, cannot be absolute. And values that are not absolute, he believes, are relative. Such values "do not really permit much of a moral judgment . . . to be placed on anybody."

Alan, a recent Oxbridge graduate student, makes a similar argument. All values, he believes, are "ultimately relativistic in the sense that there is no absolute to which I can refer which will legitimate, guarantee, or confirm one's premises. Principles, however absolute they appear, may very often, given the proper context, *clash* — which to me undermines their absoluteness claims." This conflict, he explains, cannot be decided "with reference to *principles* because the principles, in clashing, are clearly not applicable." Alan, like Nick, believes that principles, in clashing, must be "ultimately relativistic."

Each of these reasoners argues that if morality does not consist in inviolable or exceptionless principles, then it must be relative. Doug concludes that it would be impossible to capture the "tremendous complexity" of morality in rigid laws; but without rigid laws, he is left only with "arbitrary . . . rules of thumb." Jonathan concludes that without "absolute values . . . which are inviolable," such as the Ten Commandments, he is left with no morality at all. Nick assumes, similarly, that "a moral judgement . . . in the strong sense of the word" requires values that are absolute in that they "should not involve any contradictions" or dilemmas. The moral systems that do not live up to this ideal, he concludes, "do not really permit much of a moral judgment." Finally, Alan argues that when principles clash, that "undermines their absoluteness claims" — justifying his conclusion that they are ultimately relativistic.

In each case the basic argument is that because moral principles are not inviolable (that is, because they do not rule out all exceptions or overridings), they must be relative or subjective. A necessary condition for non-relative values, according to this argument, is that principles be exceptionless or inviolable. There will be reason to question this necessary condition later.

The Third Argument

Returning to Doug's interview, there is another objection to the possibility of objective moral principles:

> If someone were to design a set of moral principles, let's say Philosopher X, presumably, when he said that he had designed such a set of moral principles, he meant that I could give him a moral problem and he would be able to give me *an answer* based on those principles.
>
> My objection comes basically to this: I couldn't possibly state the problem. And in fact this is a fundamental objection. Moral decisions are inherently ambiguous decisions because moral problems are inherently ambiguous problems.

He offers an example by mentioning a problem that he believes was once posed to conscientious objectors: "Whether they would commit violence in order to keep their grandmother from being raped":

> My reaction to that question is that it is not well defined. And in order to answer it properly if it were asked of me, I would have to say: Well, first of all, is my grandmother armed herself? Does she have any weapons herself? Does she mind being raped?
>
> These may perhaps sound funny, but in a more serious vein, I might ask myself: What do I have to do to prevent her from being raped? Is it a question of closing the door? Is it a question of knocking the man down? Is it a question of shooting him in the arm? Is it a question of shooting him in the head? Is

it a question of hacking up his body with an axe? Is it out in the open where there are a lot of people? Is there a policeman on the scene already? What do you exactly mean by rape? . . .

And if he were to clarify the problem he could probably clarify it to a sufficient extent that I could answer, more or less ambiguously, that for the time being, I can't think of any more information that I would like to ask, and in all cases I can imagine — conforming to the constraints you have given — that I would prevent my grandmother from being raped.

Yet Doug asserts that even this degree of assurance in his response to such a question is due to the fact that it is "an extreme problem." Even for such an apparently clear case,

> there still comes a point where the posing of the problem becomes incredibly ambiguous — so much on the fringes of reality, so much on the fringes of understanding, so much on the fringes of judgment and interpretation, and so fuzzy, so ill-defined, so ambiguous that I could only give a somewhat ambiguous answer — for lack of an unambiguous understanding of exactly what the problem was.

Because moral problems cannot be unambiguously defined, it is not possible, Doug believes, to devise a system that determines an answer to every moral question. But, Doug assumes, if someone were to devise a moral system, presumably this would mean that his system did determine an answer to every question. This is his expectation about what a moral system would have to do to count as a moral system.

However, Doug argues against such a system in another way. Even if a complete moral system could be devised, it could not serve as a guide for human choice:

> Even if you believed that some God could set down a set of principles which would unambiguously and completely determine the proper moral decision in any situation . . . it would be so voluminous, so astronomically voluminous a system . . . [that] no human or set of humans could possibly hold it in his mind at once. And if he could, he couldn't possibly spend the time to make such a decision. It would take him a trillion years to evaluate the moral principle properly.

Complete principles are thus beyond reach — both because of the inherent ambiguity of the problems they would presume to resolve, and because of the enormous complexity of a complete system were it to be devised.

Without a complete moral system that clearly determines answers to any problem, Doug concludes that we must be left with only rules of thumb. "Instead of calling them [the imperfect and incomplete considerations we are left with] 'moral laws' or 'moral principles,' we concede that the best thing that is possible is 'rules of thumb'. . . . In the final analysis any set of principles which we design must be rules of thumb for social behavior." As was seen in the last section, these rules of thumb are thought of as arbitrary features of his psychology. Without a complete system he has no moral principles or moral laws to which he attributes any justification.

Throb is a recent Ivy League graduate living in the university community. He explains that he does not have "an absolute sense of right and wrong." The reason is, "I'm constantly being presented with questions upon which I have no definitive opinion. If you were to ask me who's right in Ireland, I don't know, man. I can't figure that out. And, I suppose, people with a real absolute sense of right and wrong can figure that out. Fundamentalists, religious fundamentalists are among those who have the strongest sense of right and wrong."

When asked whether anyone can answer these moral questions "in an absolute way" (to use his term), he replies; "No, I don't think so. I don't believe there is any absolute right and wrong. Because if I did, then I would have been able to tell you what Heinz should have done. I don't have an absolute sense of right and wrong. I just have an internal sense of some sort of ethical conduct which is probably logically inconsistent."

For Throb, as for Doug, the incompleteness which he attributes to his moral position undermines its claim to absoluteness. The alternative to an absolute position, however, is a subjective one — which he admits (as seen above) "is probably logically inconsistent."

Nick also argues from the incompleteness and the indeterminacies of any moral system he can think of, to the conclusion that these systems are subjective. Nick's argument is based on the denial of a perfect system. "In the lack of such an ideal system . . . the difference between all such systems that are in use does not really permit much of a moral judgment, I guess, in the strong sense of the word." When asked why he denies such ideal or perfect systems, he explains that "one of the arguments was that the system should be able to handle all cases that you can think of."

If he had such an absolute rather than a relative system, then Nick believes that the resolution of any problem would be predetermined; "the idea being, if you run across something new, you immediately know exactly where it would fit in. . . . As soon as you decided that new question, you'd know exactly where to slip it in the hierarchy, whereas [in] the relative case, the hierarchy is not quite as simple." In the relative case "it is not somehow predetermined completely by a previous system." He explains, "You still weigh them [values] but the decision can't essentially be determined ahead of time."

On the other hand, a defining characteristic of an absolute morality is that it would be "a system you could plug into, at all times, [and] you come up with relatively easy answers." Nick does not believe such an absolute, predetermined system is possible, but in its absence, morality must be relative. Such a nonideal or relative system "does not really permit much of a moral judgement."

Each of these reasoners argues that, lacking a moral system that clearly and completely determines answers to every moral problem, their moral positions must be relative. Doug, for example, assumes that if a philosopher X were to design a set of moral principles then presumably that would mean that "I could give him a moral problem and he would be able to give me *an answer* based on those principles." Doug then concludes that because of the complexity and ambiguity of moral principles such a system — at least in any form that could guide human choice — is impossible. But without such a perfect system, he concludes that we must be left with only rules of thumb, which he regards as arbitrary.

Throb similarly argues that he lacks an absolute sense of right and wrong, for he is constantly being presented with questions upon which he has no definitive opinion. As a result he must have merely a relative or subjective sense of right and wrong.

In a similar way, Nick argues that if he had an absolute system, he could "plug into" it at all times and "come up with relatively easy answers." But he cannot believe that morality is like that because there seem to be too many dilemmas and difficult choices that cannot be solved by a predetermined moral system. Hence, he has to conclude that he can believe only in a nonideal or relative system.

Each of these reasoners has argued from the assumption that an objective or nonrelative moral position must be complete. Given the difficulty of arriving at a moral position that has any plausible claim to completeness, they conclude that their moral positions — because they are incomplete — must be relative or arbitrary. Their argument is, in this way, based on the assumption that completeness is a necessary condition for a nonrelative moral position. That necessity, along with the other two defined above, will be questioned in the next section.

LIBERALISM AND RELATIVISM

"One belief, more than any other, is responsile for the slaughter of individuals on the altars of the great historical ideals," writes Isaiah Berlin in his "Two Concepts of Liberty." "This is the belief that somewhere, in the past or in the future, in divine revelation, or in the mind of an individual thinker, in the pronouncements of history or science, or in the simple heart of an uncorrupted man, there is a final solution."[15]

Berlin's aim is to deny such a final solution to the problems of moral and political theory — to deny that these problems can all be resolved in some way beyond reasonable dispute by principles that are compatible with one another. His denial of such a solution is part of a coherent ethical position that links the tentativeness and incompleteness of moral judgments to an assertion of the need for liberty. Since conclusive solutions are lacking, according to this position, everyone can learn from the marketplace of ideas where our tentative, conflicting, and incomplete moral notions are subject to improvement.

This ethical position of Berlin's — which will be called liberalism — is not relativism. Principles may be incomplete and they may as prima facie principles, conflict with one another, and they may lack an a priori basis — all without also being subjective, relative, or arbitrary. For example, the position that Rawls calls intuitionism has all of these characteristics, but includes no claim that moral judgments are subjective or that they lack justification.

This position is logically coherent because the conflicts among prima facie principles need not entail any logical contradictions. In other words, principles may include clauses that specify requirements for action only when a *ceteris paribus* or other-things-being-equal claim is satisfied. When such principles conflict, their claims have to be balanced or weighed intuitionistically (to use Rawls's terminology). While a position of this kind may have inadequacies because of the questions it fails to resolve, it cannot be ruled out as logically inconsistent.[16]

A similar point should be made about the incompleteness of the liberal position. The mere fact that a position does not presume to resolve every possible question should not undermine it for the questions it does purport to resolve. Consider, for example, another principle, the Pareto principle, which is explicitly incomplete. The Pareto principle prescribes choices that would make some people better off and no one worse off. But it says nothing about cases in which somebody would be made worse off no matter what is chosen. Should it count as an argument against following the Pareto principle that it fails to tell us what to do in another kind of case, namely, when we have to choose between policies that would all make someone worse off? The author believes that the fact that the principle says nothing about such hard cases cannot be used as a counterexample for the class of cases for which it does offer prescriptions.

Similarly, must principles be entirely beyond reasonable question before one can be justified in making moral judgments at all? Scientific judgments are, of course, lacking in a basis beyond reasonable question, but few would argue that they are, as a result, entirely relative or subjective in a way similar to the moral conclusions of the reasoners cited here.

There is no claim that these fundamental issues are resolved here. The point is made only that if the liberal ethical position exemplified by Berlin is a possible alternative, then the relativistic arguments cited above must be mistaken. There is no need to argue that liberalism, in this sense, is correct — only that it defines a coherent, possible position.

The arguments of the relativists were all arguments by elimination. Because their moral positions do not, it was asserted, conform to certain requirements, they must be relative. These requirements were that they be beyond reasonable question, that their principles be exceptionless, and that they be complete. The liberal position just defined, however, purports to be nonrelative even though its principles are self-consciously tentative, conflicting, and incomplete. Once the mere possibility of such a position is admitted, the conclusions these reasoners reach — that their positions do not conform to the three requirements above — could not be taken as an argument for those positions also being relative; for a moral position could lack a basis beyond reasonable question, lack inviolability, and lack completeness, but, nevertheless, be nonrelative. If liberalism is possible, in other words, then these claims against morality could all be accepted without the correctness of relativism following as a conclusion.

The moral position that would satisfy non–relativistic expectations might be called absolutism. Absolutist principles are beyond reasonable question; they hold without exception; they are complete. The relativistic reasoners previously cited have argued that because their positions do not conform to these requirements, they must be relative or subjective. Their mistake, it appears, has been to ignore a possible middle ground between absolutism on the one hand, and relativism on the other. This middle ground is defined by the ethical position of liberals such as Berlin.

A major difficulty for liberalism is that if these absolutist expectations are widely shared, then this liberal position will have a tendency to self-destruct as a coherent moral ideology, for it is an ideology that delegitimates itself in the eyes of those who come to it with such absolutist expectations. It undercuts its own legitimacy as a moral position. In other words, the ideology that morality is tentative and incomplete yields subjectivism or relativism, when it is combined with the absolutist expectations that were isolated in these ordinary reasoners.

This phenomenon is illustrated by Leo Strauss's interpretation of Berlin's ethical position as "a characteristic document in the crisis of liberalism — of a crisis due to the fact that liberalism has abandoned its absolutist basis and is trying to become entirely relativistic."[17] Strauss interprets the character of Berlin's principles (equally ultimate, conflicting, and open to disagreement) as evidence that Berlin's position can really amount to no more than relativism. In this way, Berlin's position apparently falls in what Strauss calls "an impossible middle ground between absolutism and relativism."[18] Strauss does not actually commit himself to the claim that the "middle ground" is impossible. However, it seems a fair inference from the rest of his attack on Berlin.

By approaching Berlin's liberal ethical position with absolutist expectations, Strauss leaps to the conclusion that it must be no more, at bottom, than mere relativism. For those who hold these absolutist expectations, liberalism will self-destruct in this way as a coherent moral position. In this sense, Strauss is correct to identify Berlin's position (as well as his own analysis of it) as a "characteristic document in the crisis of liberalism."

LIBERALISM AND MORAL DEVELOPMENT

While the particular claims against morality offered by these reasoners do not imply relativism, they are claims that affect Kohlberg's position. If the relativists are correct about the unavailability of principles that are beyond reasonable question, that never require exceptions, and that are complete in resolving all moral questions, then Kohlberg's description of Stage 6 must be rejected.

The reasoners did not simply assert that such principles were unavailable. Rather, they arrived at this conclusion on the basis of other assumptions that appeared plausible — for example, the lack of metaphysical postulates that would provide an undeniable basis, the distinction between analytic and synthetic truths, and the complexity of moral problems. In making these arguments they defined what has been claimed to be a coherent moral position, a position that is exemplified by a certain kind of contemporary liberalism.

Whether they are correct in their arguments supporting those three liberal claims is not a question to be settled here. However, two points should be emphasized: first, accepting those liberal claims would not commit one to relativism, and second, accepting those liberal claims would commit one to rejecting Kohlberg's account of Stage 6.

In Stage 6, Kohlberg purports to offer precisely the kinds of principles whose possibility these three liberal claims deny. Consider the first expectation.

Kohlberg's Stage 6 claims to be beyond reasonable question in that it conforms to what Kohlberg calls his Platonic assumption — that "he who knows the good chooses the good."[19] The hypothesis is ruled out that someone could understand a higher stage and also reject it. As Kohlberg explains; "If the higher stage solution is 'seen,' it is preferred to the lower stage solution, whatever the particular experiences with either stage solution. This is because part of seeing the higher stage is seeing why it is better than the lower stage solution."[20]

Hence, the higher stage cannot be both fully understood and denied. In this sense Kohlberg is making an even stronger claim for the higher stages than can be made for the geometric knowledge to which he compares them (for knowledge of this latter kind can be denied, but at the price of inconsistency). At any rate moral knowledge is held to be beyond reasonable question in a way analogous to the knowledge of geometry: "The Platonic view implies that, in a sense, knowledge of the good is always within but needs to be drawn out like geometric knowledge in Meno's slave."[21]

The highest stages would then satisfy the first expectation. They would also satisfy the second expectation (inviolability) because Stages 5 and 6 both consist in principles rather than rules. According to Kohlberg, a defining characteristic of principles is that they are inviolable. "By a moral principle we mean a mode of choosing which is universal, a rule of choosing which we want all people to adopt in all situations. . . . There are exceptions to rules but no exceptions to principles."[22]

Stage 6 would also satisfy the third expectation in that it purports to be complete. Kohlberg says of Stage 6: "The claim of principled morality is that it *defines the right for anyone in any situation.*"[23] It does this by being more differentiated than preceding stages. For example, for every valid claim to a right at Stage 6, there is a correlative determination of a duty. By contrast, Kohlberg believes Stage 5 to be inadequate in that Stage 5 rights and duties are not completely correlative. This means that some duties are not completely specified at Stage 5. There are some moral claims for which it is not clear who should do what. At Stage 6, however, this indeterminacy is remedied by making everyone's duties and rights completely correlative.[24]

Thus, Kohlberg claims to provide the very kind of theory whose possibility the relativistic reasoners deny. Kohlberg's specific suggestions about Stage 6 will not be examined here. It should suffice to note that his recent identification of Stage 6 with Rawls's theory for questions of social choice raises grave questions about whether the ambitious claims just cited are fulfilled by Stage 6.[25]

Whether Kohlberg can ultimately, in a more developed theory, refute these liberal claims remains an open question. However, the central point here is that the defense of morality against relativism need not depend upon the development of such a theory. Once the viability of the more modest, liberal alternative is admitted, then the relativistic arguments cited here must be rejected. It is for this reason that the arguments for relativism, although logically consistent, are also mistaken.

NOTES

1. Lawrence Kohlberg, "From Is to Ought: How to Commit the Naturalistic Fallacy and Get Away With It in the Study of Moral Development," in *Cognitive Development and Epistemology,* ed. Theodore Mischel (New York: Academic Press, 1971), pp. 151 – 235.

2. Ibid.

3. Ibid., p. 205.

4. Lawrence Kohlberg and R. Kramer, "Continuities and Discontinuities in Childhood and Adult Moral Development," *Human Development* 12 (1969): 93-120, 109.

5. Ibid.

6. Ibid., p. 112.

7. Kohlberg, "From Is to Ought," p. 182.

8. Lawrence Kohlberg, "Continuities in Childhood and Adult Moral Development Revisited,"in *Life-Span Developmental Psychology,* ed. Paul B. Baltes and K. Warner Schaie (New York: Academic Press, 1973), p. 191.

9. Elliot Turiel, "Conflict and Transition in Adolescent Moral Development," *Child Development* 45 (1974), p. 14.

10. Ibid., p. 17.

11. Lawrence Kohlberg and Carol Gilligan, "The Adolescent as a Philosopher: The Discovery of the Self in a Post-conventional World," *Daedalus* 100 (1971); p. 1080.

12. Ibid.

13. Kohlberg, "From Is to Ought," p. 204.

14. Kohlberg and Kramer, "Continuities and Discontinuities," p. 109.

15. Isaiah Berlin, "Two Concepts of Liberty," in *Four Essays on Liberty* (Oxford: Oxford University Press, 1969), p. 167.

16. For an account of the logic of prima facie principles, see David Lyons, *The Forms and Limits of Utilitarianism* (Oxford: Oxford University Press, 1965).

17. Leo Strauss "Relativism," in *Relativism and the Study of Man,* ed. Helmut Schoek and James W. Wiggins (Princeton: Van Nostrand, 1961), p. 140.

18. Ibid.

19. Lawrence Kohlberg, "Education for Justice: A Modern Statement of the Platonic View," in *Moral Education,* ed. T. Sizer (Cambridge, Mass.: Harvard University Press, 1970), p. 59.

20. Kohlberg, "Continuities Revisited," p. 194.

21. Kohlberg, "Education for Justice," p. 80.

22. Ibid., p. 69.

23. Kohlberg, "From Is to Ought," p. 185.

24. Lawrence Kohlberg, "The Claim to Moral Adequacy of a Highest Stage of Moral Judgment," *Journal of Philosophy* 70 (1973): 630–46.

25. Ibid. See also Lawrence Kohlberg, "Justice as Reversibility," in *Philosophy, Politics and Society,* 5th ser., ed. Peter Laslett and James Fishkin (Oxford: Basil Blackwell; New Haven, Conn.: Yale University Press, 1979). Elsewhere the author has discussed certain difficulties in Rawls's theory which would imply that it does not conform to these claims. See James Fishkin, "Justice and Rationality: Some Objections to the Central Argument in Rawls's Theory," *American Political Science Review* 69 (1975): 615–29.

7

THE TYRANNY OF THE CATEGORICAL: ON KOHLBERG AND THE POLITICS OF MORAL DEVELOPMENT

Herbert G. Reid & Ernest J. Yanarella

The current preoccupation in secondary and higher education with moral education and with the moral atmosphere of the classroom presents the critical social theorist and political educator with something of a dilemma. Encouraging this interest risks the danger of allowing it to be co-opted and defused by the prevailing structure of domination, while indicting it incurs the hazard of promoting the abundant neo-Weberian "iron cage" imagery, thus closing off possible avenues for widening the spectrum of political discourse and for advancing the tasks of critical political education.[1] More challenging in the context of today's mood of one-dimensional pessimism is taking up the positive moment of critique by uncovering the latent potentialities for moral development in the functioning operations of everyday life; for the demystifying moment of critique is hardly the most difficult task in confronting the renewal of interest in theories of moral development and moral education in school and society.

To anyone working within the tradition of critical theory, the mainstream response to the exhaustion of the liberal tradition is hardly surprising. In a society where the processes of reification have advanced to spectacular lengths (almost literally a "society of the spectacle"), a reform movement based on an ethical renewal of liberal principles and procedures is quite to be expected. What Georg Lukacs said of Bernstein's effort to reform socialism applies equally well to this latest campaign to reform U.S. capitalism and its liberal politics. This ethical reformation, Lukacs argued, "is the subjective side of the missing category of totality which can alone provide an overall view." In a reified world, "action is directed wholly inward . . . [and] the attempt [is made] to change the world at its only remaining free point, namely man himself (ethics)."[2]

One thing is certain: a concern with moral development and education will not soon subside. Contemporary political events — such as the moral bankruptcy of the U.S. Vietnam adventure and the failure of key policy makers to choose the option of "exit" and "voice" in responding to that bankruptcy, the discovery of the moral obtuseness of the arguments of the conspirators in the Watergate scandal, and the recent revelations of payoffs to foreign leaders by U.S. based corporations — have given impetus to public concern with the moral condition of liberal America. And educational psychologists and curriculum specialists have already begun to busy themselves with preparing teaching modules, educational films, and morality games designed, if not genuinely to elevate the level of moral and political discourse, at least to make our technocorporate felons more clever and sophisticated in rationalizing their private vices and public transgressions.

In its effort critically to uncover the largely unconnected insights of critical theory and phenomenology for the purposes of radicalizing the notion of moral development, this chapter is a study of critical political theory. Its basic objective is to argue for the need for a critical phenomenology of psychopolitical development serving a critical hermeneutics of the body politic. To this end, it will focus upon the highly touted writings on moral development of Lawrence Kohlberg and his associates. Then, because this effort is guided by a dialectical and phenomenological conception of critique — one involving not only the negative moment of critically exposing false appearances, but also the positive moment of restoring comprehension of actual possibilities existing within a dynamic and contradictory social whole — the chapter will conclude with a section offering a perspective on the life-world sources of psychopolitical development, which summarizes and extends the critical phenomenological analysis in the body of this critique. In order to lay the foundation for a genuinely dialectical notion of psychopolitical development, there is first an excursus into a key problematic of the Frankfurt school during the 1920s and 1930s — namely, the historical interplay between authoritarianism and instrumental rationality.

THE FRANKFURT SCHOOL, AUTHORITARIANISM, AND INSTRUMENTAL RATIONALISM: AN EXCURSUS

Martin Jay has done a commendable job in his book, *The Dialectical Imagination*, in reconstructing the essential history of the Frankfurt school from 1923 to 1950, and he is often insightful in his portrait of the intellectual ferment that occurred within the institute during the period in question.

In the 1920s, as he noted, among the Frankfurt membership a debate over the course of Soviet economic planning, industrialization, and management — in short, the "Soviet experiment" — was precipitated.[3] Frederick Pollock, and also others, participated in this debate; and what concerned them mightily was the apparent trend toward various forms of authoritarian administrative organization and scientific management. Particularly troublesome was the developing infatuation among the Soviet party elite with Taylorism — the movement further to rationalize and mechanize industrial production in the United States according to certain principles of scientific management derived from Frederick Winslow Taylor's time-and-motion studies. For example, as early as March 1918, Lenin suggested that the Bolshevik party "must raise the question of applying much of what is scientific and progressive in the Taylor system," and later urged that the party "organize in Russia the study and teaching of the Taylor system and systematically try it out and adopt it to our own ends."[4]

This uncritical importation of capitalist machine technology and its accompanying management and administrative practices portended for some members of the Frankfurt school the betrayal of the very real but ambiguous potentialities and possibilities springing from the Bolshevik revolution and the emergence of the Soviet Union. Moreover, it seemed to represent the reduplication in the Soviet state of the modes of domination and instrumental rationality that Frankfurt school studies had seen accompanying the demise of the liberalist phase of Western capitalism in the wake of the defeat of international socialism, epitomized in its fragmentation with the onset of World War I and afterward with the gradual integration and deradicalization of the proletariat throughout Europe.

With the emigration of most of the key figures of the Frankfurt Institute and its geographic relocation in the United States, the analysis of the nexus of authoritarianism and technological rationality took on a more holistic and encompassing cast. Confronted with and indeed shocked by the central tendencies in culture and economy with which they had to contend during their stay in the United States, they turned increasingly to understanding the new phase of the capitalist totality of which U.S. capitalism was its foremost example, and doing this in the context of their studies of authoritarianism in Nazi Germany. Their investigation of this incipient phase of state capitalism proceeded in terms of a critique of the "culture industry" and of a critical analysis of the authoritarian state. The former helped explain certain novel features of this developing totality — including its switch from accent on work and production to consumption through the generation of the cultural apparatus to stimulate a mass culture — while the latter clarified for them the way in which, as Max Horkheimer pointed out, the "blind, calculative rationality of business life . . . has carried over

to the authoritarian society."[5] In this respect, Pollock's essay, "State Capitalism," and Horkheimer's "Authoritarian State," both written in 1941,
represent the keystone of this attempt to encompass the latest phase of
political economy.[6] At the same time, Horkheimer and Theodor Adorno
in particular were endeavoring to deepen the historical range and foundation for understanding this new historic phase of authoritarianism in-
fecting capitalist and state socialist societies alike; and their principle means
lay in their studies of the dialectic of enlightenment — the master concept
that assisted them in comprehending the new forms of authoritarianism
in relation to the historical interweaving of scientistic enlightenment and
political domination which they situated in the Western enlightenment but
traced even more deeply to the very beginnings of Western thought.[7] What
bears emphasizing here is that during this long and complicated process
of reconceptualization undertaken by the Frankfurt school they did not
abandon truly dialectical analysis for culture critique — as some suggested — but rather, continued to practice it in their subtle investigations
by adhering to the dialectical conception of society as a sociohistorical
totality where culture and political economy are dialectically mediated
aspects of the same totality being studied.

   The purpose of this brief survey is to show that the Frankfurt theorists
during these years were struggling to come to terms with the cultural and
economic foundations of what later American critics and social theorists
would call the rise of the corporate state in the United States. Crucial to
the emergence of the increasingly technocratic and corporate form of
U. S. society for these native American theorists were at least four periods:
the late 1800s when the legal infrastructure especially was developed; the
1920s when, as Stuart Ewen has shown, advertising emerged as a form of
social production to help shape the commodity self-tailored to mass production; the 1930s, when the administrative structures of the welfare state
were forged and which in the light of the preceding analysis may be seen
as a further phase in authoritarian consolidation; and the war years from
1939 to 1945, when the institutional links of what C. Wright Mills called
the power elite were solidified.[8] What a juxtaposition of the Frankfurt
writings and the work of native critics discloses, then, is how the technocorporate phase of the U.S. capitalist economy unfolded symbiotically
amidst the ideological dynamics of the dominant liberal tradition, moving
toward technocratic-authoritarian modes of social authority which for some
academicians finally became visible in the Watergate affair.

   It is against this background and within this institutional matrix that the
discussion of moral development and the critique of Kohlberg will be
situated.

KOHLBERG'S SCHEME OF MORAL DEVELOPMENT: LOCKEAN AND KANTIAN DIMENSIONS

Except for Erik Erikson's theory of the human life cycle and his founding work linking ego psychology and historical change, no contemporary theory of psychological development has received more sustained praise and (now) mounting critical scrutiny by latter-day psychologists, educators, and philosophers than the theory of moral development growing out of the work of Harvard psychologist Lawrence Kohlberg and his fellow researchers.[9] The proximate reasons for its lure to so wide a circle of academic specialists are easy to discern. Since its inauguration nearly 20 years ago when Kohlberg first laid down the foundations for his six-stage schema of moral development in his dissertation, his studies have produced a corpus of cross-cultural research which simultaneously has challenged behavioristic orthodoxy in American psychology and has consciously and intentionally pursued the major pedagogical implications of a nonbehavioristic (and anti-Freudian) theory of moral development into the areas of moral and religious education, sex education, and criminal justice.[10]

In general terms, Kohlberg's theory and research strategy may be summarized in the following way. Working out of the cognitive developmental framework on moralization spawned by Jean Piaget, Kohlberg has hypothesized from empirical research performed by himself and others the existence of three distinct levels of moral reasoning and — within those three levels — six discrete stages of moral development. (See p. 58–59.) In positing this trilateral, six-stage ordering, Kohlberg and his associates have devised and utilized a series of short stories couched in the form of moral dilemmas, which are presented to their subjects for moral interpretation. Since the stories are literally structured as dilemmas (that is, no solution is available that does not involve negative costs), the interviewees are given the opportunity to reveal the cognitive complexity and moral sophistication of their reasoning under situations of ambiguity and conflict. From the responses of each interviewee, the subject's stage of moral development is determined by the interviewer.

Several noteworthy points in this research need to be underscored. In the first place, in regard to the methodology itself, the form of moral reasoning, not the content of the arguments used, is the basic datum of the Kohlbergian psychologist. Theoretically, two subjects might reach diametrically opposed conclusions concerning a particular moral dilemma and yet be located at the same stage of moral development by virtue of the parallel modes of moral reasoning employed. This uncoupling of the form of moral reasoning from its content and the sole focus on the former is crucial for Kohlberg, since it assures the psychologist of the scientific (that is, nonideological) and structural status of his research enterprise.[11] As for its most salient findings, perhaps the most provocative conclusion derived from limited cross-cultural data representing 12 cultures is that the six stages of moral development (uncovered in American research) have been cross-culturally validated and, in a word, may now be deemed to form a universal, invariant sequence. In Kohlberg's own words, "all individuals in all cultures go through the same order or sequence of gross stages of development, though varying in rate and terminal point of development."[12]

In addition, according to Kohlberg, the idea of a universal, invariant sequence implies — and empirical studies presumably confirm — that movement from one stage to the next higher stage (and so forth) follows sequentially without the possibility of skipping over stages; that human beings — at whatever stage — appear to be capable at best of comprehending the moral reasoning of others only one stage beyond their own present stage; that except for some Stage 4 subjects who temporarily regress to Stage 2 reasoning on their way to Stage 5 thinking, moral development is irreversible — that is, once a stage of moral development is achieved, regression to lower stages does not take place; and that "cultural teaching and experience can speed up or slow down development, but cannot change its order or sequence."[13]

In criticizing the work of Kohlberg and in particular the deeper foundations of his tacit interpretive framework, it is acknowledged that the research of Kohlberg and his followers is, and remains, an ongoing enterprise — not a completed project impervious to alteration — and that critical analyses like the present study may precipitate further changes in its prevailing ideological and philosophical grounding. What is more, however embedded in liberal ideological tendencies and Kantian epistemological biases Kohlberg's thinking may be, the potential contribution of the Kohlbergian school to radicalizing Western thought may well overflow the ideological and epistemological confines within which his work has been situated. If, for example, his research on moral development has the broader intellectual and social impact of helping to dispel the myth of "value-free" social science among its practitioners and the populace at large, the value of his writings to this larger postmodern task will not be insignificant.

KOHLBERG'S STAGES AND THE IDEOLOGICAL HEGEMONY OF LOCKEAN LIBERALISM

Critical theoretical and phenomenological perspectives grounding critical political theory yield a number of salient criticisms of the explicit conceptual structure and tacit ideological underpinnings of Kohlberg's

work, as well as of the pedagogical inadequacies of this corpus of psychological research. This critique helps to reformulate and pull together in
one framework both the socioeconomic critique of Piaget-Kohlberg presented by Susan Buck-Morss[14] and the cultural critique of Kohlberg offered
by Elizabeth Simpson[15] within the temporal dialectical totality of contemporary American society, a society that is beset by a legitimation crisis
affecting both the form and content of its dominant "historical bloc" (from
Gramsci). (Subsequent to the initial formulation of this critique, the
authors discovered Edmund Sullivan's remarkably convergent critique of
Kohlberg's theory as liberal social science ideology, which reinforces major
points of this analysis.)[16] In short, the general thesis defended in this section
is that Kohlberg's writings on moral development may best be interpreted
simultaneously as an expression of the growing exhaustion of Lockean
liberalism as a moral force in the United States, and as an effort within
the crumbling ideological edifice of liberalism to renew itself by appealing
to (and rather uncritically appropriating) the most sophisticated philosophical and ethical extension of that tradition — Kantianism.

Both as a description of the existential conditions of the United States
and as a normative vision for American society, Lockean liberalism has
been accorded a privileged place in history. As Louis Hartz, the Berkeley
school, Herbert Reid, and others have shown, owing to the special circumstances unique to the founding of America as a fragment society, this
ideology took root in the American terrain, embedded itself into virtually
every recess of social existence, and — in dialectical symbiosis with the
capitalist economy — achieved an unexcelled and almost unchallengeable
authority and status.[17] Because it permeated so widely and so deeply into
American political culture and society, its ideological character was submerged in the American psyche and its limits were lost to the national
political consciousness. As late as the 1960s, Arthur Schlesinger, Jr., could
still speak with reverence of the American genius as residing in its commitment to discrete, unconnected, and time-tested ideas rather than to an
"ideology."[18] But as early as 1955 the opaqueness of the ideological
hegemony of Lockean liberalism was beginning to give way to critical
scrutiny as C. Wright Mills, in a period of economic malaise and political
drift, wrote of the fate of liberal values in a modern world whose overriding
realities no longer reflected those values.[19] Then, too, for a brief period
in the early sixties, the New Left lifted the ideological veil of Lockean
liberal hegemony by attributing the main source of domestic upheaval and
international calamity to the inadequacies of the corporate liberal state.[20]
By 1971, Walter Dean Burnham could state without exaggeration that the
mounting crisis of American political legitimacy was truly a crisis of liberalism.[21] Indeed, so widespread was awareness of the stagnation of Lock-

eanism by the mid-1970s that a political analyst from the Harvard Business School, George C. Lodge, could make its replacement (a "new American ideology") a front-ranking and pressing order of the day on the corporate agenda.[22]

What is striking about the growing popularity of Kohlberg's work on moral development, then, is that it is occurring precisely at a time when the foundations of American liberalism are eroding in nearly all of the central institutional matrices of American society. The central norms and sanctions of liberalism sedimented into these institutions are losing legitimacy and a frantic search for a new form of legitimacy has been set in motion. But Kohlberg's psychologistic approach to moral development blinds him to the full import of all of this desperate flailing about by Americans for new means of restoring order and stability to the public and private chaos of their lives. Yet, Kohlberg to the contrary notwithstanding, his schema of moral development rests upon the tacit foundations of this historically evolved and historically changing ideology, and owes its broad appeal to the strenuous efforts of public administrators, liberal academics, and intellectuals to fortify and rejuvenate the sagging ideological bases of public authority through the strategy of ethical reform.

In his recent elaboration and defense of a hermeneutic approach to social inquiry, Charles Taylor indicted mainstream political science for adopting the mistaken view of regarding liberal-capitalist society not as one structure of meaning among many possible other ways of socially constructing reality, but rather as the "inescapable background of social action as such."[23] For these authors, the work of Kohlberg and his associates is liable to precisely the same ideology critique. That is, Kohlberg has likewise taken the dominant symbols and meanings of liberal-capitalist America as the inescapable background of moral development as such. As Taylor notes, "in this guise, it no longer need be an object of study. Rather it retreats to the middle distance, where its general outline takes the role of universal framework within which (it is hoped) actions and structures will be brute data identifiable, and this for any society at any time."[24] Seen in this way, Kohlberg's stages of moral development take on a very different character. In the first place, it seems evident that his purported hierarchical stages mask the highly tendentious ideological nature of the entire sequence of stages. In fact, those stages may be interpreted as residing wholly on a single ideological continuum within Lockean liberalism. Although less discrete than Kohlberg claims, these qualitatively different stages of moral development may better be understood as capturing gradations within the ideological framework grounding them.

Kohlberg's latent liberal allegiance, to be sure, does not express itself in the idiom of classical liberalism. Indeed, his interpretation of the universal ethical orientation of his sixth stage as based upon the "universal principles of justice, of the reciprocity and equality of human rights, and of respect for the dignity of human beings as individual persons" (see p. 59) would seem to mark his thought as standing outside the bounds of the liberal paradigm. Yet this paradigm is hardly exhausted by its classical articulation, since as a living cultural force that has existed in symbiotic relationship with capitalist institutions, it has remained historically dynamic and — within limits — historically changing. What has remained a constant, however, is the deeper core values of this historically evolving ideology; and it is here that the reform liberalism of Kohlberg and even that of some of his most subtle critics (like Kenneth Keniston) remains fixed.

In the second place, this ideology critique reveals the apparent ease with which Kohlberg and others can proclaim their schema of moral development as a universal, invariant sequence applicable to all cultures. As Simpson and others have observed, the cross-cultural data on which this allegation is based had been only selectively released and in any case remain much too limited in themselves to justify such a sweeping conclusion.[25] In addition, others have suggested that Kohlberg and his fellow researchers have shown a tendency to interpret their data in a rather perfunctory and self-serving manner.[26] Finally, apparently some of the cross-cultural studies allow the researchers to do little more than conclude that in some non-Western cultures representative of the upper stages (5 and 6) do not exist at all.[27] If it is correct to assume that a significant amount of support for the purported sequential structure and universal scope of Kohlberg's moral developmental schema springs from the covert role played by the dominant values (and their multiple forms) of Western liberalism as mediated by the American context, these and other observations are hardly puzzling. For by forgetting the historically specific and socially constructed nature of these values and symbols as they have been institutionalized in the "civilization of work," Kohlberg can forge the content of these forms of moral reasoning into a hidden universal framework informing the interpretation of the interview data from national and cross-cultural inquiries.

KOHLBERG AND KANTIANISM: PERSPECTIVES FROM CRITICAL THEORY AND PHENOMENOLOGY

To revitalize the psychological study of moral development and wrest it from the grip of Skinnerian behaviorism in American psychology, Kohlberg sought inspiration from the work of Piaget.[28] In the process of assimilating Piaget's studies in moral judgment, Kohlberg also incorporated —

indeed, at deeper levels, embraced more completely — the Kantian underpinnings of the noted French/Swiss psychologist's cognitive developmental approach. That Piaget draws significantly upon the Kantian tradition seems difficult to deny, for he opposes both crude empiricism (what he calls "geneticism without structure") and pure rationalism (what he calls "structuralism without genesis"). The point was nicely put by D. W. Hamlyn when he stated that "just as Kant's reconciliation between empiricism and rationalism came through the idea that experience is determined by categories which are a function of the mind, so Piaget's reconciliation of empiricism and nativism comes through the idea that experience develops according to structures which are, likewise, a function of the mind in its relationship to the world."[29] Following Piaget, Kohlberg embraces Piaget's Kantian reconciliation in the form of the relational (Piaget) or interaction (Kohlberg) method and understands the cognitive stages of moral development in terms of genetic structuralism; and, moreover, he further weds himself to a Kantian outlook by characterizing moral principles as categorical imperatives. With this mutual appropriation of Piagetian method and Kantian philosophical and ethical baggage come features constituting Kohlberg's enterprise which both compound native Lockean ideological proclivities in his work and add new Kantian epistemological liabilities to his developing research — proclivities and liabilities greatly illuminated by Western Marxism's critique of Kantian ethics and its overt formalism, and phenomenology's critique of idealism.

No consideration will be given here to the positive aspects of Kant's epistemological revolution in Western philosophy or to the productive role of Kantianism as a forerunner of dialectical thought in the German idealist tradition. Nor will an attempt be made to offer a thoroughgoing criticism of Piaget's rich and complex research, which is hardly exhausted by a critique of the shortcomings of the Kantian dimensions to his thinking. Rather, the focus will be on the manner in which Kohlberg's more fundamental and less reflective appropriation of Kantianism makes him vulnerable to significant criticism from the standpoint of critical phenomenology.

Kantian philosophy and ethics have been continual targets of philosophers and social theorists in the critical Marxist tradition. As the highest expression of bourgeois liberalism, Kant's thought was a natural object of critical and penetrating scrutiny by these thinkers from Lukacs to the Frankfurt school. Because of his Kantian presuppositions, Kohlberg's theoretical edifice remains vulnerable to many of the same shortcomings disclosed by these critical theorists. Among other things, Kohlberg seems most vulnerable to the charge of formalism in radically divorcing form from content in his theory of moral development. Consider his claim that the universal sequential ordering of his stages of moral development is

allegedly based upon a structured patterning of the forms of moral reasoning uncovered by his and his associates' longitudinal and cross-cultural
empirical studies. In the course of his analysis of the "antinomies of bourgeois thought" (with which Kantian philosophy — essence/appearance,
science/ethics, external determinism/inward freedom, and so on — was
riddled), Lukacs offered a historical-genetic analysis of abstract formalism
which saw this particular kind of abstraction — with its emphasis upon the
primacy of form over content and the abstract over the concrete — as a
product of the industrial stage of Western capitalism.[30] Taking as his central
guidepost Marx's insight into the way the commodity structure generates
the exchange principle, reification, and fetishism, Lukacs demonstrated in
this central chapter in *History and Class-Consciousness* how, as Buck-
Morss has indicated,

> Kant's formalism which attributed cognitive value to the abstract structure
> of verbal judgments and the rational forms of time, space, and causality,
> regardless of particular, concrete content, paralleled the capitalist concern
> for abstract exchange value rather than social use value . . . [how] Kantian
> dualism, the separation of formal mental operations from the perceptual
> objects which provided the content of thought, was the cognitive counterpart
> to the alienation of workers from the object of their production.[31]

Far from being a universal and timeless form of perceptual receptiveness
to the world, this form of cognition was itself social content of an historically evolved socioeconomic totality.

In analogous fashion, Kohlberg's cognitive stages qua abstract formal
structures may be subject to a similar critique. Buck-Morss advances her
case against Kohlberg's developmental schema by arguing that "what he
does not consider is whether form itself is content, whether the very notion
that morality can divorce form from content, far from 'culturally universal'
or 'natural,' manifests the structure of a specific society at a specific stage
of economic development.[32] As an amendment to Buck-Morss' criticism,
in the case of Kohlberg's model, the forms of moral reasoning comprising
this sequential model are filled at deeper, more submerged levels with the
Lockean liberal values historically sedimented as the hegemonic ideology
of the American social totality.

It is part of the academic conceit (if this is not too strong a term) of
Kohlberg's writings that, on the basis of such scant and apparently unre-
liable studies, a universality of scope of the stages of moral development
is imputed to all cultures and the charge of "retardation" of moral de-

velopment is laid to those "primitive" cultures and lower socioeconomic classes that fail to manifest the highest stages (social contract and principled autonomy).[33] Certainly, with respect to the former, Michael Maccoby and Nancy Modiano seem better cultural anthropologists when they offer in their recent study a contradictory interpretation of the scope of abstraction and its relative merits. In a cross-cultural and urban-rural study of American and Mexican children's abilities to determine abstract equivalences among different objects, they conclude by saying,

> If the peasant child is not dulled by village life, he will experience the uniqueness of events, objects, and people. But, as the city child grows older, he may end by exchanging a spontaneous, less alienated relationship to the world for a more sophisticated outlook which concentrates on using, exchanging, or cataloguing. What industrialized, urban man gains in an increased ability to formulate, to reason, and to code the ever more numerous bits of complex information he acquires, he may lose in a decreased sensitivity to people and events.[34]

As they show in some detail in their study, even in Mexico abstract formalism of the kind so endemic to the Western industrial world has not taken root in significant parts of this developing nation and the relationship of Mexican peasant children to other people and to nature is far more concrete, intimate, and cooperative than is the norm in advanced industrial societies.

The Frankfurt school took their critique of the logic of abstract formalism in Kantian thought one step further than Lukacs, and their criticisms carry with them even more chilling (and unexpected) implications for a depth-hermeneutic critique of Kohlberg's approach. In their excursus on Kant, de Sade, and Nietzsche, significantly entitled, "Juliette or Enlightenment and Morality," Horkheimer and Adorno situate Kant's ethical formalism within the dialectic of enlightenment and domination — one of their most important contributions to the understanding of the deep roots of technological rationality in modern thought and action.[35] The major thrust of their extremely subtle, dialectical analysis is succinctly summarized by Martin Jay when he observes:

> Once again, Horkheimer and Adorno stressed the continuity between bourgeois liberalism, in this case symbolized by Kant, and totalitarianism, here prefigured by de Sade and, to some extent, Nietzsche. Kant's effort to ground

ethics solely in practical rationality, they argued, was ultimately a failure. The Enlightenment's treatment of nature, and by extension of men, as objects was fundamentally in accord with the extreme formalism of the categorical imperative, despite Kant's injunction to consider men as ends rather than means. Carried to its logical extreme, calculating, instrumental, formal rationality led to the horrors of twentieth-century barbarism.[36]

These remarks are especially pertinent to Kohlberg's Stage 6 and to the strange and complex relationship between the types of reasoning in Stage 6 and Stage 2 that he and his compatriots have uncovered in some subjects. The depth-historical interpretation of Kant's ethics by Horkheimer and Adorno[37] suggests that the highest stage on Kohlberg's scale — which, with its characteristic emphasis on moral principle, private conscience, and personal autonomy, bares its Kantian garb — has not really transcended the preconventional stage of instrumental rationality but at its deepest levels continues to exist in dialectical tension with it and, as will be argued presently, indeed may be founded upon it.[38] Perhaps surprisingly, perhaps not, some of Kohlberg's and his associates' own research findings tend to support this philosophical interpretation. One of the most unusual findings on moral development uncovered by the Kohlberg school has to do with the apparent minority of cases of moral development in which the subjects at the upper reaches of the moral development scale undergo a regression to Stage 2 moral reasoning.

A number of longitudinal studies have noted among some subjects — particularly during the period of late adolescence or the stage of youth — a tendency to engage in a kind of temporary moral regression to Stage 2 from Stages 4 or 5.[39] After this moratorium in moral growth, most return to the earlier stage or surpass it by moving to the next stage. This phenomenon has been labeled the "Raskolnikoff Syndrome" by Kohlberg to suggest that this "regression in the service of the ego" may occur among those moving toward postconventional morality as a means of liberating the individual of guilt and anxiety and of providing him/her with a mental space for thinking through and integrating the implications of the next higher stage into his/her personal orientation.[40] Kohlberg's own interpretation of the issue of "structural retrogression" (as he calls it) has recently undergone some modification. He now rejects his earlier stance and posits a Stage 4½ to categorize the supposed transition between Stages 4 and 5 of some of his subjects.[41] For the authors, the recategorization does little to alter their fundamental point about the latent sources of regression. That is, the interpretation offered above speaks to the more critical matter of the cultural seedbed of instances of moral retrogression in Western societies, however structurally "sophisticated" their argumentative form may be. In addition, other research conducted on radicals at Berkeley and Boston has found that their radical samples were most highly represented by postconventional Stage 6s and premoral Stage 2s.[42] The Stage 2 radicals — apparently — do not really have the capacity to reason in a principled manner, but can only mimic the statements and actions of their Stage 6 compatriots, reverting to highly instrumentalist and opportunistic modes of behavior "when push comes to shove." What complicates any hard-and-fast distinction between Stage 2 radicals (called "Temporary 2s" by Eliot Turiel) and their Stage 6 counterparts is that both can comprehend higher levels of moral judgment and both oftentimes respond to political controversy in highly moralistic styles of argument.[43]

Naturally, given their skepticism of the philosophical and cultural substructure supporting the interpretational framework of Kohlberg's research enterprise, the authors do not wish to grant too much authority either to the mode of analysis — including its categorical structure — underpinning these Kohlbergian studies nor to the interpretations of the data. Insofar as these findings seem perplexing and offer clues to something significant about moral judgment, they call for a hermeneutic excavation of their meaning carried out in the spirit of Maurice Merleau-Ponty's aphorism that every significant behavioral fact anticipates a phenomenological insight.[44] An alternative interpretation of the data has already been limned by the remarks concerning Horkheimer and Adorno's critique of Kantian ethics. For now, in an effort to reintegrate perspectives on the Lockean and Kantian dimensions to Kohlberg's work, attention is called to the broad theoretical project — drawing upon the important insights and observations by close students of American political culture from Alexis de Tocqueville to the Berkeley school of political theory — of developing through depth-historical analysis and contemporary examples the special manner in which technological rationality came to represent the characteristic method of American political thought and how the New Left in the 1960s became increasingly ensnared in this familiar American mode of orientation and action — particularly expressed in its culturally-specific dialectic of pragmatism (instrumentalism) and moralism so characteristic of a submerged Lockean liberal ideology.[45] What a critical hermeneutics of American political culture and society suggests for the analyst of moral judgment is, first, that given the sociocultural depth of technological rationality in the United States, an instrumentalist mode of reasoning and behavior is an all too obvious structure for Americans, no matter what their individual capacities for moral reasoning; and second, while none of Kohlberg's research supports it, the experience of fascism in Germany and Italy makes it an open question whether or not massive regression in what Kohlberg calls moral reasoning — but what could preferably be called psychopolitical development — could take place in the United States in the future.

This competing interpretation lends added depth to Kenneth Keniston's critical assessment of Kohlberg in the context of his subtle reflections on the relationship between moral development and sociopolitical activism.[46] In the course of his critique of the "perils of principle," Keniston takes note of the paradoxical nature of the appeal to abstract personal principles by individuals (especially political actors). Some of those identified with such moral reasoning clearly fall into the category of great political philosophers and cultural synthesizers such as Socrates, Gandhi, and Martin Luther King (Keniston's examples), while others who adopted a similar type of formal moral reasoning evidently fall into the category of moral zealot, bigot, or dogmatist like the "best and the brightest," like members of the Nazi Youth Movement or like the Weatherman faction of the New Left (the authors' examples).

This apparent paradox is resolved by Keniston by arguing with the psychoanalytic school (especially Anna Freud) against the illicit move of modern developmental psychologists like Kohlberg to decouple the moral dimensions from human development in its totality, calling it analytic and arbitrary. Like Sullivan, who criticized Kohlberg's structuralism for tending "to separate the 'emotional life' from the 'intellectual life' where morality is concerned."[47] Keniston says, "Whether the highest stages of moral reasoning lead to destructive zealotry or real ethicality depends upon the extent to which moral development is *matched by development in other sectors*."[48] And, among the most critical of these related sectors of development, he singles out those involving compassion, the capacity for love, interpersonal mutuality, and empathy as essential for humanizing the highest levels of moral reasoning. In a passage reminiscent of Michael Polanyi's and Albert Camus's parallel definitions of nihilism, Keniston concludes his argument by noting how "the history of revolutions that have failed through the very ardor of their search for moral purity suggests that the combination of abstract personal principles with a humorless and *loveless asceticism* is especially likely to be dangerous.[49]

Critical theory and phenomenology contribute to a deepening and refounding of Anna Freud's important insight and its critical appropriation by Keniston. The key figures in the Frankfurt school were keenly aware of the intimate relationship between psychosexual development and moral development. With their profound concern over the transformation their homeland underwent — from the birth of the Weimar Republic to the ascendency of Hitler — Horkheimer, Adorno, and Marcuse as well as Erich Fromm strove to understand the deep historical and psychic roots of Nazism. Whether Adorno's more carefully couched observations in *The

Authoritarian Personality, Horkheimer and Adorno's more sweeping and synoptic reflections in *Dialectic of Enlightenment,* Fromm's character analysis in *Escape From Freedom,* or Marcuse's more hopeful dialectical portrait in *Eros and Civilization,* a common interest in uncovering the latent psychosexual dynamics of moral and political development and regression was apparent.[50]

One of the cardinal achievements of the tradition of critical phenomenology from Marx to Merleau-Ponty and beyond has been to radicalize even further the understanding of human development in its fullness. With reference to several of Keniston's points, leading critical phenomenologists have sought to repair the splits and dualisms into which the analytic knife of modern psychology has carved the world (cognitive/affective, subject/object, higher needs/lower needs) by recovering the life-world foundations of human development residing in such universal structures as embodiment and sociality, which exist beneath and before the analytic alienation of these living processes. Keniston's concern with restoring the embodied and social nature of human development is substantially advanced by Merleau-Ponty's work, including his critique of the cognitive developmental approach of Piaget, one of Kohlberg's mentors. Summarizing a major thrust of Merleau-Ponty's criticism of Piaget, John O'Neill states that "the cognitive approaches to child development overlook the *tacit* subjectivity which does not constitute its world *a priori* nor entirely *a posteriori* but develops through a 'living cohesion' in which the embodied self experiences itself while belonging to this world, and others, clinging to them for its content."[51] This approach does full justice to its adjective critical by indicating how these universal structures of embodiment and sociality have been occluded (even as they continue to function at deeper levels) by the sedimentation of Lockean liberal assumptions in common sense and in social science and philosophy, stressing the mind/body dualism and a particularly virulent form of possessive individualism. Developmental psychology is only beginning to make the first halting steps to transcend the hegemony of these beliefs and orientations, and Kohlberg's work illustrates how a body of theory and research critical of mainstream psychology remains so caught in its deeper current that it still largely recapitulates its major philosophical assumptions and ideological outlook.

What Merleau-Ponty said of Piaget remains applicable — even more so — to Kohlberg. Despite his clever attempts to circumvent the atomistic bases of his ethical liberalism, Kohlberg's hierarchical schema — including Stage 6 — rests squarely in the tradition of autonomous rationality. As David Rasmussen has stressed, the revolutionary, though ambiguous and incomplete, achievement of Kant lay in his grappling with and offering an epistemological resolution to the problematic of subjectivity or human identity — specifically with his concept of the mind as the active agency in constructing the world. In Rasmussen's words,

> Whereas the notion of subjectivity was unavailable to traditional societies, the Kantian man is one who freely constructs his own reality in such a way that he can be said to be the maker of his own destiny. The focus, of course, is internal, upon the achievements of the inner self, or, in terms of Kantian ethics, the focus is upon duty. The Kantian man is on a voyage of internal liberation of the self — his problem is to become what he will begin to recognize as his essential self.[52]

One fundamental difficulty in this way of addressing or rendering the problematics of subjectivity, according to Rasmussen, is that this model of autonomous rationality or autonomous man obscures the social and institutional context of human subjectivity by situating the problem of identity in a purely internal context.

In contrast, he goes on to argue, an alternative model of sociality — derived from the dialectical tradition of Hegel and Marx — radically redefines the problem of individuality and self-identity in terms of a practical struggle to overcome the predefined identity imposed upon individuals by the sociocultural totality, by reconstituting the social conditions and cultural context in which they exist in order to realize their true social nature. Thus, the human self, individuality, autonomy, identity, must be conceived in thoroughly social and institutional terms, even though particular institutional arrangement and supporting ideologies may suppress or conceal that inherent sociality. Implicit in this discussion of alternative models of rationality, then, is that the problem of moral development must be refounded upon a model of dialectical sociality and that it must be reconceptualized as an eminently political problem.

The implications of a model of dialectical sociality for moral development have been nicely summarized recently by Ben Agger when he argued that "a dialectical ethics does not concern only 'idealistic' attitudes but is fundamentally materialistic in its implications. Human beings are subject-objects who live in and through a sensuous world. Bourgeois concepts of ethics," he went on to say, "have ignored the sensuous world and man-nature relations, being concerned primarily with rights in the abstract legal sense. An emancipatory ethics goes beyond this conception and develops non-exploitative strategies for coexisting with others and with nature. Thus, an emancipatory ethics takes responsibility for political, economic, and ecological as well as strictly 'moral' dimensions of human existence, refusing to separate a person's social 'fate' and his abstract legal rights and duties."[53]

Working at the limits of liberalism, Kohlberg is evidently uncomfortable with the ideal of the autonomous self and with the modernized imagery of possessive individualism that has refurbished the Lockean liberal paradigm. And so, in defining his Stage 6 (the universal ethical principle orientation), he characterizes those "self-chosen ethical principles" as abstract "universal principles of justice, of the reciprocity and equality of human rights, and of respect for the dignity of human beings as individual persons."[54] In addition, his latent dissatisfaction with this ideal is manifested in his recent involvement with experiments in forging "just communities" as a means of fostering moral development. When he moves to ground these abstract principles theoretically, however, he turns to Rawls's theory of justice — perhaps the most extensive and ambitious contemporary effort to resuscitate and rejuvenate liberal social contract theory.[55] Much could be discussed here in regard to these theoretical underpinnings, but in the present context what deserves note is how the image of human nature guiding the foundations of Rawls's political theorizing is a conception of man as basically a self-interested creature possessing a limited sense of benevolence. In other words, in Kohlberg, no less than in Rawls, the autonomous model is not really transcended.[56]

The autonomous foundations of his ideal of moral development and the political naivete of his general approach lead Kohlberg to frame the pedagogical consequences of his research in essentially cognitivist and reform liberal terms. His cognitive developmental approach to moral education as it has unfolded over the past five years or so has stressed the need to integrate discussions of moral or civic dilemmas into courses on social studies, sex education, and other classes in order to enhance the cognitive capacities of students in the realm of ethical reasoning. Again, the emphasis in such practices, it is argued, is on form rather than content and the pedagogical rationale for this strategy is to avoid moral indoctrination.[57]

From a critical phenomenological perspective, this pedagogical approach does not begin to engage the political educative tasks dictated by the depth-hermeneutic analysis of American political culture by the Berkeley school and others — especially the impact of American constitutionalism upon American political consciousness. The writings of native political theorists like Norman Jacobson, Darryl Baskin, and Robert Pranger disclose what Kohlberg's research in its own indirect way says about the retarded level of psychopolitical development in the United States, a condition promoted by the permeation and institutionalization of Lockean liberal ideology (and other convergent strains in early modern culture) into American culture and society.[58] Seen in this way, the problem of moral education versus moral indoctrination in the implementation of Kohlberg's cognitive developmental approach is a sham issue, since these lessons in moral education covertly rest upon a liberal ideological foundation and therefore may be interpreted more often than not as instances of political indoctrination.[59] Given the depth and the extent of the problems of political myth and false consciousness stemming from Lockean liberal hegemony in the United States, what is clearly called for is a genuine strategy of political education interpreted as a form of critical hermeneutics of the body politic — a critical hermeneutics involving both a demystifying and a restorative element.[60]

This section has endeavored to perform some of these essential tasks of political education in relation to Kohlberg's theory of moral development. With its negative critique, however, this critical analysis has risked becoming merely a demystifying hermeneutics. In part, this emphasis was grounded in the concern that the social engineering of moral development may become a central tendency of public policy in the realm of American secondary and perhaps even college education.[61] The sense of moral decay is keenly felt by liberal academics and public policy makers and politicians these days and, according to a recent Gallup poll, fully three-quarters of the American populace believe that morals and moral behavior should be taught as part of the course curricula of public schools.[62] Unfortunately, the common social framework of education as presently constituted is far less likely to foster the praxis of critical reflection than it is to immerse its participants in a mimetic atemporal sea.

CRITICAL PHENOMENOLOGY AND MORAL DEVELOPMENT

It may be well in the remaining space available to try to recapitulate and amplify the positive moment of critique limned in the preceding critical examination of Kohlberg.[63] Certainly, one of the foremost themes of this critique has been the necessity of going beyond the tyranny of the categorical in any theory of psychopolitical development toward an embracement of the life-world foundations of intersubjective existence. It is here that both the limits of reification and the sources of "pre-political suffrage" are to be found. The life-world, as Paul Piccone has defined it following Husserl and Paci, is "our relation to reality as such free from any conceptual mediation our array of concepts which we use to conceptually articulate reality, and the conceptualized meanings resulting from apprehending reality through concepts. . . . [It] is also the domain in which concepts are invented and historical projects are formulated." In short, it is intermonadic and intersubjective existence, the foundation of "all the sciences and of every human praxis, insofar as the sciences and the praxes are intentional, have a function, and aim toward a *telos*."⁶⁴ As such, the *lebenswelt* is the foundation upon which the precategorical sources of psychopolitical development are grounded, the categorical expressions of psychopolitical development are articulated, and the historical projects for its quest are constructed.

So unyielding a critic of phenomenology as Jurgen Habermas gives grudging acknowledgment of this point when he admits that

> norm and value-forming communications do not always take the precise form of discourse; they are not in all cases institutionalized, but rather they are often diffuse and appear under a variety of definitions. Emanating from "the base," they penetrate into the pores of spheres of life which are formally organized. In this sense, they are a sub-political decision-making; nonetheless, they affect the political system, albeit indirectly through their impact on the normative frame of political decisions. The current debate concerning the "quality of life" is an indication of transformations of public issues affected, as it were subcutaneously.⁶⁵

Within the context of a critical phenomenology of psychopolitical development, what is called for is a thematization of this subpolitical process and more specifically the refounding of the bases of moral development (or better, psychopolitical development) upon the primordial structure of the life-world — including embodiment, historicity, and sociality. Such a thematization would exhibit the deeply social, institutionalized, and historically contingent nature of psychopolitical development. That is, it would clarify why psychopolitical development cannot be a solitary possession of a Promethean hero, or an Epicurean gardener, why it cannot emerge except by way of sedimentation and institutionalization, and why its materialization as social freedom in meaningful political participation therefore rests upon historically contingent conditions stemming in part from the renewal of political language and its role in activating a democratic movement. Seen thus, psychopolitical development as a critical concept will be understood at once as a task encompassing cultural hermeneutics, political praxis, and a socialized economy.

It deserves emphasis that psychopolitical development must be conceived in relation to "the intentionality not only utopistically projected into the future, but already functioning and intentional in the present as the level of operations of subjects reconstitutable beneath the system's ideological crust." In this respect, the radical potentialities of remembrance have a fundamental and decisive role in revitalizing critique and fostering human liberation.⁶⁶ In restoring lost or suppressed experiential dimensions to a historically evolved present, remembrance not only reawakens the "consciousness of defeat" to oppressed groups. It also reconstitutes the mediating structures that previously dichotomized their "personal troubles" and the realm of public power in such a way as to reveal the imminent possibilities of a new public life. Insofar as psychopolitical development is bound up with the generation of critical political consciousness, counter-hegemonic forms of recollection (including revolutionary nostalgia) function to dereify the ongoing reified relations and institutions and to dispel the false consciousness of subordinate classes hitherto organically integrated into the "historical bloc" organized around the ideological hegemony of the ruling class. In a society like the United States, with a tradition of antitraditionalism and an economy geared to planned obsolescence and incessant production of new artificial wants, remembrance can be revolutionary.

This recollective dimension to a critical phenomenology of psychopolitical development will find support from careful and sensitive students of early childhood development. In his concern to uncover the childhood roots to radical commitment, Keniston, in his book *Young Radicals,* has speculated on how certain distinctive sensitivities and strengths apparent in the childhood of these students were later recalled and reintegrated (subcutaneously, as it were) at higher levels and in more sophisticated forms into late adolescence and youth by these budding radicals.[67] A critical phenomenological reading of the relevant literature on early childhood development would show how Merleau-Ponty's explorations of the child's relations with others (particularly his constructs of "syncretic sociability"), Edith Cobb's investigations of the ecology of childhood imagination (particularly her discovery of a preverbal experience of an "aesthetic logic" both in nature's formative processes and in the gestalt-making powers of the child's own developing nervous system), and Ernest Schachtel's inquiry into memory and childhood amnesia (especially his critical analysis of the social and cultural causes of the schematization and conventionalization in adulthood of memory, perception, and experience), as well as Aronowitz's reflections on the two worlds of child's play (and in particular his notion of the "play element of everyday life," which may be reconceptualized as the phenomenological ground opening toward a truly democratic society beneath and beyond the instrumental framework of rationalized and alienated labor)[68] — how all of these studies of childhood deepen the suggestive, but phenomenologically ungrounded, speculations of Keniston.

In closing, one last theme of the critique of Kohlberg needs to be reiterated — that is, the need to take up and radically resituate the awesome political educative tasks for cultivating psychopolitical development; and in so doing, one should recall the introductory focus on the problematic of political authoritarianism and instrumental rationality in critical theory. The struggle for psychopolitical development in the United States, as has been shown, involves projects that are eminently political and pedagogical in character — political educative undertakings, which, beginning within the context of the ideological hegemony of American liberal-capitalistic society and its emergent technocorporate tendencies, aim beyond the framework of the dialectic of enlightenment and domination. As Berkeley school political theorists Hartz and others have shown and Gramsci's work has deepened, psychopolitical development through critical political education[69] involves the forging of a distinct counter-hegemonic strategy working at all levels and upon all aspects of society as a social totality. The authors' concern to illuminate the politics of moral development is congruent with Gramsci's reminder that "the thesis which asserts that men become conscious of fundamental conflicts on the level of ideology is not psychological or moralistic in character, but structural and epistemological." Otherwise we are likely to fall into the habit of "considering politics, and hence history, as a continuous *marche de dupes,* a competition in conjuring and sleight of hand," an orientation that reduces " 'critical' activity . . . to the exposure of swindles, to creating scandals, and to prying into the pockets of public figures."[70] Finally, there needs to be a reiteration of the Frankfurt school's concern to develop a radical strategy that breaks with the elitist, manipulative, and ultimately mythical dictates of the instrumental reason of the Western enlightenment philosophy.

Paul Ricoeur presents a reminder of what critical phenomenologists like Merleau-Ponty and Paci and the critical theorists of the Frankfurt school never forgot — namely, that one of the foremost tasks and responsibilities of the political educator is twofold: to "make apparent the ethical significance of every choice appearing to be purely economic" and to "struggle for the erection of a democratic economy."[71]

NOTES

1. See Herbert Reid and Ernest Yanarella, "Toward a Post-Modern Theory of American Political Science and Culture: Perspectives from Critical Marxism and Phenomenology," *Cultural Hermeneutics* 2 (August 1974): 91–166. For those readers lacking an elementary knowledge of phenomenology and critical theory, the above essay serves as a useful bibliographical guide to the relevant literature whose familiarity is presumed in the present study.

2. Georg Lukacs, *History and Class Consciousness: Studies in Marxist Dialectics* (Boston: MIT Press, 1968), p. 38.

3. Martin Jay, *The Dialectical Imagination* (Boston: Little, Brown, 1973).

4. Cited in Frederic and Lou Jean Fleron, "Administrative Theory as Repressive Political Theory: The Communist Experience," *Telos* 12 (Summer 1972): 80–81.

5. Max Horkheimer, "The Authoritarian State," reprinted in *Telos* 15 (Spring 1975): 3–20.

6. Frederick Pollock, "State Capitalism: Its Possibilities and Limitations," *Studies in Philosophy and Social Science* 9 (1941): 200–25; and Max Horkheimer, ibid.

7. Max Horkheimer and Theodor Adorno, *Dialectic of Enlightenment* (New York: Herder and Herder, 1972).

8. See, among others, the following native analyses: Stuart Ewen, "Advertising as Social Production: Selling the System," in *Up the Mainstream*, ed., Herbert G. Reid (New York: David McKay, 1974), pp. 130–52; C. Wright Mills, *The Power Elite* (New York: Oxford University Press, 1956); and Daniel Fusfield, "The Rise of the Corporate State," *Journal of Social Issues* 6 (March 1972).

9. This critique of Kohlberg is drawn from Herbert Reid and Ernest Yanarella, "Critical Political Theory and Moral Development: On Kohlberg, Hampden-Turner, and Habermas," *Theory and Society* 4 (Winter 1977–78): 505–41.

10. The corpus of Kohlberg's writing is sizable, and the reader is directed to a collection of his essays available through the Harvard Center for Moral Education: Lawrence Kohlberg, *Collected Papers on Moral Development and Moral Education* (Cambridge, Mass.: Center for Moral Education, 1973). Jean Piaget's most influential work for Kohlberg is his *The Moral Judgment of the Child* (London: Rutledge and Kegan Paul, 1968). For Kohlberg's most extensive statement of his theory, see "Stage and Sequence: The Cognitive-Developmental Approach to Socialization," in *Handbook of Socialization Theory and Research*, ed., David A. Goslin (Chicago: Rand McNally, 1969), pp. 347–480.

11. Lawrence Kohlberg in — among other places — his contribution, "Moral Development," in *International Encyclopedia of the Social Sciences* (New York: Crowell, Collier and Macmillan, 1968).

12. Lawrence Kohlberg, "From Is to Ought: How to Commit the Naturalistic Fallacy and Get Away With It in the Study of Moral Development," in *Cognitive Development and Epistemology*, ed. Theodore Mischel (New York: Academic Press, 1971), p. 175.

13. These four points are presented in ibid., though the last quotation is from Lawrence Kohlberg and Carol Gilligan, "The Adolescent as Philosopher: The Discovery of the Self in a Postconventional World," *Daedalus* 100 (Fall 1971): 1058.

14. Susan Buck-Morss, "Socio-Economic Bias in Piaget's Theory and its Implications for Cross-Cultural Studies," *Human Development* 18 (1975): 35–48.

15. Elizabeth Simpson, "Moral Development Research: A Case of Scientific Cultural Bias," *Human Development* 17 (1974): 81–106.

16. Edmund V. Sullivan, "A Study of Kohlberg's Structural Theory of Moral Development: A Critique of Liberal Social Science Ideology," *Human Development* 20 (1977): 352–76.

17. For a critical reconstruction of this argument in a depth-hermeneutic way, see Reid's analysis in Reid and Yanarella, "Toward a Post-Modern Theory."

18. Cited by Gary Wills, *Nixon Agonistes* (New York: New American Library, 1970), pp. 314–315.

19. C. Wright Mills, "Liberal Values in the Modern World," in *Power, Politics, and People: The Collected Essays of C. Wright Mills*, ed. Irving L. Horowitz (New York: Ballantine Books, 1963), pp. 187–195.

20. This brief period represents the zenith of the New Left as a critical movement, and is surveyed in some detail by Kirkpatrick Sale, *SDS* (New York: Vintage Books, 1973), pp. 42–203.

21. Walter Dean Burnham, "Crisis of American Political Legitimacy," *Society* 10 (November-December 1972): 24–31, esp. 30.

22. George C. Lodge, *The New American Ideology* (New York: Knopf, 1975).

23. Charles Taylor, "Interpretation and the Sciences of Man," *Review of Metaphysics* 25 (September 1971): 39.

24. Ibid., pp. 39–40.

25. Simpson, "Moral Development Research," p. 100.

26. For example, D.C. Phillips and Mavis Kelly, "Hierarchical Theories of Development in Education and Psychology," *Harvard Education Review* 45 (August 1975): 366–67.

27. Simpson, "Moral Development Research," p. 91.

28. See Kohlberg's discussion of Piaget in "Moral Development," and in "Stage and Sequence."

29. D.W. Hamlyn, "Epistemology and Conceptual Development," in *Epistemology and Cognitive Development, op. cit.*, p. 15.

30. See Lukacs' critique of Kant in the section, "The Antinomies of Bourgeois Thought," in *History and Class-Consciousness.*

31. Buck-Morss, Socio-Economic Bias," p. 39.

32. Ibid., p. 44.

33. See ibid.; and Simpson, "Moral Development Research." Were Kohlberg willing to suspend his Kantian framework, he might be able to appreciate the significance of the research of cultural anthropologists and sociolinguists on so-called "primitive" tribes and cultures.

34. Michael Maccoby and Nancy Modiano, "On Culture and Equivalence: 1," in *Studies in Cognitive Growth*, ed. Jerome Bruner et al. (New York: Wiley, 1966), p. 269. A more elaborate statement of this point would seek to reformulate and appropriate this observation in a critical phenomenological way.

35. Horkheimer and Adorno, *Dialectic of Enlightenment.*

36. Martin Jay, *Dialectical Imagination*, p. 265.

37. Horkheimer and Adorno, *Dialectic of Enlightenment.*

38. Ibid. Adorno offers a somewhat toned-down critique of Kant in *Negative Dialectics* (New York: Seabury Press, 1973).

39. Cited by Kenneth Keniston, "Idealists: The Perils of Principle," *Youth and Dissent: The Rise of the New Opposition* (New York: Harcourt Brace Jovanovich, 1971), pp. 256–61; and Charles Hampden-Turner and Philip Whitten, "Morals Left and Right," *Psychology Today* (April 1971): 40, 74 and 75.

40. Hampden-Turner and Whitten, "Morals."

41. The reader may wish to examine the multiple reasons for this change in Kohlberg's essay, "Continuities in Childhood and Adult Moral Development Revisited," in *Moralization: The Cognitive Developmental Approach*, ed. L. Kohlberg and E. Turiel (New York: Holt, Rinehart and Winston.).

42. See, for example, Norma Haan et al., "Moral Reasoning of Young Adults," *Journal of Personality and Social Psychology* 10 (1968): 183–201.

43. Hampden-Turner and Whitten, "Morals."

44. Maurice Merleau-Ponty, "Phenomonology and the Sciences of Man," *The Primacy of Perception and Other Essays* (Evanston, Ill.: Northwestern University Press, 1964).

45. See Herbert Reid, "Critical Phenomenology and the Dialectical Foundations of Social Change," *Dialectical Anthropology* 2 (May 1977): 107–30.

46. Keniston, "Idealists: The Perils of Principle." In critically appropriating Keniston's criticism for present purposes, the authors note that they depart from his reform liberal orientation in their intention to refound their critique of Kohlberg upon a genuinely postliberal and postmodern grounding.

47. Sullivan, "Kohlberg's Structural Theory."

48. Keniston, "Idealists," p. 267.

49. Ibid., p. 268.

50. Theodor W. Adorno, et al., *The Authoritarian Personality* (New York: Harper & Row, 1950); Horkheimer and Adorno, *Dialectic of Enlightenment*; Erich Fromm, *Escape From*

Freedom (New York: Rinehart, 1941); and Herbert Marcuse, *Eros and Civilization* (New York: Vintage Books, 1962).

51. John O'Neill, "Embodiment and Child Development: A Phenomenological Approach, in *Childhood and Socialization: Recent Sociology*, No. 5, ed. Hans Peter Dreitzel, (New York: Macmillan, 1973), p. 70. The comment presented by O'Neill is actually a critical reconstruction of Merleau-Ponty's critique of Piaget in the *Bulletin de Psychologie*, 236 (November 1964): esp. 130–134, 187–194, 204–210, and his development of the theme of embodiment in *Phenomenology of Perception* (New York: Humanities Press, 1962). Also relevant here is Richard Zaner's essay, "Piaget and Merleau-Ponty: A Study in Convergence," *Review of Existential Psychology* 6 (Winter 1966): 7–23, though a careful reading of Merleau-Ponty's critique discloses that Zaner overdraws the degree of convergence on key issues.

52. David Rasmussen, "Between Autonomy and Sociality," *Cultural Hermeneutics* (1973): 9.

53. Ben Agger, "Dialectical Sensibility II: Towards a New Intellectuality," *Canadian Journal of Social and Political Theory* 1 (Spring-Summer 1977): 52.

54. Lawrence Kohlberg, "The Moral Atmosphere of the School," in *The Unstudied Curriculum*, ed., N. Overley (Washington, D.C.: Association for Supervision and Curriculum Development, 1970), p. 125.

55. See, for example, Kohlberg's comment on Rawls in "Moral Development and the New Social Studies," *Social Education* 37 (May 1973).

56. For convergent lines of analysis and criticism of the Kohlberg/Rawls symbiosis, see Sullivan, "Kohlberg's Structural Theory."

57. Kohlberg's work on moral education includes the following essays: "Moral and Religious Education and the Public Schools: A Developmental View," in *Religion and Public Education*, ed. T. Sizer (Boston: Houghton-Mifflin, 1967); "Moral Development and the New Social Studies"; "A Cognitive-Developmental Approach to Moral Education," *Humanist* (November-December 1972): 13–16; and with Rochelle Mayer, "Development as an Aim of Education," *Harvard Education Review* 42 (November 1972): 449–96; and with E. Turiel, "Moral Development and Moral Education," Gordon S. Lesser, ed., *Psychology and Educational Practice* (Chicago: Scott, Foresman, 1971), pp. 410–65.

58. Norman Jacobson, "Political Science and Political Education," *American Political Science Review* 57 (September 1963): 561–69; Darryl Baskin, *American Pluralist Democracy: A Critique* (New York: Van Nostrand Reinhold, 1971); and Robert Pranger, *The Eclipse of Citizenship* (New York: Holt, Rinehart and Winston, 1968).

59. One scholar who has worried over this issue is Michael Schleifer in his essay, "Moral Education and Indoctrination," *Ethics* 86 (January 1976): 154–63.

60. This critical hermeneutics of the body politic — drawing upon the postmodern directions of Ricoeur, O'Neill, Merleau-Ponty, Rovatti, and Paci — has only begun as a collective enterprise. For some dialectical perspectives, see Reid, "Critical Phenomenology and the Dialectical Foundations of Social Changes. Also see Paul Ricoeur's important comments on hermeneutics in dialectical perspective in his *Freud and Philosophy: An Essay on Interpretation* (New Haven: Yale University Press, 1970); and John O'Neill's remarks on the body politic — *Sociology as Skin Trade* (New York: Harper & Row, 1972).

61. See, for example, the recent review of college ethics courses in the United States by Edward B. Fiske, "Growth of Ethics Courses Shows Major Changes on U.S. Campuses," New York *Times*, February 20, 1978, pp. 1 and B8.

62. George Gallup, "Many Favor Teaching Morals in Public School," Louisville *Courier-Journal and Times*, April 18, 1976, p. A7. The poll also revealed that two-thirds of the nationwide sample believed that today people generally do not lead as "good lives — honest and moral — as they used to." To get some idea how educators and policy-makers are taking

advantage of this turn in public opinion, see the special issue, "The Cognitive-Developmental Approach to Moral Education," *Social Education* 40 (April 1976).

63. The following discussion is based largely upon Herbert Reid's "Critical Phenomenology and the Dialectical Foundations of Social Change."

64. Paul Piccone, "Phenomenological Marxism," *Telos* 9 (Fall 1971), p. 24.

65. Jurgen Habermas, "On Social Identity," *Telos* 19 (Spring 1974); p. 99. See also Reid's critique of Habermas in "Critical Political Theory and Moral Development."

66. See Reid's "Critical Phenomenology," already cited and his "American Social Science in the Politics of Time . . ." *Politics and Society* 3 (Winter 1973): 201–43. The latter was followed in the same journal by Frances Hearn's "Remembrance and Critique: The Uses of the Past for Discrediting the Present and Anticipating the Future," *Politics and Society* 5 (1975): The concept of remembrance in Herbert Marcuse's work is discussed in Reid's "Critical Phenomenology."

67. Kenneth Keniston, *Young Radicals: Notes on Committed Youth* (New York: Harcourt, Brace & World, 1968).

68. See Reid's "Critical Phenomenology."

69. Some aspects of this concept of critical political education are examined in Herbert Reid and Randal Ihara, "Ideology Critique and Problems of Student Consciousness in the U.S.," *Cultural Hermeneutics* 3 (1976): 217–44.

70. Antonio Gramsci, *Prison Notebooks* (New York: International Publishers, 1971), p. 164.

71. Paul Ricoeur's "The Tasks of the Political Educator," *Philosophy Today* 17 (Summer 1973), pp. 148–49. Cf. James Palermo's "Pedagogy as a Critical Hermeneutic," *Cultural Hermeneutics* 3 (1975): 137–46.

INSTITUTIONS, MORAL BEHAVIOR, AND THE POLITY

EDITORS' COMMENTS

Moral behavior and politics are specifically joined in Part III of this volume. The papers here address the issue of how influences within institutional settings modify behavior. Can behavior ever be genuinely virtuous if pressures within institutions constrain people to put moral considerations aside? An increasingly important problem in modern social science, this conflict between the demands of morality and institutional pressures has engaged human consciousness continuously from the time of Plato and Confucius and even before. This indeed is one of those perennial problems one can never hope fully to resolve but on which guidance and clarification will always be needed.

In the first study Larry D. Spence discusses some of the ways institutional settings impede the manifestation of mature moral behavior. Basing his conclusions on findings from contemporary social psychology, he notes how individuals in experimental situations modify their behavior depending on the presence of authority figures as well as on situational constraints on their ability to make unimpeded choices. Drawing inferences from these experiments, Spence believes that modern bureaucracies foster environments that are inimical to the expression of mature moral behavior.

Daniel Candee moves from the more theoretical formulations of Spence to a discussion of the actual moral behavior of some of the actors in the Watergate crisis and to an analysis of the effect of that crisis upon the moral development of the American people generally. Candee examines statements made by Watergate participants and convincingly demonstrates how these individuals felt their behavior was modified by the conditions under which they acted.

As many of the issues associated with Watergate dealt with infringement on privacy, the next chapter by Julie Zatz is an especially apt follow-up to Candee's paper. Zatz speaks most particularly about how privacy based on the prior principle of respect for persons can foster moral development. Her arguments suggest that incorporation of this principle into political institutions and practices could act as a powerful influence upon the moral behavior of political leaders and of citizens. In many ways some of the specific points made in this chapter follow from the more general contentions presented earlier by Elizabeth Lane Beardsley.

Raising questions from the perspective of moral development theory, Gordon J. Schochet next addresses the consequences for democratic society of changes in the structure of authority in the household. The relationship between familial and political authority, the nature of the family as a political symbol, and the nuclear family as a locus of moral development are the focal points of his analysis.

8

MORAL JUDGMENT AND BUREAUCRACY

Larry D. Spence

Ethical actions are exceptional in these seedy times of the republic. It is not necessary to cite the headlines or recount the cases of mendacity, vindictiveness, and selfish manipulation that punctuate the world of politics and pollute the relationships of everyday life. People can reassure themselves that this has always been so since Adam, or reaffirm a Madisonian faith that some combination of private vices can result in public good. Even so, they share an uneasy feeling that everyone is on the take and that virtue has become quixotic. As Richard Reeves recently commented, "When my father told me to be an individual, to act like a man, he didn't mean going along, covering my ass. There are so few men, so many asses. Why?"[1]   Why, indeed? There have been many answers proposed, ranging from permissive child raising through the corruptions of affluence to lenient judges. Many are eager to point a finger, few are willing to accept responsibility. Social scientists have offered little in the way of explanation or prescription for the situation.

This chapter will present the initial stages of a theory to account for this moral morass. The explanation suggests some basic changes in the society which will make it possible to improve the level of moral behavior. However, the study is not meant as a prescription, for that would be premature. It is a critique of some current views of moral judgment and ethical action in the social sciences. The immediate aim is to promote further criticism

Besides the two editors of this volume, several scholars commented on the initial version. Their careful criticisms and questions helped the author to avoid blunders and to clarify the points he wanted to make. Thanks are due to Fred Gordon, John Pickering, Francis Sim, and Marylee Taylor.

and discussion. Therefore, an attempt will be made to make the least qualified case for the propositions of the argument to facilitate further work by others. Stated baldly, the assumptions of the argument are as follows:

Moral judgments are the necessary but not sufficient basis for ethical actions.

Moral judgments require the reasoned assessment of the consequences of human actions for human beings.

Reasoned assessments require, in the individual, emotional responsiveness, recognition of responsibility, cognitive competence, conceptual adequacy, and accurate information.

Given these assumptions, then it follows that to the extent that social institutions inhibit sensitivity, responsibility, cognitive competence, conceptual sophistication and reliability of observation and communication, they hamper the development of moral judgment and ethical actions in their members.

This chapter is concerned not so much with the justification of these propositions which have, after all, been made by others. In the first section they will be explicated in terms of a cognitive-affective view of moral judgment, which has its philosophical roots in David Hume's critique of dogmatic morality and its most mature statements in John Dewey's theory of valuation. In the next section it will be argued that the modern distinction between moral behavior as obedience and moral judgment as formal reasoning has obscured the relations between institutional structure and moral development. A survey and critique of the apparently conflicting findings on moral behavior and moral judgment of experimental psychologists such as Stanley Milgram and the developmental psychologist, Lawrence Kohlberg, are presented in the third section. While both these approaches succeed in describing some aspects of moral behavior and moral judgment in the present, they are forms of apologetics insofar as they try to derive "oughts" from the facts of their investigations. The last section of the chapter will try to show that the reasons why there are so few virtuous men and women today and so many asses are to be found in the faulty designs of our public and private institutions. While this result may be unintended, the aim is to show that it follows from a set of cultural expectations that understand the goals of institutions as both the control of human behavior and the maintenance of justice. To the extent, therefore, that the bureaucratic model of administration is applied to the affairs of human beings — whether in politics, education, or work — virtue (defined as the conduct of life according to moral principles) will be the loser. As Max Weber prophesied, bureaucratic rationalization and moral degeneration are two sides of the same process. The attempt to ensure obedience while maintaining formal principles of justice results finally in behavioral cupidity joined with abstract idealism.

THE COGNITIVE-AFFECTIVE VIEW OF MORAL JUDGMENT

Confusion and conflict mark discussions of morals, ethics, and valuation in modern times. Positions range from doctrines of ejaculatory valuation through cultural conformity and a priori formalism to simple dogmatism. That is, one is to do things because they feel good, because they maintain institutions, because they fit logical formulas, or because some extrahuman source has proclaimed them to be good. In each case, ethical acts are those of obedience to appetite, to authority, to principles, or to divinity. Evil, in turn, is what feels bad, what is unruly, what is illogical, or what goes against the will of some supernatural being. Moral judgment is just a matter of knowing what to obey and what to avoid. It is thus autocratic and absolutist in structure because good and evil appear to be arbitrary in terms of human experience or unchallengeable by human observation and reason. Even though relativism presently seems to be the basic characteristic of moral judgment, this absolutism is more fundamental. The search is for foundations, principles, and rules for judgment and conduct that are immune to experience and the criticism of consequences. The modern era in moral reasoning begins with Kant's declaration that "experience cannot teach us what is right."[2]

This confusion is taken to be symptomatic of moral degeneration; these predominant views of morality seem to be, at best, reflections of and, at worst, contributions to this degeneration. Therefore, to promote critical analysis, starting from a different and rival perspective may help in understanding how and where mistakes have been made.

The perspective will not be neutral. The author believes the current lack of virtue is a considerable threat to the existence of the United States and the human species, two things highly valued for reasons that would require another essay to detail. Also, social scientists have been so intent upon being ethically neutral that they have come to espouse an amorality that contributes to this situation. Value neutrality is a hypothetical position, like skepticism. It is intriguing as an extreme case for philosophical analysis; as a perspective on life or a prerequisite of scientific research, value neutrality, like skepticism, is humbug. To refuse to make value judgments is like refusing to make judgments of fact; the cost is the nullification of existence. Indeed, the refusal or inability to make such judgments constitutes evidence of insanity. For the sake of brevity this discussion will be directed only to those who eschew insanity.

Hume declared that "morality . . . consists not in any *matter of fact* which can be discovered by the understanding."[3] And he convincingly demonstrated that "ought" statements cannot be logically deduced from "is" statements. But he did not prove (though his statements sometimes suggest so) that moral judgments are merely expressions of self-interested approval or emotional satisfaction. Rather, he tried to show that moral judgments influence the conduct of human beings, that they always involve some reference to ends, and that they are stable, impartial, and universal. Thus moral judgments cannot be independent of affect, as they are motivated by human desires, needs, and wants. They are both cognitive and affective, involving emotions and sentiments as well as intellects. As Hume put it, "Morality is a subject that interests us above all others. . . ."[4] This interest that moral judgments hold for all is the source of their ability to exert a powerful influence on human conduct.

Hume's critique of dogmatic morality can be understood not as an attempt to distinguish moral judgments as subjective and irrational but to apply to them the same canons of critical empiricism that have been productive of useful knowledge in the physical sciences. These canons state that (1) judgments of facts cannot be certain, (2) evidence for judgments of facts must be grounded in experience, and (3) all statements that are certainly true (such as $2 + 2 = 4$) are formal and not factual.[5] When applied to morality, these canons translate to (1) moral judgments are never certain, (2) evidence for the correctness of a moral judgment must be grounded in experience, and (3) all statements of moral judgments that are certainly true are merely formal and not guides to action. This, then, is the approach to moral judgment taken here.

The assumptions are derived from a cognitive-affective view of moral judgment most closely associated with John Dewey and elaborated by others such as Jean Piaget and more recently, Eugene Meehan. The version here is offered with apologies. While the author does not agree with all the detailed propositions of these authors and does not believe the perspective to be fully developed, the basic outlines are supported. The perspective will be presented in Dewey's terms, since his influence is primary.

Moral judgments are of two types, intuitional and reflective. Ordinarily people know the right or fitting things to do in the familiar situations of their lives. They know what is right spontaneously and compellingly in the sense that they are uncomfortable if they do not act accordingly. Dewey maintained that intuitional moral judgments are based on previous experience and education. Thus, the cognitive origins of such judgments have been lost in the past. Reflective moral judgments are required when something goes wrong, and one discovers that the principles and rules of the past do not work. One becomes emotionally troubled and reacts negatively to some features of the situation.

An example will illustrate this author's interpretation of Dewey's theory of valuation. A growing child understands that it is the right thing to do to honor parents. Sometimes parents are not honored, but that makes the child uneasy if no punishment results. As the child matures, situations arise in which "honoring" must be reinterpreted to exclude or include obedience, loyalty, love, respect, and so on. The child may be dismayed at the thought of disobeying parents, at the same time that he knows he will be damaged in his own growth if he obeys. The anguish of such a situation is great, and this emotional impetus to reflective moral judgment is important, according to Dewey. The troubled child must create some new principle to guide conduct, based on a judgment of what is best under the new conditions. The child seeks to alter the disturbing features of the situation and undertakes actions that are means to that end.

Those actions are now judged according to their consequences in two ways: first, their immediate impacts, and second, their achievements of the projected ends-in-view. If their impacts are too negative or if they have unintended negative consequences, means and perhaps ends as well must be revised. If those actions do not promote the ends-in-view, new means must be tried. These judgments are, of necessity, subjective in the sense of Protagoras's dictum that "man is the measure of all things." But claims of desirability or undesirability must be capable of formulation in terms of projected standards of the quality of life. That is, the standards of judgment employed by the individual must be formulated in corrigible terms. Of course, in the case of a child or in many individual cases, judgment is private and less well articulated than if public defense and explanation were required. But even in such cases the judgment must be subject to the criticism of experience.

Ultimately, the correctness of the new judgment can be established only in practice, and a more desirable situation must be brought about without costly side affects. Thus the maturing child may decide to disobey parental injunctions about association with other children and rely instead on experience and observation to guide the choice of friends on the ground that the child's own information in this area is more complete and detailed. "Honoring" is reinterpreted to mean "becoming a grown man or woman."

After this reinterpretation moral judgment once again becomes intuitional until a new awareness is developed or until a new disturbance occurs. The point for Dewey, however, is that while moral judgments may be rationally achieved and be stable for individuals and groups over time, they are never immune to criticism and improvement. As he wrote, "Only the conventional and the fanatical are always immediately sure of right and wrong in conduct."[6]

There are difficulties with this approach to moral judgment that can and have occupied much ingenious inquiry. Unfortunately, the philosophical discussion of morals often has remained stuck at the level of these difficulties. With increased subtlety the disputes have gone beyond the training or interest of most of us, providing all the more reason for social scientists to avoid questions of value and moral judgment. The point is not to try to solve all the problems connected with moral judgments, but to achieve a journeyman philosophy that makes it possible to work on the moral troubles of the present. The cognitive-affective approach is proposed here because it can both account plausibly for moral degeneration and offer directions for research and remedy.

There are certain capacities and abilities that people must have in order to carry out the process of judgment depicted by Dewey. To begin, individuals must be capable of a direct appreciation of others, of deeds, and of objects and must be responsive to their own emotions. "Emotional reactions," wrote Dewey and Tufts, "form the chief materials of our knowledge of ourselves and others."[7] The autistic or narcissistic individual is thus incapable of moral development. This insight is the basis of the one-sided contention that all valuing is an expression of emotional response. According to that contention, "that is good" is translated to mean "I desire it," "I like it," "I feel good around it," and so on.

But this emotive theory of moral judgment fails to recognize either the seriousness or the intellectual complexity of such judgments. Selecting a course of action is not like choosing ice cream flavors. When one expresses a preference for, say, chocolate ice cream, there is no doubt about it. As that most boorish of bromides goes, "I know what I like." But when one makes the judgment that an act in a given context is good, one is faced with a situation in which only some results of that act can be anticipated and many cannot be known. This difficulty makes moral judgment more burdensome and more complicated than simply shopping or choosing an item out of a given repertoire. One is responsible not only for the choice but for construction of the range of possible choices. Since that range is always problematic, given the limits of human reason, one cannot expect to do more than approach satisfactory outcomes. Individuals choose to act or not act, knowing that at best they will produce unintentional hurt to themselves and others and at best will achieve only limited ends. Given these limits, moral judgment must then be concerned with assessment and correction, and moral action must be understood as a step in the processes of improving such judgment and not as a definitive stand to be defended to the death.

The results of actions that provide the means for assessing judgment are real and of consequence in the social world. Moral knowledge, as the tragedians have been dramatizing for centuries, is purchased at the cost of human suffering. Simple trial and error will not do. The recognition of this cost requires a sense of responsibility or the understanding that there is a choice to be made or not made and that there are consequences that must be borne and possibly rectified. This can be called responsibility commitment, conscientiousness, or seriousness. What is required is the acknowledgement, in the words of Martin Wenglinsky, that "moral judgment is one of those things which, by definition, cannot be replicated, because if you had a chance to know better, to profit from experience, you would have acted differently."[8]

While moral judgments are founded on intuitional evaluation or emotional and sympathetic responses, their social consequences are so profound as to require a method of judging capable of a high degree of accurate anticipation of consequences and a great precision of corrigibility. This requirement, wrote Dewey, forces us to see that "there is no great gulf dividing non-moral knowledge from that which is truly moral."[9] By this he meant that moral knowledge must be as reliable, precise, complex, and detailed as the ideals of the physical sciences prescribe. Moral knowledge based on uninformed preferences, prejudices, wishful thinking, autocratic fiat, or the mechanical application of formal principles is as disastrous to use in practice as a knowledge of bridge building based on fancy, on a distaste for gravity, or exclusively on the theorems of Euclidean geometry.

According to Eugene Meehan, "A choice is reasoned . . . if it involves the application of known standards to stated alternatives."[10] Moral judgments are reasoned choices that are inclusive and consistent, based on a known standard or a conceptual framework of related principles. This conceptual framework and its principles are hypothetical, just as the theories and principles of, say, physics are hypothetical. The functions are analagous; that is, the principles are guides to conduct, experiment, and research and subject to modification in the light of practice. But, Dewey and Tufts point out, moral principles are not commands, but tools for analyzing a specific situation.[11] The moral judgment of what is the right thing to do is reached by utilizing the relevant principles to analyze the situation and to assess the consequences of action in practice, not by blindly applying the principle as a rule.

The quality of moral judgment depends upon the individual's ability to conceptualize a given situation in terms of (1) its significant elements or features, (2) the relations between those elements, (3) a working model of the situation based on (1) and (2) that can generate an accurate estimate of the probable consequences of actions, (4) a set of alternative ends, and (5) an assessment of what consequences and which ends are better or worse for human life. Human life is necessary in assessing consequence because it is something that can be concretely investigated. Empirically assessing the consequence of action for "truth" or even for the will or desire of some supernatural being is impossible.

None of the above conceptualizations or explanations is easily constructed. Each requires cognitive capacities, such as logical and verbal ability and social knowledge based on experience and imagination. Indeed, moral judging itself is a complex skill that requires practice to perfect. The fact that moral philosophers often have regarded moral judging as the unyielding application of principles to choices represents an administrative bias that assumes skill to mean mechanical repetition and thus judgment to mean deciding only which rule will apply.

Jean Piaget has emphasized that moral judgment cannot be exclusively learned by obeying the instructions of moral superiors such as parents, teachers, or ministers, or by learning moral examples from books, sacred texts, or instructional films. Verbal and logical abilities can be improved through instruction, as well as the knowledge of the content of social and political values. Piaget's genetic approach to cognitive development insists that there is another kind of activity involved in the acquisition of knowledge. The first activity he calls logico-mathematical, being the process of bringing together, discriminating, ordering, counting, and the like. The second activity is physical exploration and information extraction. The child develops as it acquires a more adequate knowledge of reality, based on successive modes of acting upon the external world.[12]

The implications of a cognitive-affective view of moral judgment for patterns of human interactions were summarized by Dewey and Tufts, who stated that

> reflective morality demands observation of particular situations, rather than fixed adherence to *a priori* principles; that free inquiry and freedom of publication and discussion must be encouraged and not merely grudgingly tolerated; that opportunity at different times and places must be given for trying different measures so that their effects may be capable of observation and of comparison with one another.[13]

These implications require organizations that include the means for developing and implementing policy in terms of experimental design and public forums for reasoned argumentation and criticism. This does not mean fluid, ad hoc arrangements, for despite the emphasis placed by

Dewey, Tufts, and Meehan on the corrigible nature of the principles of moral judgment, such principles must be tenaciously held and be stable over time. The necessity of an element of tenaciousness in the development of scientific knowledge has been argued by historians and philosophers of science such as Thomas Kuhn and Paul Feyerabend. According to the argument, any and all of the important theoretical formulations of the physical sciences have been immediately faced with falsifying evidence. If, as the purists of logical positivism prescribe, Copernicus, Newton, or Einstein had abandoned their new theories in these cases, knowledge would have been aborted.

Theoretical tenacity is necessary in order for implications to be clarified, for techniques of observation, testing, and evaluation to be developed, and for new information to be produced. Similarly, while the principles of moral judgment must be open to criticism and improvement and while they must be changeable over time, they cannot undergo incessant major modifications if the implications of such principles are to be understood and their consequences evaluated. The experimental method, whether in morals or in chemistry, does not prescribe fads and fashions but a crafts-man-like attention to detail. Moral principles, whether traditional or novel, are not altered lightly. The freedom that Dewey understood as a prerequisite of moral development is laden with responsibility, responsiveness, and respect.

MORAL JUDGMENT VERSUS OBEDIENCE

What has all this to do with the structure of American political, social, and economic institutions? A great deal. If those institutions thwart the development or exercise of the capacities of responsibility, competence, and communication, then the quality of the moral judgments of the citizenry must remain poor. One understands vaguely that there is a connection between virtue and institutional design but one is generally quite confused about what it is, because the structure of institutions is based upon a very narrow and dogmatic notion of virtue. Derek C. Bok, president of Harvard, surveying recent problems of unsatisfactory moral standards in the United States, called upon private and public organizations to aid in improving them. "Business organizations and professional associations will have to take more initiative in establishing stricter codes of ethics and providing for their enforcement. Public officials will need to use imagination in seeking ways of altering incentives in our legal and regulatory structure to encourage moral behavior."[14] Notice what Bok assumes here — that moral behavior is obedience to an imposed rule or standard, that moral leadership consists in coercing or manipulating obedience, and that the moral principles of the culture are known. If all these assumptions are true, then to improve public virtue it is necessary only to increase control.

Consider that if these propositions are false, as the cognitive-affective view implies, then Bok's prescription will have the opposite effect. It will increase rather than arrest moral degeneration. It will do so because it rules out the possibility that the members of those organizations will develop their moral judgment by responding to their situations, by formulating their troubles as problems, by projecting alternative ends-in-view to solve those problems, by devising means to reach those ends, and by testing their self-generated moral judgments in use. To do any of these things, at least publicly, in the institutions that Bok wants tightened up, is tantamount to insubordination and disloyalty.

Moral confusion increases when insubordination and disloyalty are promoted as ethical alternatives. For example, in Reeves's article he describes the cases of four men who behaved ethically, or in his simplistic formulation "stood up to the system." In all four cases he describes their behavior as following a decision to obey a moral principle that was unrecognized or in conflict with the duties of their positions. In each case the decision brought personal anguish and resulted in an action condemned by superiors and peers. A major league outfielder, Curt Flood, refused to be traded because "I am a man, not a consignment of goods to be bought and sold." A reporter, John Hanrahan, refused to cross a picket line when the Washington *Post* hired strikebreakers, because he believed that "No matter how imperfect they are, unions are the only existing means workers have to get a fair shake from management." A Pentagon official, Edward Fitzgerald, "blew the whistle" on defense contract cost overruns because he refused to lie to a U.S. senator. A federal judge, Frank Johnson, handed down more than 100 unpopular decisions on desegregration in the South in the 1950s and 1960s because he thought he should, "follow the law." The results of these acts were predictable. As Reeves summarized them,

The men I searched out lost jobs and friends, endured a frightening loneliness punctuated by death threats and bombings, three of their children ended up deeply disturbed and one a suicide. All of that came to seem almost predestined: to keep the rest of us in line, established power had to make brutal examples of those who dared to challenge the order of things.[15]

This quotation is troubling, both in its confirmation of what everyone seems to expect and its implication that individuals are in the grasp of malevolent powers. Apparently the only ethical actions appropriate to the institutions of the society are heroic and perhaps suicidal. That means that such acts of standing up to the system are not to be expected.

Consider where this leaves individuals in the conduct of their working lives. For instance, any academic involved in research in any major university in the United States knows of or has participated in one or more instances of the misuse, mismanagement, or irregular juggling of public funds. Some of this results from overly rigid budget procedures that hamper reasonable but contingent allocation of funds. Some is due to individual exploitation of personnel, travel funds, equipment, and so on. And some is administrative in that overhead charged against research contracts is siphoned off as surreptitious profit and utilized to fund other activities. Consider the results of "blowing the whistle" on any of these or similar activities. Would there be public congratulation, institutional advancement, professional accolades, and greater access to funding grants? Probably not. As Reeves explains, academics, too, work in networks of polite corruption and learn to adjust to it. They learn to see this corruption not only as the way things are done or must be done in the present circumstances, but as the way they should be done. They lose the ability even to recognize corruption. As the saying goes, they "get smart," but in doing so they get a stake in the sharp differentiation of the world of values and ethics from the world of facts and accommodation. Given this view, the condemnation of the misuse of public funds is an unpopular but hardly an ethical action.

The dichotomy of moral judgment and obedience lies at the basis of moral confusion. Again Bok's article is a good example. Despite his call for tighter controls and more effective schedules of reinforcement, Bok insists that "educators have a responsibility to contribute in any way they can to the moral development of their students."[16] He further suggests that this can be done by teaching students how to recognize, analyze, and carefully reason about ethical issues. He states that such education through discussion of moral dilemmas in the classroom may have little or no effect on the ethical behavior of students. Education to promote moral development must be done on faith since, Bok concludes, moral character is profoundly dependent on forces beyond the university.

Implicit in the confusion of Bok's argument is a vicious circle that produces a series of dilemmas and paradoxes on various levels of analysis. Tightened mechanisms of social control in institutions render the development of moral judgment impossible or at least unlikely. The experienced lack of opportunity for the exercise of moral judgment makes the teaching of skills and the encouragement of capacities required for developing moral judgment seem foolish or even destructive. A therapist, Ernest Keen, states the problem this way: "The attempt to force overt honesty in a patient may subject the patient to the wrath of his bureaucratic context and do him a great disservice."[17] The problem is that such honesty is a necessary component of moral development. If honesty is dangerous, moral development is dangerous. It must therefore be eschewed or reconceptualized at a sufficiently abstract and formal level to avoid any conflict with institutional demands.

SEPARATING ETHICAL ACTION FROM MORAL REASONING

Social psychologists Roger Brown and Richard Herrnstein assert that "we have moved into a greater age of moral reasoning, as we did during the Civil War and the American Revolution."[18] It may be, as they argue, that books, magazines, newspapers, and televisions are filled with moral argument; but a close look at the frequent references to morality reveals not reasoned argument, but dismay, discomfort, and disillusion. What reasoning is going on, particularly in the social sciences, is a redefinition of obedience to authority and moral judgment that compartmentalizes them as distinct and unrelated modes of human action.

Ideas about effective social organization and ideas about moral judgment are at odds. This conflict can be viewed in various ways. Brown and Herrnstein put it in the form of a paradox: developmental psychologists have found that with age and education most people attain a reasonably advanced stage of conventional moral judgment; experimental psychologists in turn have found that in certain circumstances many and sometimes most people are capable of deceitful conformity, indifference to pleas for help from strangers, obedience to orders to hurt helpless victims, and enthusiasm for humiliating subordinates. This paradox can be dismissed, the authors say, if one does not assume "that the way people reason about moral issues determines the way they act."[19] They argue that only the cognitive or moral reasoning aspects of ethical action constitute moral judgment, while the actions themselves depend on affective factors such as degree of concern, sense of responsibility, and recognition of the existence of moral issues. The point is subtle and persuasive. It represents an important challenge to Dewey's notion that moral judgments are composed of both cognitive and affective elements.

Ethical Action

The experimental findings on which Brown and Herrnstein base their dichotomy of reason and behavior are notorious and disturbing. In each experiment various features or conditions of a social situation have been manipulated to create a conflict between accepted moral principles and the demands of the social context. Usually this has involved some major deception on the part of the experimenter and in nearly every case commonplace moral principles have been violated by anywhere from a substantial minority of one-third to a substantial majority of two-thirds of the experimental subjects.

The line of investigation began with Solomon Asch's work in the 1950s on the effects of conformity. He found that when subjects were confronted by stooges whose reports of observation conflicted with what they saw, one-third of them violated the principle of honest and accurate reporting to conform with the group.[20] Perhaps Stanley Milgram's experiments in obedience are the most famous of the series. Milgram contrived a situation in which the commands of an authority figure (a "scientist") to inflict electric shocks on a victim conflicted with the principle of not hurting another human being needlessly. As in the Asch experiment there was no lack of consensus concerning the moral principle involved among the subjects or most others, for that matter. When Milgram described the experiment to Yale undergraduates, to psychiatrists, and to psychologists, they all agreed that it would be immoral to administer high voltage electric shocks to a person learning random word pairs even if commanded by a reputable social scientist. They predicted that they would not do such a thing and that only 2 percent or less of the general population would obey such commands.

However, two-thirds of those involved in the original experiment, taken from the same population, obeyed the immoral commands and administered supposedly lethal shocks. Almost all subjects administered supposedly painful shocks. Milgram's study seems to indicate that when the situation of obedience was confronted in a purely cognitive way — through a verbal description or observed through a one-way mirror — a consensus for disobedience emerged. But when the experimental situation was confronted in its social and affective form, a majority obeyed even though they found such obedience personally painful. Milgram concluded, "Behavior that is unthinkable in an individual who is acting on his own may be executed without hesitation when carried out under orders."[21]

The general finding that more than 60 percent of the subjects obediently administered high-voltage shocks in the face of evidence that victims were suffering greatly was accounted for by proposing two differing states or sets of attitudes as determining the presence or absence of moral judgment. According to Milgram, individuals in the autonomous state understand that they are responsible for their actions, and judge morally. In the agentic state individuals understand that they are agents for carrying out the wishes of others and do not judge morally.[22] These subjective states are triggered or released by different social situations in which unethical demands occur. Unethical demands can be internally generated, releasing the autonomous mode, or they can be generated externally or socially, releasing the agentic mode. When experiencing an urge to harm another, one usually refrains because of moral judgment. But when ordered by another in certain types of institutional settings to hurt another, such moral judgment is not available. "Moral factors can be shunted aside with relative ease by a calculated restructuring of the informational and social field," Milgram states.[23]

Why should anyone, except a malevolent tyrant, want to restructure the informational and social field to eliminate moral factors from the behavior of individuals? Because, answers Milgram, obedience is a prerequisite for social organization, and social organization is a prerequisite for human survival. This is so, he argues, because social organization always is and must be hierarchical. This assertion is based on an unexamined assumption that organization and hierarchy are synonomous, and on the dubious practice of citing descriptions of dominance structures in animal societies. Having skipped over this rocky ground, he constructs a cybernetic model of hierarchy and deduces that hierarchies demand the "suppression of local control" in their components.[24] Hence, individuals in social organizations (hierarchies) must become passive elements, must enter an agentic state, in which responsibility and moral judgment are suspended. As Milgram puts it, "conscience, which regulates impulsive aggressive action, is perforce diminished at the point of entering a hierarchical structure."[25] The argument neatly suggests that there can be either social organization and obedience or social chaos and moral judgment.

Obedience is not an amoral or nonethical state. The agentic mode is based on the moral judgment that so and so is an authority and that authority ought to be obeyed. The agentic state involves the ethical values of loyalty, duty, discipline, and so on. Disobedience, Milgram admits, results in a sense of faithlessness, and he points out that the technical needs of the hierarchy "are experienced as highly personal moral imperatives by the individual."[26] The agentic state presupposes and requires that autonomous state. Thus the dichotomy is not clear and there is a paradox: social organization demands both an active and developed moral judgment and the suppression or attenuation of moral judgment. Conscience, which is diminished in Milgram's words by hierarchy, is also the basis for the obedience necessary to hierarchy. Clearly the conflict is not autonomy and moral judgment versus obedience and amorality, but between two types of morality. When an ethics based on the functioning of autonomous individuals is played off against a set of observed behaviors required by the functioning of hierarchical authority, a paradox is produced for social science and a dilemma for citizens. Both the paradox and the seeming dilemma of conscience versus authority may be a product of poor understanding. Given a limited and formal view of moral judgment and an equally limited and instrumental view of organization, perhaps this is all that can be expected.

Philip Zimbardo has conducted a series of experiments involving the manipulation of the characteristics of social situations and their impact on ethical behavior. A dramatic example of his work was the creation of a simulated prison environment. Zimbardo and his assistants (who undertook administrative roles in the mock prison) selected 22 college students, randomly assigned them the roles of guards or prisoners, paid them $15 a day, and incarcerated them in the basement of Stanford University's Psychology Building for a scheduled two weeks. The details of the situation including uniforms, rules, privacy, and so on were manipulated to promote anonymity, depersonalization. The resulting aggressive, sadistic behavior of the "guards" and the submissive, passive behavior of the "inmates" was so extreme that the experiment had to be terminated after only six days.[27]

Zimbardo concludes from this and other experiments that human evil is situation-dependent. That is, pathological behavior such as sadism or extreme passivity can be elicited with relative ease within certain institutional settings. The situational characteristics most likely to result in such behavior are presence of an authority responsible for consequences, remoteness of victims or clients, subordinate roles, and binding rules of protocol and etiquette.[28]

In contrast to these situations, producing what he calls deindividuation, are those situations conducive to individuation, — situations in which people must choose to commit themselves to a course of action and accept responsibility, for the result "shifts the locus of control of . . . behavior from external stimuli to internal cognitive controls."[29] Zimbardo points out that laboratory conditions are those that produce deindividuation and their results make it appear that human behavior is always under the control of environmental and physiological demand stimuli. The implication of this experimentation is that if manipulation of behavior is desired — for whatever reason, from the preservation of society to the making of profit — it should be brought under stimulus control. But stimulus control is achieved only when cognitive functions are bypassed. Control of human behavior in the sense of making it predictable can be achieved by creating institutional situations conducive to deindividuation. However, this produces a further set of problems because, as Zimbardo asserts, "conditions which foster deindividuation make each of us a potential assassin."[30] In short, the quest for control through the use of demand stimuli results in the creation of chaos.

Zimbardo's description of states of deindividuation and individuation characterize them as modes of emotionality without reason and rationality without emotion. There is no cognitive control in the first state and no response to biological drives such as thirst and pain, or social needs such as approval or aggression, in the second. Robert Ziller hypothesizes that individuation is a desirable state only within a supportive social situation and that deindividuation or anonymity is more desirable in a threatening environment.[31] This suggests that moral judgment is most likely to be available when it is least needed. If Zimbardo and Ziller are correct, then moral judgment is a luxury. The quest for morality could thus result in attempts to control the behavior of others. Indeed, this was Plato's view of the matter.

However, Zimbardo's and others' simulations of social situations involving superordinate roles and rules of obedience do not indicate that one can expect the exercise of moral judgment by controllers any more than by controllees.[32] Most investigations of the consequences of the exercise of control have focused on subordinates rather than superiors. David Kipinis notes that there is a tradition that postulates the corrupting influence of power on the powerful. On the basis of the few studies done of the consequences of exercising control on controllers, Kipinis offers a "metamorphic model" of such effects:

> The metamorphic model assumes that the control of resources, in conjunction with a strong power need, triggers a train of events that goes like this: (a) with the control of resources goes increased temptation to influence others' behavior to satisfy personal wants; (b) if powerholders use strong and controlling means of influence to satisfy these personal wants and compliance follows; (c) there arises the belief that the behavior of the target person is not self-controlled but has been caused by the powerholder; as a result (d) there is a devaluation of the target person's abilities; and (e) a preference to maintain social and psychological distance from the target person; (f) simultaneously the power-holder's evaluation of himself changes so that he views himself more favorable than the target person.[33]

Complicating the picture is Kipinis's contention that isolation, loneliness, and emotional lack provide a powerful impetus to seek to control the behavior of others. If, in striving to become individuated, one succeeds only in becoming a caricature, such as the image of the self-made man or woman, the western movie hero, or the Raymond Chandler detective, a likely result will be a craving to control. Likewise, if social arrangements promote isolation, a similar need to dominate will occur.

What can be concluded from these investigations in social psychology? Milgram argues that his findings show that nature has designed a fatal flaw in each of us; everyone, he says, possesses "the capacity to abandon his humanity, indeed, the inevitability that he does so, as he merges his unique personality into larger institutional structures."[34] The flaw is one's incapacity to judge morally in hierarchical organizations. But as this discussion has tried to show, Milgram's own descriptions of the behavior of his subjects indicates that nearly all of them attempted to act ethically in the light of their understanding of the principles governing the situation, and of their interpretation of the significance of the experimental setting. The danger to the survival of the species revealed in these studies is a misunderstanding of moral judgment as a purely cognitive activity and a misunderstanding of social organization as a matter of hierarchy.

Seeing a flaw in man's capacity to abandon humanity in entering hierarchies is like seeing a flaw in man's capacity to suffocate on entering an oxygenless atmosphere. It is much more reasonable to conclude that the threat to humankind lies in institutions that are designed to require the manipulation of people so that they must lose their humanity. Milgram and other investigators in this area are subject to Weglinsky's charge that they are guilty of "provoking people into evil by hiding the truth so that it is difficult to come up with a correct solution."[35] Perhaps these investigators also are subject to the effects described in Kipinis's metamorphic model and have come to believe that the behavior of the experimental subjects was not self-controlled but merely a result of the investigators' manipulations. The image of a defective but obedient humanity evoked by this work certainly implies that more investigations into how to control such hopeless creatures must be undertaken. But who can be trusted to do that? Over this dilemma, Machiavelli would weep with envy.

Moral Reasoning

If the present age is a great one of moral reasoning, then the work of Lawrence Kohlberg over the last decades is a major contribution. Working out of a cognitive developmental viewpoint, Kohlberg has done an outstanding job of criticizing both socialization theories of moral education that understand it to be indoctrination, and the cultural-relativist theories of moral judgment that understand it to be obedience to socially defined rules.[36] His critiques and his investigation of the development of types of moral reasoning in children and adolescents have forced both social scientists and educators to confront the claims of a morality based on something more than emotionalism and conformity.

Kohlberg claims that his studies demonstrate universal ontogenetic trends toward a moral reasoning as conceived by Western philosophers of ethics and that this development is different from the internalization of the arbitrary norms of a given culture.[37]He states two general empirical claims: first, "that there are universal moral concepts, values or principles," and second, "that the marked differences between individuals and cultures which exist are differences in stage or developmental status."[38] His evidence for the first claim is that "almost all individuals in all cultures use the same thirty basic moral categories, concepts, or principles" and "all individuals in all cultures go through the same order or sequences of gross stage of development, though varying in rate and terminal point of development."[39] The second claim is based on the finding "that factor analysis indicates a single 'stage' factor cutting across all moral situations, and all aspects of morality on which the individual is assessed."[40] Beside these empirical claims, Kohlberg insists that "my major philosophical claim [is] that the stimulation of development is the only ethically acceptable form of moral education."[41]

In turn, all these claims are based on research that involves the presentation of a series of stories of moral dilemmas to subjects, each of which asks for a judgment about the course of action taken in the story. The stories are all true dilemmas in the sense that some recognized moral principle supports each option offered. Subjects are not scored on what action they judge to be right but on the reasons they give for choosing. Answers are scored by means of content analysis and assigned to one of six stages of moral development. Kohlberg's stages range from preconventional levels of avoiding punishment and seeking gratification, through conventional levels of conformity and obedience, to postconventional levels of social or universal ethical principles. Kohlberg's investigations have been criticized on methodological grounds and, indeed, present difficulties in terms of scoring and definition. These problems will not be dealt with here; rather, the present concern is with the philosophical adequacy and political implications of Kohlberg's work.

Kohlberg's theory of moral judgment is attractive because of its stress on cognitive abilities over indoctrination and conformity. It has been praised generously elsewhere.[42] But several features and propositions of the theory have led this author to take a closer look and to conclude that it is not the alternative to behavioristic theories of morality it purports to be, but merely an idealistic complement. Like the moral philosophies of Plato and Kant, Kohlberg's theory is ultimately an apology for institutions of social control. Initially, two problems stood out — Kohlberg's concept of role taking and his naive idea that so-called "just communities" could be conducted on a democratic basis within authoritarian institutions, like schools and prisons, whose major functions are custody and control.

In adapting his theory from Piaget's earlier work, Kohlberg substituted the concept of role taking for cooperation. Piaget insisted that the experience of cooperating with peers was necessary for the development of autonomous moral judgment.[43] This idea was similar to the ideas of Rousseau, Mill, and Cole, who understood the act of participating with peers in determining the rules and roles of a given social context as educative and even enobling.[44] In this view, institutional arrangements that are participatory and democratic promote the moral development of citizens. Dewey said the same thing.

Kohlberg's translation of cooperation into opportunities for role taking looks like a simple substitution of jargon until it is discovered that role taking does not necessarily involve peers or direct participation. Role taking means several things, including having sympathy for others, adopting Adam Smith's perspective of the "generalized other," holding to the Kantian principle that each person must be treated as an end and never as a means, participating in "justice structures" that dictate reciprocity and equality, sharing expectations and/or values, and finally, deriving moral decisions from Rawls's principle of justice.[45] Given these meanings, Kohlberg concludes that role taking is more easily accomplished by decision makers. He writes that leadership positions in institutions are prerequisites for development of a certain kind of sensitivity to others. Thus, "the group leader must role-take all the subordinate's roles and be aware of their relations to one another, while the subordinate is only required to take the role of the other [i.e., the leader]."[46] This assertion flies in the face of much experience and research on the isolation of leadership roles in organization and the autistic attitudes produced in such roles by the lack of accurate feedback.[47]

This ambiguous translation, followed by an apparent ignorance of relevant organization research on taking the perspectives of others in subordinate and superordinate roles, is troublesome. But such a mistranslation is necessary to justify findings that middle-class children develop faster and attain higher stages of moral development than working-class children.[48] Kohlberg denies that this finding is based on any class bias in his stage theory. He argues that the advanced moral judgment of middle-class children is due to the superior opportunities for role taking in middle-class families which purportedly stress participation, communication, emotional warmth, sharing in decisions, awarding responsibility to the child, and pointing out consequences of actions to others.[49] But such opportunities are a far cry from what Piaget understood as the means for delivering the child "from the mystical power of the world of the adult."[50]

Kohlberg may be asserting covertly that the moral reasoning appropriate to those who occupy decision-making roles in hierarchical institutions is superior. This is the only way one can make sense of statements such as "The psychological unity of role-taking and justice at mature stages of moral consciousness is easily recognized."[51] This psychological unity seems to mean that one can judge morally according to the principles of justice to the extent that one can take into account all the roles in a given situation. Since role taking is a prerequisite for recognizing situations as involving moral conflict, then only the decision makers' empathy or concern for the welfare of others defines when and where moral judgment is appropriate.[52] Subordinates may complain or resist, but a moral conflict exists only if the superior can and does sympathize. The subordinate may feel wronged and even give reasoned arguments for those felt grievances, but such objections can be rejected as inappropriate to the role. Not only do superiors define roles in the first place (which Kohlberg does not recognize); they decide when there is a moral conflict and how to resolve that conflict.

Kohlberg puts this rather grandly by proclaiming: "To act in a way you want all humanity to act is to recognize the claims of all humanity."[53] But to act in such a way is to act from the perspective of an extrahuman legislator or administrator, for it presumes that one knows how all humanity ought to act. Of course, one cannot know such a thing, not knowing all of humanity, nor can one know the individual claims of humanity in any empirical sense. Thus, perspective is necessarily imaginary, abstract, formal, and unconcerned with specific people and concrete consequences. The danger is that this formulation leaves no way for the administrator at the highest levels of moral judgment to comprehend the information of others as a means of correcting fallible human judgment.

For example, a teacher may make a principled commitment to treat all students in the class absolutely equally. That is, the teacher chooses to disregard the consequences of the instruction on the cognitive development of the students. In effect, this advantages some students whose preparation is superior or simply similar to that of the teacher; for intentionally or not, the class work will be designed for them. Others, however, will be disadvantaged. The latter may argue that the principle is retarding their intellectual progress and present evidence supporting their claims. Further, they may point out that their lower achievements may retard their future ability to earn a living and so on. In any case, there is no obligation to alter the principle, for if the teacher exemplifies Kohlberg's morally advanced person, it is understood that the dissident students are judging the situation, not simply according to different standards, but according to lower standards. They are too materialistic, too concerned with mere appetite, unable to view the situation in a disinterested manner, and so on. To the extent that the teacher cannot convince them that they are wrong, he is justified in regarding their claims as symptoms of their lack of moral development. The teacher's obligation, then, is to provoke or to seduce them, by whatever means or manipulation, to agree with his judgment.

Unfortunately, this built-in discrediting of the judgments of others makes the development of a self-critical attitude on the part of the "morally advanced" unlikely. It also evokes the ire and the resistance of opponents. As this author reads Kohlberg, he becomes more and more convinced that he prefers to be heard, not helped; be listened to and argued with, rather than be an object of another's condescending sympathy. In sum, he prefers that people take seriously, not his role, but his claims, reasons, evidence, and criticisms. To paraphrase Dostoyevsky, "I prefer to be a human being and not a piano key."

In Kohlberg's theory, only those who view moral choice from the perspective of a disinterested spectator or are forced by something called "justice structures" to share expectations, values, and rules can achieve the levels of abstraction necessary for the highest stages of moral development. It is not surprising that Kohlberg estimates that only 25 percent of the population develop beyond Stage 4. Someone, after all, has to mind the store of everyday reality.

Investigations into the problems of reinterpreting cooperation as a form of role taking that comes close to both simple imitation and applying formal conventions to social situations have made it possible to see how different Kohlberg's ideas of moral judgment are from those of Hume and Dewey, and how close they are to the moral dogmatism they oppose. In language and perspective, Kohlberg is close to Kant, but from time to time glimpses of the sophistry of Plato emerge from the background. Two problematic characteristics of Kant's philosophy are shared by Kohlberg — formalism and unfalsifiability. In this volume, David Candee, Roy Feldman, and others have noted that Kohlberg's theory is focused on the form but not the content of moral judgments. However, the theory is formal in a much more fundamental sense because morality itself is defined as "*a unique sui generis realm.*" Kohlberg spells out the definition this way:

> Like most deontological moral philosophers since Kant, we define morality in terms of the formal character of a moral judgment, method, or point of view, rather than in terms of its content. Impersonality, ideality, universalizability, preemptiveness, etc. are the formal characteristics of moral judgment. These are best seen in the reasons given for a moral judgment, a moral reason being one which has these properties.[54]

It follows from this definition that moral discourse follows unique and nonscientific rules, and the autonomy of morality must be protected from the disruptions of nonmoral concerns such as will, desire, emotion, the arbitrary specifications of concrete situations, facts, instrumentality, and so on. But a formalistic conception of morality tends to become vacuous or irrelevant as a guide to action. By means of formalism morality may be preserved, but ethics is destroyed.

Kohlberg makes two claims to preserve the ethical relevance of his theory. First, he argues that there is no great discrepancy between moral reasoning and moral action. The relation between judgment and action is to be considered as a correspondence between the general maturity of an individual's judgment and the maturity of his or her actions. Kohlberg goes further and asserts that "the moral force in personality is cognitive."[55] These and similar statements about the relation imply that although morality is an autonomous, cognitive realm, it can and does act upon the real world. The real world, while being the stuff on which morality operates, can, in turn, affect morality only by corrupting it, frustrating it, or destroying it. Kohlberg paraphrases Plato approvingly with "He who knows the good chooses the good."[56] This statement seems to be an empirical claim.

Kohlberg offers a second claim to deny the inference that his theory of moral judgment is vacuous. He states that "not only is there a universal moral form, but the basic contents principles of morality are universal."[57] In other words, the principles derived from Stages 5 and 6 of moral judgment are not just formal; they are substantive. In particular, "justice [is] the basic moral principle."[58] This principle, justice, is defined "interchangeably" as everyone is equal, impartiality, reciprocity, and respect for personality. Supposedly, it can show not only how to analyze a situation, but how to act. It seems debatable, however, whether such a principle of justice, adopted from John Rawls, can compel or suggest any definitive course of action in a real-life situation. That is because it does not (however interchangeably defined) specify any particular ends or purposes to be achieved.

For example, take the Heinz dilemma. A man is faced with a situation in which his wife is dying for want of a rare drug. The supplier, a druggist, wants a large and unaffordable price for the drug. The question is, should Heinz steal the drug? Supposedly this is a true dilemma and the interest is in how subjects reason about it and not what course of action they choose. But to score at Stage 6, Kohlberg states categorically (which places his own moral reasoning at Stage 6 or higher) that subjects must say that Heinz is obligated to steal the drug because it is demanded by the principle of respect for personality.[59] This principle implies the goal of saving the wife's life. Consider, however, that someone like Socrates could refuse to steal the drug on exactly the same principle. If respect for personality translates into maintaining life, as Kohlberg interprets it here, Socrates could argue as follows: that society is necessary for the maintenance of human life (or for that matter, the notion of human personality, the idea of morality, and so on); that society is itself dependent upon allegiance and obedience of members; that since an act of theft would set a dangerous example of disloyalty and disregard for law, it could aid in the destruction of society; and that therefore, Heinz should refrain from theft to prevent a larger destruction of human life, even though this means his wife must die.

Kohlberg and his supporters can object that Socrates has used Stage 5 reasoning, since all differences of moral judgment are differences in stages. But that defense does not meet the objection that the principles of Stage 6 do not imply a specific end or a particular course of action in the described situation. They require, rather, some definitive interpretation by Kohlberg or one of his trained scorers.

A dilemma like Heinz's in the real world could not be decided without specifying an end. Other, so-called nonmoral considerations also would have to be investigated. For example, does Heinz have the skill and courage to successfully steal the drug? What are the chances of being caught, regardless of skill? Indeed, what are the chances of being shot or convicted? Would the wife die without Heinz's income or his care if he did time in the penitentiary? Might the wife consider public shame worse than death? Such questions only illustrate the difference between this author's moral reasoning and Kohlberg's. The distance between these two positions can best be estimated by considering that those moral philosophers who score at Stage 6 on this dilemma would be unlikely (due to lack of experience, courage, and perhaps, ability) to commit a successful burglary. In short, the objection is that morality is not a formal textbook operation. As Meehan points out, "The empirical environment acts as a constraint on man, and his organizations must function within those limits; in imagination, the constraints are removed, for the whole supporting structure that gives meaning to events must be imagined or ignored. But in imagination all things are possible."[60]

Kohlberg's theory of moral judgment is vacuous, first, if there is no demonstrable relation between what he measures as levels of moral judgment and actual ethical behavior, and second, if the principles of the highest stages do not force specific choices in concrete situations. Since data such as those reported by Feldman do support the first, and analysis of Stage 6 principles indicates an amorphous generality that cannot force logical conclusions, the theory is in difficulty. Some recognition of this may be present in Kohlberg's writings, since he takes certain steps in argumentation that make his set of assertions about moral reasoning unfalsifiable in principle.

Kohlberg writes that "the basic referent of the term 'moral' is a type of *judgment* or a type of *decision-making process* not a type of behavior, emotion or social institution."[61] Thus, "impersonality, ideality, universalizability, preemptiveness, etc., are the formal characteristics of moral judgment."[62] What is moral then is a restricted type of judgment or decision that has those characteristics. Dewey and Tufts, however, warned that "the important point is that any restriction of moral knowledge and judgments to a definitive realm necessarily limits our perception of moral significance."[63] What Kohlberg calls his formal definition of morality restricts the ability to perceive moral significance. It reduces the ability, for example, to ascertain responsibility. Is Heinz responsible for the political disintegration of his community or the life of his wife? Is he responsible for the nursing care of his wife, for ascertaining the potency of the drug, for his wife's sense of pride in the community? No formal concept of justice or restriction of the moral realm will help to answer such questions — only to exclude them from attention. Why, then, does Kohlberg ignore the warning of Dewey and Tufts, their rejection of formalistic moral principles, and their contention that "the need for constant revision and expansion of moral knowledge is one great reason why there is no gulf dividing nonmoral knowledge from that which is truly moral"?[64]

Morality must be defined formalistically, as well as the restricted nature of moral knowledge proclaimed by Kohlberg, in order for Stages 5 and 6 to be established as the highest expressions of moral judgment on grounds that are not obviously arbitrary. Once this superiority is established, then differences in moral judgment can become differences in development. The philosophical grounds of any and all opponents are undermined by such proclamations as

> [W]e are claiming that stage 5 is the first of two and only two possible novel, consistent, systematic, and stable modes of moral judgment which provide answers to the skeptical and relativistic questioning which constitutes the dawn of moral philosophy . . .; regardless of the diversities of meta-ethical positions of moral philosophers, there are only two broad structures of normative ethics (together with their mixtures) open to philosophical elaboration.[65]
>
> Regardless of psychology, then, our conception of morality has a strong philosophical base. Anyone who tries to criticize it must provide a stronger positive alternative.[66]

Again and again Kohlberg charges that there are no positive alternatives to his position. This charge is nonsense since he nowhere demonstrates that the cognitive-affective alternative is not adequate. The positions of Hume, Dewey, and Meehan all contrast with Kohlberg's by being experimental, concerned with the consequences, and involving affect. But these alternatives can be denied so long as morality is defined formalistically.

Kohlberg's theory is impregnable to the extent that his claims to be able to define the rules of moral discourse are accepted. The only reasons offered for accepting these claims are that they are based on the hallowed authority of traditional moral philosophers such as Plato and Kant, and that they relieve the discomforts of skepticism and relativism. That will not do. Kohlberg's position is even more untenable when he slips to deny his critics any moral standing. For example, at one place he paraphrases Socrates' views of morality (actually Plato's) as a summary statement of the implications of his theory and research. The paraphrase contains metaphysical statements of dubious status and yet Kohlberg concludes: "Most psychologists have never believed any of these ideas of Socrates. Is it so surprising that psychologists have never understood Socrates? It is hard to understand if you are not stage 6."[67]

A number of philosophers have not believed the ideas of Plato, nor does this author. What stage of moral development does that indicate? Conventional, at best, and thus as Candee points out in his chapter, in need of law and the ruling guidance of those capable of superior moral reasoning. Thus critics can be taught, improved, or managed, but their logical, pragmatic, or empirical objects are not to be considered as possible falsifications.

Kohlberg writes: "In fact . . . basic hierarchies of moral values are primarily reflections of developmental stages in moral thought. Anyone who understands the values of life and property will recognize that life is morally more valuable than property."[68] Really? Suppose one does not agree; then by definition one does not understand. If one does not understand, there is no point in listening to that person's arguments, observations, alternative framework of analysis, and judgment. Since this formulation insures that Kohlberg cannot be wrong, then either he is not a human being or he cannot correct the propositions or principles of his theory. Given this formulation, it must be admitted that Kohlberg always wins — but only for converts.

Kohlberg's theory has all the characteristics of what Feyerabend calls apologetic ethics: rejection of human responsibility for the foundations of moral judgment, the enlistment of "higher values" in the preservation of institutions, and the promotion of feelings of superiority by persons most loyal to those values.[69] There is no wish to impugn Kohlberg's motivation or intentions. His writings give evidence of a man of some liberality who values democracy, freedom, equality, fairness, and individualism. The historic figures that he offers as examples of individuals who reasoned at Stage 6, such as Socrates, Jefferson, Lincoln, Martin Luther King, Jr., are all exemplars of ethical men. But the danger of Kohlberg's theory is that in order to operate as a guide to moral judgment and action its formalistic principles must be interpreted. A person of extraordinary sensitivity and sensibility may interpret it in reasonable ways, but such people are rarely available and, when they are, their human failings and limitations hamper their accomplishments. Kohlberg suggests that humanity has not been prepared for the prophets of Stage 6, but perhaps these great reformers were not prepared for humanity — especially their own.

BUREAUCRACY AND MORALITY

Brown and Herrnstein's admonition to give up the idea that there is a strong connection between moral reasoning and moral action is a way of refusing to think through the meaning and implications of the research briefly reviewed here. The experiments were all concerned with moral reasoning and choice as well as action. The people involved had to decide whether to state what they saw truthfully or to adhere to the majority judgments of the group, whether to defy a culturally designated authority, or to hurt a poorly behaved victim, or whether to act or not upon the license invoked in play acting a repressive situation. However people acted in these situations, there is no evidence that they did not reason, only that their reasoning had surprising outcomes from the experimenters' viewpoints.

The social situation intervened in these cases as a cognitive and not simply an affective factor. Obedience is an act based on a moral judgment that some directive is authoritative, that is, based on a recognized and accepted set of values and rules. Affectively, most of the subjects showed or reported extreme discomfort, but disregarded it instead of taking it as a clue to the altered and deceptive nature of the situation. The fact that so many did not attend to their own pain is some evidence that their situations were not dominated by affect and demand stimuli.

The obedience of Milgram's subjects, the sadomasochism of Zimbardo's students, and the aggrandized egos of Kipinis's supervisors are all in part the results of a particular morality. That morality is identical to that of Kohlberg's Western philosophers of ethics. It is a major justification of hierarchy, for it is based on the assumption that moral action is always obedience to moral principles, and that such principles are above criticism and revision. Moral principles, in turn, are assumed always to be derived from extrahuman and certain foundations. To reason and to act morally, according to this view, is to overcome emotion, desires, needs, appetites, pains, and material demands of whatever sort in the name of higher principles. Further, the belief in such higher principles entails belief in "higher" people and "lower" people. Higher people recognize higher principles, no matter what the impact of those principles are on human life. Lower people hold the wrong principles, no matter what human needs are served.

Another view of this research results if Dewey's model of moral judgment is taken not just as what ought to be the case, but as a reasonable description of how adults actually make such judgments. Dewey makes it possible to see that attending to the observations of peers and obeying authority are based on an intuition of trust, an intuition that persists if clues to changes in the situation are well and deliberately hidden. In the case of Zimbardo's experiments, it is seen that abuse of others is based on habitual distrust of symptoms of stress and pain; this distrust can generalize to the pain of others if the clues of the situation indicate their unworthiness. One may wish to say that the quality of moral judgment in these cases is defective, but it should be recognized that the quality of any judgment is no better than the motivation and information on which it is based. If institutions by design or default employ devious motivations and misinformation, moral judgment will suffer. In trying to understand the characteristics of moral judgment in the present, the common error is to overlook its institutional foundations. As Floyd Alport warned in 1933,

> Standardized, corporate ways of thinking and behaving have become habitual, and have therefore lapsed for the most part into unconsciousness. Not realizing that the elements of this system are psychological in character and really lie *within* human beings, we tend to project them as "economic forces" outside ourselves, and to imagine that they are as inevitable in influencing human action as climate and gravitation.[70]

While Kohlberg does not offer examples that could be contrasted with these experimental situations, he and his associates do claim to improve moral judgments by manipulating temporary situations within hierarchies like prisons and schools. Feldman has reviewed the results of some of these attempts in this volume. He concludes that "just" communities operate primarily as techniques of social control on subjects and points out the arbitrary manipulation of the communities by administrators. He finds no moral growth and no rehabilitation results. It is predicted here that if further studies of "just" communities were undertaken over time, the following trends would emerge. As subjects advance in stages of moral reasoning they will become able to justify any and all actions required by institutional conformity and expediency by means of higher, more abstract principles. They would be expected to learn, like Plato, how to justify lying to subordinates; like Aristotle, slavery; like Saint Augustine, the suppression of critical thought; like Jefferson, the denial of women's political rights. A relationship would be expected between moral reasoning and ethical action, similar to that in the story told by the former commandant of the extermination camp at Treblinka, Franz Strangl, who was charged with the deaths of more than 900,000 people:

> I remember one occasion — they were standing there just after they'd arrived, and one Jew came up to me and said he wanted to make a complaint. So I said yes, certainly, what was it. He said that one of the Lithuanian guards (who were only used for transport duties) had promised to give him water if he gave him his watch. But he had taken the watch and not given him any water. Well, that wasn't right, was it? Anyway, I didn't permit pilfering. I asked the Lithuanians then and there who it was who had taken the watch, but nobody came forward. Franz — you know, Kurt Franz — whispered to me that the man involved could be one of the Lithuanian officers — they had so-called officers — and that I couldn't embarrass an officer in front of his men. Well, I said, I am not interested in what sort of uniform a man wears. I am only interested in what is inside a man. Don't think *that* didn't get back to Warsaw in a hurry. But what's right is right, isn't it? I made them all line up and turn out their pockets.
>   In front of the prisoners?
>   Yes, what else? Once a complaint is made it has to be investigated. Of course we didn't find the watch — whoever it was had got rid of it.
>   What happened to the complainant?
>   Who?
>   The man who lodged the complaint?
>   I don't know, he said vaguely.[71]

Note the abstract principle of justice, namely, the value of each human being as a personality, expressed in the cited or implied bureaucratic rules: all people, however humble or unfortunate, can register complaints; contracts must be honored, even by the stronger; all people, however exalted or powerful, are accountable for their actions; observance of the principles of justice is more important than individual advantage; and all complaints of whatever origin must be investigated. Strangl's level of moral reasoning can be seen to be remarkably high, but his actions were in this case remarkably inept. The culprit was not caught ("of course") and the man who complained was exterminated.

Kohlberg is right to insist that ethical action is informed by reason. But he fails to pay adequate attention to the converse — that moral reasoning is informed by action. Experimental moral action would require confrontation with the authority structure and the very principles of hierarchical institutions imbedded in Kohlberg's own theory of stages. In the absence of opportunities for such experimentation, then, a limited, formalistic moral reasoning is the only possible outcome.

Thinking through the implications of both kinds of research without drastically separating action and reasoning can produce the suspicion that the ethical values and principles of Western philosophers which justify our institutional designs are in need of revision. That suspicion, in turn, requires that social scientists recognize their own responsibility to cease to worship the given social order in which they live and work. While one must be careful and must not become a hero, ways can be sought to criticize and demystify the institutional forms and their supporting ethics that occasion apologetic, ineffective, and dangerously deficient moral judgments.

Dewey observed that "tools can be evolved and perfected only in operation." If, in line with him, moral judgment is regarded as a tool for living an improved social life, its development is impossible without testing in use. But there can be no such use of moral judgment in this sense without subordinating doctrines of institutional form of human choice and will. So long as social scientists regard human institutions as the determined products of biological or social evolution or the embodiments of laws deduced from timeless principles, moral development is impossible. The result of this inability or unwillingness to apply an experimental method to moral concerns and institutional design is, as Dewey charged, an "infantile state of social knowledge." The research briefly reviewed here reflects this state and its major characteristics of a "withdrawal from reality and an unwillingness to think things through."[72]

The reality withdrawn from is threatening and confusing. It must be resolutely ignored every day. Stated in the baldest terms, the major feature of that reality is that present institutions do not work. They are not efficient in terms of their use of people, their consumption of resources, their production of goods, and their delivery of services. In the bureaucracies of the state, of education, and of industry, it costs too much to do too little with too much constriction of human life and intelligence. That constriction involves the curtailment of creativity and the blunting of moral judgment. The refusal on the part of social scientists to think things through is the intellectual version of that constriction. Its form, as Alport wrote, is a social science illusion "that certain man-made systems of organization and the fictions by which they are supported are the beginning and the end of wisdom, the meaning of life itself."[73] Thinking things through does not mean thinking like someone else whose view of reality may be wrong, and is certainly incomplete. If present institutions are working well or better than is apparent, at least questions should be asked about their performance; they should not simply be assumed to be adequate. All the statements about the rationality, speed, efficiency, effectiveness, coordination, economies of scale, and morality of hierarchical institutions seem to be reiterations of the rationale for trying out these forms of organization in the first place. As rationales they are perhaps adequate, but they are not measurements of actual performance.

As the modern organizational form, based on a wedding of traditional hierarchy with a division of labor combining task specialization and professional expertise, bureaucracy is much decried. However, it is assumed to be an evolved and thus an advanced form of organization, and its obvious failures are blamed on human nature. Consider that the failures of bureaucracies may be due to faulty assumptions. Modern organizations aim at efficiency of control based on the hidden premise that human experience can be "divided into physical and spiritual realms, immediate and mediated modes, concrete and symbolic forms, lower and higher activities."[74] By subordinating the physically immediate and concrete to the spiritual, mediated and symbolic, rational truth, logical beauty and formal justice can be achieved. The irrationality of this premise is revealed by the resulting practice of rigorously attending to process at the expense of ignoring outcomes.

Bureaucracies produce a structure of formal rationality at an abstract level, while structuring individual human experience as meaningless and purposeless. Within this experience consistent moral reasoning and ethical activity is impossible. This is the point that Weber tried to make in asserting that the achievement of formal rationality by means of the relentless application of techniques of control creates a stratification of meaning in which substantive rationality is not possible. Ralph Hummel writes that in the untranslated essay "On Some Categories of a Sociology of Understanding" Weber describes this stratification as analogous to the way mathematics is understood. That is, there is a small elite who understand the rational generation of the rules of calculation, while everyone else, more or less, applies the rules habitually on the basis of blind faith.[75] The elite do not know how mathematics is used concretely and are contemptuous of the faith that leads to many errors, in terms of the most basic principles, but satisfactory results in terms of application. Most people, for example, understand the statement, $2 + 2 = 4$, as empirically true, while the mathematician understands it as a tautology. Weber describes four levels of understanding:

> The rational institutions of society, be it a compulsory or a voluntary association, are imposed or "suggested" by one group for specific purposes although individuals in the group may already differ on the intent. The institutions are interpreted more or less similarly and applied on a subjective basis by the second group, the "organs" of institutionalization. The third group, in turn, understands these institutions subjectively insofar as adherence to them is absolutely necessary in private dealings; this group converts the

institutions into means serving as standards for (legal or illegal) action — because these institutions evoke specific expectations in regard to the behavior of others (the "organs" as well as the fellow members of the compulsory or voluntary association). The fourth group, however, and this is the "mass," simply learns to behave according to "traditional" routines that approximate in some way the meaning of the institutions as it is understood on the average; these routines are maintained most often without any knowledge of the purpose or meaning, even of the existence, of the institutions in question.[76]

Weber's levels of initiators, administrators, users, and clients can be mapped onto Kohlberg's moral stages in the following way:

Initiators who freely choose ethical principles (goals, objectives, and so on) to be applied universally, comprehensively, and consistently. (Kohlberg, Stage 6)

Administrators who produce procedural rules aimed at maintaining institutional stability and ensuring consensus. (Kohlberg, Stage 5)

Users whose acts are conformist in that they strive for good behavior through obedience to superiors or seeking the approval of others. (Kohlberg, Stages 3 and 4)

Clients who habitually acquiesce under threat of punishment or reward. (Kohlberg, Stages 1 and 2)

Without quibbling over whether there should be four or six strata of understanding or moral reasoning, it can be seen that the two rankings are quite similar. Kohlberg's research findings may be a partial confirmation of Weber's scheme of stratified meaning. According to Weber, hierarchical organizations shatter and fragment human experience to the extent that the commonality of reason, meaning, and morality is lost. Founded by idealists who aim at certainty and fidelity of transmission, the form requires different patterns of consciousness at different levels of the organization. Purposes and principles abound in the upper reaches, pragmatism and instrumentalism dominate the lower levels. What Kohlberg calls stages are only overdeveloped fragments of moral reasoning produced by the organized restriction of activity. If one's life depends on obedience or the avoidance of obedience, then a primary consideration in any ethical decision is the likely reward or punishment to follow. If one's life depends on exacting the obedience of others, then a primary consideration in any ethical decision is the reasoned justification that makes it incorrigible.

Turn this hierarchy on its side and it becomes an inventory of some elements of moral reasoning (that is, will this action damage one, satisfy one, satisfy others, damage others, promote order, be fair, and be rationally defensible?) Or it can be seen as a description of Dewey's cycle of moral judgment (that is, intuitional judgment results in unmet needs or harm to others, setting off the reflective process of attending to the social configuration of the situation, the projection of ends-in-view, devising of means to those ends, and the testing of the entire structure of judgment and action in practice). Viewed in these ways, no one element of the inventory or moment of the cycle can be justified as superior or more highly developed than any other. The hierarchy of these elements or moments is supplied by the political formula of bureaucracy that "organization must be an embodiment of the endeavor to place the brains over the multitude and subject the multitude to the brains."

Of present institutions and their morality, Ralph Hummel writes:

Hierarchy is an essential part of the control mechanism that turns modern bureaucracy into a power instrument without compare. Bureaucracy's power is unstable unless the use of hierarchy — and its position of absolute dominance over the individual's sense of right and wrong, proper and improper — can be justified.[77]

The moral development of self or of one's fellow citizens unless one is willing to challenge the justification of hierarchy and the stability of bureaucracies. Kant's philosophical idea — that in the moral realm "everybody is a businessman" who cannot escape the precepts of theory or call for the improvement of those precepts on the basis of experience — must be rejected.[78] The mortician role of the social sciences, eager to bury the hopes of democratic and participatory institutions because of the metaphysical faith in the inevitability of hierarchy, must also be rejected. These rejections will make it possible to proceed with the tasks initiated by John Dewey — the development of corrigible valuations and the creation of nonhierarchical organizations.

NOTES

1. Richard Reeves, "The Last Angry Men," *Esquire* 89 (March 1, 1978).

2. Immanuel Kant, *On the Old Saw: That May Be Right in Theory But it Won't Work in Practice* (Philadelphia: University of Pennsylvania Press, 1974), p. 74.

3. David Hume, *A Treatise on Human Nature,* Book 3, Part 1, Section 1, in *Hume's Moral and Political Philosophy,* ed. Henry D. Aiken (New York: Hafner, 1962), p. 42.

4. Ibid., p. 31.

5. Aiken, *Hume's Philosophy,* p. xxxi.

6. John Dewey and James H. Tufts, *Ethics* rev. ed. (New York: Henry Holt, 1932), p. 294.

7. Ibid., p. 297.

8. Martin Weglinsky, "Review of *Obedience to Authority*," *Contemporary Sociology* (January 1975), p. 617.

9. Dewey and Tufts, *Ethics*, p. 312.

10. Eugene Meehan, *The Foundations of Political Analysis* (Homewood, 111.: Dorsey Press, 1971), p. 151.

11. Dewey and Tufts, *Ethics*.

12. Jean Piaget, *The Moral Judgment of the Child* (New York: Collier Books, 1962).

13. Dewey and Tufts, *Ethics*, p. 364.

14. Derek C. Bok, "Can Ethics Be Taught?" *Change* (October 1976), p. 26.

15. Reeves, "Angry Men," p. 41.

16. Bok, "Can Ethics Be Taught?" p. 26.

17. Ernest Keen, *Three Faces of Being: Toward an Existential Clinical Psychology* (New York.: Appleton-Century-Crofts, 1970), p. 331.

18. Roger Brown and Richard J. Herrnstein, *Psychology* (Boston: Little, Brown, 1975), p. 309.

19. Ibid., p. 289.

20. Solomon Asch, *Social Psychology* (Englewood Cliffs, N.J.: Prentice-Hall, 1960).

21. Stanley Milgram, *Obedience to Authority* (New York: Harper & Row, 1974), p. xi.

22. Ibid., p. 133.

23. Ibid., p. 7.

24. Ibid., p. 131.

25. Ibid., p. 132.

26. Ibid., p. 186.

27. C. Haney, C. Banks, and P. Zimbardo, "Interpersonal Dynamics in a Simulated Prison," *International Journal of Criminology and Penology*, 1 (1973): 69–97; "A Study Of Prisoners and Guards in a Simulated Prison," *Naval Research Reviews* (September 1973): 1–17.

28. Philip Zimbardo, "The Psychology of Evil: Or the Perversion of Human Potential," (Springfield, VA.: National Technical Information Service, 1975), Microfiche.

29. Philip Zimbardo, "The Human Choice: Individuation, Reason, and Order versus Deindividuation, Impulse and Chaos," in *Nebraska Symposium on Motivation*, ed. William J. Arnold and David Levine (Lincoln: University of Nebraska Press, 1969), p. 238. See also Philip Zimbardo, ed., *Cognitive Control of Motivation* (New York.: Scott, Foresman, 1969).

30. Zimbardo, "Human Choice," p. 304.

31. Robert Ziller, "Individuation and Socialization: A Theory of Assimilation in Large Organizations," *Human Relations* 17 (November 1964).

32. See N. J. Orlando, "The Mock Ward: A Study in Simulation," in *Behavior Disorders: Perspectives and Trends*, ed. O. Milton and R. G. Wahler (Philadelphia: Lippincott, 1973).

33. David Kipinis, *The Powerholders* (Chicago: University of Chicago Press, 1976), pp. 178–9.

34. Milgram, *Obedience*, p. 188.

35. Weglinsky, "Review of *Obedience*," p. 617.

36. See Lawrence Kohlberg, "From Is to Ought: How to Commit the Naturalistic Fallacy and Get Away with it in the Study of Moral Development," in *Cognitive Development and Epistemology*, ed. Theodor Mischel (New York: Academic Press, 1971).

37. Ibid., p. 155.

38. Ibid., p. 176.

39. Ibid.

40. Ibid., p. 177

41. Ibid., p. 153.

42. Larry D. Spence, *The Politics of Social Knowledge* (University Park: Pa.: Penn State Press, 1978).

43. Jean Piaget, *The Moral Judgment of the Child* (New York: Collier, 1962).

44. See Carole Pateman, *Participation and Democratic Theory* (New York: Cambridge University Press, 1970).

45. Kohlberg, "From Is to Ought".

46. Lawrence Kohlberg, "Development of Moral Character and Moral Ideology," in *Review of Child Development Research*, ed. Martin L. Hoffman and Lois W. Hoffman (New York.: Russell Sage Foundation, 1964), p. 399.

47. For example, see Peter Nokes, "Feedback as an Explanatory Device in the Study of Certain Interpersonal and Institutional Processes," *Human Relations* 14 (1961); Orville G. Brim, "Family Structure and Sex Role Learning by Children: A Further Analysis of Helen Koch's Data," *Sociometry* 21 (1958); or the discussion of this point in Spence, *Politics of Social Knowledge*.

48. Kohlberg, "From Is to Ought."

49. Ibid.

50. Piaget, *Moral Judgment*, p. 402.

51. Kohlberg, "From Is to Ought," p. 192.

52. Ibid.

53. Ibid., p. 211.

54. Ibid., p. 215. A "deontological ethics" is one that does not make the theory of obligation dependent upon a theory of value. Such an ethics is based on the idea that an action can be known to be right despite its motivation and its consequences. See Dagobert D. Runes, ed., *Dictionary of Philosophy* 15th ed. (Paterson, N.J.: Littlefield, Adams, 1964).

55. Kohlberg, "From Is to Ought," p. 230.

56. Ibid., p. 232.

57. Ibid., p. 177.

58. Ibid., p. 220.

59. Ibid., p. 213.

60. Meehan, *Foundations of Political Analysis*, p. 167.

61. Kohlberg, "From Is to Ought," p. 214.

62. Ibid., p. 215.

63. Dewey and Tufts, *Ethics*, p. 312.

64. Ibid.

65. Kohlberg, "From Is to Ought," p. 204.

66. Ibid., p. 218.

67. Ibid., p. 232.

68. Ibid., p. 176.

69. Paul Feyerabend, *Knowledge Without Foundations* (Oberlin: Oberlin College Press, 1961).

70. Floyd H. Alport, *Institutional Behavior* (Chapel Hill, N.C.: University of North Carolina Press, 1933), pp. 198–99.

71. Gitta Sereny, *Into That Darkness: From Mercy Killing to Mass Murder* (New York: McGraw-Hill, 1974), pp. 169–70. See also Rudolf Hoess, *Commandant of Auschwitz* (New York: World, 1959) for similar stories.

72. John Dewey, "From the Public and Its Problems," in *Directions in American Political Thought*, ed. Kenneth Dolbeare (New York: Wiley, 1969), pp. 284, 286.

73. Alport, *Institutional Behavior*, p. 477.

74. Terence Des Pres, *The Survivor: An Anatomy of Life in the Death Camps* (New York: Oxford University Press, 1976), p. 164.

75. Ralph P. Hummel, *The Bureaucratic Experience* (New York: St. Martin's Press, 1977).

76. Max Weber, *Gesammelte Aufsatze zur Wissenschaftslehre,* 3rd ed. (Tubingen: J.C.B. Mohr, 1968), pp. 472–73, trans. Ralph Hummel, pp. 85–86.

77. Hummel, *Bureaucratic Experience,* p. 119.

78. Kant, "On the Old Saw."

9

THE MORAL PSYCHOLOGY OF
WATERGATE AND ITS AFTERMATH

Daniel Candee

Rarely do issues arise that are as tailored for a social scientist studying the role of moral development in politics as was Watergate. Although the torrents of media attention that were lavished on the event have dried up, the principles that relate moral thinking to public action remain uniquely revealed. Furthermore, the point has been reached at which the impact that Watergate had on the broader structures of government and on public attitudes can now be assessed. However, before examining the depth and direction of Watergate-induced changes, it will be useful to examine the moral psychology that contributed to the actual event.

KOHLBERG'S THEORY OF MORAL DEVELOPMENT

By now most psychologists are familiar with the work of Lawrence Kohlberg (1969, 1971).[1] Kohlberg is not primarily concerned with the content of moral choices but with the reasoning or "structure" underlying such choices. By structure is meant the types of considerations a person uses in resolving a moral problem and the principles or logic by which these considerations are tied together. Moral reasoning is measured by presenting people with situations in which conventional values conflict. A typical story involves a husband, Heinz, who must decide whether to steal a drug to save his dying wife, after all reasonable and legal offers have failed. An appeal to conventional folkways cannot resolve this dilemma.

The first portion of this paper was previously published as "The Moral Psychology of Watergate," *Journal of Social Issues*, 1975.

One is taught, "Thou shalt not kill," but one also learns, "Thou shalt not steal." In these types of dilemmas an individual is forced not only to examine his or her reasons for accepting such values, but more importantly, to think about the relationship of life to law in this situation and in general.

By following the responses of the same individuals over a period of years and in several cultures, it has been found that the structure of moral reasoning develops through a series of six stages. The stages are of increasing complexity; each stage builds upon and further expands the reasoning of the stage before. While all persons follow the sequence invariantly (none proceed out of order), few ever achieve full development. Therefore, a cross-section of the population will reveal large numbers of persons at every moral stage.

The first two stages are characteristic of children between 6 and 14 years of age. Here, "right" is not yet separated from "pragmatic." At Stage 1, right is whatever avoids punishment. At Stage 2, it becomes the satisfaction of the needs and desires of oneself and occasionally those of others. Though it might appear that many of the Watergate participants reasoned at these stages, in reality they did not.

By the third stage, typically reached during high school, an individual has differentiated "right" from "practical." However, right and wrong are determined by what one's parents, the community, or any other moral authority deem a "good boy" or "good girl" should do. Psychologically, Stage 3 reasoning is directed at maintaining interpersonal relationships and caters to the emotions of the concerned parties. The problem at Stage 3, though, is that people one would like to make happy often require one to commit conflicting actions. This was the plight of Herbert Porter, an assistant to Jeb Magruder at the Committee to Re-elect the President, as he explained why he told the grand jury that money which had gone to Gordon Liddy to finance the Watergate break-in had actually been given for a "more legitimate" purpose (infiltrating student radical organizations):

Porter: Well, Senator Baker, my loyalty to one man, Richard Nixon, goes back longer than any person that you will see sitting at this table throughout any of these hearings. I first met Mr. Nixon when I was 8 years old in 1946, when he ran for Congress in my home district. . . . I felt I had known this man all my life — not personally, perhaps, but in spirit. I felt a deep sense of loyalty, I was appealed to on this basis.
Baker (in a preceeding question): At any time, did you ever think of saying, I do not think this is quite right? (*Porter:* Yes I did.) What did you do about it? (I did not do anything about it.) Why didn't you?
Porter: In all honesty, probably because of the fear of group pressure that would ensue of not being a team player.[2]

Porter's reasoning forms a consistent structure of conventional morality. At Stage 3 right is determined by group norms. It is not surprising, therefore, that Porter is positively appealed to on the basis of favors established by his reference group (the Nixon campaign), and negatively by the fear of sanction by that group. Unfortunately for Porter, besides being less than fully moral, decisions based on loyalty are not always even practical. When Porter's name was mentioned to the former president on one of his infamous tapes, Nixon responded, "Who?"

The progression to Stage 4 is marked by the awareness that individual relationships are part of a larger society. Roles become structured with definite duties and privileges. The overriding concern in Stage 4 is to maintain a system that allows the society to function smoothly and avoids chaos. Such a system need not be conventional society. It may be one's ideal system, a humanistic, religious, or communal one. But if the system itself is seen as more basic than the rights of its individual members, it is being viewed from a Stage 4 perspective.

A classic instance of such reasoning seems to have motivated former Plumber's chief, Egil Krogh, to have authorized the break-in at the office of Dr. Fielding, Daniel Ellsberg's psychiatrist. Recalling his reasoning at the time, Krogh reflects,

> I see now that the key is the effect that the term "national security" had on my judgment. The very words served to block my critical analysis. . . . to suggest that national security was being improperly invoked was to invite a confrontation with patriotism and loyalty and so appeared to be beyond the scope and in contravention of the faithful performance of the duties of my office. . . . the very definition of national security was for the President to pursue his planned course.[3]

As Krogh saw it, his primary duty was to fulfill the requirements of his role, not to insure human rights. The requirements, which he viewed as maintaining the nation, really meant maintaining the president.

Compared to earlier stages, Stage 4 reasoning has a sophisticated view of the law, but it is not wholly adequate; inherent contradictions remain. Since Stage 4 reasoning does not inquire into the basis of law, it has difficulty handling situations where two reasonable conceptions of the law conflict. This shortcoming seems to have lead Jeb Magruder to mistake the reelection of the president for a moral emergency. In explaining his role in the Watergate cover-up, Magruder states,

> During the whole time [that] we were in the White House . . . we were directly employed with trying to succeed with the President's policies. We saw continuing violations of the law done by men like William Sloane Coffin.

He tells me my ethics are bad. Yet he was indicted for criminal charges. He recommended on the Washington Monument grounds that students burn their draft cards and that we have mass demonstrations, shut down the city of Washington. . . .

So consequently, when these subjects came up although I was aware they were illegal we had become somewhat inured to using some activities that would help us in accomplishing what we thought was a cause, a legitimate goal. Now, that is absolutely incorrect: two wrongs do not make a right.[4]

Magruder's fatal flaw was that he did not realize that violations of the law are of different kinds. Coffin's infraction was committed openly, in the belief that it was a crucial and direct link in the saving of lives in Vietnam. Magruder's action was covert and was not necessitated by a concern for human rights. As in the case of former President Ford, who justified the pardon of Richard Nixon because it was tendered out of conscience, Magruder justified his perjury, at least at the time, because it was done for a cause he believed in. The problem, which is left largely unresolved at Stage 4, is how to determine when one's conscience is right or when the cause one believes in is just.

The solution to this problem, which is accomplished at Stages 5 and 6, requires that one see morality not as a tool for maintaining society but as a reflection of the very reasons societies exist. While Stage 4 achieves the awareness of a social system, Stages 5 and 6 proceed to ask, "What is the moral validity of that system?" The response to both of these issues, at the higher stages, is in terms of the features all human beings desire to maximize, their physical life and their liberty. Liberty, the ability to make one's own decisions and to pursue one's inclinations necessarily includes the freedoms of speech, assembly, and action. From the moral viewpoint such rights are basic to human beings and exist prior to societies. As a procedural matter these rights must be adjusted when they conflict with the equally valid assertion of such rights by another. However, any action that purports to support a law or maintain a system at the expense of individual rights would be logically, and thus morally, incorrect, since the very legitimacy of the system is the maximization of such rights.

No Stage 5 reasoning could be found among the Watergate participants. However, as seen in the following statement by former Special Prosecutor Archibald Cox, it lay at the very crux of their most sophisticated critics.

If man is by nature a social being — if we are destined to live and work together — if our goal is the freedom of each to choose the best he can discern — if we seek to do what we can to move toward the realization of these beliefs, then the rights of speech, privacy, dignity and other fundamental liberties of other men such as the Bill of Rights declares, must be respected by both government and private persons.[5]

EMPIRICAL SUPPORT

If conventional moral reasoning led the Watergate characters to err, at least they were not alone. In a survey of 370 people (predominantly college students drawn from a variety of New England and midwestern campuses) the motives that influenced the reasoning of the Watergate participants were found to affect the reasoning of private citizens as well. Persons who had been given the Moral Judgment Interview were asked to decide some of the same dilemmas that confronted the participants. In every instance where one alternative more clearly followed from the principles of a democracy, the percentage of persons endorsing that alternative was greater for those at Stage 5 than for those at Stage 3 or Stage 4.

The results for a number of questions are presented in Table 9.1. While these results are more fully reported elsewhere[6] comments will be made on some of them here. The first question in Table 9.1 asks "Should the Watergate defendants have been allowed to conduct a public campaign to raise funds for their defense?" This is, of course, a right well established in a democracy. Accordingly, nearly all persons who reasoned at Stage 5, despite their candidate preference, chose to allow the defense fund — 89 percent of those who had voted for McGovern in the 1972 election, and 80 percent of the Nixon supporters. In contrast, roughly 50 percent of both Nixon and McGovern voters at Stage 4 and only 35 percent at Stage 3 favored the defense fund. In their zeal to condemn the Watergate participants, many Stage 3 and 4 subjects denied them the very rights the participants had denied to others.

Question 2, focusing on the conflict of Jeb Magruder who had to choose between due process and the overt obligations of his job, was phrased as follows:

> Jeb Magruder was one of the top officers in the Committee to Re-elect the President. After the Watergate break-in had occurred Magruder was faced with a conflict. On one hand, as an officer of the Committee to Re-elect, he had a duty to see that Nixon was not embarrassed nor his chances for re-election hurt. On the other hand, he thought of telling the truth. Assuming that Magruder thought the break-in could be successfully covered up what should he have done? (a) Admitted the burglars had been hired by the Committee to Re-elect, (b) Tried to cover it up, assuming that it would have worked, (c) At the time there was no clear answer.

Again the expected pattern was found. The proportion of persons who believed that Jeb Magruder should have admitted his association with the

TABLE 9.1

Distribution of Watergate Responses by Moral Development Stage and Candidate Preference
(percent of subjects responding)

	McGovern			Nixon		
	3	4	5	3	4	5
Moral Stage:[a]	(92)	(62)	(50)	(79)	(31)	(11)
1. Should the Watergate defendants have been allowed to conduct a public campaign to raise money for their defense?						
Yes	34	55	89	36	48	80
2. Should Magruder have admitted the burglars were hired by CREP or covered up?[b]						
Admitted	54	89	96	52	56	81
3. Herbert Kalmbach asked his superior, "Is this a proper assignment and am I to go through with it?" He was told it was. If it later turns out that Kalmbach was collecting hush money would you consider him responsible?[b]						
Yes	31	44	66	20	12	45
4. If impeachment alone were held today, based on what you know at this time would you be for or against impeachment?						
For	86	96	97	40	64	100
5. If the President were already impeached and a vote were held today on removing him from office would you be for or against removal?						
For	91	94	97	24	46	83

Note: Figures in parentheses indicate number of respondents. The number of respondents may vary from question to question due to subject omissions, don't-know answers, and the like.

[a] Determined by highest stage for which subject had 25 percent or more of his/her responses. Stages 1, 2, and 6 are eliminated from this table because of their infrequency.

[b] The wording of the question has been shortened for presentation here. Actual questionnaires are available from the author.

Source: Adapted from Daniel Candee, "Structure and Choice in Moral Reasoning, *Journal of Personality and Social Psychology* 34 (1976).

Watergate burglars increases monotonically with moral stage.

There is, however, another interesting feature of the Magruder results. For Stage 3 subjects there was virtually no difference in their support of criticism due to candidate preference. Among Stage 4 subjects, however, the difference was considerable. Only 56 percent of Stage 4 Nixon supporters considered Magruder wrong, compared to a full 89 percent of Stage 4 McGovernites. It is not surprising that while moral development sets broad limits on one's political evaluation, an individual will always judge esteemed causes as favorably as possible within those limits.

A similar pattern emerges in the case of Nixon's personal lawyer, Herbert Kalmbach (Question 3). Kalmbach was asked by John Erlichman to raise what later turned out to be "hush money" for the burglars. While Kalmbach may truly have been misled, there is still the question of whether he took reasonable precautions.

For Stage 3 subjects the issue was relatively clear. Kalmbach did what any good subordinate would do; he asked his superior. Since his superior told him the assignment was proper, Kalmbach is free of responsibility. Stage 4 subjects, however, were more concerned with whether Kalmbach's behavior was precise enough to meet the requirements of his role, though the definition of these requirements varies. Therefore, the disagreement between Stage 4 McGovernites and Nixonites is considerable.

Unlike Stage 3 and 4 subjects who tend to see any action of a legitimate authority as itself legitimate, Stage 5 persons are able to evaluate the action directly. From the viewpoint of Stage 5, advisors can be used to supply one with information but cannot themselves pass final judgment on the propriety of an action. Thus, Kalmbach's question, "Is this a *proper* assignment?" was insufficient to relieve him of responsibility. What he should have done was to ask directly, "What is this money going to be used for?" and make his own decision as to its propriety. In contrast to the lower stages, 66 percent of the McGovern voters and 45 percent of the Nixon supporters at Stage 5 believed that Kalmbach was responsible.

The final question to be discussed here involves the issue of impeachment (Questions 4 and 5). Understandably, nearly all subjects who voted for McGovern in 1972 favored both Nixon's impeachment and removal. However, among subjects who voted for Nixon, those at Stage 5 were significantly more favorable to the idea of impeachment and removal than were their Stage 3 counterparts. Stage 5 subjects seem to have been more willing to hold Nixon accountable for the admittedly suspicious evidence that had emerged before and during the course of this study (November 1973–May 1974). Stage 3 subjects may have been sufficiently awed by the office of the presidency or desirous of believing in Nixon's good motives to oppose impeachment. Naturally, the percentages of Nixon voters who favored removal were below those for impeachment, since many persons looked upon a Senate trial as a means of exoneration. However, the pattern by moral stage remains constant.

INTERPRETATION OF DATA

A major issue that appears in the thinking of both the participants and the public is the distinction, in a democracy, between the areas that allow for diversity and those that should be absolute. An area that should be absolute is the protection of fundamental rights — above all, the rights to life and liberty. The maximization of these rights is the very legitimation of society, the reason that society is an improvement over what Thomas Hobbes called "the state of nature." On the other hand, areas where diversity can exist concern such policy matters as government intervention versus laissez faire, a loose versus strict interpretation of the Constitution, and a centralized versus decentralized government.

The central confusion of the Watergate participants was that in their effort to advance issues of the relative kind, that is, their own conservative policies, they violated rights that were absolute. In discussing the testimony of several Watergate participants it was noted that their reasoning seemed to be at Stages 3 and 4. At these stages the concept of rights takes on no special significance. At Stage 3 rights are seen as behavior which, if followed, will win social approval. At Stage 4 rights are seen as important to a system but not the very basis of it. It is understandable, at these stages, that in competition with other good motives such as "loyalty to a man" (Porter), "being a team player" (Porter), or "service to one's country" (Hunt), the concept of rights may not fare well.

The reason these other motives are powerful enough to compete with the concept of rights, at Stages 3 and 4, is that, in themselves, they refer to virtues. All other things being equal, loyalty, for example, has the beneficent quality of teaching one to keep commitments and creates bonds of trust. Thus, given the goals of getting Nixon elected and furthering his policies, the Watergate participants could feel that they were achieving these goals by means that had some degree of morality to recommend them. However, they were also aware that the moral issue was not unequivocal. That is why Porter could agree that he "did not think things were quite right," but at the same time could lie out of a sense of loyalty. What Porter probably saw was a conflict between truth and loyalty, both of which had considerable weight. Given such a finely balanced choice, the pressures of the Nixon team to "win at all costs," probably tipped the scale.

The explanation of Watergate set out here is that the participants were enthusiastic but essentially ordinary people who responded to the pressures of the campaign with decisions that from a Stage 3 or 4 point of view seemed right or at least permissible. This view also explains how men, who in other areas of their lives acted with such probity, could perform actions that from the perspective of Stage 5 were unethical. In short, the Watergate actors seem to have been morally confused rather than morally malicious. Watergate was not a case of simple political graft. Unlike most political scandals, there was little personal reward to the participants.

EFFECTS OF WATERGATE

What has been the effect, particularly the moral effect, of the Watergate affair? Four outcomes seem most important. First, Watergate had a profound and generally spiritualizing effect on those who participated in it. Second, it led directly to legal and structural changes in the governmental system. Third, while Watergate may have ultimately provided renewed faith in the institutions of government, it led, at least in the short run, to a decrease in confidence in the leaders who head those institutions. Fourth, the public mood set by Watergate was instrumental in the election of Jimmy Carter. Carter, in turn, produced a foreign policy that differed markedly from his immediate predecessor's in its strong emphasis on human rights.

Moral Growth

The first outcome, the spiritualizing of former Nixon aides Colson and Magruder, and the dedication to antipoverty work of John Erlichman may, if accepted as sincere, seem puzzling. However, such events serve only to underscore the fact that Watergate was a crime of misplaced morality, not maliciousness. Many of the Watergate participants believed they were carrying out a righteous cause, a crusade. Since Watergate itself always had a peculiar moral basis, it is understandable that those who were destroyed by it should take moral or spiritual solace.

In the case of at least one of the participants the event was a catalyst for structural moral growth. For Krogh, participation in Watergate seems to have spurred development from maintaining a system of presidential prerogative (Stage 4) to evaluating the moral basis of a democracy (Stage 5). Compare Krogh's statement, cited earlier, in which he defined national security as allowing the President to pursue his personal course, with the following reflections delivered as he was being sentenced for directing the break-in at the office of Ellsberg's psychiatrist:

> But however national security is defined, I now see that none of the potential uses of the sought information could justify the invasion of the rights of the individuals that the break-in necessitated. The understanding I have come to is that *these rights are the definition of our nation.* . . . (emphasis added)
>
> I hope they [young men and women who are fortunate enough to have an opportunity to serve in government] will recognize that the banner of national security can turn perceived patriotism into actual disservice. When contemplating a course of action, I hope they will never fail to ask, "Is this right?"[7]

Have the American people as a whole gone through any such moral growth? Nearly everyone who followed Watergate was probably stimulated, to some degree, to ponder the contradictory testimony and inconsistent definitions of "right" that were given by the Watergate participants. To the extent that this situation left people with a somewhat more sophisticated view of the government, Watergate was a valuable national experience. However, although there are no data, theory and other research would suggest that few persons experienced the profound structural change in thinking that seemed to take place in Krogh. While many persons may have become more aware of governmental irregularities, few probably used their knowledge of these irregularities to gain new insight into the principles by which the entire sociomoral world should be governed. Moral stages are, by their very nature, the most basic and hence most slowly mutable structures in a person's sociomoral thinking. Experience with moral education in secondary schools and colleges indicates that students who participate in structured moral discussions weekly for 26 weeks advance an average of one quarter of a stage. Thus, it is unlikely that there would be many instances of significant growth among the many persons who followed Watergate vicariously. Structural growth is most likely to have occurred among those who paid the closest attention to Watergate and who thought, in the most coherent manner, about the basic issues of government that it raised.

Public Attitudes

While one would not expect to find evidence of great structural change on the basis of Watergate, many instances of content change would certainly be expected. There should have been a greater public awareness of moral issues in government, at least a temporary loss of confidence in political leaders, and a call for reforms in governmental operations. Indeed, this is exactly what is found.

The interpretation of any specific attitude change in the post-Watergate and post-Vietnam era must be seen in the light of the dominant trends in attitude change, generally, during these years. The direction of public thought since 1972 has been toward a greater concern for success in one's individual life, a reaction against big government, and a greater concern with local rather than national or international issues. Even before Watergate the massive protests against so public and so omnipresent an issue as Vietnam had disappeared from the scene. Gone also was the challenging rhetoric that extended the subject of the Vietnam War into a more rudimentary analysis of the American political system. Watergate, which for most people was a spectator event, marked a transition between an active involvement with national issues that characterized the Vietnam era and the relative lack of involvement with national issues seen today.

Evidence of the shift in public opinion toward a concern with self and with local issues can be seen in a Harris survey of April 1977[8] The three activities most frequently engaged in by a representative sample of Americans (selected from a list of activities embracing various values) were "seeking out those experiences that make you feel peaceful inside" (89 percent); "wanting to experience life directly rather than observe it through television" (86 percent); and "wanting to test your own creative abilities" (84 percent). Other items that received substantial endorsement were "like to participate in community decisions that affect your life" (73 percent); "like individual experiences better than group experiences" (69 percent); and "feel that 'bigness' in almost anything leads to trouble for individuals who can't stand up to it" (60 percent). Thus, the public mood after Vietnam and Watergate was not one of inaction, but rather of personal, local, and directly controllable action.

This general background of values is reflected in specific attitudes toward government and national institutions. The Harris poll of March 1976[9] revealed that the mean percentage of persons having "a great deal of confidence" in the leaders of each of 11 major U.S. institutions fell steadily in the decade from 1966 to 1976. For example, the percentage of persons expressing a great deal of confidence in the leaders of the federal executive branch fell from 41 percent in 1966 to 28 percent in 1974 and to only 11 percent in 1976. Congress fared even worse, ranking last among the 11 institutions covered. However, the decline in leadership confidence was not limited to the national government alone. Although the leaders in medicine enjoyed the greatest degree of confidence at every time period, trust in them eroded too, falling from 73 percent in 1966 to 42 percent in 1976. Of particular interest to academics may be the fact that confidence in university educators ranked second, enjoying a 61 percent rating in 1966, though only a 31 percent score in 1976. Interestingly, the only group that did not suffer a loss of confidence over this time was television newspersons, and, to a lesser degree, the press. This is no doubt due to the fact that the news media were credited, in the public's view, with having exposed both Watergate and Vietnam.

While the erosion of confidence was severe, there is evidence that it has begun to be reversed. Comparable Harris poll data for 1977 shows an increase in public confidence in nearly every national institution. The greatest beneficiary of this trend is the presidency, where the proportion of persons expressing a "great deal of confidence" rose from 11 percent in 1976 to 31 percent in 1977.[10]

Although the mood of Americans in the immediate aftermath of Watergate was one of disinterest in national government, the public did hold quite definite opinions concerning the direction that government would have to take in order to regain its trust. As expected, the role of political morality was central. This can be seen in three areas: the qualities desired in a new president, the priorities for Congress, and the priorities for the White House. As evidenced by the recent upswing in confidence, many of these actions have been taken.

The qualities desired in a new president are revealed by a mid-continent survey of 1,000 Minnesota adults taken several months before the 1976 election.[11] There honesty was found to be the trait overwhelmingly deemed most important for the next president to possess. Sixty-one percent of the sample mentioned honesty first, followed by interest in the well-being of people (9 percent), integrity (7 percent), intelligence (3 percent), leadership (3 percent), courage, God-fearingness, and experience (all 2 percent). The prominence of moral issues is also seen in the priorities for the new Congress. A Harris poll in August 1976 found the most important issue facing the new Congress to be "clean up corruption in government" (cited by 88 percent of the sample as "very important") followed by "listen to the people more" (83 percent) and "show trust in people more" (79 percent).[12] Turning to priority items for the next president (Harris Survey, March 1976) it is found that while "fighting inflation" headed the list (cited as a major concern by 94 percent of the sample), "restoring confidence in government" was tied for second (88 percent) and "restoring integrity to government" ranked seventh (84 percent) out of 30 items.[13]

Next, in the light of the specific values and attitudes that emerged in the aftermath of Watergate, this discussion will examine the governmental changes that were made and the kind of leadership that was elected.

Legislation

The first national election following President Nixon's resignation in 1974 saw the greatest number of insurgent liberal Democrats sent to Congress since the New Deal. Thus, one immediate political outcome probably attributable to Watergate was the demise of those legislators most associated in the public mind with the manifestations of improper government, namely incumbents and Republicans.*

The first order of business undertaken by the post-Watergate 94th Congress (particularly by the House of Representatives) was the passage of legislation that substantially reformed the committee system and congressional proceedings. While support for such reforms had been building over the previous six years, it was catalyzed by Watergate. The need to regain the public's lost confidence in government and the liberal ideology of those elected in 1974, both direct outgrowths of Watergate, combined to insure that the historic revisions would take place. In the House, reform included transferring the power of making committee assignments within the Democratic party from the Democratic members of the Ways and Means Committee to those on the Steering and Policy Committee. Furthermore, all committee chairpersons became subject to automatic election by the entire Democratic caucus, a provision that resulted in the deposition of several senior chairmen for only the second time since 1925.[14]

In the area of campaign practices, reform included the public financing of federal elections, limitations on the amount of private contributions allowed, and the public disclosure of the names of substantial contributors. New codes of ethics were passed by both houses of Congress which limit a congressperson's external income, require almost complete disclosure of personal assets, and curtail abuses of the franking privilege. The passage of a list of specific prohibitions distinguishes these codes from previous loosely worded ones. In the area of surveillance, post-Watergate legislation was marked by the creation in the Senate of a permanent select committee empowered to monitor activities of the CIA and to share monitoring duties for the FBI and the Defense Department. The creation of this committee followed revelations by a Senate investigating panel of CIA payments,

---

*Whether the liberal wing of the Democratic party will be able to retain its unusually high representation into the 1980s remains to be seen. Adverse trends are suggested by the steady climb in the plurality of voters who consider themselves conservative (though favoring most traditional liberal legislation), in the slightly less liberal voting record of freshmen congresspersons in the second session of the 94th Congress compared with the first (see *Congressional Quarterly*, November 20, 1976, p. 3206), and in the net replacement of several liberal senators with conservatives in the national election of 1978.

wiretaps, and assassination plots — all activities that were also practiced by the Watergate perpetrators.

The direct influence of the public's mood in bringing about these reforms can be seen in Senate Majority Leader Byrd's remark that it was "absurd that the Senate has to demean itself by enacting a code of conduct, but in a climate of public distrust it is a necessity."[15] The need to present a clean ethical face was no doubt instrumental in the House's reprimand of Congressman Robert Sikes (D-Fla.) and in the forced resignation of House Administration Committee Chairman Wayne Hays (D-Ohio). Sikes had been accused of sponsoring legislation in Congress to remove restrictions on land he owned in Florida, while Hays was charged with retaining a mistress on the government payroll. The Sikes reprimand was the first instance since 1969 of a House vote to punish one of its members.

The lasting effect of the congressional legislation, as well as similar actions in state legislatures and the revision of ethical codes in many professional organizations, was to reduce the types of situational pressures that had pushed the Watergate participants to commit crimes. Since the moral reasoning of most individuals is such that it looks to conventions to determine right and wrong (Stages 3 and 4), the most direct way of insuring right action is to make right action the norm. Indeed, an important function of laws in a democracy is to reduce the need for each individual to reconstruct the ethical basis for every community-affecting action in his or her own mind before it is undertaken. If a particular law is consistent with principled thinking, then it will encourage people to behave in the manner they would have deemed right if they themselves had constructed an analysis of the situation from a principled (Stage 5 or 6) perspective. In this way the reforms of Watergate will continue to affect the conduct of government officials long after the public's heightened awareness of ethical issues has worn off.

Presidential Reasoning

In the area of presidential politics the ultimate resolution of the moral crisis that was Watergate was the election of a self-professed moralist. Three themes in Jimmy Carter's philosophy — morality, humility, and human rights — are evident in both his inaugural address and in his later speeches. All three themes represent direct reversals of the philosophy that characterized the Watergate-plagued Nixon administration.

The theme of morality appears several times in President Carter's inaugural address, including his reference to "the special obligation to take on those moral duties" which the definition of our nation in terms of spirituality and human liberty bring.[16] President Nixon's administration was essentially pragmatic and nonmoral, a philosophy conducive to the expansion of presidential powers. In comparison, President Carter's awareness of moral boundaries may, in a limited way, have been one cause of his using such powers, at least during the first 18 months.

The second theme, humility, is nowhere better expressed than in Carter's inaugural admonition to the American people: "Your strength can compensate for my weakness, and your wisdom can help to minimize my mistakes." That statement stands in stark contrast to the doctrine of presidential omnipotence that characterized the Nixon administration.

Third, perhaps no theme has become more identified with Carter than has been the theme of international human rights. Presidents Kennedy and Johnson both devoted much energy to the issue of domestic civil rights (for example, voter registration, nondiscrimination in hiring, and so on), but no president since Woodrow Wilson has ventured to try to impose the protection of human rights (for example, freedom of speech, freedom of travel, and freedom from political repression) on the internal affairs of other countries. Indeed, Carter's early foreign policy was geared to reward those who respected human rights and to punish those who violated them. While the policy was sometimes only a temporary obstacle to aid (all South American countries that were originally denied aid were later able to work out arrangements), and was sometimes even detrimental to long-range foreign policy goals (it seems to have slowed detente with the Soviet Union), it is also credited with some success. There is considerable sentiment for the position that Carter's human rights policy was instrumental in the Soviet Union's lenient treatment of dissident Alexander Sakharov and in Chile's decision to free scores of political prisoners. Furthermore, unlike that of previous presidents, Carter's criticism was not limited to adversaries of the United States. In March 1978, more than a year after his inauguration, Carter completed his meeting with leaders in Brasilia by issuing a separate communique in which he criticized the human rights record of the present Brazilian government. However, unlike the early Carter, the now-veteran president also indicated that his condemnation of the Brazilian record would not be allowed to prevent the expansion of trade between the United States and its South American neighbor.[17]

While Carter's philosophy is clearly one to which morality is central in content, what are the structures or principles of his thought? Are moral values simply replacements for the Nixon administration's emphasis on loyalty and patriotism, or are they embedded in a more developed conception of the sociomoral world?

The moral reasoning of Richard Nixon was basically Stage 4. Although a manipulative and suspicious person by nature, he nevertheless sought to justify his many usurpations of political power by appealing to the Stage 4 principle of "system maintenance." Nixon's claim was that without the privilege of surreptitious tapes and private communications the "office of the presidency" would not be able to survive.

In contrast to Nixon who was constantly forced to use his limited understanding of democratic principles as a defense, Carter truly seems to use the principles of democracy as a guide. The first paragraph of his inaugural speech contains the following quote which Carter attributes to his former high school teacher, "We must adjust to changing times and still hold to unchanging *principles*" (italics added). Carter's decision to begin his speech by distinguishing principles (which are permanent) from customs (which are "changing times") suggests one element of Stage 5 thought. In the slightly extended version of his inaugural address that was prepared for overseas viewing, Carter stated, "We cannot guarantee the basic right of every human being to be free of poverty and hunger and disease and political repression. We can and will cooperate with others in combating these enemies of mankind."[18] This statement suggests that he may see human rights as existing prior to society, and indeed forming a standard toward which democratic institutions should strive. These represent two additional characteristics of Stage 5 thought.

However, on the basis of Carter's three major documents (the Inaugural Address, the Address to People of Other Nations, and the Address to the United Nations), his moral reasoning cannot definitely be placed at Stage 5. The difficulty is that politicians in their public remarks are not prone to elaborating the bases upon which their statements are made. Thus, it is not clear *why* Carter considers freedom from poverty, hunger, disease, and repression to be basic rights. It is not clear *why* he believes that principles should be the cornerstone of a foreign policy. Such probing questions would have to be asked before one could categorize Carter's thinking with the certainty with which a well-conducted personal interview is classified.*

For this reason, it is possible that Carter's lack of a clear statement justifying why human rights should take precedence over political expediency stems from his failure to understand the logical priority of rights. From the structural point of view, Carter's moral content may merely define a system that is no more cognitively developed than was the essen-

---

*The problem of elaboration was not, of course, as great in the earlier analysis of the reasoning of those who participated in Watergate. In that case, the principal parties were asked to publicly defend, that is, create their best argument for, behavior that was manifestly questionable. The Watergate situation was, therefore, more akin to the standard test stories in which a respondent is asked to defend one or the other choice of action in a moral dilemma. Ultimate justifications are more readily given under those circumstances than in the case of presidential addresses.

tially nonmoral system of Nixon. Occasionally presidents are given the opportunity to prove the depth of their conceptions by creating political structures that define new sets of relations between people. Wilson's League of Nations is a paramount example. However, Carter has neither created nor been handed this opportunity. Thus, on the evidence now available, we must classify the moral reasoning of Carter as a mixture of Stages 5 and 4.

CONCLUSION

Where is the nation likely to go from here? The dangers of excess that were exposed by both Watergate and Vietnam have curtailed America's role as the military policeman of the world. Whether the United States will have any greater success in being the moral policeman of the world remains to be seen. At the presidential level, the election of a chief executive who displays a greater degree of Stage 5 (principled) thinking than either of his predecessors, and who is conscious of the moral limitations of his office, should prevent, at least for the present, a brush with tyranny such as was experienced during the Nixon years. On the wider governmental front, the structural changes that resulted from post-Watergate legislation will probably outlive the public's immediate interest in ethical concerns. The permanent effect of making open government, public financing of campaigns, and surveillance of intelligence-gathering agencies the law will be to establish a new standard of what citizens can expect from government and of what politicians can be expected to deliver. While governmental behavior may not fully match these new expectations, it will not remain too far behind.

NOTES

1. Lawrence Kohlberg, "Stage and Sequence: The Cognitive-Developmental Approach to Socialization," in *Handbook of Socialization Theory and Research,* ed. D. Goslin (Chicago: Rand-McNally, 1969); and "Indoctrination Versus Relativity in Value Education," *Zygon* 6 (1971): 285–310. The goal of this article is to demonstrate how Kohlberg's theory of moral development aids in the explanation of a political event. Other chapters in this volume more critically examine Kohlberg's theory itself.
2. *The Watergate Hearings* (New York: Viking, 1973), p. 227.
3. Text of Krogh's statement about his role in the Plumbers' break-in at the office of Ellsberg's psychiatrist, New York *Times,* January 25, 1974, p. 16.
4. *Watergate Hearings,* p. 258.
5. Archibald Cox, "Ends," New York *Times Magazine,* May 19, 1974.

6. For a complete statement of 20 questions regarding both Watergate and the case of Lt. Calley, see Daniel Candee, "Structure and Choice in Moral Reasoning," *Journal of Personality and Social Psychology* 34 (1976): 1293–1301. In'that study, significant correlations between stage of moral reasoning and theoretically predicted content choices were found for 17 of the 20 questions.

7. Text of Krogh's statement, p. 16.

8. Harris Survey, April 1977, reported in *Current Opinion* 5 (1977): 105.

9. Harris Survey, March 1976, reported in *Current Opinion* 4 (1976): 42.

10. Harris Survey, February 1977, reported in *Current Opinion* 5 (1977): 37. (See also Yankelovich, Skelly and White, Survey, March 1977, reported in *Facts on File,* April 9, 1977, p. 251.)

11. Mid-Continent Survey, 1976, reported in *Current Opinion* 4 (1976): 108.

12. Harris Survey, August 1976, reprinted in *Current Opinion* 4 (1976): 128.

13. Harris Survey, March 1976, p. 43.

14. *Congressional Quarterly,* April 2, 1977, p. 591.

15. *Facts on File,* April 9, 1977, p. 251.

16. President Carter, Inaugural Address, January 20, 1977.

17. New York *Times,* March 31, 1978.

18. President Carter, Address to People of Other Nations, January 20, 1977.

10

THE RIGHT TO PRIVACY: AN ISSUE IN MORAL DEVELOPMENT

Julie Zatz

One of the most pressing ethical dilemmas of contemporary society is whether to use the law as a vehicle for moral development. While the law is generally regarded as providing a process for settling disputes and regulating human conduct, there is little agreement over the kinds of issues that ought to be submitted to that process. Historically, there has been a wide array of opinion regarding the moral developmental potentialities of law. Political thinkers such as Augustine and Thomas Hobbes regarded law as an instrument of social control in a world of malevolent and morally underdeveloped individuals. Others such as Jeremy Bentham believed that law could promote social harmony and personal development by enabling individuals to make informed decisions about the probable consequences of their actions. While John Locke, John Stuart Mill, and Thomas Jefferson felt that collective well-being and individual self-development were best assured by minimizing legal restriction of human conduct, others such as Plato claimed that these ends could be achieved only through the legal enforcement of particular moral norms.

Law has a role to play in the moral developmental process in the sense that its function is to secure the fullest possible conditions for the exercise of personal freedom. Such freedom is an essential part of the process whereby persons acquire a facility for the kind of independent principled thought characterizing the highest levels of moral maturity. According to Lawrence Kohlberg, a critical element in the developmental task of learn-

Most of this article was written prior to the author's joining the staff of the National Academy of Sciences. The National Academy of Sciences, the National Research Council, and the Committee on Child Development Research and Public Policy are not responsible for any part of what is presented here.

ing to function independently is the maintenance of social conditions hospitable to the evolution of capacities for individuation, self-respect, and interpersonal growth.[1] In this discussion it will be argued that the Kohlbergian theory of moral development implicitly presupposes the need for personal privacy in facilitating the social interaction necessary for higher levels of self-development. To the extent that this argument is valid, it can also be argued that the legal repression of certain kinds of personal behavior may impair the process of moral development and in so doing obstruct the attainment of one of its most important goals: an ethical orientation toward others based on a principle of respect for the dignity of human beings as differentiated persons.[2] It is this ethical orientation that is also at the core of what is meant throughout by "the right to privacy"*

The principle of respect for persons characterizes the most highly sophisticated levels of moral judgment described by Kohlberg in his stage theory of moral development.[3] According to Kohlberg, there are several stages of moral development through which one consecutively passes, gradually acquiring the capacity to assess situations objectively and to perceive oneself in the position of others. By taking roles moral situational dilemmas are continuously confronted and resolved and this in turn progressively converts perceptions of rules from external authoritarian commands to internal ethical principles.

A highly developed cognitive orientation is contingent upon the availability of opportunities to foster critical analytical capacities for measuring one's own standards of conduct against the requirements of law. In the process of moral development law begins to be perceived as an instrument of social change rather than as a set of rules that preserves the status quo and has the character of natural necessity. Eventually conduct is conditioned by an internalized system of independent personal values with which one complies in order to avoid self-condemnation.[4] The core of this value system is the principle of respect for persons; the behavioral observance of this principle is a manifestation of the achievement of a mature and morally principled cognitive orientation.

---

*For the purposes of this study, the right to privacy is characterized as a set of claims that specifically rely upon arguments about respect for persons. While the fledgling privacy literature is rich in efforts to define the right to privacy in idiosyncratic operational terms, there is a prior need to develop an adequate conceptual framework for accommodating the many substantively diverse claims to privacy being raised today. Such claims range from the desire to protect one's sexual life-style from public inquiry to the desire to maintain control over the collection, use, and dissemination of personal information. Nevertheless, implicit in this study is the assumption that the arguments that sustain various contemporary claims to privacy all depend upon the premise that persons should be treated in ways that are consistent with recognition and respect for human dignity.

There are some fundamental underlying assumptions about human nature contained in Kohlberg's theory, which support the link between the principle of respect for persons and the moral development process. The principle of respect for persons stipulates that "every human being in so far as he is a person, is entitled to [a] minimal degree of consideration."[5] This contention is predicated on the supposition that there are ways of treating persons that are fundamentally inconsistent with a recognition of their human dignity. According to one analyst, the Kohlbergian scheme of moral development presupposes that: "(1) [people] ought to be autonomous (i.e., not controlled by fear or intimidation but enjoying independent participation); (2) men ought to treat each other with respect and dignity; (3) men are capable of rationality; (4) justice should be based on the equality of reciprocity between individuals; [and] (5) human beings can learn generalizable principles as well as specific behaviors."[6]

It is argued here that privacy contributes to moral development. Privacy affords opportunities for confronting the kinds of situational dilemmas and exercising the type of independent personal judgment that lead to the fostering of a mature morality. Contemporary claims to privacy rely upon arguments about the importance of respect for persons and typically raise questions about the justifiable limits of social control posed by the legal enforcement of morality. Such claims to privacy include those of women choosing to have an abortion, those of individuals seeking to protect their sexual life-style from public scrutiny, and those of the terminally ill wishing to die with dignity.[7] Because the legal enforcement of morality aims at producing social conformity rather than preserving individual autonomy, it is maintained that it circumscribes personal opportunities to act in ways that do not hurt others. The protection of such opportunities is implied by the right to privacy, for as further discussion will show, it is principally by means of increasing occasions for self-determination, particularly in matters of purely personal concern, that privacy is fully recognized. Therefore, following from this logic, to the extent that the legal enforcement of morality disregards one's privacy and hence one's human dignity, it also impairs the process of moral development. Indeed, this is what makes the case for the right to privacy such an important issue in moral development.

The discussion begins by examining the nature of the concept of privacy, indicating some of the major purposes served by a commitment to it. From this basis for understanding the function of privacy, the next step is to consider how the recognition of claims to privacy enhances moral development. Claims to privacy raise significant questions concerning the appropriate balance between individual freedom and societal constraint. According to the principle of respect for persons, the presumption will generally be in favor of personal freedom, for such freedom will enhance moral maturation. Thus it is argued that the legal enforcement of morality detracts from the moral developmental process by discouraging the exercise of personal choice and initiative and censoring individual interaction.

THE NATURE OF PRIVACY

In past and present American experience, the concern for privacy has involved a common desire to determine freely the extent and circumstances of interaction with others. With the growing erosion of possibilities for making choices of this kind, the need to guard against the arbitrary and capricious intrusion of others and especially government into personal lives appears all the more pressing.

In speaking of privacy, there is implied the existence of several related physical and psychological conditions that are part of the spectrum of relationships with the environment. These include solitude, intimacy, and anonymity.[8] Exclusive focus on any one of these conditions, either for general discussion or for a more precise characterization of privacy, fails to provide the breadth of analysis necessary for a satisfactory understanding of the place and purpose of privacy.

People seek solitude as an opportunity to be left alone by others while they pursue personal interests, reflect upon their actions, plan their futures, and the like. However, while solitude is possible only as an aspect of privacy, the equation of the right to privacy with "the right to be left alone"[9] is too narrow; it is neither a realistic statement of what a legal right should be nor is it adequate to the richness of the concept of privacy itself. "While privacy is often referred to as the individual's choice of aloneness, it is an interactional concept. By this we mean that however it is defined, it presupposes the existence of others, the possibility of interaction with them and the desire to minimize or control this interaction."[10] Part of what it means to live in a community and enjoy political rights is that all must accept a degree of restraint upon their personal lives. Such restraints are both occasioned and limited by the amount of social organization necessary for the community to function effectively. Furthermore, to predicate a claim to privacy solely upon the desire to be left alone fails to capture the importance of social interaction in developing moral maturity. Therefore, privacy must be considered as a value that "does not exist in isolation but is part and parcel of a system of values that regulates action in society."[11]

Intimacy is an intrinsic part of a private or personal sphere of action. It has been argued that it is a distinctly modern notion. The tendency of contemporary liberals to mark off some forms of private life as essential to self-development stands in stark contrast to the classical Greek association of freedom with public activities and nonfreedom (or privacy) with the province of women, children, and slaves.[12] People's innermost, essential, and self-affecting feelings and thoughts are those they choose to share with individuals to whom they feel most intimately attached. Such intimacy may imply feelings of love and affection that reinforce the inclination to share parts of oneself only with certain others. Or individuals may enter into intimate relationships with persons for whom they have no such feelings, such as doctors, lawyers, or clergy. In any event, to confide in other persons suggests a relationship of trust and respect. Such relationships place a mutual requirement of confidentiality upon the shared experiences and information. Without some guaranteed sphere of privacy there could be no intimacy; there would be no opportunity to share oneself, more or less, with some but not with others. Such opportunities are essential to the process whereby the nature of relationships with others can be understood, developing the capacity to define those relationships in terms of reciprocal rights and duties. As Kohlberg himself suggests, "Moral role-taking involves an emotional or sympathetic component, but it also involves a cognitive capacity to define situations in terms of rights and duties, in terms of reciprocity and the perspectives of other selves."[13]

Privacy is sought not only by withdrawing occasionally into states of solitude and intimacy; it is also sought in more public settings by protection against continual, systematic, and deliberate physical surveillance. The condition of anonymity ordinarily serves as a buffer against unwarranted interference with the ability to relax and act spontaneously in settings where one is unlikely to be recognized by others.

While there must be different expectations regarding privacy in public as opposed to purely private settings, it would be a mistake to conclude that privacy has no place beyond the confines of the home or the closed door. To be observed in public in the sense that one is noticed momentarily before quickly merging into the "situational landscape"[14] is the price of living in society. All but the most eccentric would accept and indeed welcome the necessity of running such "risks," for without them social interaction is virtually impossible. Recognition in this casual sense poses no substantial threat to legitimate expectations of privacy and facilitates occasions for spontaneous interpersonal contact and exchange.

However, it is a different matter altogether to be systematically watched, to have one's movements and activities noted and recorded. Such surveillance goes well beyond the boundaries of chance observation, inhibiting spontaneous social interaction. Under such circumstances, expectations of anonymity are falsified and privacy thereby violated. What is lost is the opportunity to venture out in public and remain unrecognized, at ease in the knowledge that actions can be freely undertaken and thoughts openly expressed without fear of deliberate observation and reprisal.

Taken together, the conditions of solitude, intimacy, and anonymity indicate some of the major contexts within which people seek to satisfy their interest in privacy. While particular claims to privacy vary in substance, all are predicated on the importance of preserving individual autonomy and maintaining a respect for persons. Indeed, personal authenticity and independence, which are core values in any free society, cannot be achieved without the assurance of occasions for private thought and conversation. For most people, life in a perpetual limelight would mean the end of such activities as well as the loss of any opportunity for emotional release. Under such circumstances, individual diversity and the promise of new and different experiences in daily existence would suffer and individual self-development would be impaired.

It is in this perspective that different claims to privacy can best be understood. Some of these claims assert an immunity from the dictates of social norms respecting personal conduct, such as those by women seeking abortions, or by homosexuals seeking protection from public harassment. Other claims to privacy object to the unrestricted collection, use, and dissemination of personal information. But regardless of the particular substance, each claim to privacy depends upon the principle of respect for persons for reasons that will now be addressed.

THE PRINCIPLE OF RESPECT FOR PERSONS

The notion of respect for persons is by no means a new one. Human beings have had long-standing interests in deciding matters of purely personal concern without outside interference, in not being spied upon at home or followed about in public, in dying with dignity, and the like. What makes the protection of these interests so urgent today are the new methods for attacking them. Even though interests such as these have always been important, they have never been so threatened as they are now as a result of technological developments by which life can be artificially and indefinitely prolonged or voiceprints and pictures obtained without the knowledge of the subject. With the utilization of these technologies there is a loss of control over what is known about individuals or what is done to them. Such control is an important part of the principle of respect for persons and the process by which they mature and grow morally. "The need and ability to exert . . . control . . . over self, objects, information, and behavior . . . is a critical element in any conception of privacy."[15]

According to Kohlberg, moral development is a process through which individuals achieve progressively higher stages of moral maturity by confronting social situations that call customary rules into question and demand increasingly sophisticated levels of moral judgment. Each stage of the moral development process represents a step in the transformation of one's cognitive-structural orientation. Accordingly, one moves from a preconventional morality, wherein law is perceived as a series of sanctions backed by physical force, to a more conventional perception of law as a set of external rules designed to preserve the social order, until finally one achieves a postconventional orientation toward law as the embodiment of an internalized system of general ethical principles. At the highest stage of moral development, such internalized ethical principles guide personal conduct, serving as the benchmark against which formal legal proscriptions are measured. Ultimately respect for law (rather than mere submission) relies upon the law's adherence to a core of universal principles of which the principle of respect for persons is a fundamental part.

The moral development process depends upon the availability of opportunities for individual conflict resolution through the vehicles of role-taking and participation in independent decision making. The principle of respect for persons underscores this process by stipulating that prima facie all human beings have a right to develop to their fullest potential, exercising personal discretion and choosing particular courses of action in any way they feel best serves their interests without impairing the interests of others. Accordingly, a person is understood in this context as

> . . . a subject with a consciousness of himself as an agent, one who is capable of having projects and assessing his achievements in relation to them. To *conceive* of someone as a person is to see him as actually or potentially a chooser, as one attempting to steer his own course through the world, adjusting his behavior as his apperception of the world changes, and correcting course as he perceives his errors. It is to understand that his life for him is a kind of enterprise like one's own, not merely a succession of more or less fortunate happenings, but a record of achievements and failures; and just as one cannot describe one's own life in these terms without claiming that what happens is important, so to see another's in the same light is to see that for him at least this must be important.[16]

Thus, respect for persons implies both a facility for looking at one's own actions from the standpoint of others and a corresponding willingness to modify the intrusive aspects of one's behavior out of regard for the interests of others.

This use of reciprocity in ethical judgment is most characteristic of the highest stages of moral development in which ethical orientation is predicated upon subjective norms and values. In order to appreciate the condition of others, one must be able to comprehend the essential nature of one's own condition.

> All social knowledge implies an act of sharing, of taking the viewpoint of another self or group of selves. . . . The motivational problem usually proposed to socialization theory is the question of why the "selfish" or impulsive infant develops into a social being. . . . The answer of development theory is that the self is itself born out of the social or sharing process, and therefore, motives for self-realization or self-enhancement are not basically "selfish" in the perjorative sense, but require sharing. . . . developmental theories assume a primary motivation for competence and self-actualization which is organized through an ego or self whose structure is social or shared.[17]

Self-development is a process marked by a growing capacity to cultivate a sense of personal identity through which it is possible to differentiate oneself from others. By engaging in self-selected projects and developing personal preferences and points of view free from the compulsion of others, self-knowledge and self-confidence are gradually acquired. The capacity for self-awareness contributes to the moral developmental process, for it is impossible to appreciate the way in which the actions of others are important to them if one cannot comprehend the significance of one's own actions for oneself.

One of the necessary conditions for personal development is the ability to act out beliefs and preferences in any manner that does not conduce to the harm of others. Such an ability depends upon a sphere of personal privacy within which the individual is sovereign, free to experiment and reason in an atmosphere that lacks both surveillance and sanctions. Actions undertaken pursuant to such expectations of privacy are considered authentic in the sense that people have reason to believe that they are in command of their actions and understand the dynamics of the context within which they occur. Any action of another that has the effect of reducing the significance of people's actions for themselves by falsifying their expectations of privacy violates the principle of respect for persons upon which the American notion of individual self-development proceeds.

Needless to say, there are important exceptions to the rule just pronounced. Otherwise, the principle of respect for persons would be little else than an open invitation to hypersensitivity. These exceptions are briefly stated as follows: a previous waiver of the right to privacy; a mistaken impression that behavior is entitled to be protected as private; the absence of a direct and substantial intrusion upon privacy; and the presence of some compelling reason for overriding the right to privacy. Intrusive behavior predicated upon these exceptions would not necessarily violate privacy according to the principle of respect for persons or vitiate interest in self-development. While there is no wish to engage in an extended discussion of these exceptions, some elaboration is clearly required.

The principle of respect for persons would not sustain one's right to privacy if one had deliberately chosen to waive that right. However, three conditions must hold in order for such a waiver to be valid: the waiver must have been freely given; it must have been given for some specific purpose; and it must have been given in advance of the event for which it was required. A waiver given under such circumstances is assumed to legitimate the subsequent behavior of others toward an individual.

The principle of respect for persons and claims to privacy that derive from it are applicable only when the activity in question is private, either by its very nature (that is, a private activity) or because of the circumstances in which it occurs (that is, privately, in private). In the first instance people's activities are private because intrinsically they consist of those aspects of their lives about which they feel most intimately. Such aspects are often marked by the feelings of personal pride or shame that are experienced most profoundly in relation to them.

By contrast, an activity may be private insofar as its private nature is dependent upon the private context of its occurrence. In such cases, however, expectations of privacy are unwarranted if there is a failure to insure the privacy of that context adequately. Obviously, different sorts of activity will require different degrees and kinds of care. Nevertheless, it is essential to remember that the possession of a right to do something or to be free from the interference of others carries with it a concomitant obligation to exercise that right responsibly. Responsibility in this case implies taking steps to insure that others do not inadvertently or unavoidably intrude upon one's privacy.

As a practical matter the principle of respect for persons must also be limited to substantial and direct intrusions upon privacy. The principle should not be interpreted as supporting every complaint stemming from annoyance at what is perceived to be rude and insensitive behavior. Yet it is impossible to stipulate a precise formula by which to identify true violations of privacy, in part because of the fact that what one person may regard as a fundamental intrusion another may view as a mere irritation.

In recognition of this difficulty it has been suggested that individuals try to identify those aspects of their lives that bear the closest connection to their sense of personhood.[18] These aspects include one's physical person, possessions, and attitudes respecting particular events and institutions that the conventions of the culture make it relevant to regard as part of the sense of personal identity (for example, sexual attitudes and preferences, familial arrangements, political opinions, religious beliefs). Because these phenomena may be regarded as essential to a sense of self-perception, to obstruct or alter the development of the ability to make personal choices respecting such matters would ordinarily comprise the basis for claims to a violation of privacy. Such claims would be predicated upon the ground that there is a substantial connection between all of these things and the principle of respect for persons.

Alleged intrusions of privacy must also be direct in terms of their impact before the principle of respect for persons may be justifiably invoked. Ordinarily, it is not enough simply to claim that a substantial connection exists between something about which individuals have strong feelings and the conditions under which they can enjoy their privacy. Unless it can be demonstrated that knowledge of the invasion of the privacy of another person has directly caused an individual to modify or abandon his own course of action, his claims to privacy must rely upon showing that the intrusive action was directed against that individual personally.

Even if the intrusion complained of is not mitigated by a previous waiver of the right to privacy, nor by some mistaken expectation that one was entitled to protection against the intrusion, and is substantial and direct, there remains a final kind of qualification to the applicability of the principle of respect for persons. Simply stated, a claim to privacy may be overridden by a claim of some other kind, the recognition of which is deemed more important by courts and legislatures. Under such circumstances the right to privacy must be foregone to the extent required by the counterclaim and cannot depend upon the principle of respect for persons to alter this result.

Once again, there is no neat formula by which to resolve the occasions and degrees of such forfeitures. However, using the principle of respect for persons as a rough measure, it is possible to indicate generally the factors that should be taken into account in limiting personal privacy.

As a general rule individuals may not exercise any of their rights to the detriment of others. The difficulty comes in determining when such detriment or harm has occurred. Claims to privacy that assert a fundamental right to be free of societal control and interference in matters of purely personal concern are most often weighed against society's interest in stemming what it regards as essentially antisocial behavior. Yet, if the most optimal conditions for the cultivation of self-potential are to be preserved, it is important to construe the type of harm that society has a right to protect itself against in the narrowest possible terms. Furthermore, as will be argued, regulatory schemes that go beyond those aspects of individual conduct with which society can be justifiably concerned and seek instead to legislate morality for its own sake can only diminish the possibilities for self-development and reduce respect for law in the process.

However, there may be some occasions that require the forfeiture of a right even if that right is not used for some legally detrimental purpose. While people's concern for the protection of personal privacy arises from a desire to guard against any arbitrary or undue interference with their lives, a certain amount of intrusion is the price everyone pays for living in society. For example, persons may be asked to provide information about themselves as a condition for receipt of certain kinds of social and economic services. On such occasions, if they wish to receive these services, they must submit to the loss of some privacy. Ordinary expectations about the degree and conditions under which privacy can be enjoyed are also forfeited in the case of public figures. Under no circumstances, however, does such a quid pro quo imply a total divestiture of the right to privacy. If it is acknowledged that all persons, by virtue of their being persons, have a right to privacy irrespective of whether in any given situation their privacy must be overridden, the principle of respect for persons will limit the extent of the usurpation.

In summary, the principle of respect for persons stipulates that individuals not act in ways that will impair the freedom of choice and opportunities for action by others. In order to sharpen the focus of the principle, it has been subjected to the kinds of qualifications outlined above. Accordingly, any intrusion upon personal privacy that is not accounted for by these qualifications violates the principle of respect for persons.

Such intrusions are also significant from the standpoint of moral development because they discourage occasions for independently formulating standards of ethical conduct by limiting participation in decision making and the exercise of personal discretion. While law cannot itself transform cognitive structures, it can increase the possibilities for personal interaction and conflict resolution, and thereby stimulate complex logical thought leading to more ethical behavior. When law becomes an instrument of repression, it limits social exchange and therefore risks institutionalizing a conventional level of moral thought. By contrast, minimal legal constraints on behavior promote critical self-examination and, at the same time, foster a more highly developed morality.

THE RIGHT TO PRIVACY AND THE ENFORCEMENT OF MORALITY

Moral development is an ethical maturation process by which individuals progress through a series of increasingly complex reasoning stages as a result of interaction between their emerging cognitive structures and the social environment. The role of law in this process as a prime socializing agent has been alluded to elsewhere.[19] Ideally, it aims at enhancing the development of reflective and interactive principles that ultimately condition one's understanding of concepts such as rights, duties, and obligations and the way in which these concepts affect one's relationships with others.[20] Law can be an effective educative tool through which the principle of respect for persons takes on meaning by minimizing the disruption of personal initiative and facilitating opportunities for self-development. Functioning in this manner, law helps to preserve the conditions that stimulate moral maturation.

Moral development theory is predicated upon assumptions about people's capacities to develop independent reasoning and experiential potentials. Through reflection and social interaction they come to appreciate the desirability of maximizing as much personal freedom as is compatible with noninterference with the freedom of others.[21] Arguments about the importance of privacy also take account of the importance of personal freedom for ethical development. Such arguments stress the significance of the relationship between increased occasions for the exercise of unimpeded personal discretion and the growth of autonomous principles of ethical thought and conduct. Accordingly, claims to privacy inevitably raise questions about the extent to which it is legally justifiable to interfere with an individual's actions. Such claims become especially compelling when no direct and substantial harm to others is posed by the activity in question. In such cases, it can be argued that the importance of self-determination and free choice more than outweighs whatever interests society might have in forcing compliance with its designated norms. As Justice William O. Douglas stated, "Liberty in the constitutional sense must mean more than freedom from unlawful government restraint; it must include privacy as well . . . [which is] the beginning of all freedom."[22]

The right to privacy is violated whenever the law is invoked for the sole purpose of proclaiming the inherent goodness of particular rules. This is the case because the principle of respect for persons upon which any particular claim to privacy depends is ordinarily compromised if the law intrudes upon a person's ability to act in ways that do not limit the freedom of others. Moreover, this tendency has serious implications for the moral development process in that by placing arbitrary constraints upon the scope of personal freedom, law undermines its own socializing potential.

Clearly the law is unlikely to encourage the growth of independent accommodative ethical principles if its primary function is to require the adoption of rigid patterns of behavior. Cognitive development depends upon increasing levels of personal participation and decision making regarding the affairs of one's own life. This type of enhanced involvement is best occasioned by the disequilibrium generated when customary attitudes and new types of situational demands come into conflict. Because claims to privacy are predicated upon the same sorts of needs for the unimpaired exercise of personal freedom and increased opportunities for personal choice and initiative as those essential to moral development, violations of privacy posed by the legal enforcement of morality are likely to impair the maturation of one's moral perspective.

The precise nature and extent of the damage to the moral development process by excessive reliance upon criminal penalties to discourage immoral behavior and punish "victimless" crimes will vary according to a person's level of cognitive maturity. For example, some persons will adhere to the requirements of law in order to avoid the penalties attached. At this preconventional level, compliance will not be conditioned upon an understanding or appreciation of the nature of the norms the law is attempting to inculcate. Nor are such persons stimulated to do more than merely conform to the law's expectations. Persons at this level perceive their environment entirely in terms of the authoritarian features within it and structure their actions accordingly. Thus, habitual reliance upon law as a mode of constraint at this point in the development process may reinforce the tendency to value power and authority for their own sakes and do very little to encourage respect for the integrity of law and the social order as a whole.

The adverse effects of the "criminalization" of immoral behavior for persons at the conventional level of moral judgment may be more complex, owing to the tendencies of such persons to perceive their own self-worth in terms of compliance with legal rules. A good action is one that is approved by others (Stage 3), and consists of obeying the law as a means of showing respect for the society of which one is a part (Stage 4). To the extent that the law is viewed as a repository of social values, individuals' self-perception will reflect the degree to which they adhere to the norms the law imparts. There is a danger that persons at this level will regard themselves as social deviants whenever their behavior is deemed illegal. Such effects upon self-perception are felt even when the individual is not explicitly identified and brought to trial. The nonenforcement of legal proscriptions against deviant behavior (which is often offered as an explanation for not decriminalizing such activities) does little to diminish the sense of social ostracism and individual worthlessness experienced by persons in this position.[23] A negative self-perception of this may change behavior—if only temporarily—and it has the potential of prolonging cognition at this conventional moral level.

Moreover, this type of legal stigmatization may have the effect of creating or further entrenching certain types of deviant subcultures. Persons convinced of their uselessness may begin to systematically engage in various activities that reinforce this image.[24] In so doing, such persons may eventually impair the legitimately constituted rights of others. Hence, the excessive criminalization of individual behavior could well result in the perpetuation of a social climate of tension and hostility.[25] Such conditions are hardly hospitable to the promotion of tolerance of individual diversity and the capacity to accommodate and integrate various social perspectives that characterize the most advanced level of moral development.

It has been suggested that the legal enforcement of morality may result in compliance without understanding at the preconventional level or the creation of a deviant self-image at the conventional level. However, the negative effects of legal moralism are not felt only at the lower levels of moral development. The phenomenon of overcriminalization can also trigger disobedience and disrespect for law among those who have advanced to the point of being conditioned by their own internalized value structures (postconventional level).

Once persons are able to differentiate what is good from what is bad from the perspective of general ethical principles and are no longer exclusively dependent upon the approval of others, they will tend to obey the law if it comports with their understanding of these principles. Laws that proscribe immoral behavior for its own sake inherently disregard individuals' estimation of their own interests, substituting society's better judgment in its stead. Inasmuch as laws of this general type violate the fundamental precepts of the principle of respect for persons, those who are more highly advanced morally may choose to disregard such laws by either openly engaging in acts of civil disobedience or getting around them in less obvious ways. Either response diminishes respect for law in its optimal capacity as an instrument of social change.

It is suggested, therefore, that with respect to the kind of personal conduct that poses no substantive harm to others, less legal restriction may significantly enhance moral development. The protection of such conduct is a primary focus of contemporary claims to privacy. These claims are directed in one way or another toward the maximization of individual opportunities for personal experimentation without sanction or surveillance. Clearly, self-determination and the unimpeded exercise of personal judgment contribute significantly to development. Without such opportunities cognitive maturation bogs down, for there is less chance of interaction between a person's emerging cognitive structures and environmental input. When the law aims at achieving social conformity, it does so at the cost of individual autonomy and principled moral development.

It has been argued that the protection of personal privacy is implied by the meaning of the principle of respect for persons, which in turn is one of the most fundamental precepts of the moral development process. Moreover, it is claimed that unwarranted constraints upon privacy may limit the progressive maturation of individual and group morality. Thus, the appropriate function of law should be to enhance the occasions for the enjoyment of privacy so as to assure a growing respect for persons and broader exercise of personal choice and initiative, the behaviors that characterize the highest stages of moral development.

NOTES

1. Lawrence Kohlberg, "From Is to Ought: How to Commit the Naturalistic Fallacy and Get Away With It in the Study of Moral Development," in *Cognitive Development and Epistomology,* ed. Theodore Mischel (New York: Academic Press, 1971), pp. 151–235. Kohlberg's thesis is stated in universal terms but it has been criticized for its cultural bias. (See, for example, Elizabeth L. Simpson, "Moral Development Research: A Case Study of Scientific Cultural Bias," *Human Development* 17 (1974): 81–106.) Inasmuch as this chapter addresses the relationship between Kohlberg's moral development theory and the right to privacy in the Anglo-American context, such criticisms are not relevant here.

2. Ibid.

3. Kohlberg, "From Is to Ought." Also see Stanley Benn, "Privacy, Freedom, and Respect for Persons," in *NOMOS XIII Privacy,* ed. J. Roland Pennock and John Chapman (New York: Atherton Press, 1971), pp. 1–26.

4. Lawrence Kohlberg, "Development of Moral Character and Moral Ideology," in *Review of Child Development Research,* vol. 1, ed. Martin and Lois Hoffman (New York: Russell Sage Foundation, 1964), p. 400.

5. Benn, "Privacy," p. 9.

6. Daniel Friedman, "Political Socialization and Models of Moral Development," in *Handbook of Political Socialization,* ed. Stanley Allen Renshon (New York: Free Press, 1977), p. 339.

7. For a formulation of the classic debate over the extent of legitimate control of society over persons and the enforcement of morality, see Patrick Devlin, *The Enforcement of Morals* (Oxford: Oxford University Press, 1965); and H.L.A. Hart, *Law, Liberty and Morality* (Stanford, Calif.: Stanford University Press, 1963).

8. Alan Westin, *Privacy and Freedom* (New York: Antheneum Press, 1968). For another typological evaluation of the multidimensional nature of privacy, see Robert S. Laufer and Maxine Wolfe, "Privacy as a Concept and a Social Issue: A Multidimensional Developmental Theory," *Journal of Social Issues* 33 (1977): 22–41.

9. Samuel Warren and Louis Brandeis, "The Right to Privacy," *Harvard Law Review* 4 (1890): 193–220.

10. Laufer and Wolfe, "Privacy as a Concept," p. 207.

11. Arnold Simmel, "Privacy Is not an Isolated Freedom," Pennock and Chapman, *NOMOS,* p. 71.

12. See Hannah Arendt, *The Human Condition* (Chicago: University of Chicago Press, 1958).

13. Lawrence Kohlberg, "Development of Moral Character," p. 395.

14. Westin, *Privacy and Freedom*, p. 15.

15. Robert S. Laufer, Harold M. Proshansky and Maxine Wolfe, "Some Analytic Dimensions of Privacy," in *Environmental Psychology: People and Their Physical Settings*, ed. Harold M. Proshansky, William Ittelson and Leanne Rivlin (New York: Holt, Rinehart and Winston, 1976), p. 210.

16. Benn, "Privacy," pp. 8–9.

17. Lawrence Kohlberg, "Stage and Sequence: The Cognitive Developmental Approach to Socialization," in *The Handbook of Socialization Theory and Research*, ed. David A. Goslin (Chicago: Rand McNally, 1969), p. 416.

18. Benn, "Privacy."

19. For example, "Symposium: Socialization, the Law and Society," issue editor June L. Tapp *Journal of Social Issues* 27 (1971): 1–234; June Tapp and Felice Levine, "Legal Socialization: Strategies for an Ethical Legality," *Stanford Law Review* 27 (1974): 1–72.

20. Tapp and Levine, "Legal Socialization."

21. See John Stuart Mill, *On Liberty* (Indianapolis: Bobbs-Merrill, 1975). (originally published in 1859)

22. Justice William O. Douglas, *Public Utilities Commission v. Pollack* 343. U.S. 451, 467 (1951).

23. See Edwin Schur, *Crimes Without Victims: Deviant Behavior and Public Policy* (Englewood Cliffs, N.J.: Prentice-Hall, 1965).

24. Ibid.

25. See Norval Morris and Gordon Hawkins, *The Honest Politician's Guide to Crime Control* (Chicago: University of Chicago Press, 1971).

11

FROM HOUSEHOLD TO POLITY

Gordon J. Schochet

The household, wrote Cicero, *"est principium urbis et quasi seminarium rei publicae"* — "is the foundation of the city [and] what we might call the 'seedbed' of the state."[1] The child grows into the adult who becomes the member or citizen of civil society. Cicero's observation — an echo of Aristotle's more familiar assertion that the household experiences of ruling and being ruled were essential preparations for citizenship — was not lost to his successors. Discussion of the relationship of the familial association to the polity was a leitmotiv of Western social and political thought until the nineteenth century. Conspicuously absent from non-Marxian political thought in the twentieth century, the household now seems to be regaining its once central position, as historians, social critics and reformers, students of political socialization, and even philosophers turn their attention to this most fundamental of social institutions.

Historically, the family has served three distinguishable functions in political philosophy. Most familiar is the view of the household as the precursor of civil society, discernable in the teleology of Aristotle and the crude anthropological and developmental speculations of Thomas Hobbes, John Locke, and David Hume. In the second place, the family has been viewed as an important social institution from which significant information and conclusions about politics can be inferred. The process here is usually comparative, metaphorical, or analogical. Examples are Plato's insistence in the *Republic* that members of the Guardian and Philosopher-King and Queen classes should regard each other as brothers, sisters, mothers, and fathers, and Sir Robert Filmer's less heralded dictum that the powers of kings are identical to those of fathers. Finally, there is the view, straight out of the concentric universes of the great chain of being and the har-

monious *Elizabethan World Picture* (as E.M.W. Tillyard called it), that
the family is a rudimentary form of association that fits into the larger
scheme in so important a way as to deserve attention.

Clearly, these are not utterly separate categories. A teleological theory,
for instance, is more than an account of political origins; it is equally a
statement about how the family fits into society as a whole. Similarly, the
developmental theories of Hobbes and Locke were aimed at showing how
much, on the one hand, and how little on the other, could be validly
inferred about the polity from the household. Equally clearly, precisely
what is said about the household in any of these three senses will depend
upon what the family is presumed or understood to be, which itself is a
matter of argument and ideological speculation, as well as of cultural (or
historical) context, to say nothing of perception. The picture is complicated
a bit more by emphasizing that one sometimes encounters references to
the family that are designed to alter one's perceptions of politics and
perhaps even to transform those very institutions. For instance, Mary
Shanley has found significant alterations in the use of the marriage contract
as a political metaphor in seventeenth- and eighteenth-century England;
as the marriage contract became more voluntary and marriage itself was
increasingly seen as resting upon consensual bases, the appeal to that
contract to account for civil relationships served to underscore what was
taken to be the voluntary nature of politics.[2] And by the end of the seventeenth century, arguments are encountered to the effect that as such
social relationships as those between parents and children, wives and hus-
bands, and masters and servants are reciprocal and even contractual, so
must the political relationship between ruler and subject rest upon a contract.[3]

The disappearance of the family from Anglo-American political thought
in the nineteenth century is undoubtedly related to the triumph of the
narrow and putatively liberal distinction between public and private and
the consequent exclusion of the private realm, including the family, from
political discourse. Renewed interest in the family, correspondingly, reflects a dissatisfaction with at least this aspect of what is taken to be liberal
ideology and a concern on the left and the right about the present state
of society. From one vantage, the traditional, nuclear family is seen as a
repressive institution that demeans women and children and perpetuates
objectionable but fundamental inequalities. On the other side, the family
is regarded as implicated in the "crisis of authority" that is presumed to
define so large a part of modernity, and attempts to "shore up" our tot-
tering culture necessarily include the revitalization of the household. Both
kinds of perspectives have been complemented by the rapid growth of the
relatively new academic field of family history and by the debates among

historians over how and how much the family has changed in the past 300 years, as well as by the even newer attempts by philosophers to discuss the normative structure of household relationships. Additionally, the family has assumed an unprecedented importance as an object of debate and public policy. Increases in the number of working mothers and the growth of day-care centers as alternative child-rearing institutions, increases in the legal divorce and remarriage rates, relaxation of traditional sexual restraints, and the legalization of abortion have all served to focus attention on the household and its relation to the wider social and political systems. The day of the family is clearly upon us, and the subject is becoming a preoccupation.

So far, however, little of this preoccupation has been incorporated into general or emerging political theories. Cicero, and Aristotle before him, seem to have been asserting that primitive experiences somehow shape the rest of people's perceptual lives. The perception, recognition, and acceptance of political authority are, at best, parasitic, derivative, or tertiary activities, but it is difficult to determine how these early familial experiences relate to one's later life in the wider society. It is not clear what factors can intrude upon and facilitate or interfere with the movement from the early and relatively unquestioned experiences of childhood to the thinking participation of democratic citizenship.* Somehow the child grows up to become a citizen and participates in a world that is at once more demanding, less secure, and presumably more rational than the world of its household.

These points can be restated in the form of a rudimentary theory of political symbolization and perception. Politics and political perceptions, it is suggested, are necessarily symbolized and therefore learned; that is, politics is always *represented*, for political understanding is the epiphenomenal result of the expansion of notions and conceptions that are already comprehended. These prior notions are metaphorically and analogically extended and transformed into symbolizations of something that was previously unknown. In this manner, an entirely new perceptual entity is brought into being.

Because it is the initial source of social learning and provides the earliest set of perceptions that can be modified into representations of something else, the household has been an obvious and long-standing political symbol. This perceptual expansion of the family renders new, different, and otherwise strictly meaningless (because perhaps not even perceived) experiences intelligible and enables the child to accommodate them to its perceptual world. In these terms, what is subsequently called authority is an expansion

---

*Note that "democracy" is used here as a political ideal and not in either the descriptive or "stable democracy" sense employed by many political scientists.

of familial experiences, a conversion of something that was previously understood into a symbol that encapsulates and provisionally accounts for something totally alien. Thus, the process of symbolization as discussed here is necessarily creative, for it brings something into being. (Making something "intelligible" and "giving meaning to" something seem to entail this sort of "creation;" without "meaning," something cannot be said perceptually to exist.)

The relationship between something represented in a symbol and the perceptual antecedent of the symbol is generally nonisomorphic, and it is the eventual appreciation of this lack of congruence that gives rise to discussion and debates about the adequacy of a symbol. At this stage, the phenomenon or experience represented in a symbol may well have its own perceptual identity and need not be symbolized (any longer). Alternatively, a different and seemingly inappropriate symbol may be introduced as a means of changing a perception and therefore of changing the nature of reality. This is especially true of politics if the author's view of the political realm as at least experientially epiphenomenal is accepted. Even in cultures that appear to have firm and irreducible understandings of politics, discourse about the political realm is frequently representational or symbolic. The point of such symbolization is not so much to create as it is to alter. Accordingly, political debate in England at the end of the seventeenth century was characterized by the attempt to replace the familial metaphor with a contractual one.[4]

A political consciousness that grows perceptually out of the household will be a reflection—however altered or distorted — of that familial structure. Thus it should be possible, at least in principle, to discover a relationship between the family and the polity such that in the development of an individual's political awareness the household is both causally and conceptually prior. This view is obviously oversimplified, but a correction of some of these difficulties will have to await a fuller elaboration of the theory. The general point to be argued here is that significant changes in the structure of the household and in the primitive authority-implicated experiences of children will impinge upon political awarenesses in ways that are potentially quite profound. It should be pointed out, however, that the author is not committed to a strict and narrowly deterministic interpretation of the causal priority of the household to the polity. Other factors certainly contribute to the growth of political awareness, and as the example of the contractual metaphor in seventeenth-century England suggests, it is possible to argue self-consciously against the imposition of familial images onto politics. Again, however, these qualifications are somewhat beside present purposes, which are to view the family from the Ciceronian perspective as *seminarium rei publicae.*

Paul Goodman once complained of the growing tendency to deprive children of the freedoms of childhood in contemporary families. He felt that by being given important, participatory roles in their families, young children were having too much responsibility thrust upon them at precisely the ages when they should be enjoying the leisurely benefits of nonparticipation and of having someone else make decisions for them. (This was not the more frequently heard complaint about too much permissiveness in the household, but the two issues are surely related.)

Goodman's contention can be incorporated into the author's derivation of the origins of political consciousness from the family. Assuming that many children do not experience the authoritative structure that traditionally characterized the household, it may follow that unless something replaces legitimate parental power in their perceptual worlds, these children will never develop the referents that could eventually be expanded to accommodate what one would call "political authority." As adults, they will lack what could be termed a "representational memory" of primitive authority, a memory that once functioned for the major or dominant part of a culture and was part of its essential nature.[5] One may conjecture either a changing (but not yet fully altered) familial setting throughout a culture or permanently differential systems of symbolic imposition within a single culture. One may further assume, correspondingly, either that the larger cultural and social patterns have not (yet) changed to match the changes in the household, or that there are dominant cultural patterns that do not conceptually comprehend or correspond to all the symbolic systems but seek to contain them politically. In either case, the result will be an incoherence or dissonance at the levels of political perception and practice.

In these terms, the assertion of a traditional authority that requires, relates to, or is symbolically reminiscent (in the above sense of representational memory) of experiences and perceptual developments people have not had will have to be irrelevant and unintelligible. The participatory, overly democratized family can thus be seen as the virtual antithesis of that seedbed of traditional authority. When an authority that has been "created" and justified by an unexperienced (perhaps because historically prior and now no longer operative) way of ordering and participating in the world asserts itself, it can have no meaning. The consequence is, in a fundamental sense, a clash of irreconcilable world views.

Something very much like this sort of clash seems to be at the root of the so-called "crisis of authority" in Western society. Significant numbers of people from nontraditional systems of symbolic imposition — many of them, no doubt, from participatory households — are confronted by authority structures they cannot comprehend, do not accept, and are therefore seeking to transform. This can be seen in part in the attempts to democratize procedures in various institutions on the generally salutary ground that people are entitled to participate in the making of decisions that impinge upon their lives and interests. There is the danger, however — a danger that has been seized upon and dramatically exaggerated by social critics who fear and bemoan the social and political transformations sought by the advocates of expansive democratic participation—of considerable overdemocratization and the destruction of vital institutions, as well as the elimination of important sources of nonrational social sustenance. There is a certain·complicating irony in the fact that the demands for greater democratization have been extended to the very household setting that, it is suggested, is among the causes of that demand in the first place. As the remainder of this essay will attempt to make clear, however much the insistence upon widespread participation in most social institutions may be shared, and despite the author's agreement with the claim that the traditional family has been the vehicle for the suppression, exploitation, and abuse of women and children, there are serious, undesirable consequences to the weakening of parental (that is, shared by both parents) authority in the household.

The concern here is with the means of establishing those personality traits, behavioral habits, and intellectual qualities that are necessary to sustain participation by adult citizens in an ideal democratic polity. Full membership in such a polity is demanding, for democracy confronts its citizens without formally institutionalized authority at its top, and depends, on the contrary, on the rational and self-consciously moral wills of its members for the furtherance of their common objectives. In short, what is meant by democracy in this context is a civil society that is founded upon the moral autonomy of its citizens, but is committed to social justice as a common and public goal and presupposes the willingness and ability of its citizens to do the good. There still remains a vague inability to account for the transformation of the child into the citizen.

The moral development theory of Lawrence Kohlberg provides an interesting and important means of dealing conceptually with that transformation, and at the same time suggests ways in which the process can go wrong. The structural categories of moral development theory also provide a framework in terms of which a fuller version of the theory of symbolic political perception could be presented, and it should be stressed that the enlargement and transformation of symbolized experiences and perceptual memories proceed developmentally and in accord with an individual's cognitive ability to comprehend and utilize "higher" (because conceptually later) symbols. Central to Kohlberg's explanation of individual moral development are the sequential ordering of the stages and the enticing quality of the next higher stage: people pass through the stages in order and are induced to move up only by the appeal of the reasoning at the next higher stage, in part because they cannot understand reasoning that is more than one stage higher. Therefore, the structures of the most significant agencies facilitating moral development must match the level of individual comprehension both if people are to develop properly and if social structures are to function. If, for instance, a child at Stage 1 or 2 — which are essentially self-interested and pleasure-pain calculating — is confronted consistently by social structures appropriate to Stage 5, the motivations and inducements for the child to move to Stage 3 will both be absent. (Recall that the perspective of Stage 5 is that of the rational individual who understands contractual commitments, the needs and entitlements of others, and the importance of group decisions.)

The concern, of course, is with the regulai exposure of young children to modern, democratic-participatory familial structures that require the reasoning of Stage 5 persons. The movement toward participatory households is not an especially new phenomenon. Child-rearing practices and parent-child relations in America have been becoming democratized since the nineteenth century. As Alexis de Tocqueville observed,

It has been universally remarked that in our time the several members of a family stand upon an entirely new footing towards each other; that the distance which formerly separated a father from his sons has been lessened; and that paternal authority, if not destroyed, is at least impaired.

Something analogous to this, but even more striking, may be observed in the United States. In America the family, in the Roman and aristocratic signification of the word, does not exist. All that remains of it are a few vestiges in the first years of childhood, when the father exercises, without opposition, that absolute domestic authority which the feebleness of his children renders necessary and which their interest, as well as his own incontestable superiority, warrants. But as soon as the young American approaches manhood, the ties of filial obedience are relaxed day by day; master of his thoughts, he is soon master of his conduct. In America there is, strictly speaking, no adolescence: at the close of boyhood the man appears and begins to trace out his own path. . . .

Thus at the same time that the power of aristocracy is declining, the austere, the conventional, and the legal part of parental authority vanishes and a species of equality prevails around the domestic hearth. I do not know, on the whole, whether society loses by the change, but I am inclined to believe that man individually is a gainer by it. I think that in proportion as manners and laws become more democratic, the relation of father and son becomes more intimate and more affectionate; rules and authority are less talked of, confidence and tenderness are often increased, and it would seem that the natural bond is drawn closer in proportion as the social bond is loosened.[6]

Tocqueville recorded and celebrated the apparent beginnings of a process that is now in a much more advanced stage. What is distressing about the contemporary notion that even young children have participatory entitlements in their families is that it represents the final triumph of the voluntary association model of social groups and the convergence of political and familial structures.

Harry Eckstein, among other students of political stability, claims that a stable polity's various social and political structures tend toward mutual congruence: "a government will be stable if its authority pattern is congruent with other authority patterns of the society of which it is a part."[7] He lists "families, schools and occupational contexts" as "the most basic (that is, the most absorbing and demanding) segments of life."[8] If this view is correct, it may have destructive consequences for democratic political systems, for households that are congruent with such a system would tend to block the moral development of their child members in ways already suggested. One would assume that such children would be frozen at relatively early stages of moral development and that they would never acquire the sense of justice and the abilities to handle choice, power, and responsibility that are so important to adult democratic participation. Indeed, it can be suggested that adults who emerge from these childhood experiences will be neurotically maladapted and that their behavior will be self-centered and self-interested. Such people could wreak havoc when they enter the public as well as the private bureaucratic systems, for they will attempt to manipulate the openness of the democratic process for their own advantage in much the same way that democratically reared children manipulate their parents.

A further difficulty grows out of the "mass society" criticism of democratic individualism, which can be restated in ways that contribute directly to this author's developmental reservations about the theory of political congruence. It is sometimes alleged that the open, participatory institutions of democratic polities create anxieties because of their built-in lack of permanent, substantive standards. Instead of a coherently meaningful world of which one can be a part, the individual is confronted by conflicting rights, litigiousness, and widespread voluntarism. In order to function in such a world, people need integrated, coherent personalities; that is, a democratic polity requires citizens with the sense and experience of authority that would provide a foundation on which that democracy could rest. Traditionally, the authoritative and integrating institutions in society have been religion, work, and the family. Religion and work have already become voluntary, democratized associations and so have lost a considerable part of their ability to provide integration. The household seems destined to go the same way, as major institutions move toward congruence, and there is nothing to take its place.

The author's work on seventeenth-century England shows a clear congruence between family structure and ideology, on the one hand, and political structure and ideology on the other.[9] It may be that this congruence reinforces the stability of an authoritarian political system, but as has been indicated, there is reason to believe that it is inimical to the health of a democratic polity. Robert A. LeVine some time ago offered a series of hypotheses about the congruence of familial with community and political authority patterns:

1. The degree of congruence is inversely related to the amount of social stratification.
2. The degree of congruence is inversely related to the specialization and stability of supra-community political structures.
3. Among societies of a given level of political integration (such as the local community or nation level), the degree of congruence is directly related to the presence of corporate descent groups, the degree of localization of descent groups, and the use of kinship terms within territorial units.
4. Among societies of a given level of political integration, the degree of congruence is inversely related to the presence of procedures for secondary socialization such as schools, institutionalized peer groups, and military training programs, through which actors in the political system must pass.[10]

It is suggested, with LeVine (and research on the propositions is urged), that political and social structures may have no tendencies toward congruence in complex, differentiated societies, but that they do have impacts upon one another in ways that moral development theory suggests.

NOTES

1. Marcus Tullius Cicero, *De Officiis*, I, xvii, 54, trans. H. G. Edinger, Library of Liberal Arts (Indianapolis: Bobbs-Merrill, 1974), p. 27.
2. Mary L. Shanley, "Marriage Contract and Social Contract, in Seventeenth-Century English Political Thought." *Western Political Quarterly* 32 (1979): 79–91.
3. Gordon J. Schochet, "Patriarchalism, Politics, and Mass Attitudes in Stuart England," *Historical Journal* 12 (1969): 413–439.
4. Gordon J. Schochet, *Patriarchalism in Political Thought* (Oxford: Blackwell, 1975).
5. Some of these notions are the result of crude borrowings from and reworkings of points made in Clifford Geertz's profound essay, "Ideology as a Culture System," originally published in *Ideology and Discontent*, ed. David Apter (New York: Free Press, 1964), pp. 47–56, and reprinted as ch. 8 of his *The Interpretation of Cultures* (New York: Basic Books, 1973).
6. Alexis de Tocqueville, *Democracy in America*, trans. Henry Reeve, rev. and ed. Phillips Bradley, 2 vols. (New York: Vintage Books, 1954), vol. 2, pp. 202, 205.
7. Harry Eckstein, "A Theory of Stable Democracy," reprinted as Appendix B to his *Division and Cohesion in Democracy: A Study of Norway* (Princeton: Princeton University Press, 1966), p. 234.

8. Ibid., p. 249.

9. Schochet, "Patriarchalism, Politics, and Mass Attitudes"; and *Patriarchalism in Political Thought.*

10. Robert A. LeVine, "The Role of the Family in Authority Systems: A Cross-Cultural Application of Stimulus-Generalization Theory," *Behavioral Science* 6 (October 1960), p. 295.

LEARNING TO BE A VIRTUOUS CITIZEN

EDITORS' COMMENTS

Speculation over the centuries on the relationship between moral behavior and politics has included the persistent assertion that people can be taught to be virtuous. Many societies today, most notably Marxist ones, are fervently committed to the notion that moral values can be imparted, and it is but a short step, even for the Anglo-American culture, from moral development theory to moral (or values) education. Yet knowledge about moral education is scant and hardly precise. It is not clear whether it can be done or whether it ought to be done, and there is certainly no agreement about its prospective content. The chapters in this part advance some preliminary ideas about how citizens can be taught to be virtuous. The chapters are in no sense, however, a practical guide to what has been called political socialization. Rather, they are an amalgam of theoretical and empirical insights into the current state of this multifaceted issue.

In the first paper, Edward Schwartz returns to a critical view of Kohlberg's work; his concern is whether current moral development theories of a cognitive developmental nature can give adequate instruction concerning the behavioral attributes of Kohlberg's highest stages of moral judgment. He argues that the highest stages of moral reasoning have been associated in historical documents with calls for different forms of social behavior. These discrepancies, according to Schwartz, make the problem of devising morally mature, universal, behavioral prescriptions difficult, if not impossible.

Robert E. O'Connor's chapter is more specific. Using results from surveys of university students in England and France, O'Connor seeks to determine the influences that lead to types of moral reasoning. He points out the considerable differences in the settings of the various universities, but his most significant finding is that socialization within the home appears to be the major factor in the development of individuals with mature moral reasoning capabilities. In some ways this argument makes specific for modern university students previous suggestions put forth by Gordon J. Schochet. O'Connor concludes that it may be difficult for those interested in the development of moral reasoning to discuss this issue fruitfully without discussing the ways in which politics is dealt with in the home.

In the third paper, Jack L. Nelson focuses on the relationship between citizenship instruction in the United States and the goals of educators with regard to moral education. The link between the two has generally been very close, but Nelson points out that traditional means of citizenship instruction have operated to impede rather than to enhance the capacity for the development of mature moral individuals. In conclusions that reflect Irving Louis Horowitz's doubts that institutional education can ever truly foster moral development, Nelson points out how citizenship instruction, designed to create members of modern national states, by its nature generally hinders moral development. In Nelson's view, moral development requires an unrestricted capability to examine the implications of moral dilemmas, while citizenship instruction, in his opinion, is structured in such a manner as to minimize this very possibility.

In the final chapter Roy E. Feldman discusses the application of Kohlberg's theories to programs in prisons and schools where the stated goals have been to develop more mature moral orientations among inmates and pupils. Feldman points out that the assertions about the success of these programs have not been borne out by actual results. He is skeptical about the applicability of Kohlberg's theory and suggests that much work will be required before adequate moral development education techniques can be put into practice.

12

TRADITIONAL VALUES, MORAL EDUCATION, AND SOCIAL CHANGE

Edward Schwartz

THE STAGES OF DEVELOPMENT: THE CONTENT OF THE STRUCTURE

For those who participate in movements for justice, the growing debate over moral development and moral education offers a new opportunity to examine the exact relationships among traditional values, political education, and social change. In the United States, especially, the issue is of great interest, given the strong emphasis on values that emerges from most major social movements and the related failure of Marxism to gain a substantial following among working people and the poor. Whether or not it can be proved that ethics can shape economics and politics, most Americans believe that public issues and institutions ought to be held accountable to moral principles.[1] Even contemporary socialist intellectuals here have had to devote considerable attention to conflicts in the ideological and cultural superstructure, given their inability to persuade most Americans that a dialectical analysis of history is a better guide to the future than are the values of the past.[2] Thus, discussions of domestic reform rapidly devolve into disputes over principles, and fairly traditional principles at that.

On this basis, both the intent and the content of Lawrence Kohlberg's six-stage theory of moral development, and the related use of moral dilemmas as means of inducing citizens to move up the stage ladder, should come as welcome news to the various movements. Certainly Kohlberg sees his own work as contributing to social change. In "Education for Justice: A Modern Restatement of the Platonic View," written in 1970, he stresses the "revolutionary nature" of moral education, pointing to Martin Luther

King as one of a "long list of men who have had the arrogance not only to teach justice but to live it in such a way that other men felt uncomfortable about their own goodness."[3] The schools, he concludes, "would be radically different places if they took seriously the teaching of the good."[4] This is not Kohlberg the scholar speaking but Kohlberg the activist, for whom moral education can become a dramatic vehicle for political reform.

Moreover, Kohlberg's theory itself elaborates on several assumptions that liberal and radical idealists over the past 25 years have entertained about moral development. First, it suggests an inseparable connection between cognitive skill and moral reasoning, always a gratifying notion to intellectuals. The relationship lies at the heart of Kohlberg's system. In his "Restatement of the Platonic View," he takes great pains to challenge "a brand of common sense first enunciated by Aristotle," by which there are "two spheres, the moral and the intellectual, and that learning by doing is the only real method in the moral sphere." This "Deweyite thinking," he contends, "has lent itself to the Boy Scout approach to moral education which has dominated American practices in this field and which has its most direct affinities with Aristotle's views." Kohlberg's description of these practices should strike a familiar note to graduates of American public schools:

> American educational psychology, like Aristotle, divides the personality up into cognitive abilities, passions or motives, and traits of character. Moral character, then, consists of a bag of virtues and vices. . . .
> Given a bag of virtues, it is evident how we build character. Children should be exhorted to practice these virtues, should be told that happiness, fortune, and good repute will follow in their wake; adults around them should be living examples of these virtues; and children should be given daily opportunities to practice them. Daily chores will build responsibility; the opportunity to give to the Red Cross will build service or altruism, etc.[5]

Kohlberg insists that this approach to moral education does not work. He argues that unless teachers follow the Platonic mode of helping students learn how to *think* about moral issues, the students will treat morality as just another set of intrusions of the older generation upon the younger one.

Second, Kohlberg's theory stipulates that individuals achieve a high level of moral maturity only when they can rationalize decisions on the basis of principles that transcend the rules that govern the operation of existing institutions. At the primitive level of Stage 1 or 2, people behave ethically only out of fear of being punished or in expectation of private gain. At Stage 3, one aims to please, especially those in authority. Stage 4 people obey the rules — to the point, some might say, of being "hung up" on them. People reach Stages 5 and 6 only when they can grasp abstract concepts—the terms of a social contract or, ultimately, universal ideals that go beyond the social contract.

At a minimum Kohlberg is saying that one must reach the highest level of moral reasoning in order to conceive of alternatives to existing institutions. Moreover, the way in which he formulates the stages — especially Stage 6 as embodying a "universalized reverence for human life" — suggests that moral maturity will bring with it a dissatisfaction with any established order. Thus, if radicalism historically has fostered a concern for human rights over property rights, then Kohlberg's Stage 6 tilts decidedly leftward. Certainly, his choice of Socrates, Christ, and Martin Luther King, Jr., as Stage 6 personalities does little to dispel this impression.

The third proposition that Kohlberg advances is strategic: that with the right procedure for moral education, a teacher can achieve the proper moral result without ever appearing to impose a particular point of view. The technique itself involves the use of moral dilemmas in the classroom. These are "open" situations, where a student must decide between ethically unpalatable alternatives. Should a man steal a drug to save his wife's life? Should Martin Luther King have called for mass disobedience of laws requiring racial segregation in the South? These are the sort of moral dilemmas that Kohlberg has in mind. He insists that if students confront these issues on the basis of moral arguments one stage higher than their own, they will increasingly justify their decisions on grounds of abstract principles, rather than merely parrot the rules and practices of existing institutions. That is, they will advance in stages of development, as students in Kohlberg's classes have done.

> In practice, then, our experimental efforts at moral education have involved students at one level, say Stage 2, to argue with those at the next level, say Stage 3. Then the teacher would support and clarify the Stage 3 arguments. Then he would pit the Stage 3 students against the Stage 4 students with a new dilemma. Initial results with this method with a junior high school group indicated that 50 percent of the students moved up one stage and 10 percent moved up two stages. In comparison, only 10 percent of a control group moved up one stage in the four-month period involved.[6]

While these are classroom techniques, they are perfectly consistent with strategies employed by the movements of the 1960s designed to hold unjust practices of dominant institutions accountable either to constitutional law or to what Martin Luther King, Jr. called the "full meaning of the creed" of the Declaration of Independence.

Thus, the hypotheses that Kohlberg is testing about moral reasoning and education correspond dramatically to strategies used by the Left to promote moral sensitivity to injustice in society. Kohlberg believes that young people will acquire maturity in ethical reasoning if they learn how to think, rather than merely react to the commandments of their schools. In the process, he says that they must look beyond the laws and institutions for guidance, rather than accepting all rules without question. Most important, he would accustom students to view ethical conflict as a creative, dialectical process leading to a capacity for abstract reasoning about principles, as opposed to teaching morality as a science of order, which new values would only destroy.

A careful examination of what Kohlberg is saying, however, reveals a more conservative set of assumptions than he himself admits. Those who focus on the revolutionary implications of Stages 5 and 6 risk overlooking the mass of men and women who live lives of quiet desperation at Stages 1 through 4. For those acquiescent souls there will be no revolution unless some ruler breaks the laws. Even then, the revolution will serve only to restore the rule of law. The guardians and philosopher kings at the highest level of moral maturity will have had to learn first how to reason on the basis of conventional law and morality, with all their orthodoxies and edicts obscuring the universal vision. On this basis, whether a person could ever reach Stage 6 in a society without a social contract — much as a Preamble to the Constitution or a Declaration of Independence as a civic launching pad to pure thought — is doubtful.

In short, Kohlberg's argument suggests that people first must grasp the moral assumptions underlying the institutions and laws of their own societies before they can articulate the principles that go beyond them. The stages are "hierarchical integrations," by which subjects, "comprehend all stages below their own," but "not more than one above their own."[7] On this basis, Stage 6 personalities — educators and activists alike—must ground their defense of abstract principles in the laws of their own societies if they hope to be understood by those who have reached levels no higher than Stage 4. By implication, moreover, the "universal reverence for life" embodied in Stage 6 itself must find some reflection in the specific rules and institutions of the polity, or idealists and visionaries will have no way of conveying to citizens the precise moral assumptions they have in mind.

It is useful, therefore, to separate the areas in which Kohlberg's theory provides useful insights into the relationship between values and politics from those in which it does not. The argument here is that Kohlberg's system supports empirically the case made by classical and a few modern political philosophers for an integrated system of moral and civil authority, upon which leaders and citizens can ground their arguments for political change. It equally reinforces the proposition advanced by Gilbert K. Chesterton and others that proposals for reform receive the greatest attention when cast in terms of traditional values or even the law — in Kohlberg's categories, at the lower stages of development.

Kohlberg fails to show how citizens can sort out values when faced with competing systems of authority. The problem is built into his theory. His formulation of Stage 6 confuses the capacity to think about universal principles of justice with the principles themselves. These, by his own admission, may differ from writer to writer, from system to system. What he does not acknowledge is that the character of the contracts, laws, and rules among these various systems will differ as well. Their content will differ, and the decisions required by them will differ. A Stage 4 Chinese Communist is not a Stage 4 resident of New Brunswick, New Jersey, even if they both believe in obeying the rules. To say that the structure of their arguments will tell more about their character and their behavior than the precise content of the rules that they must obey is to direct the discussion of moral education almost entirely away from its traditional concern for human conduct, to the processes of thought that justify it.

Moreover, when alternative visions of the good life compete for authority within the same society — as the Golden Rule and the Declaration of Independence can be said to compete in the United States — Kohlberg's kind of moral education offers no way for students and citizens to sort out their preferences between the two. These problems deserve serious examination, given the growing popularity of Kohlberg's theories among educators and the increasing use of his techniques in American schools.

THE MORALITY OF THE POLITY

As Kohlberg knows, the general proposition that political institutions shape moral attitudes is no newer than Plato. It was on this basis, in fact, that classical philosophers constructed their arguments for specific laws and institutions. In the *Republic,* Plato argued that a government would not only determine the relationships among different social classes, but the character of the individuals within them. An aristocracy would produce aristocrats — citizens who would value honor above all else. A democracy, as he defined it, would create hedonists with no sense of values beyond their own private wants. A tyranny would spawn little tyrants among the people, conceived in the image of their ruler. Thus, it was critically important that there be a "right ordering" in a republic between the philosophers, the guardians, and the artisans in order to foster the right ordering of each individual's soul.

At least a few post-sixteenth-century philosophers retained Plato's insistence on seeing the civic culture as the primary force shaping the moral attitudes of citizens. Thomas Hobbes devoted the third part of the *Leviathan* to an analysis of the political theory of the Bible and defended buttressing the church with the authority of the state. The punishments available to religious institutions by themselves were simply not tough enough. The "Use and Effect of Excommunication," for example,

> . . .whilest it was not yet strengthen with the Civill Power, was no more, than that they, who were not Excommunicate, were to avoid the company of them that were. It was not enough to repute them as Heathen, that never had been Christians; for such they might eate, and drink; which with Excommunicate persons they might not do. . . . As for keeping them out of their Synagogues, or places of assembly, they had no power to do it, but that the owner of the place, whether he were Christian, or Heathen. And because all places are by right, in the Dominion of the Common-wealth; as well hee that was Excommunicated, as hee that never was baptized, might enter into them by Commission from the Civill Magistrate. . . .[8]

The result was

> . . . that upon a Christian, that should become an Apostate, in a place where Civill Power did persecute, or not assist the Church, the effect of Excommunication had nothing in it, neither of damage in this world; nor of terrour; Not of terrour, because of their unbelief; nor of dammage, because they returned thereby into the favour of the world.[9]

Jean Jacques Rousseau was outrightly contemptuous of Christian leaders for failing to take Hobbes's advice. Indeed, he blamed Christianity for favoring a virtuous individual with no loyalty to the sovereign over the moral force that the state itself could command:

> There remains, then, the religion of man, or Christianity, not as we see it today, but as we find it in the Gospels — which is quite a different thing. By virtue of this holy, sublime and true religion, men, as all being children of the same God, look on one another as brothers, and the society which unites them remains firmly knit even in death. But this religion, since it has no particular relation to the body politic, leaves to the laws the force which they derive from themselves, and adds nothing to it. In so far as that is so, one of the chief bonds of the social fabric remains ineffective. But the evil goes farther, because, so far from attaching the hearts of the citizens to the State, it weans them from it, as from all merely earthly concerns. I know of nothing more at odds with the spirit of society.[10]

Finally, in recent years, Sheldon Wolin has urged theorists to conceive of politics as the classical philosophers did — as a vehicle to pursue shared moral ideals, rather than as an arena for a loosely regulated war among interest groups, or a process that emerges when bureaucratic procedures fail, or both. Wolin's plea for a recovery of political vision to give ethical direction to society brings the classical tradition up to date.[11] Like Plato, Hobbes, and Rousseau, he insists that private values will always depend upon the public authority that gives rise to them.

THE POLITICS OF MORALITY

Kohlberg's hypothesis that the development of moral reasoning proceeds from arguments based on force and legal conventions, to justifications grounded solely on abstract principles, reinforces the claim of an integral connection between political and moral authority. The implication, moreover, is that activists who want to strengthen society's commitment to justice will find greatest success when they appeal to its own civic covenants. Kohlberg is specific on this point:

> The most fundamental values of a society are termed moral, and the major moral values in our society are the values of justice. According to any interpretation of the Constitution, the rationale for government is the preservation of the rights of the individuals, i.e., justice. From our point of view, then, moral education may legitimately involve certain elements of social reform if they bear directly on the central values of justice. . . .
> The delicate balance between social reform and moral education is clarified by the example of Martin Luther King if you recognize that King was a moral leader, a moral educator of adults, not because he was a spokesman for the welfare of the Negroes, not because he was a minister of religion, but because, as he said, he was a drum major for justice. His words and deeds were primarily designed to induce America to respond to racial problems in terms of a sense of justice, and any particular action he took had value for this reason and not just because of the concrete political end it might achieve.[12]

Here, again, Kohlberg is not the first person to make such an argument. Chesterton in his book, *Orthodoxy,* advocated using traditional values to defend revolutionary ideals on grounds quite consistent with the moral development theory that Kohlberg is now expounding.

> A strict rule is not only necessary for ruling; it is also necessary for rebelling. This fixed and familiar ideal is necessary to any sort of revolution. Man will sometimes act slowly upon new ideas; but he will only act swiftly upon old ideas. If I am merely to float or fade or evolve, it may be towards something anarchic; but if I am to riot, it must be for something respectable. . . .
> Thus we may say that a permanent ideal is as necessary to the innovator as to the conservative; it is necessary whether we wish the king's orders to be promptly executed or whether we only wish the king to be promptly

executed. The guillotine has many sins, but to do it justice, there is nothing evolutionary about it. The favourite evolutionary argument finds its best answer in the axe. The Evolutionist says, "Where do you draw the line?" The Revolutionist answers, "I draw it *here:* exactly between your head and body." There must at any given moment be an abstract right and wrong if any blow is to be struck; there must be something eternal if there is to be anything sudden. Therefore for all intelligible human purposes, for alterering things or for keeping things as they are, for founding a system for ever, as in China, or for altering it every month as in the early French Revolution, it is equally necessary that the vision should be a fixed vision.[13]

More recently, John Schaar has insisted that the "fixed and familiar ideal" most conducive to radical change is a civic ideal. In his "In Defense of Patriotism" he develops a notion of "covenanted patriotism," whereby a citizen displays loyalty to the country by adhering to the highest principles of its social contract. The argument amounts to a theoretical explication of what Kohlberg now calls Stage 5.

This is the only conception of patriotic devotion that fits a nation as large and heterogeneous as our own. It sets a mission and provides a standard of judgement. It tells us when we are acting justly and it does not confuse martial fervor with a dedication to country . . . the covenant is not a static legacy, a gift outright, but a burden and a promise. The nation exists only in repeated acts of remembrance and renewal of the covenant through changing circumstances. Patriotism here is more than a frame of mind. It is also activity guided by and directed toward the mission established in the founding covenant. This conception of political membership also decisively transcends the parochial and primitive fraternities of blood and race, for it calls kin all who accepted the authority of the covenant. And finally, this covenanted patriotism assigns America a teaching mission among the nations, rather than a superiority or a hostility toward them. This patriotism is compatible with the most generous humanism.[14]

Schaar concludes that it is crucial for activists to refer authority to a covenant in making their claims lest they forego the authority that it represents. The radicals of the 1960s, who did not approach political education in this way, failed to "persuade their fellow Americans, high or low, that they genuinely cared for and shared a country with them."[15]

Kohlberg's conclusions about moral education in the classroom confirm this view. His findings suggest that people cannot understand ethical arguments that are divorced from the system of authority they respect. In Kohlberg's classes, specifically, students are not able to cope with solutions to moral dilemmas defended at more than one stage higher than their own.

For society, this implies that a Stage 3 citizen, who supports the president "because we have to support the president," will be receptive only to arguments grounded in law; that a Stage 4 citizen will have to hear a reference to a social contract before taking seriously any principle contained within it; and that only those who already believe in the Declaration of Independence will be ready to accept what "life, liberty, and the pursuit of happiness" require at a universal level. American reformers who choose to argue for higher principles outside of this framework, then, will do so at their peril. This was Chesterton's complaint about Marxists and anarchists of his day; and Schaar's, about the New Left. It is now Kohlberg's warning to future generations of reformers who want to bring about an improvement in social values through movements for political reform.

Yet all this makes sense only if the highest moral ideals of a country's visionaries are at least consistent with its civic principles. Stage 6 can reflect a more universal ethic than Stage 5, but it cannot represent a radically different conception of ethics from Stage 5. It can require that a person give to humankind what the social contract guarantees only to citizens. It cannot claim that a person owes something substantially different to humankind from what the social contract claims he owes to citizens.

Premodern philosophers understood this problem well. It was the reason Plato went into such great details to describe the social structures of the best city in the *Republic* and to explicate the rules governing the second-best city in the *Laws*. His object was to foster the same kind of moral values in citizens regardless of the level of civic authority they could understand. Aristotle, similarly, argued that under a constitution that did not reflect the highest moral ideals, the best man would not necessarily be the best citizen, since he would be in a constant state of uncertainty about what his ethical duty required.

To Hobbes such a situation would lead not merely to a conflict between political and religious obligation but to confusion about God's actual demands:

> The most frequent pretext of sedition, and Civill Warre, in Christian commonwealths hath a long time proceeded from a difficulty not yet sufficiently resolved, of obeying at once, both God, and Man, then when their Commandments are one contrary to the other. It is manifest enough, that when a man receiveth two contrary Commands, and knows that one of them is God's, he ought to obey that, and not the other, though it be the command of his lawfull Soveraign . . . or the command of his Father. The difficulty therefore consisteth in this, that men when they are commanded in the name of God, know not in divers cases, whether the command be from God, or whether he that commanded, doe but abuse God's name for some private ends of his own.[16]

Hobbes's solution to these dilemmas was to bring the substantive principles of the polity into accord with Christian principles, while encouraging the church to view the state as the proper enforcer of God's will.

Kohlberg, however, avoids the substantive conflicts between these rival conceptions of civic and religious virtue, and focuses exclusively on the potential tensions between the two kinds of authority, regardless of content. Consider the discussion of the clash between Stage 6 and Stage 5, derived by Kohlberg from Martin Luther King's *Letter From a Birmingham Jail:*

> One may well ask, "How can you advocate breaking some laws and obeying others?" The answer lies in the fact that there are two types of laws, just and unjust. One has not only a legal but a moral responsibility to obey just laws. One has a moral responsibility to disobey unjust laws. A just law is a human law that is not rooted in eternal law and natural law. Any law that uplifts human personality is just, any law that degrades human personality is unjust. An unjust law is a code that a numerical or powerful majority group compels a minority group to obey but does not make binding on itself. This is difference made legal.[17]

"King makes clear," Kohlberg concludes, "that moral disobedience of the law must spring from the same root as moral obedience to the law, out of respect for justice." He elaborates:

> We respect the law because it is based on rights, both in the sense that the law is made by the principle of equal political rights. If civil disobedience is to be Stage 6, it must recognize the contractual respect for law of Stage 5, even to accepting imprisonment. That is why Stage 5 is a way of thinking about the laws which are imposed upon all, while a morality of justice about the laws which are imposed can never be anything but a free, personal ideal.[18]

Thus, it is not a willingness to live by a specific kind of ideal that signifies moral maturity, but the ability to understand and adhere to an ideal regardless of the law.

What happens, however, when the "free, personal" ideals adopted by the visionaries of a society are themselves in conflict? In what way, for example, could the techniques of moral analysis developed by Kohlberg sort out the differences between the three abstract conceptions of justice quoted below, offered, respectively, by Plato, the Puritans, and John Rawls?

> And, in truth, justice was, as it seems, something of this sort; however, not with respect to a man's minding his external business, but with respect to what is within, with respect to what truly concerns him and his own. He

doesn't let each part in him mind other people's business or the three classes in the soul meddle with each other, but really sets his own house in good order and rules himself; he arranges himself, becomes his own friend, and harmonizes the three parts, exactly like three notes on the harmonic scale, lowest, highest, and middle. And if there are some parts in between, he binds them together and becomes entirely one from many, moderate and harmonized. . . . In all these actions he believes and names a just and fine action one that preserves and helps to produce this condition, and wisdom the knowledge that supervises this action; while he believes and names an unjust action one that undoes this condition, and a lack of learning in its turn, the opinion that supervises the action."[19]

There are two rules whereby we are to walk towards another: JUSTICE and MERCY. These are always distinguished in their Act and in their object, yet they may both concur in the same Subject in each respect. . . .

There is likewise a double law by which we are regulated in our conversation, one towards another. . . . By the first of these laws, man as he was enabled so withall is commanded to love his neighbor as himself. Upon this ground stands all the precepts of the moral law, which concerns our dealings with men. To apply this to the works of mercy, this law requires two things: that every man afford his help to another in every want or distress, that he perform this out of the same affection, which makes him careful of his own good according to that of our Savior: Matthew (7:12).[20]

A conception of social justice, then, is to be regarded as providing in the first instance a standard whereby the distributive aspects of the basic structure of society are to be assessed. This standard, however, is not to be confused with the principles defining the other virtues, for the basic structure, and social arrangements generally, may be efficient or inefficient, liberal or illiberal, and many other things, as well as just or unjust. A complete conception defining principles for all the virtues of the basic structure, together with their respective weights when they conflict, is more than a conception of justice; it is a social ideal.[21]

In truth, there is no way within Kohlberg's system to resolve these tensions, and therein lie its limitations. If one is to reason on the basis of the authority of a stage predicated upon an ideal beyond the rules, one must implicitly accept the ideal. No doubt most Americans, nurtured in Lockean liberalism, do share a notion that justice is equivalent to individual rights, as Kohlberg says it is. Yet once a person was able to reason on the basis of this principle, that person would also be able to draw inferences from the religious notion that justice depends upon service to others in accordance with God's will, and from Plato's conception of justice as the right ordering of the community. This new "maturity" would give the idealist not a fixed standard, but a new set of moral dilemmas — this time between conflicting conceptions of the good to which appeals to higher authority would provide no answers. In short, by avoiding any serious discussion of the nature of justice — by implying that such a consideration is not even relevant to moral development, as he conceives it — Kohlberg ends up championing a form of moral education that could lead merely to a more sophisticated form of moral confusion.

THE CONTENT OF THE LAWS

For advocates of social change, however, this historic debate over different conceptions of justice has been at least as significant as the tension between the "eternal law" and the civil law that faced Martin Luther King. Conflicts do not occur only at Stage 6; they exist at all of them. Consider the stark contrasts between Plato's republic and that of the United States. Where liberal education in the United States leads Americans to conceptualize an abstract notion of the individual, with inalienable rights against all governments, Plato hoped that his polis would encourage citizens to see the virtue of the properly structured group.

Thus, the right ordering for Plato of wisdom, spirit, and appetite in the soul required a political environment in which the theorists would rule, in which the soldiers would live collectively,and in which the farmers and merchants would accept a subordinate political position in exchange for economic security and reciprocity. The government would replace the nuclear family altogether, separating children from parents at an early age for an education that would integrate them thoroughly into the community. In short, Plato's Stage 6 conception of justice ended up defining the laws and institutions that were to govern the mass of citizens at Stages 1 through 5.

Or examine how the stages would operate in relation to the authority of Scripture:

Stage 1:   Fear of Punishment. People behave morally out of fear of hell or excommunication.

Stage 2:   Instrumental Hedonism. People behave morally in order to gain private favors from God.

Stage 3:   Good Boy (in this case, Choir Boy). People learn to "Love the Lord thy God, with all thy heart, with all thy soul, and with all thy might."

Stage 4:   Orientation to Authority, Law, and Duty. People adhere to the rituals of the church or synagogue.

Stage 5:   Social Contract. People live by the Ten Commandments.

Stage 6: Universal Principles. People live in accordance with the Golden Rule, or its comparable formulation within Judaism.

A schema of this sort seems to lend support to the argument that the cognitive structure of all ethical systems is the same, regardless of their content. Can the content be ignored, however? For the Puritans who signed John Winthrop's "Model of Christian Charity," the universal goal was, "to improve our lives to doe more service to the Lord" (Stage 6). This principle demanded adherence to a two-part covenant (Stage 5):

There is likewise a Double Lawe by which we are regulated in our conversacion towards another. . . . By the first of these lawes man as he was enabled soe withall is commanded to love his neighbor as himself upon this ground stands all the precepts of the morall law. . . . The Lawe of the Gospell propounds likewise a difference of seasons and occasions: there is a time when a christian (though they given not all yet) must give beyond theire abillity, as they of Macedonia . . . likewise community of perills calls for extraordinary liberallity and soe doth community in some special service for the Church. Lastly, when there is noe other means whereby our Christian brother may be relieved in this distress, wee must help him beyond our ability, rather than tempt God, in putting him upon help by miraculous or extraordinary means. . . .

The covenant called for obedience to specific rules, "and a more than ordinary approbation of the Churches of Christ to seek out a place of Cohabitation and Consorteshipp under a due forme of Government both civill and ecclesiasticall" (Stage 4). It depended upon an encompassing love of God — "being delighted to shewe forthe the glory of this wisdome in the variety and difference of the Creatures and the glory of his power" (Stage 3). In return, God would favor the community with his blessing — "wee shall find that the God of Israell is among us, when tenn of us shall be able to resist a thousand of our enemies. . . ." If the people failed to live up to their commitments, God would punish them — "but if wee shall neglect the observacion of these Articles which are the ends wee have propounded . . . the Lord will surely breake out in a wrathe against us be revenged of such a perjured people and make us knowe the price of the breache of such a Covenant" (Stage 1). By remaining true to their ideals, however, they would create a commonwealth whose members would be devoted not only to God, but to one another:

Wee must be knitt together in this worke as one man, wee must entertaine each other in brotherly Affeccion, we must be willing to abridge ourselves of our superfluities, and for the supply of others necessities, wee must uphold a familiar Commerce together in all meekenes, gentleness, patience, and liberallity, wee must delight in each other, make others Condicions our owne rejoyce toegether, allwayes haveing before our eyes our Commission and Community in the work, our community as members of the same body.[22]

Once again, Stage 6 justice had defined the terms of Stage 4 laws and customs, creating a system of moral obligation vastly different from the present system.

CONCLUSION: THE LIMITS OF THE THEORY

Finally, consider the many issues between ethical systems that arouse heated debate today. Should the ideal community operate on the basis of collective, leadership, on the assumption that all members are equal in their claim to authority; or should it assume that some people are inherently more capable than others, and that the moral problem, therefore, is to insure that the proper leaders emerge? Does the preservation of the "right ordering" of the values within this community justify military self-defense against a tyrant, or does the sanctity of human life rule out murder for any reason — implying that no war can ever be said to be just? Should the community view the pursuit of material abundance as being inherently corrupt, or merely its misuse? These questions have plagued more than one social action organization since the early 1960s, even to the point of splitting them apart. They require Stage 6 reasoning in the sense that neither the law nor even the Declaration of Independence can resolve them. Yet their resolution one way or the other will have an enormous impact on the society as a whole.

Kohlberg is aware of all these issues, but they seem to be irrelevant to his concern for the form of moral arguments, regardless of content. In his "Restatement of the Platonic View," he points out that he conceives of justice "as equality instead of Plato's hierarchy" but refuses to "spend time on my disagreements with Plato."[23] In his discussion in the *International Encyclopedia of the Social Sciences* of how people at various stages would approach the value of human life, he argues that at Stage 6, "Life is valued as sacred and as representing a universal value of respect for the individual,"[24] a formulation that leaves open whether there are just grounds on which it might be sacrificed. In an assessment of moral development within various religions, he acknowledges that there are "considerable differential emphases" on "entreperneurial achievement" in the Protestant ethic, the Jewish ethic, and the Catholic ethic, but contends that these should not "obscure the common moral ideas and principles which seem to develop equally in all."[25]

Yet to anyone who wants to pursue moral education in America, these issues are of great significance. What is more, a simple appeal to an abstract conception of justice does not offer a clear way to resolve them. Whose justice does one choose — Plato's, the Puritan's, or Jefferson's? Determining the exact nature of Martin Luther King's "eternal law" becomes the issue, rather than establishing its ultimate authority over people's lives.

At this point what appears to be only a theoretical problem with Kohlberg becomes practical. Authority is not monolithic in the United States; it is divided. The founding fathers refused to go along with what the classical tradition, and even Hobbes and Rousseau, believed to be essential to a coherent system of moral and political values — namely, that the government had to reflect and espouse the highest ethical vision of its society. The cultivation of virtue simply is not the primary purpose of government in the United States, if one is to accept James Madison's arguments in the *Federalist Papers*. It is, rather, to preserve private liberty, including the liberty of competing ethical traditions to make their claims upon conscience and consciousness. If there are now moral dilemmas in the country between traditions — between Catholicism and secular humanism, for example — it is not by political default but by design.

Thus, any serious system of moral education in the United States must find a way for students and citizens to sort out their competing versions of what justice is in order to determine which of them ought to govern the· laws and institutions. The uncertainty about how to do this in a way that respects both religious liberty and the separation of church and state is what has paralyzed efforts to bring explicit programs of moral education into the schools. It also accounts for the reluctance of many activists to cast their arguments in terms of high moral principles. An appeal to one ethical ideal in America may not only ignore those who do not accept it; it may offend them, as partisans on both sides of the abortion debate, for example, have discovered. For many reformers, then, the alternative seems to be to reduce such conflicts to their lowest denominator, that is, to Stage 2 questions of interests, costs, and benefits that deliberately obscure the values from which those interests, costs, and benefits are being derived. Better to confuse the public, it appears, than to arouse it.

From the standpoint of raising the level of moral debate, of course, the reductionist solution is no solution at all. It cannot work even on its own terms. The moment someone asks, "Who benefits?" and "Why?" the discussion must shift to a higher level of abstraction. In Kohlberg's terms, the discussion must shift to a higher stage of moral reasoning. Indeed, to the extent that Kohlberg is now indicating ways for citizens to engage in those debates without tearing one another apart, he is performing an invaluable service. Yet there is a limit to his procedure as well. It can help one find the morality behind the law but not the morality behind the morality. For that the content of an argument must be examined, not merely the structures of authority it represents. This dilemma, it would seem, remains the major challenge facing both moral educators and social activists in the years ahead.

NOTES

1. Andrew M. Greeley, *Unsecular Man: the Persistence of Religion* (New York: Delta, 1972).

2. See, especially, Barbara Bick, *Culture and Politics: Notes From a Conference* (Washington, D.C.: Institute for Policy Studies, 1976).

3. Lawrence Kohlberg, "Education for Justice: A Modern Restatement of the Platonic View," in *Moral Education*, ed. Theodore Sizer (Cambridge, Mass.: Harvard University Press, 1970), p. 66.

4. Ibid., p. 83.

5. Ibid., p. 59.

6. Ibid., p. 82.

7. Lawrence Kohlberg, Continuities in Childhood and Adult Moral Development Revisited," in *Life-Span Developmental Psychology: Personality and Socialization*, ed. Paul B. Boltes and K. Warner Schaie (New York: Academic Press, 1973), p. 186.

8. Thomas Hobbes, *Leviathan,* ed. C.B. Macpherson (Middlesex, England: Penguin, 1968), Part III, Ch. 42, pp. 536–37.

9. Ibid., p. 537

10. Jean Jacques Rousseau, *Social Contract,* ed. Ernest Barker (New York: Oxford University Press, 1962), Book 4, Ch. 8, p. 303.

11. Sheldon Wolin, *Politics and Wisdom,* (Boston: Little, Brown, 1959).

12. Kohlberg, "Education for Justice", p. 68.

13. Gilbert K. Chesterton, *Orthodoxy* (Garden City, N.Y.: Doubleday Image, 1959), pp. 106–109. *Passim*

14. John Schaar, "The Case for Patriotism," in *New American Review #17* (New York: Bantam, 1975), p. 62.

15. Ibid.

16. Hobbes, *Leviathan,* XLIII, p. 609.

17. Kohlberg, "Education for Justice," p. 76.

18. Ibid., pp. 76–77.

19. Plato, *The Republic,* ed. and trans. Alan Bloom (New York: Basic Books, 1968), Book IV/443 c-444a, p. 123.

20. John Winthrop, "Model of Christian Charity," in *The Puritans: A Sourcebook of Their Writings,* ed. Perry Miller and Thomas H. Johnson (New York: Harper, 1938), p. 195.

21. John Rawls, *A Theory of Justice,* (Cambridge, Mass: Harvard University Press, 1971) p. 58.

22. Winthrop, "Model of Christian Charity," pp. 197–199.

23. Kohlberg, "Education for Justice," p. 58.

24. Lawrence Kohlberg, "Moral Development," in *International Encyclopedia of the Social Sciences* (New York: Crowell, Collier and MacMillan, 1968), p. 490.

25. Lawrence Kohlberg, "Moral and Religious Education and the Public Schools: A Developmental View," in *Religion and Public Education,* ed. Theodore Sizer (Boston: Houghton-Mifflin, 1967) p. 180.

13

PARENTAL SOURCES AND POLITICAL CONSEQUENCES OF LEVELS OF MORAL REASONING AMONG EUROPEAN UNIVERSITY STUDENTS

Robert E. O'Connor

This chapter proposes to look at the moral development of undergraduates at three European universities and to relate the findings to the childhood socialization experiences of the undergraduates. It will then examine the relationship between moral reasoning and a number of political variables. Do postconventional moral reasoners hold political values that are different from those of preconventional or conventional moral reasoners? Ideally, this study would include data gathered during the childhood of the respondents as well as measures of moral reasoning and political attitudes attained later in their lives. However, as is often the case in socialization studies, the study depends upon respondent recall for the childhood measures. Although dependence on recall does suggest caution in the interpretation of findings, the respondents in this study probably made more accurate statements than do many other adult samples;[1] almost all of the respondents were between the ages of 18 and 21, so their childhood experiences were not distant memories. Almost all had parents who were still alive, so their memories were not infused with the glorifications often associated with deceased parents. And all had undergone at least one year of college education, which presumably included training in how to respond accurately to questions.

This paper is a secondary analysis of data collected by the author in a 1970 study of the sources of student political activism.[2] The advantages of doing a secondary analysis have been enormous in terms of time and money. The "free" use of almost 900 interviews gathered in three nations is an opportunity not to be belittled. However, the costs of doing a secondary analysis are also considerable. The original socialization measures were designed as part of operationalizations of various models purporting to account for student activism. The measures were not designed to test hypotheses of childhood influence on moral development. If the study had been designed for this latter purpose, more aspects of parental behavior would have been examined. Also, multiple measures of concepts measured in this study by one or two items would have been employed. Nevertheless, in spite of these substantial variations from an ideal study, findings do emerge that suggest that different types of parental behavior systematically affect moral development.

The original study, which provided the data for this paper, also provides a response to the "so what?" question. A cynic might ask why anyone should care which parental behaviors are likely to result in what kinds of moral development. The cynic might argue that, unless the Kohlberg variable can be shown to relate to behavior, such efforts to account for different levels of moral development might be better directed elsewhere. The earlier study found, however, that moral reasoning was the single best predictor of political activism among the 50 not explicitly political variables in that analysis.

SETTING AND SAMPLING

Samples of students were contacted in the fall of 1970 at the Universities of Essex in England, St. Andrews in Scotland, and Montpellier in France. These universities were selected to maximize diversity within the limits imposed by the temporal, financial, and lingual resources of the researchers. Since the original study sought to account for variance in activism, schools with different quantities of activism at that time were chosen. The University of Essex is a new university with a modern curriculum and a reputation for left-wing activism. The University of St. Andrews is an ancient school with a traditional curriculum and a reputation for conservatism. The University of Montpellier falls somewhere between the extreme positions of Essex and St. Andrews on these dimensions.

The student body of the University of Essex probably differs from a random sample of British university students by underrepresenting conservatives. Founded in the early 1960s in a nation that places great value upon tradition, the University of Essex immediately evokes negative reactions from traditional Britishers. Another reason conservative students would prefer a different school is Essex's reputation for radical politics. This reputation is not undeserved, since the university in its brief history has been the site of building occupations, countless demonstrations, a shouting-down of right-winger Enoch Powell, and an inept attempt to ignite the local branch of Barclay's Bank.

The University of St. Andrews was selected because it serves as a contrast to Essex. Although both institutions are coeducational and each includes nearly 2,000 students, St. Andrews takes great pride in its centuries of tradition and is markedly conservative. Essex student elections, for example, raise serious issues such as the proper role of the university in a democratic society. At St. Andrews, students assiduously attend to the forms of democracy with much campaigning and postermaking; but it is all hollow, as the campaigns are virtually issue-free contests between personalities who proclaim that they are the most experienced candidates or will do the best job. Few specific campaign promises are even made or issues raised.* In 1970, Essex had practically no right-wing political activity, whereas St. Andrews had a very active Conservative Association whose honorary chairman was Powell. Thus, the student body of St. Andrews probably overrepresents the conservatives in comparison with a random sample of all British university students.

The University of Montpellier differs from both Essex and St. Andrews in size, setting, and the regional homogeneity of its students. As the French government requires that, with few exceptions, students attend the university of their area of birth, over 80 percent of Montpellier students are natives of the Languedoc region. Montpellier students therefore would seem to be representative of French students to the degree that Languedoc is like the rest of France. Languedoc is disproportionately agricultural (16.5 percent of the people versus 9.9 percent for all of France), under-industrialized (20.4 percent workers versus 28.0 percent for all France), elderly, and copiously supplied with small businesses (8.8 percent merchants and only 6.3 percent clerks).[3] The university's urban setting and scale (almost 25,000 students) also is quite distinct from the small-town campuses and small student bodies of Essex and St. Andrews, in political traditions and in the national culture in which it exists. The French school lacks both the brief but extraordinary history of activism of Essex and the staid, almost otherworldliness of traditional St. Andrews.

Ideally, for a study of students, a random sample would be selected from lists of all students currently in attendance. Instead, samples of addresses of students in the previous year were drawn by use of a table of random numbers. Everyone living at the addresses selected was then contacted, regardless of the number of returns to the same address that were necessary in order to contact all residents of the address. This sampling approach, the best approximation to a truly random method, was utilized

---

*As though to make the point, in November 1970 the students at St. Andrews elected to .the rectorship—usually an honorary position but one with great potential since the rector is a voting member of the university's five-member governing board—John Cleese, an English comedian.

for three reasons. First, sampling by address increases the actual degree of anonymity while creating an aura of anonymity. Never did the researchers find themselves asking for a specific person whose name they knew. The total anonymity seems to have been a major factor responsible for the high completion rates of 96 percent at Montpellier, .95 percent at Essex, and 92 percent at St. Andrews.

Second, sampling by addresses introduced a clustering that enabled the researchers to secure many completed questionnaires daily. The researchers handed the written questionnaires to students, then waited while the students completed their responses. This enabled several students to work on the questionnaire simultaneously with great savings of time for the researchers.* The third reason for the adoption of a cluster sampling design was an inability to obtain a list of students' names with addresses at Essex and Montpellier for the current academic year. Even if straight random sampling were preferable, it could not have been carried out at these two universities, which do not make public students' names with addresses.†

For Essex, a sample size of one hundred addresses was selected. This number was thought to be adequate for producing sufficient numbers of completed questionnaires to ensure that true population values lie within 5 percent of the sample estimates. The N of 376 realizes this criterion. For the St. Andrews sample, a much smaller number of addresses was chosen because the researchers in the earlier study did not expect to find any activists and therefore would not need the larger N required for slight differences between activists and nonactivists to be statistically significant. For Montpellier, a sample of approximately ninety addresses was chosen to ensure that the St. Andrews N of 185 would be substantially exceeded. The resulting 325 completed questionnaires permit inference making with almost the same confidence as in the Essex sample.

---

*The median time for completion was approximately 30 minutes, with the mean being somewhat longer.

†One bias with this approach is that students living in larger groups are oversampled. Students would more likely have been included in the sample if they lived in a commune of 15 students than if they lived alone because the sample was of addresses rather than names. This bias is significant as it is related to activism, the dependent variable. Students living in apartments shared with other students are more active than students boarding with families in bed-and-breakfast arrangements. Students in their own flats are almost invariably in groups; students in bed-and-breakfast abodes generally live alone. Fortunately, the researchers anticipated this bias and attempted to compensate for it by including the addresses of first-year students, who live disproportionately in bed-and-breakfast dwellings, in the master lists from which sample addresses were selected. Oversampling bed-and-breakfast addresses compensates for the oversampling of individuals who live in larger groups. Although the bed-and-breakfast addresses often were found to include first-year students, these students were excluded from this study. First-year students would almost invariably appear to be nonactive politically because their short tenure at university before the administration of the questionnaire afforded them little opportunity for political activism.

MORAL REASONING

Lawrence Kohlberg's concept of moral reasoning is the dependent variable of this part of the study.[4] Through intensive interviewing, Kohlberg places respondents into six categories. Kohlberg's categories have been reduced here to a trichotomy of preconventional, conventional and post-conventional moral reasoners. The extensive (almost 900 interviews) rather than intensive (much time with only a few respondents) nature of this project limits the ability to probe each respondent to make difficult, sensitive measurement determinations. As a trichotomy, moral reasoning may have lost some of its elegance, but retains both its theoretical importance and, as noted above, its ability to predict behavior. Perhaps treatment of this variable as a trichotomy avoids splitting of some hairs that empirically cannot easily or usefully be split. In any event, it was possible to attain intercoder reliability of well over 90 percent in the treatment of moral reasoning as a trichotomy.

Kohlberg was read as saying that preconventional individuals are really amoral, in that right action for them is defined as actions satisfying their own needs regardless of the consequences for others. For preconventional individuals, rights are ownership rights, permitting one to do what one pleases with one's possessions. The only aspects of a behavior that would make it "bad" for the preconventional individuals would be finding it unenjoyable or being punished for doing it. Preconventionality is most clear in the amorality of the young child who has not yet learned the difference between right and wrong. However, preconventionality is in no way limited to children or to students. One adult writes, "So far, about morals, I know only that what is moral is what you feel good after and what is immoral is what you feel bad after and judged by these moral standards, which I do not defend, the bull-fight is very moral to me because I feel very fine while it is going on . . . and after it is over I feel very sad but very fine."[5]

A typical preconventional response to a dilemma posed in the questionnaire was given by a St. Andrews student. The question was whether it was right for a husband to steal a small amount of money from an avaricious cruise company in order to buy a ticket from the company for a life-saving cruise for his ill wife. The student wrote:

R.   The husband should not have broken into the office because it was rather stupid. As far as he was concerned it was right and remained right as long as he wasn't found out. The idea of breaking into the offices of the cruise company seems odd. Why pick them? Why not have his wife do the act if she wants to be saved?

Q. In the absence of a law setting a limit to the price, did the owner have a right to charge so much for the ticket?

R. Yes, he did, he was trying to run at a profit. . . .

Q. If the husband does not feel very close or affectionate to his wife should he still steal the money to buy the ticket?

R. There would hardly be any point.

Q. Would you steal the money to save your wife's life?

R. Probably, if I still loved her.

This respondent is clearly preconventional. The theft, for him, is right as long as he is not caught and punished. Right is not determined by law or by what is necessary to preserve human life. In fact, there would hardly be any point in helping to keep his wife alive if he no longer felt close to her. If he still loved her, though, he would steal the money. Right for this respondent is a matter of furthering his own selfish interests. Right for him resides neither in law nor in principled behavior.

The second category of the trichotomy derived from the work of Kohlberg is that of conventional morality. Here is the "good boy" orientation. A conventional individual defines right action in terms of the approval of others, especially authorities, in maintaining the social order for its own sake, in doing one's duty, and in showing respect for authority. Although Kohlberg might differ, conventional morality has been coded for this study to include any contractual-legalistic orientation that seems to evade moral issues.* A typical response of this type follows. The dilemma is again that of a theft of money from an avaricious cruise company to enable the purchase of a life-saving ticket.

R. Undoubtedly wrong. Whatever the situation concerning his wife, it would not warrant the committing of any crime. Simply because fate has treated you unkindly, there is no reason why you should try to take it out on someone else or on the rest of society; the crime of theft is no less immoral because you are desperate for money. The psychological motivation is apparent, especially since he stole from the company concerned because this would give a touch of irony which would appeal to a mind in desperation. Thus, although he was probably not the criminal type, what he did was wrong because theft is an immoral action. The difficulty here is of course to try and look at the problem objectively.

---

*Kohlberg breaks the trichotomy into six stages, the fifth of which gives much emphasis to the importance of maintaining contracts. Here individuals have been coded at this stage, which is difficult to distinguish from the law-and-order stages, as conventional. The intent is not to imply that conventional moral reasoners are necessarily unprincipled, but that they choose obedience to authorities as their ultimate value in justifying their behavior. This choice is not only justifiable, but actually is preferable from a Hobbesian perspective.

Q. The husband was caught a month after he stole the money and brought before a magistrate. Should the magistrate send the husband to prison? Why?

R. Yes, because he has committed a crime.

The third Kohlberg category consists of postconventional individuals. They manifest a principled orientation in which behavior is justified by appeals to abstractions such as the Golden Rule and the categorical imperative. To a postconventional individual, logical consistency and universality are important. The orientation is to conscience as the directing agent and includes a salient respect for the sanctity of human life — as in the following response to the same dilemma:

R. In this case the theft can be justified because a human life is more important than money and in such a situation human life comes before all other considerations.

Q. The husband was arrested a month later and brought before a judge. Should he be sent to jail? Why? Why not?

R. No, he ought to be acquitted because his goal went in the direction of justice whereas the intransigence of the proprietor resulted from his (monetary) stake in it.

Q. If the husband does not love his wife a great deal, should he steal the money for the ticket anyway?

R. He must do it because a human life is at stake and this has the same value if he loves his wife or not.

Q. Would you steal the money to save your wife's life?

R. That depends on the circumstances but in the impossibility of doing otherwise the response is affirmative.*

All respondents were coded as preconventional, conventional, or postconventional according to their responses to two moral dilemmas.[6] The dilemmas were modified slightly to take into account cultural factors that would have caused confusion if the unmodified dilemmas had been used. In addition the dilemmas just posed — that of the morality of a husband stealing a small amount of money from an avaricious cruise company in order to buy a ticket from the company for a life-saving cruise for his ill wife, the other dilemma asked if a doctor should save his wife's life or the lives of two other persons in a situation involving access to kidney dialysis equipment. Two coders made independent evaluations of the responses,

---

*This response was made by a French university student and translated by the author.

which were coded independently from the other sections of the questionnaire in order to minimize biases. The coders agreed on well over 90 percent of their initial independent judgments and were able to reach agreement on the few other respondents through a careful rereading and discussion. Table 13.1 reports that there were significant differences among the student bodies at the three universities. The Essex and French patterns are similar, with pluralities of postconventional students, but the French sample has clearly the higher proportion. At St. Andrews almost half of the students were conventional in their moral reasoning.

In the analyses that follow, moral reasoning has been treated as a nominal rather than ordinal variable. Although Kohlberg seems to argue that changes are always step by step from lower to higher stages, the evidence for this conclusion is not overwhelming.[7] There are no known studies that demonstrate that some students do not enter a university at a conventional state, pass through a preconventional stage of a mindless "freedom," and then advance to postconventionality. Also treatment of moral reasoning as a nominal variable does not, within the purposes of this paper, lessen the theoretical significance of the concept. Unless otherwise noted, all relationships are two-by-two tables in which the dependent variable is preconventionality, conventionality, or postconventionality.

TABLE 13.1

Moral Reasoning
(percent of sample)

	Essex	St. Andrews	Montpellier
Preconventional	29.8	21.9	20.9
Conventional	28.4	45.4	22.8
Postconventional	41.8	32.8	56.3

Note: The significance levels for the differences between the Essex and St. Andrews responses were .05 for the preconventional level, .0001 for the conventional, and .05 for the post conventional; for Essex and Montpellier .01 N.S., and .0001, respectively; and for St. Andrews and Montpellier, N.S., .0001, and .0001.

Source: Compiled by the author.

PERMISSIVENESS

Although many words have been written and spoken in praise or damnation of permissiveness, general agreement on what the concept means has not been attained. To Benjamin Spock, permissiveness involves the absence of harsh punishments, the open acceptance of sexuality, and the encouragement of individuality and self-expression.[8] In other minds, however, permissiveness is equated with an anything-goes approach to parenting. Rather than attempt to develop a detailed measure of permissiveness, and quite possibly move beyond the recall powers of the respondents in this study, the researchers were content to define permissiveness by what it is not. There seems to be general agreement that a permissive upbringing is one that is not strict and one in which parents do not order their children about without providing reasons for the commands. Respondents were coded as permissively reared if they disagreed with two statements: "When I was a child, my parents very often told me to do things without explaining to me why these things should be done," and "My parents were very strict in raising me." Students who disagreed with only one of these statements or who agreed with both were coded as not permissively reared.

Martin Hoffman and Herbert Saltzstein found that parents who used inductive rearing methods (that is, focused on the consequences of children's actions for others) rather than power assertion were less likely to produce preconventional children.[9] Following this finding, it is hypothesized that permissiveness is positively related to postconventionality and negatively related to preconventionality. Table 13.2 reports that these expectations are borne out, but only among the French students. Among French students with permissive upbringings, 62.6 percent were postconventional; among French students without permissive upbringings, only 52.6 percent were postconventional.

TABLE 13.2

Correlation of Moral Reasoning with Permissiveness

	Essex	St. Andrews	Montpellier
Preconventionality	.18	−.03	−.29*
Conventionality	−.08	−.01	−.02
Postconventionality	−.06	.08	.20*

*Significant at .05 level.
Source: Compiled by the author.

Permissiveness cannot be entirely dismissed as irrelevant in explaining the moral development of Essex students. Table 13.3 repeats Table 13.2, but includes only students from upper-income families. Here there is some evidence in support of spoiled-brat notions of permissiveness. Among Essex upper-income students with permissive upbringings, 42.4 percent were preconventional; among students of the same privileged class without permissive upbringings, only 21.9 percent were preconventional.

TABLE 13.3

Correlation of Moral Reasoning with Permissiveness among Upper-Income Students

		Essex	St. Andrews	Montpellier
Preconventionality		.45*	−.09	−.36
Conventionality		.06	−.04	.05
Postconventionality		−.39*	.14	.27
	N =	65	55	38

*Significant at .05 level.
Source: Compiled by the author.

Permissiveness, even as crudely measured as in this study, does foster postconventionality and reduce preconventionality among French students. These expected relationships, however, break down among the British students and actually are reversed among upper-income youths at Essex. It can be theorized, with some support in the literature,[10] that a French and an upper-class English student, both coded as permissively raised in this study, actually are likely to have had significantly different upbringings. The French student would most likely have had inductive training in which his parents focused on the consequences of his behavior for others. In contrast, the upper-income English student, also coded as permissively reared, would most likely have had parents who allowed him to do as he pleased. The French student would disagree with "When I was a child, my parents very often told me to do things without explaining to me why these things should be done," because his parents told him why he should act in a particular manner. The affluent Essex student also would disagree with the statement, but because his parents rarely told him to do anything. Both these students would be coded as permissively reared, although their upbringings were critically different. Here is an area where further study, with more subtle measurements of permissiveness beyond the dichotomy indicated here, would seem fruitful.

MORALISTIC SOCIALIZATION

Does parental stress on the difference between right and wrong help to bring about postconventionality? Does frequent church attendance produce a similar result? The second question can be answered simply: the frequency of church attendance as remembered by respondents from their childhood fails to correlate with any of the three moral reasoning variables. The first question requires a more complex response.

Table 13.4 shows that a moralistic socialization, as measured by agreement that "my parents used to impress upon me very strongly the difference between right and wrong," is certainly not predictive of postconventionality. There was a slight tendency at all three schools for moralistic socialization to correlate with conventionality. Perhaps parental harping on right-wrong differences is usually accompanied by views that authorities provide appropriate yardsticks for what is right and wrong. "Do what's right" may be taught to be the equivalent of "Do what the authorities say," clearly the point of view of a conventional moral reasoner.

TABLE 13.4

Correlation of Moral Reasoning with Moralistic Socialization

	Essex	St. Andrews	Montpellier
Preconventionality	−.29*	.01	−.13
Conventionality	.25	.23	.17
Postconventionality	−.10	.02	−.03

*Significant at .05 level.
Source: Compiled by the author.

The effects of this moralistic socialization by parents were especially strong among upper-income students at St. Andrews and Montpellier. As noted in Table 13.5 the variable is strongly positively related to conventionality and negatively related to preconventionality. Although not reported in tabular form here, this same pattern was found among lower-income students at Essex. Parents who stress right-wrong differences seem likely to reduce the chances that their offspring will be preconventional, increase the chances for conventionality, and have no effect on probabilities for postconventionality.

TABLE 13.5

Correlation of Moral Reasoning with Morality Socialization among Upper-Income Students

		Essex	St. Andrews	Montpellier
Preconventionality		−.14	−.70[a]	−.43[b]
Conventionality		.29	.68[a]	.58[b]
Postconventionality		−.18	−.13	.13
	N =	65	55	38

[a] Significant at .01 level.
[b] Significant at .05 level.
Source: Compiled by the author.

COMPETITIVE SOCIALIZATION

Some parents provide storng encouragement for their children to do well in school, and stress career goals for their offspring. Other parents are reluctant to place such an emphasis on striving for success. It is hypothesized that the former parents, who are labeled competitive, are more likely to produce undergraduates of conventional moral reasoning. "Making it" generally involves success within definitional constructs of the dominant culture. It involves accepting the legitimacy of the rules of the game and doing well within those rules. This is clearly the realm of the conventional moral reasoner.

Students were coded as competitively socialized if they agreed that two statements were valid or very valid: "My parents gave me strong encouragement to do well at school so that I could get into a good university," and "My parents have always encouraged me to aim for a career goal and to work hard to achieve it." Students who found only one of these statements to be valid or who disagreed with both of them were coded as not competitively socialized.

As evident in Table 13.6, the hypothesis that a competitive socialization leads to conventional moral reasoning has slight credibility among the St. Andrews students, but none at all among Essex and Montpellier students. At Essex, the number of competitively socialized students among preconventional moral reasoners is disproportionate. It is hypothesized that differences between Essex and St. Andrews may be accounted for by the different experiences of working-class students at the schools. At Essex, much of the rhetoric from student leaders involves a glorification of the working class. Competitively socialized lower-income students at Essex may rebel at this striving for middle-class respectability and the rejection of their own class backgrounds. Their môral reasoning may regress from conventional to preconventional. At St. Andrews, hearing no rhetoric invoking the splendors of the working class, lower-income students would retain the conventional moral reasoning produced by their competitive socializations. The findings reported in Table 13.7 lend support to this argument. A competitive socialization correlates with conventionality among St. Andrews lower-income students and with preconventionality among those at Essex.

TABLE 13.6

Correlation of Moral Reasoning with Competitive Socialization

	Essex	St. Andrews	Montpellier
Preconventionality	.24*	−.20	−.00
Conventionality	−.09	.21	.00
Postconventionality	−.22*	−.04	.01

*Significant at .05 level.
Source: Compiled by the author.

TABLE 13.7

Correlation of Moral Reasoning with Competitive Socialization among Lower-Income Students

		Essex	St. Andrews	Montpellier
Preconventionality		.29*	−.53*	.03
Conventionality		.04	.47*	.03
Postconventionality		−.19	.01	−.09
	N =	177	69	110

*Significant at .05 level.
Source: Compiled by the author.

"RED DIAPER" SOCIALIZATION

As a final effort to account for moral reasoning through parental socialization, it is hypothesized that undergraduates with politically active, left-wing parents will be found in disproportionate numbers among post-conventional reasoners. Left-wing ideologies reject the naive hedonism of preconventionality and the acceptance of the status quo of conventionality. Left-wing politics generally involves the rejection of much behavior by authorities as inconsistent with principles such as democracy and equality. It is hypothesized that left-wing parents teach their offspring that political behavior must be evaluated in terms of its congruence with principles and that, as a consequence of this teaching, the offspring are likely to develop postconventional moral reasoning.

Students were coded as having a "red diaper" socialization if either of their parents was viewed as "moderately liberal, very liberal, or further left" and if either of their parents was viewed as "moderately active, active, or very active." Students without a left-wing parent, an active parent, or left-wing and active parents were coded as lacking a "red diaper" socialization.

Table 13.8 shows that the researchers' expectations were realized, especially among the St. Andrews students. Of the students with "red diaper" socializations at St. Andrews, 43.9 percent were postconventional moral reasoners; only 29.2 percent of students without left-wing socializations attained postconventionality. The French correlation coefficients run in the expected direction, but are small. A closer analysis of the data demonstrates that the parental activism dimension of "red diaper" socialization shows no relationship to the moral reasoning variables, but that the pa-

TABLE 13.8

Correlation of Moral Reasoning with "Red Diaper" Socialization

	Essex	St. Andrews	Montpellier
Preconventionality	.02	−.08	.01
Conventionality	−.38[a]	−.24[b]	−.19
Postconventionality	.21[b]	.31[b]	.15

[a] Significant at .01 level.
[b] Significant at .05 level.
Source: Compiled by the author.

rental attitudinal dimension is strongly related to conventionality and post-conventionality. The correlation coefficient between having a left-wing parent and conventionality is − .40; that between having a left-wing parent and postconventionality is .30. Only 15.9 percent of the French students with a left-wing parent were conventional moral reasoners; 30.8 percent of the French students without a left-wing parent were conventional moral reasoners. Clearly, having a left-wing parent makes a difference.

Conventional moral reasoners form almost a political mirror image of postconventional moral reasoners. The former place themselves on the Right more frequently, express a greater willingness to limit free speech, are more likely to oppose the Cuban revolution and are more willing to trust authorities. These attitudes are not surprising in individuals who justify their behavior to themselves in terms of community standards generally defined by authorities.

The only exceptions to this portrayal of postconventional moral reasoners are the free speech issue in Essex and the questioning of authorities in France. These exceptions may both be accounted for by the lack of variance on the matters in each locale; at Essex, almost everyone supports free speech, and at Montpellier, almost no one is willing to give authorities the benefit of the doubt.

POLITICAL IMPLICATIONS

Earlier study demonstrated that moral reasoning is indeed related to political activism, at least of the left-wing variety, as postconventional moral reasoners were shown to be disproportionately active. As Table 13.9 demonstrates, moral reasoning is also related to a series of political attitudes. Postconventional moral reasoners are more likely to place themselves on the Left when given a six-point scale, are more likely to support the Cuban revolution, are more likely to disapprove of limiting freedom of speech for anyone, and are more likely to feel that the decisions of political leaders should be questioned.* They might be summarized as members of the idealistically romantic Left.

---

*The actual wording of the question is: "What position is closest to your political view? Farther left, very liberal, moderately liberal, moderately conservative, very conservative, farther right." The three Likert items are (1) The Cuban Revolution generally should be applauded; (2) Even though freedom of speech for all groups is a worthwhile goal, it is unfortunately necessary to restrict the freedom of speech of certain political groups; (3) Political leaders generally have access to information which the public cannot see and therefore their decisions should not be questioned too readily.

On every question in Table 13.9, preconventional moral reasoners are found to lie between conventional and postconventional moral reasoners. Knowing that certain students are preconventional gives little information about their political views or level of activism. This is not surprising since preconventionality, as a naive hedonism, seems to discourage the development of ideologies that might guide behavior.[11] Ideologies perform important functions, as they provide guidelines for behavior.[12] An individual without an ideology may have to expend extra effort deciding how to decide what should be done in many instances. An individual with an ideology has a decision rule to guide his behavior.

TABLE 13.9

Correlation of Political Attitudes with Moral Reasoning

	Essex	St. Andrews	Montpellier
Position on right-left continuum			
Preconventionality	.18[a]	.28[a]	.15
Conventionality	−.71[d]	−.52[d]	−.54[d]
Postconventionality	.48[d]	.36[b]	.30[c]
Suppport of the Cuban revolution			
Preconventionality	.06	−.16	−.13
Conventionality	−.61[d]	−.40[d]	−.33[d]
Postconventionality	.48[d]	.30[b]	.32[d]
Support of freedom of speech			
Preconventionality	.06	−.02	.01
Conventionality	−.17[a]	−.16	−.44[d]
Postconventionality	.09	.22[a]	.31[d]
Disagree that authorities should not be questioned too readily			
Preconventionality	.08	.21	.03
Conventionality	−.46[d]	−.32[b]	−.20[a]
Postconventionality	.35[d]	.21[a]	.13

[a] Significant at .05 level.
[b] Significant at .01 level.
[c] Significant at .001 level.
[d] Significant at .0001 level.
Source: Compiled by the author.

Preconventionality, by hindering the adoption of ideologies, is inherently unstable. Nonetheless, individuals may find the "freedom" of preconventionality or postconventionality after occasional walks on the wild side. Thus, whereas the moral-reasoning trichotomy may be normatively developmental, it is uspected that empirically some individuals go from conventionality to preconventionality and then perhaps to postconventionality. At least, this is a conjecture worthy of empirical examination through study of the moral reasoning of adults through time.*

CONCLUSIONS

Four conclusions emerge from this study. First, one's level of moral reasoning is significantly related to parental socialization experiences.[13] How one grows up does affect one's moral reasoning as an undergraduate. Table 13.10 summarizes the 10 (12, if one considers left-wing parents in France) significant relations found among the 36 examined. If relationships are found in a secondary analysis with crude, dichotomous measures, how much more might be learned with a well-designed, sophisticated search for the sources of levels of moral reasoning? Clearly an extension to nonparental sources (for example, schools) also would contribute a great deal.

TABLE 13.10

Significant Relationships between Socialization Variables and Moral Reasoning Level

	Essex	St. Andrews	Montpellier
Preconventionality	− Moralistic + Competitive		− Permissive
Conventionality	+ Moralistic − Red Diaper	− Red Diaper	− (left-wing parent)
Postconventionality	− Competitive + Red Diaper	+ Red Diaper	+ Permissive + (left-wing parent)

Note: Plus sign indicates positive relationship; minus sign indicates negative relationship.
Source: Compiled by the author.

*There are no known studies that examine changes in the moral development of college students or other adults. The closest is the work of James Rest, previously cited, who tested high school seniors and then retested his subjects two years later. It is to be hoped that he will continue retesting these individuals at two-year intervals.

Second, the "red diaper" socialization variable seems most measurable in distinguishing the socialization experiences of postconventional moral reasoners from those of conventional moral reasoners. This suggests that political attitudes are more than a consequence of moral reasoning but, through the socialization behavior of parents, they may strongly influence moral development. It may be difficult to discuss moral reasoning fruitfully without discussing politics.

Third, the findings are consistent at all three universities. In no instance does a socialization variable that relates positively to a level of moral development at one school relate negatively to the same level of moral development at another school. This consistency is especially strong when levels of moral reasoning are correlated with political attitudes. The cross-national similarities give more credibility to the findings than would occur if this paper were a case study.

Finally, among these students in 1970, conventional moral reasoners were found to be disproportionately right-wing, postconventional moral reasoners were found to be disproportionately left-wing, and preconventional moral reasoners were between the extremes. Moral reasoning, then, is not merely an esoteric concept of interest only to philosophers and theologians. It is a measurable variable that can help political scientists understand political attitudes and behavior and may even be essential to that understanding. It is to be hoped that just what moral reasoning can contribute to the understanding of political phenomena will soon cease being a matter of conjecture and become a debate over the interpretation of many systematic studies.

NOTES

1. The problem of the reliability of reported attitudes is discussed by Kent L. Tedin, "On the Reliability of Reported Political Attitudes," *American Journal of Political Science* 20 (1976): 117–24. Studies have shown that, at least in the case of adolescents, subjects' reports of parental behavior are accurate. See W. C. Becker, "Consequences of Different Kinds of Parental Discipline," in *Review of Child Development Research*, ed. Martin Hoffman and Lois Hoffman (New York: Russell Sage Foundation, 1964), pp. 169–208; E. S. Shaefer, "Children's Reports of Parental Behavior: An Inventory," *Child Development* 36 (1965): 413–48; and S.H. Cox, "Intrafamily Comparison of Loving-Rejecting Child-Rearing Practices," *Child Development* 41 (1970): 435–48.

2. For a discussion of that study, see Robert E. O'Connor, "Political Activism and Moral Reasoning: Political and Apolitical Students in Great Britain and France," *British Journal of Political Science* 4 (1974): 53–78; and, for a more detailed discussion, see Robert E. O'Connor, "The Activist Examined: Political and Apolitical Students at the Universities of Essex, St. Andrews, and Montpellier." Ph.D. dissertation, University of North Carolina, 1971.

3. These figures come from Institut national de la statistique et des études économiques, *Annuaire Statistique de la France* (Paris: A. Colin, 1969), p. 39.

4. See Lawrence Kohlberg, "The Development of Children's Orientations Toward a Moral Order—Sequence in the Development of Moral Thought," *Vita Humana* 6 (1963): 11–33; and Lawrence Kohlberg and Richard Kramer, "Continuities and Discontinuities in Childhood and Adult Moral Development," *Human Development* 12 (1969): 93–120.

5. Ernest Hemingway, *Death in the Afternoon* (London: Jonathan Cape, 1932), p. 8.

6. In Kohlberg's own early studies, the interviews were with children and were entirely orally conducted. The adaptations used in this study are from Norma Haan, M. Brewster Smith, and Jeanne Block, "Moral Reasoning of Young Adults: Political-Social Behavior, Family Background, and Personality Correlates," *Journal of Personality and Social Psychology* 10 (1968): 183–201.

7. Kohlberg does state, "Fifteen-year longitudinal data on fifty American males in the age periods 10–15 to 25–30 demonstrate movement is always forward and always step-by-step." Lawrence Kohlberg, "Continuities in Childhood and Adult Moral Development Revisited," in *Life-Span Developmental Psychology: Personality and Socialization,* ed. Paul B. Baltes and K. Warner Schaie (New York: Academic Press, 1973), p. 12. This conclusion is contradicted in other studies. See James Rest, "Longitudinal Study of the Defining Issues Test of Moral Judgment: A Strategy for Analyzing Developmental Change," *Developmental Psychology* 11 (1975): 738–48; and R. Kramer, "Changes in Moral Judgment Response Patterns during Late Adolescence and Young Adulthood: Retrogression in a Developmental Sequence." Ph.D. dissertation, University of Chicago, 1968.

8. Benjamin Spock, *Baby and Child Care* (New York: Duell, Sloan and Pearce, 1945).

9. Martin L. Hoffman and Herbert D. Saltzstein, "Parent Discipline and the Child's Moral Development," *Journal of Personality and Social Psychology* 5 (1967): 45–57.

10. See Ian Weinberg, *The English Public School* (New York: Atherton Press, 1967); Laurence Wylie, *Village in the Vaucluse: An Account of Life in a French Village* (New York: Harper & Row, 1964); J. C. Brown, "Education of the French Administrative Class," *Public Personnel Review* 28 (1955): 17–27; Margaret Mead and Martha Wolfenstein, eds., *Childhood in Contemporary Cultures* (Chicago: University of Chicago Press, 1955); and James Nathan and Richard Remy, "Comparative Political Socialization: A Theoretical Perspective," in *Handbook of Political Socialization*, ed. Stanley Renshon (New York: Free Press, 1977) pp. 85–111.

11. Richard Merelman argues that the development of morality is a requisite for the development of ideology. See Richard Merelman, "The Development of Political Ideology: a Framework for Analysis of Political Socialization," *American Political Science Review* 63 (1969): 750–67. Although Sullivan, Marcus, and Minns found no relationship between moral development and ideological development, their treatment of moral development as an ordinal variable with six categories differs from the conceptualization put forth here and, it is suspected, produced an attenuation of correlation. See John L. Sullivan, George E. Marcus, and Daniel R. Minns, "The Development of Political Ideology: Some Empirical Findings," *Youth and Society* 7 (1975): 148–68.

12. On the functions of ideologies, see Daniel Katz, "Attitude Formation and Public Opinion," *Annals* 367 (1966): 150–62; and Giovani Sartori, "Politics, Ideology, and Belief Systems," *American Political Science Review* 63 (1969): 398–411.

13. This finding extends to adults similar findings involving children. See Martin L. Hoffman, "Childrearing Practices and Moral Development: Generalizations from Empirical Research," *Child Development* 34 (1963): 295–318. Few studies examine the relationship between childhood socialization experiences and adult development. This has been a criticism of the relevance of much of the socialization research. See Donald Searing, Joel Schwartz, and Alden Lind, "The Structuring Principle: Political Socialization and Belief Systems," *American Political Science Review* 67 (1973): 415–32.

14

THE UNCOMFORTABLE RELATIONSHIP BETWEEN MORAL EDUCATION AND CITIZENSHIP INSTRUCTION

Jack L. Nelson

A recurring theme in educational literature is the need to educate citizens. Stated as a dominant goal of the schools, citizenship education has few dissenters. Preparation for citizenship is a primary justification for the very existence of schools, compulsory attendance by children, and the teaching of all required subjects. Teaching students to read, to manipulate numbers, to appreciate art, music, and literature, to have a physically sound body, and to recite information from history and the social sciences rests partly upon the judgment that these areas of knowledge contribute to being a good citizen. In particular, the required teaching of national history and government in the public schools is a direct result of pressures (often political) to develop in children a conception of citizenship. Citizenship education, a common goal of most subjects in the schools and a specific goal of social studies instruction, is enjoying renewed interest in the United States.[1]

A second theme of recurring emphasis in the schools is moral education. In a variety of forms and titles, including character development and values education, the essential concept in moral education has been to produce the good person. Moral education, like citizenship education, has been a dominant goal of schooling in most subjects, and a particular interest in social studies curricula. Moral education, also, has enjoyed a revitalization of interest in recent years.[2]

These two themes have typically been perceived as convergent and complementary goals in American educational history. There is a continuing belief that citizenship and moral education are identical. A survey of state educational agencies reported in 1977 that the most frequently expressed state policy was that "ethical/values education must be integrated with citizenship education; and schools should teach the skills which enable students to think and act with American civic ethics."[3]

Terrel H. Bell, former U.S. commissioner of education stated his view of the relationship: "I am in full accord that citizenship education cannot and should not be divorced from moral education. The two are intimately related, and moral education may well be the single most important component of the more general concept of citizenship education."[4] Among the grounds Bell uses to support his contention that the schools should provide moral-citizen education in a form that links the two is a statement from the 1974 *Guide for Teaching Ethical and Moral Values in Alabama Schools,* to the effect that in recent years there has been "a clearly evident decline in the spirit of patriotism and disregard for religious, moral and ethical values on the part of young people and adults as well."[5] In this context, as in virtually all of the literature on the subject, it is assumed that the qualities of citizenship to be taught in the schools are necessarily consistent with the qualities of moral thought and action to be taught.

Learning to be a citizen, it is argued, is learning to be moral. Citizenship is defined in terms of certain approved behaviors that are considered moral. Definitions of citizenship and morality are strikingly similar in school terminology, and schools are expected to educate for both. This paper explores differing definitions of each theme and suggests an arena in which education for citizenship and for moral development may be incompatible goals of the schools.

Politics and schooling are long-term associates. The political order establishes, justifies, controls, and criticizes the schools. The schools provide one type of formal and systematic mechanism for the political socialization of new generations and offer an opportunity for examination by students of the political order. While the political socialization function of schools is deeply implanted in the goals and practices of citizenship education, the examination opportunity is much less obvious and is typically avoided in school activities. Recent interest in moral education, which can incorporate examination of the moral standards of the political order, poses therefore a sensitive problem for schools.

Can instruction designed to produce loyal and obedient citizens in a political order coexist with instruction designed to encourage autonomous moral reasoning?

FUNCTIONS OF THE SCHOOLS

American schools have had a large variety of responsibilities and pressures. They have been charged with responsibility for the development of

reading, writing, and number skills, physical abilities, intellectual processes, work habits, religious and political rituals, aesthetic interests, historical and scientific information, leisure-time activities, social attributes,
automobile driving techniques, home management details, sexual practice
knowledge, and personal adjustment. Schools, in addition, have been subjected to community pressures of social conformity, mediocrity, and anti-
intellectualism.

Within the framework of these expectations, the two themes of citizenship and morality have historically predominated as essential goals of the
schools. While the operational definitions of these goals have differed
widely, they are basic rationales for establishing, altering, and continuing
the schools. A basic justification for decisions about who is to be educated,
for how long, and in what subjects rests upon one or both of these fundamental educational goals. Reading is taught as a skill necessary for active
citizenship and moral knowledge. Compulsory education for all children
emerged in democracies partly as a product of the argument for preparation
of citizens for self-government.

Manifest functions of the schools have focused on preparation of students
to fulfill social and intellectual expectations incorporated in the concepts
of citizenship and moral conduct. Latent functions of the schools include
preparation of students to conform, to be relatively docile, to fit into
socially prescribed roles, and to accept authority uncritically.[6]

The potential disparity between the manifest and latent functions of
schools is often ignored until one encroaches upon the other. When the
hidden curriculum of the school is exposed — for example, when students
have been overtly taught values relative to dissent and protest in American
history, but are not permitted to engage in protest in their own school or
community — the thoughtful students and teachers recognize the disparity.
Manifest functions of schooling for enlightened citizenship and moral development are commonly expressed in educational literature and school
documents. Latent functions stressing adherence to moralistic precepts of
citizenship behavior, dogma, and ritual are commonly practiced in the
schools and expected in society.

Jules Henry describes the nature of educational institutions, and the role
of social studies in them, as follows:

American classrooms, like educational institutions anywhere, express the values, preoccupations and fears found in the culture as a whole. School has no
choice; it must train the children to fit the culture as it is. School can give
training in skills; it cannot teach creativity. . . . An intellectually creative
child may fail, for example, in social studies, simply because he cannot understand the stupidities he is taught to believe as "fact." He may even end

up agreeing with his teachers that he is "stupid" in social studies. *Learning social studies is, to no small extent, whether in elementary school or the university, learning to be stupid* (emphasis added).[7]

AGENTS OF SOCIALIZATION

Schools, of course, are not the only agents of socialization. A variety of formal and informal institutions influence the values, attitudes, and behaviors of youth with regard to citizenship and morality. Certainly the family educates in both realms; religious institutions, mass media, and peer groups also exemplify prominent agents of political and moral socialization. Schools are, however, the most consistently organized, experienced, and controlled of the socialization agents. They are public; they exist to transmit the cultural heritage; they are the most subject to political and economic pressure; they are formally organized and relatively consistent throughout the country; they transmit experiences widely shared by virtually the entire population.

Although there is a mixed body of research findings on the relative actual influence of schooling on the political attitudes of youth,[8] there is no dispute over the pervasiveness of schooling in American society. Within the schools political education in the United States is justified on the grounds that courses in government, civics, and American history are necessary for good citizenship. There has been a presumed positive linkage between the moral concept of "good" and the political concept of "citizen."

THE DUALITY OF MORAL CITIZENSHIP IN AMERICAN EDUCATIONAL HISTORY

Schools have long had the burden of preparing young generations to have socially acceptable moral standards. It could be argued that schooling in morals is a basic condition for the existence of schools. Certainly church-related schools make this a dominant claim, since they consider instruction in religious beliefs to be the basis of moral thought and behavior. In the United States, where church-related schools are in the minority, public education has had a long history of involvement in moral education. There is a corollary history of schooling for citizenship, variously defined as civics, government, politics, and citizenship education.

Moral education is enjoying a rebirth of interest in the United States, Canada, Australia, and England. There is a cyclical history of peaks and valleys in the degree of attention paid to attempts to instill proper morality in the minds and actions of youth. Recent political events, including the Vietnam War and Watergate, have been responsible for much of the current interest in moral education in the United States, but efforts to produce the good, the right, the just, and the wise citizen through schooling in moral precepts or proper manners have permeated American educational history. Those efforts, however, led Michael Scriven, in 1975, to the conclusion that the "history of moral education in the United States is, by and large, a history of failure."[9]

This history of presumed failure has not dissuaded educators, school boards, state legislatures, and parents from eagerly pursuing some sure-fire system for implanting goodness in youth. The earliest legal documents (1642) establishing public education in the United States indicate an understanding of the dual mission of the schools with regard to moral education and citizenship training, and illustrate the public belief that schools "the moral person make":

> This court, taking into consideration the great neglect of many parents and masters in training up their children in learning and labor and other employments which may be profitable to the commonwealth, do here upon order . . . [town officials to have the power to determine the status of children's education] . . . especially of their [the children] ability to read and understand the principles of religion and the capital laws of this country . . . .[10]

The more famous Massachusetts Bay Law of 1647 includes this compelling statement: ". . . it being one chief product of the old deluder, Satan, to keep men from the knowledge of the Scriptures, as in former times by keeping them in an unknown tongue. . . ." That same law went on to require the establishment of schools to provide children with the ability to read the Scriptures and, thus, foil the old deluder, Satan.[11]

George Herbert Palmer, Alford Professor of Philosophy at Harvard, wrote in 1908 that the "problem of moral education is an old one — older indeed than schools . . . there is an increasing conscious dependence upon the school as a moulder of character."[12] Palmer went on to note ways that such moral education could take place, including direct and systematic teaching of principles in the classroom through "regular courses in 'morals and manners', 'ethics', 'behavior', 'civics', and the like"; and indirect teaching by "maintaining a high moral tone in all the work of the school . . . supervision of the social activities."[13]

In an early insight into an educational problem that persists into the current relationship between moral education and citizenship instruction, Palmer responded to his own rhetorical question of what is the central aim of teaching by stating that it is the "impartation of knowledge" and that those things that further this aim should be pursued, while anything that hinders it should be rejected. It is in the context of this defined central aim of teaching that Palmer noted:

> When schoolmasters understand their business it will be useless for the public to call to them, "We want our children to be patriotic. Drop for a time your multiplication table while you rouse enthusiasm for the old Flag." They would properly reply, "We are ready to teach American history. As a part of human knowledge, it belongs to our province. But though the politicians fail to stir patriotism, do not put their neglected work upon us."[14]

Although Palmer argued that formal instruction in ethics should be reserved for college, he understood the public confusion about the nature of primary and secondary level education and especially the education for national loyalty that had been prevalent in the public schools for at least a decade at the time of his writing. This confusion between moral education and citizenship training continued as each cycle of advocacy and criticism occurred.

The address of Reverend Benjamin Larrabee, upon his inauguration as president of Middlebury College in 1891, incorporated the well-accepted notion that morality and citizenship were so interwoven that moral education was a basic category of citizenship education.

> No instance can be found in the history of man, in which mere intellectual cultivation has proven an adequate protection to public virtue; but it is an unquestionable fact, that, in instances not a few, national morals have been at the lowest point of depression and debasement, when literature has been at the zenith of its glory; yet in the light of undisputed facts, in defiance of all the lessons of history, some of our statesmen and scholars, would have us believe, that general intelligence is the panacea for all our moral and political maladies. . . . The intellectual elevation of a nation without some degree of moral instruction, is neither safe nor desirable. . . . How often are the most gifted powers and the most rigid discipline of intellect, associated with the lowest depravation of moral principle, yet intellect is one of our national idols . . . and what christian or patriot can be indifferent as to the manner in which these youth shall be educated. . . . If not under the control of moral principle, they will become the instruments of social wretchedness and a public ruin.[15]

Larrabee continued by referring to the need for teachers who are virtuous, and he cited the case of a college president who was "an avowed infidel" and who, as an educational influence, was blamed for training "members of the Legislature, and such as held other stations of influence, to be doubting, and in many instances, to be scoffing at divine truth."[16]

Religion was obviously the moral basis for Larrabee's remarks and it dominated the education of students in moral precepts and citizenship from the time of the earliest schools in America. Cotton Mather's *A Family Well-Ordered*,[17] published in 1699, contains two sections: one for parents, in which Mather argued that the home was to develop reading and writing, encourage an interest in mathematics, but most importantly, emphasize religion; the second, addressed to the obligation of children to their parents, teachers, ministers, and public officials. Obedience and labor were the primary virtues proposed by Mather and the social context of these virtues was the continuing application of religious principles in the everyday affairs of citizens.

This religious indoctrination for citizenship was also true of the learning materials included in the *New England Primer* (1690). These incorporated moral lessons like:

> In Adam's Fall
> We Sinned all.
>
> . . .
>
> A Dog will bite
> A Thief at night.
>
> . . .
>
> The Idle Fool
> Is whipt at school.[18]

Secondary school textbooks built moral learning into the instructional content of many subjects, usually with the intent of developing good citizens. Two examples from early texts in reading and history illustrate this point. The purpose of publishing *The Young Gentleman and Lady's Monitor and English Teacher's Assistant* (1795) was set forth as follows: ". . . calculated to eradicate vulgar prejudices and rusticity of manners; improve the understanding; rectify the will; purify the passions; direct the minds of youth to the pursuits of proper objects. . . ."[19]

And Caleb Bingham's *A Historical Grammer of Universal History* (1802) used a catechetical method of questions and answers including the following:

Was idolatry established during this period?

A. The children of Noah, in the beginning of it, preserved the worship of
    the true God; but afterwards, the morals of men became altogether
    corrupt, and superstition introduced idolatry.[20]

Certainly a discussion of moral and citizenship education through
textbooks cannot overlook the McGuffey readers which were among
the most dominant books used in schools for generations, well into
the twentieth century. One can open a McGuffey reader to almost
any page and discover a moral lesson that was designed to elucidate
good citizenship while offering appropriate language instruction. The
third reader, for example, has prayers, sayings, poems, and a collection of stories, each of which ends with a statement of manners and
morals: for example, "It cured him entirely of his low and insolent
manners";[21] "You must have this fearless spirit, or you will get into
trouble, and will be, and ought to be, disliked by all";[22] "One doer
is worth a hundred dreamers";[23] "Beware of the first drink!";[24] "Now,
which of these boys, do you think, grew up to be a rich and useful
man, and which of them joined a party of tramps before he was thirty
years old?"[25]

TEACHERS AS MODELS

Teachers as well as texts have been continuously expected to share the
double burden of moral (religious) and citizenship education. An illustra-
tion of this early in American history is the contract issued to a newly
employed schoolmaster in Flatbush, New York, in 1682. The schoolmaster's defined duties included having students read prayers, leading in the
singing of psalms, requiring pupils to "be friendly in their appearance and
encourage them to answer farely and distinctly,"[26] keeping the church
clean, helping the minister, serving funeral invitations, digging graves, and
assisting in baptisms.

Not only have teachers historically had the responsibility for teaching
morality and citizenship, they have also had to act out their own teachings
under scrutiny. In the eighteenth century The Society for the Propagation
of the Gospel in Foreign Parts required potential schoolmasters to present
certificates bearing attestations to the following specifics: age, marital status, temper, prudence, learning, "sober and pious conversations," zeal in
the Christian religion, affection for the present government, and conformity to the doctrines and discipline of the Church of England. Rules for

teachers posted by a school principal in New York in 1872 included notes that women teachers who married or "engaged in unseemly conduct" would be fired and that any teacher who smoked, drank, frequented pool or public halls, or got shaved in a barber shop would be under suspicion for lack of integrity, worth, and honesty. A teacher's contract in the 1930s in North Carolina incorporated a promise to abstain from dancing and immodest dress, not to go out with men except to stimulate Sunday School work, and not to fall in love.[27]

Despite the current liberalization of schools and the unionization of teachers, there remains a public expectation that teachers will exhibit a higher set of moral and citizenship standards than is expected of other members of the community. Thus, teachers who are professed homosexuals, who undergo sex-change surgery, who engage in open dissent against the government, or who fail to conduct flag salutes in classrooms are usually in jeopardy. Indeed, in each of these specific instances teachers have been dismissed from their positions, although no claims regarding professional incompetence were made. There is, in fact, a long and sorry history of restrictions on the academic freedom of teachers under the concept that effective moral and citizenship education require that the teacher be a model of acceptable morality and citizenship.[28]

Widely publicized programs of study for schools in the mid-twentieth century continued the belief that citizenship and morality are coterminous educational activities. Following World War II, the term "character education" identified a strong movement for moral education to instill certain attitudes and behaviors in youth in the United States. A survey of school practices in the public schools, published in 1949, contains the following recommendations for character education:

> The general atmosphere of the schools must be morally and spiritually helpful. . . . One of the earliest tasks in character development is that of inculcating an understanding and appreciation of authority as a social necessity; and of stressing the fact that respect for law and authority should come from within the child — rather than be imposed upon him from without. . . . A school which has no moral or spiritual program for youth is neglecting the most essential element in the making of a good citizen.[29]

A further suggestion was that character education permeate the school, but that it be given a focus under one or more of the following titles, all of which illustrate the presumed interchangeability of moral and citizenship education:

Citizenship training
Promotion of citizenship ideals
Training in moral and spiritual ideals
Good citizenship program
Moral and spiritual development
Development of personal and social ideals
Moral and spiritual values
Moral ideals and practices
Standards of good citizenship
Democratic ideals for a good American.[30]

In legal enactments that founded schools a century before the United States was established, in laws regulating schools through to the present time, in the writings and speeches of educators, in the most prominent teaching materials, and in common expectations for schools and teachers, moral education and citizenship training are regarded as virtually synonymous.

THE STRAINED RELATION: MORAL EDUCATION

There is, however, a strain in the presumed relationship between preparing good citizens and teaching morality. Current literature in moral education and citizenship education leads to multiple possibilities and suggests that the traditional undifferentiated concept of the good student/citizen needs reconsideration.

Moral education has evolved from rigid indoctrination in absolutistic values and behavior patterns to a range of approaches to moral learning. Similarly, citizenship education has shifted from a singular structure of essential information, viewpoints, and socially approved conduct to a variety of possible educational rationales. There still exists a dominant tradition of literature and school practice built on the presumption that moral and citizen education are indistinguishable avenues for implanting prescribed social and political values in students. There are, however, potential conflicts in the adoption of differing orientations to citizenship education and moral development

Table 14.1 indicates the range of approaches currently advocated for moral education and suggests that these differences are due to varying purposes and intellectual sources.

TABLE 14.1

Approaches to Moral Education

Type	Purpose	Example Sources
Idealistic inculcation	Transmission of acceptable social morality	Theology, traditional behavior
Cognitive development	Movement from lower to higher states of moral reasoning	Stage theory, structuralism, developmental psychology
Analysis/inquiry	Application of thinking process to moral questions	Scientific method, reflective thought
Clarification	Self-justified personal choices	Self-actualization theory, humanistic psychology

Source: Adapted from Douglas Superka, "A Typology of Valuing Theories and Values Education Approaches." Ph.D dissertation, University of California, Berkeley, 1973.

Idealistic inculcation presumes that a set of ideals, virtues, and morals drawn from dominant theology or tradition must be assimilated by each generation. This set of moral precepts may be perceived as universal and everlasting, as in religious dogma; they may be viewed as perennial and cross-cultural, as described by C. S. Lewis in *The Abolition of Man;* [31] or they may be put in the form of a political or economic ideology, as in definitions of an American creed or of free enterprise. One differentiating characteristic of this approach to moral education is that the set of morals and definitions of moral behavior associated with idealistic inculcation are not subject to dispute or critical examination. Moral education, in this approach, intends to instill a prescribed morality as the basis for moral thought and action. Concepts of the good, the right, and the just are externally determined for the student.

Another characteristic of the idealistic inculcation approach is the expectation of student conformity to the ideal despite evidence within the society of behavior that is at variance with the ideal. In many aspects of social life there is little relationship between the reality of moral standards as practiced and the ideals prescribed for students in school. In effect, the society expects the schools to educate children to a more rigorous standard of morality than the society expects of its typical adult members.

This form of moral education is of the longest duration in schools, and continues the most widely used.

Cognitive development approaches to moral education are based upon theories about processes of human development in reasoning. Developmental theory has been a significant addition to the study of education. The early twentieth-century work of Jean Piaget, for example, established that children go through stages of cognitive knowledge as they grow, and that each of the stages is structurally different.[32] Piaget's developmental analysis formed one of the bases for the work of Lawrence Kohlberg in examining the stages of development in moral reasoning. Other developmental theorists have proposed sequential frameworks for moral development,[33] but Kohlberg's theory has been the most influential as well as the most criticized.[34]

A characteristic the Kohlberg theory shares with idealistic inculcation is the concept of a universal moral code. A distinction must be made, however, between the two approaches on several grounds. First, inculcation expects uncritical acceptance of particular moral viewpoints and behaviors, while cognitive development is concerned with structures of reasoning about moral dilemmas. Second, inculcation provides a dominant morality regardless of a student's age, while development presumes a hierarchy of stages, each of which has a distinctive concept of morality with the last-stage being superior. Third, inculcation presumes conformity to a prescribed set of morals, while development presumes conformity to a stage-sequential pattern of reasoning. Fourth, inculcation provides a moral framework drawn from traditional belief systems, while development provides one drawn from social scientific research incorporating empirical evidence. And finally, inculcation does not envision morally autonomous individuals, while the end state of developmental approaches is some form of moral autonomy.

Analysis/inquiry approaches to moral education are based upon the application of logical processes of thinking to moral issues.[35] There is an emphasis on rationality, including the stating of moral postulates, identification of opposing moral hypotheses, examination of evidence, logical tests of evidence and consequences, and the drawing of tentative conclusions based upon elements of reason. Morality is perceived as open to inquiry and critical judgment. Essential elements of morality can be subjected to scrutiny in order to obtain tested beliefs. These beliefs, grounded in rational thought, form the basis for moral judgments about human issues. Questions of morality arise in human situations of conflict, and moral education should provide students with a set of tools for the rational handling of moral conflicts.

Analysis/inquiry incorporates cognltive processes but does not begin with a notion of a predetermined moral-reasoning hierarchy, as would be found in cognitive development theories, or from an uncritical set of moral standards, as in inculcation approaches. The primary emphasis in analysis/inquiry is on the process of rational examination and on openness to new evidence.

Clarification approaches to moral education are the least structured and most individualistic of those described in the literature. The dominant work in the field is by Louis Raths et al.,[36] who formalized ideas from humanistic psychologists into a procedure for acquiring self-determined values. This procedure included the steps for choosing freely from among alternatives after consideration of consequences, prizing and affirming the choice to others, and acting on it repeatedly. In contrast to inculcation (where an externally derived morality is imposed upon students), cognitive development (where hierarchical structures for moral reasoning are presumed), or analysis/inquiry (which requires rational testing of evidence), clarification sets no external standards and relies upon internal determination of moral thought and behavior.

Clarification, as the name suggests, aims to assist students in clarifying values without the superimposition of moral standards or reasoning. Students are encouraged to become self-analytic and individualistic. Personal preferences, publicly proclaimed and acted upon, are the sources of classroom activities in clarification.

The four moral education approaches can be analyzed according to their comparative degrees of relativism and absolutism as follows: clarification and analysis/inquiry are more relativistic, and cognitive development and inculcation are more absolutistic.

EDUCATION FOR CITIZENSHIP

As noted earlier, citizenship education is similar to moral education in its evolution from a single approach involving indoctrination to a range of approaches. Table 14.2 indicates this range. As in the variety of approaches to moral education shown in Table 14.1, each of the types of citizenship education identified in Table 14.2 incorporates several different individual viewpoints about education.

TABLE 14.2

Approaches to Citizenship Education

Type	Purpose	Role Model
Social/national loyalty	Conformity to social/national expectations: responsible, trustworthy, courteous, voter; uncritical support of nation-state; negative views of contranational ideas.	Model citizen, selected U.S. patriots
Junior social scientist	Training in concepts and methods of social sciences; analysis, neutrality	Social scientist
Social criticism/ activism	Critical thinking, decision making, active participation	Thoughtful dissident, Activist

Source: Adapted from Jack L. Nelson and John U. Michaelis, *The Social Studies* (Englewood Cliffs, N.J.: Prentice-Hall, in press).

Social/national loyalty is the oldest and most entrenched of the types of citizenship ·education approaches. It is the type most closely related to inculcation forms of moral education. The essential concern of social/national loyalty is the production of citizens who conform to behavior considered socially acceptable and unquestioningly subscribe to national chauvinism. There are two dominant subtypes in this approach: "good" behavior and nationalistic education. They are typically combined in schools but they can be differentiated.

"Good" behavior preceded nationalism in the school's efforts to train young generations in proper conduct. Throughout the history of education (as seen in the examples from the regulations and texts noted earlier), attempts to form the character of youth, along lines deemed consistent with moral precepts and social acceptability, have permeated schools. The good citizen in school is one who attends regularly, is not tardy, respects authority, turns in work on time, sits up straight, speaks when spoken to, dresses appropriately, follows directions, and otherwise willingly follows school and teacher rules. The assumption is that this patterning transfers to model citizen behavior in the society at large.

Nationalistic education emerged in the nineteenth century in the United States to replace religious indoctrination in schools as the most prominent form of moral citizenship education.[37] It differs from "good" behavior training in the sense that nationalistic education provides an ideological framework of beliefs that are to be assimilated, in addition to a set of specific behaviors like flag salutes. Nationalistic education incorporates instruction designed to portray the most positive views of the nation-state and the most negative views of ideas, symbols, and people considered to be contranational. In the United States, for example, students are required to learn positive views of American history and negative views of communism.

The junior social scientist approach to citizenship education is a more recent development in schools. The basis of this approach is the assumption that terms, concepts, and modes of inquiry used in the social sciences are useful in comprehending the nature of social existence. Much of the content taught in classrooms is vocabulary development and data that are available from standard works in fields like sociology, anthropology, economics, history, psychology, geography, and political science. Systems analyses or behavioristic conceptual frameworks are the organizing principles of courses and programs.[38] An analytic and relatively neutral approach to society, human interaction, and social phenomena is taken. Students are taught procedures for document comparison, surveys, table and graph analysis, interviewing, and similar social science methods.

Values, including moral principles, are examined as artifacts of societies. The attempt to be value-neutral is evident in this approach, although it is much less apparent than the corollary attempt in the social sciences, practiced by scholars in those fields in their research. What are taught in the elementary and secondary schools are interpretations of select social scientific studies.

Social criticism/activism approaches vary in emphasis, but embody a concern for civic education that examines social issues.[39] Proponents start from a basic assumption of social change and the concept that citizens have a right and a responsibility to be participants in their society. This includes critical examination of social issues, involvement in decision making, and active pursuit of improvement in society. It also includes attempts to apply more democratic principles to the operation of schools, where students are perceived to be citizens. The content of criticism/activism approaches deals with social conflict, problems, or issues, while the methodology is some form of critical thinking.

Social criticism may be emphasized in schools without a concomitant emphasis on social activism. Criticism is essentially concerned with the stimulation and development of critical thinking processes with regard to social or individual issues. It does not have to lead to activism, although that is one possibility. Criticism opposes the approach normally associated with social and national loyalty. Social criticism opens areas of dogmatism and value conformity to scrutiny. It differs from the social science approach in that criticism deals with issues and problems rather than a particular formal structure of knowledge or a single-discipline viewpoint.

Social activism is derived from criticism in the sense that investigation of social issues and ethical considerations leads students to decisions to participate in improving society. Activism can also follow from uncritical agreement to participate or unexamined acceptance of authority, but no major advocates of social-activism approaches to citizenship take that position. To the extent that social and national loyalty approaches incorporate uncritical participation, they are similar to activism, but it is a superficial similarity. The purpose of activism, as in criticism, is social improvement through critical thinking.

DISCUSSION OF THE RELATIONSHIPS

As Table 14.3 suggests, there are areas of compatibility and incompatibility among possible relationships between types of moral education and types of citizenship education.

The compatibility of idealistic inculcation of morals and social/national loyalty is illustrated in the introductory material in this chapter. This combination of externally imposed morality and citizenship training is the most traditional and widespread approach to social studies instruction in schools.

A California statute, passed in 1943 and still in force, exemplifies this particular combination of moral citizenship education:

Each teacher shall endeavor to impress upon the minds of the pupils the principles of morality, truth, justice, patriotism and a true comprehension of the rights, duties and dignity of American citizenship, including kindness toward domestic pets and the humane treatment of living creatures, to teach them to avoid idleness, profanity, and falsehood, and to instruct them in manners and morals and the principles of a free government.[40]

TABLE 14.3

Possible Relationships Between Moral and Citizenship Education

Moral Education Types	Citizen Education Types		
	Social/National Loyalty	Junior Social Scientist	Social Criticism/ Activism
Idealistic inculcation	Highly compatible	Compatible only in those areas of general cultural bias	Incompatible
Cognitive development	Compatible ony in early developmental stages	Compatible in empiricism	Compatible at later developmental stages
Analysis/ inquiry	Incompatible	Compatible in methodology; limited compatibility in structure of content	Highly compatible
Clarification	Compatible in areas of cultural bias	Incompatible	Compatible in areas of rational judgment and social analysis

Source: Compiled by the author.

This law was used in 1969 and 1970 as a basis for recommendations by the California State Department of Education to the State Board of Education for moral education, which would commit the schools, including higher education institutions, to "rededication to American moral standards" based on religion, and which would prohibit instruction that draws from "secular Humanism," Communism, Marxism, or various forms of "sensitivity training."[41]

Social and national loyalty forms of citizenship education are compatible with early developmental stages in cognitive developmental types of moral education. The early stages, according to Kohlberg's research, incorporate preconventional moral reasoning (Stage 1 — obedience to rules to avoid punishment; Stage 2 — obedience to rules to obtain rewards), and conventional moral reasoning (Stage 3 — conformity to stereotypical behavior to avoid disapproval; and Stage 4 — orientation to law and order and following authority). Stages 1 and 2 are dominant from ages four to ten, while Stages 3 and 4 dominate in preadolescence.

Loyalty-based citizenship education, which incorporates unquestioning respect for traditional authority, is consistent with what appears to exist in young students' moral reasoning. Developmentalists, however, do not support programs of moral education that limit students to lower stages of reasoning. Their intention is to move students through the early stages and toward more thoughtful application of moral principles and a level of autonomy in moral reasoning and behavior. This is one area of conflict between the most common type of citizenship education and the most widely researched type of moral education. Loyalty-based citizenship education is incompatible with analysis and inquiry forms of moral education, since there is a direct conflict between unquestioning acceptance of authority and open inquiry.

Social and national loyalty can be considered compatible with certain aspects of clarification approaches to moral education, where dominant cultural views have been assimilated by students who then simply affirm cultural biases in considering any moral choices. Clarification depends upon individual moral choice among alternatives, prizing and acting upon that choice. Where students have been indoctrinated, as in loyalty-based citizenship education, the choices are predetermined and individual prizing and acting is pro forma. Where indoctrination has not occurred, clarification approaches are incompatible with social and national loyalty. Because it is not clear that loyalities have been firmly entrenched in youth, there is considerable suspicion among the advocates of loyalty-based programs that clarification techniques are amoral or immoral, and are thus incompatible.[42]

Junior social scientist, or discipline-based education is less compatible with inculcation of morals than is social/national loyalty. There is, however, compatibility in those areas of social science where there is general cultural bias, such as support for capitalism, or where the schools are required to present a single view of historical and social scientific knowledge. In these latter areas of compatibility social science subjects are used merely as vehicles for nationalistic education, and not for training in social science techniques. State-mandated courses in American history and government, with prescribed educational outcomes, are examples. In Nebraska, the law states:

In at least two grades of every high school, at least three periods per week shall be devoted to the teaching of civics during which courses specific attention shall be given to the following matters: (a) the Constitution of the United States and the State of Nebraska, (b) the benefits and advantages of our form of government and the dangers and fallacies of Nazism, Communism, and similar ideologies, (c) the duties of citizenship. . . .[43]

And in Florida, the statute reads as follows:

The public high schools shall each teach a complete course of not less than thirty hours, to all students enrolled in the public schools entitled "Americanism versus Communism." . . . The course shall be one of orientation in comparative governments and shall emphasize the free-enterprise-competitive economy of the United States as the one which produces higher wages, higher standards of living, greater personal freedom and liberty than any other system of economics on earth. . . . No teacher or textual material assigned to this course shall present communism as preferable to the system of constitutional government and the free-enterprise-competitive economy indigenous to the United States.[44]

The Nebraska law is an example of the kind of law that is common in many states that require American history and civics instruction. As the section quoted shows, such instruction is not intended to be neutral. Pointing out the benefits of American citizenship and the detrimental nature of contranational views are required aspects of the course.

The Florida statute, in addition to revealing the intellectual difficulties inherent in trying to compare an amorphous Americanism with the relatively clearly defined political system of communism, provides no basis for open inquiry into the issue. It requires the teacher and teaching materials to adhere to a prescribed political and economic viewpoint.

The more neutral forms of social science education, which are descriptive and informational, are not necessarily compatible with moral inculcation. Although they convey cultural values, including belief in science and rationality, they are much less morally loaded than social and national loyalty forms of citizenship education. To the extent that social science education strives for value neutrality, it avoids explicit moral education.

Teachers are trained in academic disciplines and tend to teach them in the form of accumulation of factual information. Teacher education programs typically consist of a subject major, some general education, and some professional education course work. The bulk of that preparation is devoted to factual content and is essentially devoid of moral deliberation. Since teachers tend to teach as they have been taught, the factual content in teacher training is the basis of subsequent school teaching, and moral questions are avoided partly because teachers have had little experience or preparation in dealing with them.

Social-science-based citizenship education is compatible with cognitive development types of moral education in their mutual concern for empirical verification and theory. Social science, as taught in the elementary and secondary schools, however, tends to be descriptive and factual, while moral development programs involve confronting moral dilemmas and improving moral reasoning. In this context social science and moral development have very limited contact and, although they are not opposing views, they differ considerably. To the extent that the social sciences are positivistic, they are incompatible with cognitive development moral education which presumes a hierarchy of values and moral reasoning.

Social science approaches are compatible with analysis/inquiry moral education in the application of rational methods of thinking, but have limited compatibility with the nature of the content examined. Social science inquiry draws on data, concepts, and generalizations produced in several fields, while analysis/inquiry examines issues and conflicts. Analysis and inquiry approaches to moral education use knowledge from the social sciences and other fields but are not bound to single-discipline perspectives.

Social science citizenship education is incompatible with clarification forms of moral education in the sense that social science represents a body of specific knowledge validated externally by scholarly authorities, while clarification is a more personal and individual selection of values and actions. Clarification techniques encourage personal preference in value choices; social science rests on information derived from scholars in several fields and is not readily subject to student preference.

Social criticism and activism types of citizenship education are incompatible with idealistic inculcation of morality. Inculcation requires uncritical learning of moral precepts and behaviors, while criticism and activism presume the use of student critical judgment for the purpose of improvement of the society. Criticism incorporates the concepts of dissent and the acceptability of holding minority views, neither of which are appropriate to inculcation except as rhetoric. Inculcation might include statements about minority and dissident rights as moral values in American history, but would not advocate activism among contemporary students. The good student, according to moral inculcation, is not one who criticizes authority, states dissenting views on social issues, or takes action in order to protest.

Criticism and activism citizenship education is compatible with later stages of cognitive development approaches to moral education. In the hierarchies posited by various developmental theorists the higher stages .are more thoughtful and critical. Development leads toward moral autonomy which includes the exercise of social criticism and activism based on moral reasoning. If the theory of development is accepted, then criticism/ activism approaches appear to be less useful during early stages of moral development because students at lower stages would not be able to comprehend more sophisticated moral reasoning and would not be able to act as autonomous and responsible moral beings. In the combination of cognitive development and criticism/activism there would be one period in student maturation in which student criticism would be restricted to moral reasoning based on simple views of punishment and reward, and another period in which it would be based on higher moral principles of justice and equality.

Criticism/activism approaches to citizenship are highly compatible with analysis and inquiry types of moral education. They share methodologies, basic rationales, and intentions. Advocates of criticism and activism support inquiry and reflective thinking as processes for making decisions. Basic to both types is a belief in human rationality and in the ability of people to solve problems and make decisions. Their mutual intention is to open issues to inquiry, seek and evaluate data, draw tentative conclusions, and determine courses of action. The subject of inquiry can be social, moral, or a combination of both. Citizenship is defined dynamically as a concern for turning change into progress. Ideas about moral thought and action are open to criticism; and social criticism and activism are based upon ethical judgment.

Social criticism/activism forms of citizenship education are compatible with clarification types of moral education where clarification depends upon rational judgment that leads to thoughtful action. These approaches differ where clarification becomes more personalistic, based on individual aspirations rather than on goals of social improvement. Clarification procedures are heavily loaded toward self-analysis and introspection, while criticism/activism procedures are loaded toward social analysis and involvement in society. Clarification does not oppose social analysis but such analysis is not its major objective. Clarification also accepts personal emotion, claims of individual preference, and idiosyncratic behavior more than does social criticism/activism which expects principled justifications for correcting society.

PRACTICAL IMPLICATIONS OF DISPARITIES BETWEEN FORMS

The relationships suggested in Table 14.3 and the subsequent discussion are based upon analyses of rationales and statements of educational strategies proposed by advocates of various types of moral and citizenship education. It is entirely possible for individual teachers to combine approaches that would appear to be incompatible — for example, using clarification techniques in a social-science-based course. In these instances teachers are knowingly not using the approaches to lead to their stated purposes, or they are confused about disparities among approaches and are willing to try anything, or the rationales and strategies proposed for each type of citizen and moral education have no meaning in practice.

The primary conflict in political education is the divergence between the responsibility of schools to develop support for basic social patterns and structures and education's responsibility to train individuals for enlightened social change. The former responsibility implies the positive transmission of a heritage and the expectation of conformist thinking and behavior concerning it from students. The latter responsibility entails social criticism and the expectation of dissident thinking and behavior from students. This dilemma, as stated, suggests only two alternatives at polar ends of an educational scale, whereas in reality there are various possibilities, with most American schooling emphasizing the uncritical positive transmission of national citizen ideas, attitudes, and behaviors, while simultaneously advocating and sporadically practicing social activist education.

Harold Berlak succinctly states that the "idea that schools for the young could take as priority or sole goal the encouragement of fundamental social criticism is foolishness, as is the more rampant contemporary myth that schools are nothing more than well-oiled machines for imprinting the society on the young.[45] He goes on to note, however, that curricular reforms in political education have not encouraged a critical examination of society, institutions, or social relations. Rather, the newer forms of citizenship education are mainly improvements in the teaching of academic disciplines from a presumably neutral position.

The heritage transmission concept of citizenship education, with minor modifications, currently predominates in the schools. The reconstructive concept, which stresses social activism as an aspect of student work, is virtually nonexistent, and only slightly noted in the literature about citizenship education. While there are a number of scholars who currently advocate "active" citizenship education, the teaching of this concept in schools is blunted by approaches that fit into the existing framework of schools and that offer no likelihood that real social criticism or reconstructionism will occur. The existing domination of schooling by political forces that require positive inculcation of national values is not easily subject to minor attempts to stress active citizen roles for students. The general condition of the field is commitment to the transmission of existing dominant values in both practice and literature. A content examination of the relationship between reconstructionist educational philosophy and the views of writers in areas relating to citizenship education demonstrates that citizenship educators do not advocate reconstructionist ideas.[46]

The most popular approach to citizenship education is through courses in American history, government, and related disciplines. This approach, required by state legislatures and school boards, mirrors the nature of teacher education, which is heavily based on the production of history majors and reflects the influence of academic scholars in higher education. The standard curriculum of schools across the United States includes at least one year of American history at each level: elementary school, junior high school, and high school. It also includes at least one year of government or civics and incorporates a substantial amount of government and history in other social studies courses in economics, sociology, or geography.

Law-related education is similar to the academic discipline approach to citizenship education. It is typically based on the idea that answers to social (and moral) questions lie in legal action. There is, therefore, presumed to be a body of answers and a framework of legal history for understanding them. While some law-related education attempts to raise moral issues that go beyond discussions of the law itself, most are designed to inculcate a respect and support for law as the means for resolving conflicts. The good citizen is one who knows and obeys laws, or uses legally constituted means for changing laws. This aspect of citizenship education applies also to economics education programs, where the intent is to train good citizens to know and support free-enterprise capitalism on the assumption that that is and should be the economic system of the United States.

Under cognitive development or analysis/inquiry forms of moral education, the moral education content of history, civics, law-related, or economics courses could be substantial. Questions regarding the bases of laws and the grounds for obeying or disobeying laws are filled with moral dilemmas and issues. Concepts of justice, equality, and truth are essential for a comprehensive approach in any social studies course. But the usual teaching approach and the text materials that are used incorporate factual information or social scientific concepts (for example, supply-demand, structure of government, court system) that convey moral ideas but do not pose moral dilemmas. It is the unusual teacher who suggests that students can think and act on moral principles that are different from the norms expressed in citizenship education.

APPLICATION OF MORAL DEVELOPMENT IDEAS

The scientific aura surrounding the application of moral dilemmas used in Kohlberg's research creates a new condition for teachers. The teacher training programs and classroom practices being adopted on the basis of cognitive moral development theory assume that the theory has been demonstrated and has scientific support. The result is that teachers are being trained as technicians to operate moral development classrooms.[47] This training includes both the use of moral dilemmas, which were used as research tools by Kohlberg, and the utilization of a teaching strategy designed to elicit from students selected moral reasoning responses according to the Kohlberg hierarchy of stages. This teaching technique assumes that the teacher operates at a moral reasoning level beyond that of the students, that the teacher can accurately assess the developmental level of any student, that morally superior reasoning will be recognized by the teacher, and that the behavioral implications of potentially autonomous moral reasoning can be countenanced in a conservative school setting.

The movement to translate Kohlberg's work into classroom activities for citizenship education appears to be premature. Although Edwin Fenton, who has been a major figure in translating Kohlberg's research into direct teaching activities, argues that cognitive moral development "has the best claim as a system which helps develop specifically democratic values based on principles enumerated in the *Declaration of Independence* and the *Constitution*,"[48] there is no research support for this claim, and analysis of actual teacher methods leads to an opposite conclusion. Teacher training programs and materials are prescriptive rather than open, and more likely to inculcate "right answers" in moral reasoning than to develop autonomous moral reasoning. The applied program fits an established model of citizenship instruction, but does not appear to fit the framework of cognitive moral development theory.

In the practical application of developmental moral education, where the teacher is largely a technician posing prescribed moral dilemmas in a prescribed pattern and holding an answer book filled with "right answers" to fit prescribed stages of moral reasoning, a comfortable relationship with social/national loyalty forms of citizenship can exist, since the students are restricted in their moral reasoning. In the theoretical form of cognitive moral development education, students would be free to explore those moral dilemmas that are of the most immediate concern in the school and society, arriving ultimately at reasoning that could be superior or inferior to that of their teachers, parents, and community leaders. Such training could create a very difficult relationship with the standard forms of citizenship education, especially if the reasoning is beyond the comprehension of those at lower stages.

It is true that the Henry David Thoreaus and Martin Luther Kings of any young generation are in school, where they have their moral development encouraged or stunted. It is also true that the established social order demands instruction in those attributes that preserve and protect it. This is an uncomfortable relationship.

MORALIZING AND CENSORSHIP

Another relationship that is uncomfortable occurs when citizenship education is perceived as social/national loyalty or social science but when analysis/inquiry approaches are used in moral education. Analysis/inquiry encourages exploration of controversial topics and controversy is not an expectation of the standard forms of citizenship education. Moralizing and censorship are the practical consequences.

While it is possible to deal with moral questions in forms that encourage moral development, the actual classroom practice is to moralize rather than to raise moral questions. The content and teaching of history, government, and other courses typically ignore or discourage open inquiry or moral debate. The school has a traditional role as a social institution in conveying the right and proper answers to youth and expecting good attitudes and behavior in return. Most parents, school boards, administrators, and teachers are comfortable in a setting where specific right answers are available.

In addition, the general school environment is characterized by great reluctance to deal with controversial issues. As one of the more conservative social institutions, and one more open to public view than most, the school is particularly sensitive to pressures that prevent it from exploring issues that arouse dispute. Examples of censorship in schools abound. A nationally publicized episode, for instance, focused on questions involving morality as portrayed in different cultures. The incident emerged from the use of materials for elementary school students which examined the life-styles of an Eskimo group. These materials were the product of years of work by Jerome Bruner and others and their use involved elementary school children in inquiry into moral reasoning. A congressional investigation into federal funding effectively chilled school interest in the materials.[49] The use of other controversial materials in schools in Kanawha County, West Virginia, led to strikes, picketing, and physical violence by members of the public.[50] The immediate effect was the removal of these materials from the schools, but the long-range effect has been to dull the interest of schools across the country in dealing with value-laden questions. Some schools now prohibit values education (moral education), as though such an action can be legislated, and other schools are especially wary of such courses.

Censorship of moral questions involving religion, patriotism, and sex are commonplace in schools.[51] No academic year passes without a number of examples of book banning, exclusion of controversial speakers, or other forms of censorship. These are typically predicated upon controversies over values that imply moral positions. Anyone examining the depth and breadth of censorship and the general reluctance of schools to engage in controversy must pause at the suggestion that free deliberation of moral questions is a likely school activity. Perceptions of people in school and community settings suggest that self-imposed censorship and avoidance of controversy are more likely.[52] Clarification forms of moral education have been subjected to similar censorship on the grounds that they are un-American, individualistic, and hedonistic.

Although the existence of censorship is not a sufficient ground for arguing that moral education cannot take place in schools, it is a major consideration when examining the possible nature and form of any moral education program, and it is important to a discussion of the relationship between citizenship education based on community norms and moral education based on a theory of moral development.

The uncomfortable relationship between citizenship education based on blind obedience or neutral social scientific data and moral education based on critical thinking or individual choice creates a paradox in education similar to that described by Bertrand Russell in 1928:

> Education should have two objects: first, to give definite knowledge, reading and writing, language and mathematics, and so on; secondly, to create those mental habits which will enable people to acquire knowledge and form sound judgments for themselves. The first of these we may call information, the second intelligence. The utility of information is admitted . . . [but] it is not desired that ordinary people should think for themselves, because it is felt that people who think for themselves are awkward to manage and cause administrative difficulties. . . . We are faced with the paradoxical fact that education has become one of the chief obstacles to intelligence and freedom of thought.[53]

The traditional forms of uncritical rational/social loyalty citizenship education and inculcation of moral thought and behavior are compatible and dominant in schools. The other highly compatible combination is social criticism or activism citizenship education and analysis/inquiry approaches to moral education. The latter combination is considerably more popular in the literature but much less practiced in the schools than is the former type. Other combinations of citizenship and moral education types are less compatible.

Schools have manifold purposes. As agents of socialization they are responsive to social norms of behavior and belief. These norms have historically been expressed in the dual goals of citizenship and moral education. The commonly accepted view is that moral and citizenship education are virtually identical. That view has a long tradition in the literature and practice of schools.

Another view is that moral education may be in conflict with citizen education. This view notes that morality may not be coincidental with law, government, national history, social habits, or personal manners. To the extent that moral reasoning can lead to autonomous judgment and action, the state, which supports and controls the schools, is threatened. The mentality of the schools, governed by tradition, community, finances, and public review, has consistently been conservative of the common morality. This produces in schooling an uncritical transmission of prescribed citizenship attitudes and behaviors and a concept of moral education based on indoctrination.

Opportunities in schools for developing autonomous moral judgment are essentially nonexistent. Opportunities for assimilating the standard moral precepts and their application to civic life are pervasive and required. Socially accepted views of the good, right, and just are the overwhelming standards against which student attitudes and behaviors are measured. Institutional rewards go to those who deviate least from the norms. Schools are devoted to perpetuating the values of the dominant social strata, and in expressing moral standards that idealize those values.

The schools, as creatures of the political environment and responsive to it, are not likely locations for challenges to the moral framework within which that political environment operates. The theoretical position that the schools, among all social institutions, constitute the best hope for the new social order, strikes a responsive but despondent chord.

NOTES

1. Robert D. Barr, James Barth, and S. Samuel Shermis, *Defining the Social Studies,* Bulletin 51 (Washington, D. C.: National Council for the Social Studies, 1977); James Shaver, *Building Rationales for Citizenship Education,* Bulletin 52 (Washington, D. C.: National Council for the Social Studies, 1977).

2. Harry S. Broudy, *Moral/Citizenship Education: Potentials and Limitations,* Occasional Paper No. 3 (Philadelphia: Research for Better Schools, Winter, 1977); Douglas Superka et al., *Values Education Sourcebook,* (Boulder, Col.: Social Science Education Consortium, 1976); Norman Bull, *Moral Education,* (Beverly Hills, Calif.: Sage, 1969); John Wilson et al., *Introduction to Moral Education* (Baltimore, Md.: Penguin, 1967).

3. Mark Blum, *Ethical-Citizenship Education Policies and Programs: A National Survey of State Education Agencies.* Technical Report (Philadelphia: Research for Better Schools, Spring, 1977), p. v.

4. Terrel H. Bell, *Morality and Citizenship Education: Whose Responsibility?* Occasional Paper No. 1, (Philadelphia: Research for Better Schools, Winter, 1976) p. 1.

5. Ibid., p. 3.

6. Joel Spring, *The Sorting Machine* (New York: David McKay, 1976); Michael Katz, *Class, Bureaucracy and Schools* (New York: Praeger, 1971); Jack L. Nelson and Frank Besag, *Sociological Perspectives in Education* (New York: Pitman, 1970).

7. Jules Henry, *Culture Against Man* (New York: Vintage Books, 1965), p. 287.

8. M. Kent Jennings and Richard Niemi, eds., *The Political Character of Adolescence: The Influence of Families and Schools* (Princeton: Princeton University Press, 1974); Judith Torney et al., *Civic Education in Ten Countries* (New York: Wiley, 1975).

9. Michael Scriven, "Cognitive Moral Education," *Phi Delta Kappan* 56 (1975), p. 689.

10. "A Massachusetts Bay Law of 1642," in *Prologue to Teaching,* ed. Marjorie Smiley and John Diekhoff (New York: Oxford Press, 1959).

11. Massachusetts (Colony), *Records of the Governor and Company of the Massachusetts Bay in New England.*

12. George Herbert Palmer, *Ethical and Moral Instruction in Schools* (Boston: Houghton-Mifflin, 1908) p. v.

13. Ibid., p. viii.

14. Ibid., p. 27.

15. Benjamin Larrabee, *Moral Education* (Middlebury, Vt.: Maxham, 1891), p. 9.

16. Ibid., p. 9.

17. Cotton Mather, "A Family Well-Ordered," in Frederick Mayer, *American Ideas and Education* (Columbus, Ohio: Merrill, 1964), p. 50.

18. *New England Primer,* 1690, in Mayer, *American Ideas.*

19. J. Hamilton Moore, *The Young Gentleman and Lady's Monitor and English Teacher's Assistant* (Hudson, Ashbell, Stoddard, 1795) in John Nietz, *The Evolution of American Secondary School Textbooks* (Rutland, Vt.: Tuttle, 1966).

20. Caleb Bingham, *A Historical Grammer of Universal History* (1802) in Nietz, *Evolution of Textbooks.*

21. *McGuffey's Third Eclectic Reader,* (New York: American Book Co., 1879, 1896).

22. Ibid.

23. Ibid.

24. Ibid.

25. Ibid.

26. Marjorie Smiley, and John Diekhoff, eds., *Prologue to Teaching* (New York: Oxford Press, 1959).

27. Nelson and Besag, *Sociological Perspectives,* Ch. 12.

28. See, for example, Bessie Pierce, *Citizens' Organizations and the Civic Training of Youth* (New York: Scribner's, 1933); Howard K. Beale, *Are American Teachers Free?* (New York: Scribner's, 1936), and *A History of Freedom of Teaching in American Schools* (New York: Scribner's, 1941); Donald Robinson, "The Teachers Take a Birching," *Phi Delta Kappan* (February 1962); Nelson and Besag, *Sociological Perspectives;* Harmon Ziegler, *The Political Life of American Teachers* (Englewood Cliffs, N.J.: Prentice-Hall, 1967).

29. Henry Lester Smith, *Character Education* (Washington D. C.: National Education Association, 1949), p. 20.

30. Ibid., p. 21.

31. C. S. Lewis, *The Abolition of Man,* (New York: MacMillan, 1947).

32. Jean Piaget, *Moral Judgment of the Child* (London: Kegan Paul, 1932); and *The Construction of Reality in the Child* (New York: Basic Books, 1954).

33. Jane Loevinger, "The Meaning and Measurement of Ego Development," *American Psychologist* (March 1966): 195–206; Robert F. Peck and Robert J. Havighurst, *The Psy-*

chology of Character Development (New York: Wiley, 1960); Abraham Maslow, Toward a Psychology of Being, 2d. ed. (New York: Van Nostrand, 1968).

34. Lawrence Kohlberg, "The Child as Moral Philosopher," Psychology Today (September 1968): 25–30; Lawrence Kohlberg and R. Kramer, "Continuities in Children and Adult Moral Development," Human Development 12 (1969): 93–120; Richard S. Peters, "A Reply to Kohlberg," Phi Delta Kappan 56 (1975): 678; also see Richard S. Peters, Ethics and Education (London: George Allen and Unwin, 1966); Scriven, "Cognitive Moral Education," pp. 689–94; Jack R. Fraenkel, "The Kohlberg Bandwagon: Some Reservations," Social Education 40 (1976): 216–22.

35. Lawrence Metcalf, ed., Values Education (Washington D. C.: National Council for Social Studies, 1971); Jack L. Nelson, Introduction to Value Inquiry (Rochelle Park, N. J.: Hayden, 1974).

36. Louis E. Raths, Merrill Harmin, and Sidney Simon, Values and Teaching, 2d ed. (Columbus, Ohio: Merrill, 1978); also see Sidney Simon, Value Clarification (Columbus, Ohio: Merrill, 1972).

37. See, for example, Pierce, Citizens' Organizations; Bruce Raup, Education and Organized Interests in America (New York: Putnam's, 1936); William Gellerman, The American Legion as Educator (New York: Teachers College Press, 1938); Henry S. Commager, The American Mind (New Haven: Yale University Press, 1950); Ray Allen Billington et al., The Historian's Contribution to Anglo-American Misunderstanding (London: Hobbs, Dorman, 1966); Jack L. Nelson, "Nationalistic Vs. Global Education: An Examination of National Bias in the Schools and its Implications for a Global Society," Theory and Research in Social Education 4 (1976): 33–50.

·38. Irving Morrissett, ed., Concepts and Structures in the New Social Science Curricula (New York: Holt, Rinehart and Winston, 1967); and The Social Studies and the Social Sciences (New York: Harcourt, Brace and World, 1962).

39. Shirley Engle, "Decision-Making: The Heart of Social Studies Instruction," Social Education 24 (November 1960): 310–4, 306; Harold Berlak, "Human Consciousness, Social Criticism, and Civic Education," in Shaver, Building Rationales; Fred Newmann, Education for Citizen Action (Berkeley, Calif.: McCutchan, 1975); Dan Conrad and Diane Hedin, "Learning and Earning Citizenship Through Participation," in Shaver, Building Rationales.

40. California State Education Code, Art. 4, Sec. 9031, 1975.

41. Guidelines for Moral Instruction in California Schools: A Report Accepted by the State Board of Education (Sacramento: California State Department of Education, May 9, 1969), pp. 31, 61.

42. Ibid.

43. Nebraska School Laws: 79–213.

44. Section 230:23(4) (1) Florida Statutes.

45. Berlak, "Human Consciousness," p. 35.

46. William Stanley, "Social Reconstructionism and the Recent Developments in the Social Studies." Unpublished paper presented at Social Science Education Consortium Conference, Columbia University, March 25, 1978; and "The Philosophy of Social Reconstructionism and Contemporary Curriculum Rationales in Social Education." Ed.D. dissertation, Rutgers University, 1979.

47. Edwin Fenton and Lawrence Kohlberg, Learning to Lead Moral Discussions: A Teacher Preparation Kit (Pleasantville, N. Y.: Guidance Associates, 1976); Ronald Galbraith and Thomas Jones, "Teaching Strategies for Moral Dilemmas," Social Education 39 (1976): 16–22.

48. Edwin Fenton, The Relationship of Citizenship Education to Values Education, Occasional Paper No. 2 (Philadelphia: Research for Better Schools, Winter 1977), p. 24.

49. Peter B. Dow, "MACOS Revisited." Unpublished paper prepared for the Science Curriculum Implementation Review Group of the U. S. House of Representatives Committee on Science and Technology (May 13, 1975).

50. *A Textbook Study of Cultural Conflict* (Washington, D. C.: National Education Association, 1976).

51. See, for example, Beale, *Are American Teachers Free?*; Jack Nelson and Gene Roberts, *The Censors and the Schools* (Boston: Little, Brown, 1963); Maurice Hunt and Lawrence Metcalf, *Teaching High School Social Studies* (New York: Harper and Row, 1968); Jack L. Nelson and William Hering, *Developing a Position on Academic Freedom and Censorship* (Boulder, Col.: Social Science Education Consortium, 1976).

52. David Naylor, "An In-depth Study of the Perceptions of Public School Educators and Other Significant School Related Groups Concerning Aspects of Nationalistic Education," Ed.D. dissertation, Rutgers University, 1974; Mark Schuman, "An Examination of Social Studies Teachers' Perceptions of Situations Depicting Nationalistic Education," Ed.D. dissertation, Rutgers University, 1976; Stuart Palonsky, Jack L. Nelson, and David Naylor, "Perceptions of Political Restraint in Social Education Classes," unpublished paper presented at College and University Faculty Assembly, National Council for the Social Studies, November 1976.

53. Bertrand Russell, *Sceptical Essays* (London: George Allen and Unwin, 1928), pp. 129–30.

15

THE PROMOTION OF MORAL DEVELOPMENT IN PRISONS AND SCHOOLS

Roy E. Feldman

INTRODUCTION

This chapter is primarily based on the author's evaluation of Lawrence Kohlberg's Just Community prison programs, which were designed to promote moral growth.[1] These data are supplemented by data and observations collected by E. R. Wasserman and her colleagues on Kohlberg's Just Community program in the Cambridge Cluster School.[2] The prison data reported here are substantially different from other published reports on the results of Just Community prison programs,[3] and do not support many of the claims made for the success of such programs. Some of the claims that have been made can be characterized as promotional,[4] and the programs have operated in a fashion that by design has made it extremely difficult to evaluate them rigorously.

This paper argues that the relationship between Kohlberg's theory of moral development and the programs implemented in both the prison Just Communities and the Cambridge Cluster School Just Community is weak at best. Evidence is presented that the programs are, in effect although not necessarily by intent, programs of institutional maintenance. They create and promote institutional loyalty by persuading the participants that they are being given an opportunity to increase their control over the rules that govern their lives in the institution. The mechanism offered to the prisoners and students is alleged to be "participatory democracy." There is some evidence, however, that the one-man-one-vote definition of participatory democracy offered by the promoters is illusory. Furthermore, important cognitive and behavioral outcomes claimed for the prison program have not been found.[5] The reincarceration rate for the Just Community graduates is as high as or higher than the rates for comparison groups.[6] However, prisoners and students in these Just Community programs do appear pleased with the social climate produced by the programs. This is an important finding[7] that may justify some components of the programs. However, it appears to be independent of the promotion of moral growth or rehabilitation.

In sum, this paper presents evidence to support the following conclusions: first, operational programs that assert that they will promote moral growth have been popular because they are consistent with general cultural values in the United States and with the liberal values of the elite; second, claims made and implied for the Just Community programs have an ambiguous relationship to Kohlberg's theory of moral development and go well beyond the data available; third, Just Community programs in corrections and in the Cambridge Cluster School do not appear to be either participatory democracies or social systems meeting the promoters' claim of one-man-one-vote;[8] fourth, Just Communities have operationally elevated an alleged democratic process into an end in itself without adequate checks against the tyranny of the majority; and fifth, the Just Community, tempered by unilateral intervention by conventional authority, appears to be a functional management technique of social control which utilizes peer pressure to urge conformity to middle-class values, and it is perceived in this way by virtually all the senior administrators under whose auspices these Just Communities operate.

THE APPEAL OF MORAL DEVELOPMENT

Popular concern with moral development, moral education and values education is clear from the plethora of journals, newsletters, books, periodicals, and monographs on the subject that have appeared in the 1960s and 1970s.[9] E. V. Sullivan[10] argues that at least part of the appeal of moral development theory, and the appeal of moral development programs, can be attributed to the North American social context of the Vietnam War and post-Watergate concerns with the place of values in education. Sullivan argues that because the 1960s represented a period in which value-free social science was under attack, Kohlberg's theory was welcomed with open arms both by the social sciences and by educators.[11] Furthermore, Sullivan notes that Kohlberg's theory of moral development "has existed in an era in which any *developmental* theory has been a very attractive option. . . . Since the concept of development implies progress, we can understand why a culture that demands progress should draw from theoretical perspectives that build this notion into their very ontology."[12] Certainly the internal consistency of the theory itself, and its effectiveness in tying Jean Piaget's work to that of John Dewey and the advocacy of democracy as the effective means of progress also helped increase its acceptability and popularity.

This chapter, however, is not attempting an evaluation of the formal elegance, internal consistency, or validity of the theory in the area of normal human development. These are not central to the major points of the paper, and the interested reader can examine the work of J. Gibbs,[13] and ·Kurtines and Greif[14] for formal and methodological criticism of Kohlberg's theoretical claims. The concern here is to illustrate and raise questions about the important role alleged applications of the theory are now playing in corrections[15] and in education,[16] and to suggest that empirical verification by independent investigators of important parts of the theory has not yet been achieved.

Kohlberg's theory and especially his operational programs for schools and prisons have benefited from popular misinterpretation of the terms "moral growth," and "moral development."[17] These terms as used by Kohlberg and his colleagues have a restricted, technical, operational meaning: a positive change in score on Kohlberg's Moral Judgment Interview,[18] an instrument that scales the subject's verbally stated reasons for endorsing hypothetical courses of action. However, moral growth and moral development have strong social and behavioral implications to the layman.

The technical definitions and usage of moral growth and moral development are perfectly unobjectionable. However, because the meanings are different from the layman's understanding of these terms, and because conditions of moral growth are still hypotheses, a special responsibility falls upon the social scientist who advocates the implementation of a program alleged to promote moral development. The next section attempts to assess the degree of responsibility assumed by Kohlberg and his supporters in promoting moral development programs.

THE PROMOTION OF MORAL GROWTH

Kohlberg as well as advocates of the values clarification approach to moral education assert their opposition to any use of indoctrination in moral education. Indoctrination is dismissed as ineffective in promoting moral behaviors and growth in moral judgments, and as undemocratic.[19] Kohlberg's theory of moral development states that there are six invariant and universal stages of moral reasoning.[20] The attainment of successive stages is dependent upon passage through all preceding stages, but the attainment of a given stage is not a guarantee of the attainment of the next stage of moral reasoning. According to Kohlberg, "the stimulation of development is the only ethically acceptable form of moral education."[21] On the basis of a relatively small number of studies by Kohlberg's students, which suggest that it might be possible to stimulate movement through the stages by some form of intervention,[22] Kohlberg and his associates embarked upon a larger program of social interventions in prisons and in the Cambridge Cluster School. Even if one takes at face value the assertions that the interventions reported in the preliminary studies were, in fact, followed by increases in reported level of moral reasoning, the following qualifications would still be in order: first, fewer than half of the subjects showed an increase in level of moral reasoning; second, the average increase measured following intervention was very small; and third, the increases were not of any demonstrated social significance. No behavioral significance was even claimed for the amount of change reported at the levels of moral reasoning under study. Given these qualifications, it is important to examine Kohlberg's own assumptions and the claims that he and others have made on behalf of the proliferating moral development programs.

THE CLAIMS OF THE PROMOTERS

Kohlberg's use of the term moral development is quite different from the usual understanding of the term moral which typically has some behavioral referent. Kohlberg's referent is the subject's judgment, that is, the structure of the reason given for preferring a particular course of action, not the substantive course of action recommended. It is particularly Kohlberg's orientation to formal structure rather than content that has the potential for seriously misleading administrators of institutions that set up moral development programs.* The latter are concerned primarily with the behavioral and substantive aspects of morality. Yet despite Kohlberg's assertion that "It is almost self evident that no psychologist would engage in moral research with the notion that the use of such research is the creation of instrumentalities of manipulation and control to be made available to adult 'socializing agents,' "[23] claims like those reported below often seem to indicate the contrary. And much of the acceptability of moral development programs seems attributable to the resultant confusion.

Consider the following claims:

---

*Interviews by the author with senior administrators of Just community prisons in Connecticut, Nevada, and Kentucky and interviews with senior administrators in the Cambridge school system indicate that they were looking for concrete behavioral results of moral development programs such as the Just Community.

. . . it is not surprising to find that principled subjects are considerably less likely to cheat than conventional subjects.[24]

Moral judgment, while only one factor in moral behavior, is the single most important or influential factor yet discovered in moral behavior.[25]

The Just Community [prison] program aims to develop in inmates the ability to solve social and moral problems in a consistent and responsible manner. It is based on the theoretical work of Professor Lawrence Kohlberg. . . . He has shown that development is stimulated by the experience of collective decision-making in which the open discussion of competing views and interests helps everyone to understand the *need* for complex social institutions.[26]

. . . research results have shown that there is a significant increase in ethical development among program members, as compared with control groups. [Recruitment Form Letter sent out by Dr. Joseph E. Hickey,[27] Fall, 1976 "to provide training and consultation for the establishment of similar units."]

We have created a fair self-governing community which operates within the constraints of a larger total institution and correctional system. Half the original women have been placed in either work release or parole programs. Most of them seem to be doing quite well. None have failed as of this writing.[28]

. . . nearly one-third of the group [of female Just Community inmates] shifted more than half a moral stage* — e.g., stage 2 to 2(3).[29]

Initial recidivism results are encouraging. . . . Overall preliminary results indicate a program recidivism rate of 16% after a mean of two years in the community. While this is roughly half of the mean recidivism rate for similar offenders within the state of Connecticut, a controlled, comparative three-year report will not be available until 1977. . . .[30]

Among the general educational goals which can be reached by using a program of moral discussions are the following: . . . As a result of several years of moral discussions in an integral part of social studies classes, the typical high school student who began as a freshman thinking in a mixture of Stage two and three terms will think predominantly at Stage four.[31]

. . . the development of Just Community Schools has brought a new perspective to the matter of moral action. Observers report that these schools influence the behavior patterns of many of their students. They attend classes more regularly. They take greater responsibility for their own behavior and for the behavior of others. They show greater respect for students in the school who come from different racial, ethnic, or social backgrounds. These changed behaviors are probably not the result of changes in the moral stages of the students involved, but they are the indirect result of developing a

---

*Such a shift would be one-third of a stage, as the Global Score possibilities were 2, 2(3), 3(2), 3(4), and so on.

school based firmly on the findings of research in cognitive moral development. In the long run these changes in action may hold great significance for American education.[32]

. . . classroom activities built around moral discussions have facilitated moral development.[33]

As we have seen, once a person has reached a given higher stage he will always be able to see the world and his decisions in those terms. While there is no foolproof correlation between stage and action, individuals who are in prison are Stages 1 and 2. Furthermore, those who experience growth after their initial incarceration have a far better than average chance of staying out of trouble once they are released.[34]

Among paroled inmates, conventional inmates (those who have reached Stage 3 and 4) are less likely to be reincarcerated than preconventional (Stage 1 and 2) inmates. Thus inmates who move to the conventional level through Moral Development Programs are more likely to stay out of legal difficulties than those who do not move.[35]

. . . the moral development program tries to provide inmates with the elements of experience they have missed and which have led to moral stagnation.[36]

Children who come from families and who associate with friends who use Stage 1 and 2 arguments almost exclusively have little opportunity to advance up the moral scale. Society deprives them of a full opportunity for ethical development unless some societal institution such as school or church intervenes. Society should intervene. Educational intervention to stimulate universal stages of moral development is constitutional. . . . It is socially useful; persons who think at a higher moral level reason better and act in accordance with their judgment more frequently than less developed thinkers. We have every reason to intervene educationally; we have no reason not to do so.
    . . . As a minimum goal of civic education we should aim to raise the level of moral thinking of all children to the stage that will enable them to understand the Principles behind the Declaration of Independence and the Constitution. That is the Societal Maintenance Stage, Stage 4. Getting most high school seniors to Stage 4 thought will be no easy task. To reach this goal, family, community, and school must work together to establish societies based on principles of justice, the principles involved in Stage 5 and 6 thought.[37]

THE PROGRAMS

Moral development programs call for organizing an institution or unit of an institution to maximize conditions hypothesized to produce moral development. This has typically involved training teachers or correctional officers in group dynamics, Kohlberg's theory of moral development, peer counseling, and leading moral discussions so as to provide a controlled challenge to whatever moral reasoning stages were existent in the unit. Kohlberg's proposed guidelines for the Just Community school essentially paralleled those for the Just Community prison:

> 1. The governance of the School should be one of *participatory democracy* with students and teachers having equal rights and a vote of one . . . all major issues of school governance, rules and policy should be made in a (weekly) community . . . meeting.
>
> 2. The governance structure and community meetings should stress solutions of issues through *considerations of fairness and morality*.
>
> 3. The curriculum or academic classes of the school . . . should involve developing *moral discussion* and should stress basic concepts of democracy, law, and justice. Classroom discussions of morality, law, and democracy should be integrated with the real-life decisions and policies of the small school community meetings and with the school's relation to the larger school system and society.[38]

Five direct conditions for moral growth are specified: "These include amount and stage of (i) role taking, (ii) judgments of fairness, (iii) treating decisions as moral issues, (iv) presence of conflict (of two sides), and (v) participation in, and concern about community decisions."[39] Four indirect conditions of moral growth are specified. These involve positive perception of "(i) school program, ideals, goals, (ii) rules and discipline, (iii) staff personality and relations to students, and (iv) peer-group personalities and relations. . . ."[40]

ARE THE PRISON AND SCHOOL JUST COMMUNITIES PARTICIPATORY DEMOCRACIES OPERATING ON THE BASIS OF ONE-MAN-ONE-VOTE?

This question follows directly from the claims of the operators of the prison and school Just Community programs.[41] This section presents data that suggest a negative answer to the question, given the claims of the promoters and most ordinary definitions of participatory democracy and one-man-one-vote. The evidence is based primarily upon two years of observations of prison community meetings in Niantic, Connecticut, at which one-man-one-vote decision making is claimed to be the mechanism of participatory democracy. Virtually all of these meetings were tape-recorded and random samples of the meetings were subjected to a content and process analysis.* The data answer the following questions: (1) Who made decisions at community meetings? (2).How did inmates and students perceive the decision making? (3) Who spoke to whom at these meetings? (4) At what rates did these verbalizations occur? (5) What was discussed at community meetings? The schedule and function of these meetings is given in Appendix A of this chapter; Appendix B shows the method of analysis.

In the prison Just Communities the institution of weekly community meetings and twice-weekly small group meetings did give inmates and staff an opportunity to express their ideas and feelings before the group. At "constitutional convention" meetings (called marathons) held approximately every 10 weeks, inmates had a say in the making of many of the rules that governed their lives in the institution. However, decisions occurred infrequently in the random sample of meetings selected for analysis in spite of a procedure that searched for a decision if an issue was posed in decision-making terms (see Appendix B). The findings are consistent with the evaluators' subjective impressions that decision making was not a frequent event at community meetings (see Table 15.1).

TABLE 15.1
Unit Decisions by Staff or Community
(percent)

	Community Decision	Staff Decision
Women's Just Community (N = 17; 18 sessions)	47	53
Women's Response unit (N = 3; 3 sessions)	67	33
North Building I (N = 4; 8 sessions)	75	25
North Building II (N = 5; 9 sessions)	40	60

Note: Staff or community population may consist of inmates alone.
Source: Compiled by the author.

*Unit meetings of all Connecticut Just Community units and of the Response Program were tape-recorded and a statement-by-statement analysis of who said what to whom was performed on a sample of meetings to determine meeting process, rates of communication by inmates and staff and an inventory of all topics that occurred in the tape-recorded selections drawn in the random selection process. Technical details of sampling and coding are given in Appendix B of this chapter.

Some decisions were ambiguous, some were never made, and some were postponed to a later date. Moreover, not all decisions were the result of community votes. Some were made unilaterally by staff, and some by inmates alone without the participation of staff. Table 15.1 indicates that decisions were made by the community as a whole or by the inmates 47 percent of the time in the women's Just Community, 75 percent of the time in the men's Just Community (1975–76), 40 percent of the time in the men's Just Community (1976–77), and 67 percent of the time in a modified behavior modification program used for comparison (called the Response program).

Kohlberg has defined participatory democracy as one-man-one-vote.[42] However, it would be naive to think that this statement of principle precluded the possibility of disproportionate influence exercised by staff administrators or outside consultants, or the possibility of unilateral decision making by the staff. For example, community meetings of the Just Community women's unit at the Connecticut prison did not appear to be very democratic in comparison with the Just Community ideology. This judgment by the evaluators was independently corroborated by a senior administrator of the program and a staff member of the unit itself in addressing the unit at a community meeting:

> We worked it out, the staff and me . . . I admit that a lot of the things that I do are not always democratically done, nor do I say it's moral development, but in the back of it I think it is because you see what I do I really anticipate that growth will come from it. Something has to happen . . . in this group to make us want to do it a little differently. Now nothing you have done, nothing you have come up with has worked. . . . Now this is what we've decided to do . . . (tape-recorded).

At one point, the staff announced to the inmates (unilaterally) that small groups would be required to meet every day: "Telling about yourself is beneficial; the women who did that are back on the street. We used to be more helpful, [and] got them closer to their families. . . ."

Evidence of unilateral staff decision making in the prison Just Communities substantially impairs the claims of democratic governance. Inmates were permitted to participate in decision making so long as the resultant decisions were tolerable to the traditional authorities of the prison. The inmates were aware of this state of affairs and some pointed explicitly to the discrepancy between the claims for the Just Community and the reality. The staff were aware of this reality and periodically suspended the format of mock democracy when dissatisfied with the outcome. Wasserman has illustrated similar unilateral action by the teachers in the Cambridge Cluster School Just Community.[43] A senior administrator there described staff members' occasional unilateral enforcement of their traditional values as a kind of blackmail: students had to go along with the staff or risk the loss of benefits.

Substantive Contents of Unit Meetings

Prison Just Community unit meetings rarely made reference to topics that would have been consistent with program ideology. References to fairness, justice, trust, and respect were very infrequent in comparison with other topics raised at these meetings.* Actually these topics (fairness, and so on) comprised a dramatically higher proportion of the topics referred to in community meetings of the behavior modification program. The rarity of these topics in Just Community meetings is quantitatively indicated by a content analysis of a random sample of meetings in all of the Connecticut Just Community units and in a parallel analysis of Response unit meetings (see Table 15.2 and Appendix B).

What were the essential features of the weekly Just Community unit meetings observed in the Connecticut prison? They were in large part discussions of inmates' violations of community rules, institutional regulations, and federal and state laws. Staff and other inmates applied implicit and explicit verbal sanctions to alleged violators; disciplinary procedures and penalties were often applied as well. Just Community unit meetings in the women's prison unit cited negatively valued behaviors in 25 percent of all sampled instances. Examples of negatively valued behaviors were theft, violence, drug and alcohol violations, sexual behavior violations (according to institutional regulations), and escape. The rates for men were 28 percent (1975–76) and 55 percent (1976–77). The Response program rate was zero. In contrast, the citations of positively valued behaviors (for example, fairness, trust, respect, maintaining confidentiality, sharing unit resources) for the women's unit were 6 percent; the rates for the men's unit were 1 percent (1975–76) and 7 percent (1976–77). For the Response program the rate was considerably higher, 39 percent.

Just Community programs gave inmates the assurance that minor violations would be handled within the Just Community unit meetings, and inmates were warned that specified more serious offenses could or would (this was ambiguous in practice) be dealt with outside of the Just Community by the institutional administration. A variety of allegations of vi-

---

*It was not necessary to use the term "fair" explicitly in order for a statement to be coded as "fairness." Statements that attempted to balance conflicting rights or interests were also included.

TABLE 15.2

Content Analysis Aggregation of Topics
(percent of references)

Topics	Women's Just Community (N = 710; 18 sessions)	Women's Response Unit (N = 64; 3 sessions)	North Building I (N = 283; 8 sessions)	North Buidling II (N = 348; 9 sessions)
Unit rules/procedures/program reference/ expulsions/disciplinary procedures/ curfews/decision-making/half-way house/furlough/parole/too many short-termers in unit	43.0	54.5	49.0	22.0
Citation of positively valued behaviors: fairness/trust/respect/confidentiality/sharing/spending community funds	6.0	39.0	1.0	7.0
Citation of negatively valued behaviors: theft/violence/threats/sexual and drug violations/community hostility and tension cited/explicit racial hostility expressed/refusal to work/escape/ tampering with security system	25.0	0.0	28.0	55.0
Personal criticism of inmate on unit	1.0	0.0	5.0	—*
Praise of staff or inmate	0.0	5.0	0.0	—*
Interprets feelings/situation; self-revelation request	4.0	0.0	5.0	—*
Swimming/rock concert	13.0	0.0	0.0	9.0
Other: 5 references to any topic	8.0	1.5	12.0	5.0
Total	100.0	100.0	100.0	100.0

* > 1 percent.
Source: Compiled by the author.

olations of institutional, state, and federal rules and laws were handled within the confines of the Just Community units (for example, physical violence, possession of contraband, tampering with the institutional security system). This was of benefit to the inmates and a mixed blessing to the staff and administration: it eased the load of violations the administration had to handle, but it increased the risk that the flow of information would be incomplete; it also increased the burden of unit staff members who felt they had to take some action. For example, the discovery of a drug or a hypodermic syringe in a common area of the unit, but not in the possession or in the room of an inmate, would result in a community meeting and an effort by the staff and some inmates to determine the ownership of the contraband. Although it appears that these kinds of events were reported to the prison administration by most of the unit supervisors, there were clear inmate benefits to having the members of the unit investigate these events rather than the administration of the institution or the state police.

As Table 15.2 indicates, references to fairness and justice or discussion of moral dilemmas rarely occurred. Discussion did not occur in community meetings even in a mechanical fashion; for example, someone in the community might have been required to ask (as a ritual), "Is there a question of fairness involved in this issue?" On the rare occasions when issues of fairness were raised in meetings of the Just Community, they were usually raised by two trainers who periodically attended these meetings. But the trainers themselves did not regularize the raising of issues of fairness and were not successful in transmitting a method of raising such issues to the Just Community staffs.

There is no question that the supervisors and staffs of the Just Communities were personally concerned with fairness.* They cited this concern frequently to the evaluators and knew that helping the community examine conflicts as issues concerning fairness was an important program objective. But this was very difficult for them to achieve in the context of community meetings. Some trainers reported that they found great resistance among inmates to their presentation of hypothetical dilemmas in small groups, and so they abandoned the effort. One trainer who led small groups reported that it was extremely difficult to cast conflicts as moral issues (or issues of fairness) and that this did not happen frequently. Another trainer, after being reassured of confidentiality, asserted that there was a substantial gap between the program in effect and the program ideals of justice through democracy.[44] One of the most experienced senior staff trainers of the Just Community claimed on numerous occasions, both to the evaluators and to other members of the training staff, that one of the Just Community

---

*This was also true of the Response program.

unit supervisors was such a dominating force in community meetings that democratic procedures were hindered. On the other hand, the status discrepancy between inmates and prison staff is an inherent part of incarceration.

Failure to implement an ideal statement of program goals and procedures should not be judged harshly. Probably no programs in correctional institutions or elsewhere reach this level of achievement (certainly not evaluation programs). What *was* implemented in these Just Community units was a program of regular community meetings, marathon (constitutional convention) meetings, and house meetings. Small groups also met, but not as regularly as the Just Community Manual specified, and often without the presence of the consultant/trainers whose function was to instruct staff and inmates about the methods and objectives of these small groups. Although the topics of discussion were rarely cast in terms of fairness and justice, the topics enumerated at the beginning of this section *were* discussed, often at great length and with the expression of great emotion. Indeed, interactions among inmates and staff appear to have been a key element of the programs as implemented.

Interactions at Unit Meetings

A quantitative analysis of the interactions among staff and inmates in prison unit meetings does not reveal a distinctive pattern of interactions in Just Communities as distinct from the comparison programs. A higher proportion of inmates appeared to participate in the meetings of the women's Just Community unit than in Response program meetings, but the balance between staff and inmate participation was virtually identical across programs. The proportion of questions to assertions was also virtually the same. The rates of inmates speaking to fellow inmates was basically the same in the Response and the Just Community programs. Staff and inmates in the Response program tended to address the community as a whole substantially more than staff addressed particular inmates or inmates addressed staff. In contrast, Just Community communications tended to be directed more often at individuals (see Table 15.3).

A clinical analysis of unit meeting dynamics suggests that the Just Community utilized group dynamics typical of other therapeutic communities and that different processes in the male and female Just Communities nevertheless led to similar positive evaluations of the social climate of the respective units. Moreover, the social climate in the Just Community units was more positive than in the Response unit.

TABLE 15.3

Process Analysis Data: Verbalization Rates for each Unit
(percent of total verbalizations recorded)

	Women's Just Community (N = 800; 18 sessions)	Women's Response Unit (N = 111; 3 sessions)*	Men's Just Community North Building I (N = 337; 8 sessions)	Men's Just Community North Building II (N = 592; 9 sessions)
Staff verbalizations	38.0	34.0	38.0	40.0
Statements	27.0	25.0	27.0	26.0
Questions	11.0	9.0	11.0	14.0
Inmate verbalizations	62.0	66.0	63.0	60.0
Statements	53.0	53.0	49.0	50.0
Questions	9.0	13.0	14.0	10.0
Inmate verbalizations to inmates	32.0	33.0	43.0	29.0
Inmate verbalizations to staff	34.0	19.0	28.5	38.0
Inmate verbalizations to community	34.0	48.0	28.5	33.0
Staff verbalizations to inmates	45.0	26.0	56.0	47.0
Staff verbalizations to community	44.0	74.0	40.0	48.0
Staff verbalizations to staff	11.0	0.0	4.0	5.0

*Meetings were very infrequent in this unit.
Note: In all cases staff here includes supervisor, correctional officers, and program trainers.
Staff verbalizations·plus inmate verbalizations total 100 percent.
Source: Compiled by the author.

Clearly, Just Community meetings had their own dynamics and rituals not reflected in the quantitative analyses presented in Tables 15.2 and 15.3. There was ritualized talk in the women's unit about how "the Program has helped me [to] improve," and there were references to people who had previously been in the program and had "now succeeded on the outside." Occasionally, former inmates who were program graduates returned as visitors to the women's unit and said how good the program had been for them (and incidentally, how it appeared to have "fallen" since they had left the prison). More frequently, former program participants were reincarcerated in the women's Just Community unit. (During the course of this evaluation, male Just Community graduates were not permitted to return to the Just Community if rearrested or resentenced.) Women recidivists reentering the Just Community program almost invariably talked about how the program had "fallen" and needed "to get back to where it should be." The evaluators tended to view these kinds of statements as ritualized exhortations to the community to "be good," and not as negative evaluations of the program.

Tears were frequently seen at community meetings and the simultaneous crying of four or five residents was never a surprising event at the women's meetings. It sometimes appeared to the evaluators that community meeting dynamics were guided by combinations of staff and inmates toward the "achievement" of tears and the subsequent giving of physical and emotional support, which was invariably followed by a sense of community well-being, "togetherness," and general good will. Whether the crying followed an inmate's confession of some illicit act or some other kind of personal self-revelation, it was typically the culmination of the issue and any consequent disciplinary procedures seemed anticlimactic.

The author believes that such rituals are an important explanation of the highly positive social climate scores reported for the women's Just Community unit. The intense emotional interactions, within a group setting, among inmates and staff, were one of the most salient events in the women's Just Community unit at the prison. Even staff statements that were critical of specific inmates' behaviors were almost always made with apparent concern and personal warmth. Although equal personal warmth was often observed between staff and inmates in the Response unit, it did not take place in a group setting fraught with intense emotional outbursts and followed by warm support. In the Response unit inmate-staff affect was typically expressed in a one-to-one setting, and a common framework of intense emotional experiences involving the entire community did not appear to exist.

Though emotion was the most salient aspect of the women's solidarity with the Just Community, and this emotional affiliation with the group helps explain the positive social climate perceptions of staff and inmates, the same factors did not appear in the male Just Community units. Confessions of unreported or undetected violations were virtually never observed as they were in the women's unit. It appeared that group solidarity among male inmates, to the extent that it existed, was based upon protecting their stay in the program and avoiding expulsion to the more secure institution from which they had come. The salient feature of group dynamics was a power struggle between inmates on the one hand and staff on the other.

Inmates described by the staff and their peers as leaders in the male Just Community described some of their behavior in meetings as an effort to test the limits of inmate autonomy. They knew, they said, that staff statements about democratic governance could not be true and that, ultimately, equal power of staff and inmates was not possible in a prison. They sought what they called "the bottom line," the point where decisions would have to be made by the staff rather than by the community as a whole (a majority of which consisted of inmates). The purpose of this search appeared to be to prove their belief that the community was not truly democratic.

Staff also perceived a power struggle and often discussed the community in terms of a contest for power or control between themselves and inmates. One unit supervisor, referring to the inmates, said at a staff meeting:

> It kinds of boils down to the whole thing: "If you [inmates] want to f——
> with us the we're going to f——with you. . . . And we [the staff] can do it
> a lot better than they can — I mean from a power vantage point. . . ."
>   The point behind it is if you [staff] people are feeling uncomfortable and
> you're feeling like the community or the individuals in it are putting you in
> a bad position, as far as your job goes, then you have the right and obligation
> to take a unilateral move — I mean I think that should be the last step, but
> I think that's entirely possible and necessary at times, and yet it's not an easy
> thing to do. You stand to take a lot of flack for it. You stand to shake the
> credibility of the staff . . . in the situation, but at the same time if we go the
> other alternative in not keeping them serious and not having things dealt with
> then you're really going to ultimately get really f——d around, and it's better
> to take a stand on it (tape-recorded).

Because of the constant testing of staff by male unit inmates, it was probably easier for the staff there (compared with the women's Just Community unit) occasionally to stigmatize the male inmates both as individuals and in terms of the group. This is illustrated by one staff member's statement at a community meeting:

> We are not saying that everybody has to be an angel, you've got to be a good
> boy, because you guys aren't. You know you basically are a bunch of f——
> ing hoodlums [yelling of objections from inmates]. But see, you cop an attitude
> behind that [get upset at my statement] and you don't have to because if I
> didn't like you as people, I wouldn't be here (tape-recorded).

Inmates "kept cool" and did not report on known violations of community and institutional rules or violations of law they knew were being committed by fellow inmates. They even refused to identify those they were "sure" were stealing items from fellow inmates. The highest good for the male inmates appeared to be staying in the program rather than returning to the prison from which they had come.

The attitudes of a majority of the staff in the male unit were genuinely sympathetic to the inmates' plight of confinement and restriction. They tried to help the inmates perceive that they understood that violations would occur, but that for the good of the community these acts must be committed discreetly. Staff asserted that these behaviors would not be permitted to jeopardize the program. Inmates were occasionally criticized by the staff for the blatant nature of the violations rather than for the violations per se — for example, throwing contraband containers out the window of the unit where they would be found on the ground the next morning rather than disposing of the evidence.

Liberal and conservative staff alike viewed the expulsion of an inmate from the program as the worst thing that could happen to him. This appeared to be partly because of staff and trainer perceptions that living conditions at the alternative prison were terrible, partly because some believed that they could help the inmates and the other prison could not, and partly because expulsion of an inmate both revealed an institutional violation that might not otherwise become widely known, and implied that the Just Community had failed to deal effectively with the inmate. Staff loyalty in the male Just Community units was typically more to the program and its administrators than to the institution or the Department of Correction. According to the confidential reports received by the evaluators from the male Just Community staff members, one unit supervisor had to be and was replaced by request of the Just Community director, because loyalty to the administrators of the institution was perceived to be stronger than loyalty to the administrator of the Just Community program. This was not true at the women's Just Community unit, where loyalty to the administration of the institution appeared to be paramount.

Institutional regulations aside, marathon meetings, held approximately every three months, did in fact establish rules of the unit. Interviews with inmates clearly showed that they believed that they had written or approved rules governing their unit at the marathon meeting, and the evaluators agreed with that judgment. The community meetings, moreover, did deal with a wide variety of rule infractions (both rules made by the unit and those of the institution and sometimes of the state). The community meetings did "promote the controlled conflict and open exchange of opinions"[45] that are prescribed by the program manual, but conflicting ideas of what was right and what was wrong were very rarely discussed in the light of what was fair.

If moral growth could be demonstrated in the individuals involved in the Just Community programs, one could not argue that the discussion of community concerns in terms of fairness and justice was a relevant variable. One could argue, however, that inmates' perceptions that they had been treated fairly were an important factor in the promotion of moral growth. The next section, however, shows that there was no demonstrable evidence of moral growth among the inmates of the Just Communities.

EVIDENCE FOR THE DEVELOPMENT OF MORAL MATURITY AMONG THE INMATES OF JUST COMMUNITIES

Contrary to the report by Scharf and Hickey,[46] no evidence was found for the development of moral judgments among the inmates of Just Communities examined in Connecticut. It is possible that there was a time when such development occurred. However, there appear to be about the same proportion of individual decreases in the measurement of moral maturity as increases during the fall 1975 through summer 1977 period of this study. This finding could, in part, reflect scoring error due to low inter- and intracoder reliability in scoring Moral Judgment Interviews. One coauthor of the scoring manual and a second expert scorer have acknowledged that the reliability for scoring Form B of the Moral Judgment Interview is unsatisfactorily low.* Some scorers interviewed by the evaluators acknowledged that they had scored individual Moral Judgment Interviews of some other studies on more than one occasion and sometimes they did acquire knowledge of the chronology of the Moral Judgment Interview protocols. That is, they knew which Moral Judgment Interviews occurred at earlier and which at later dates. This suggests the possibility that unconscious bias of some scorers could produce measurements that indicate moral growth. This could easily happen if the Moral Judgment Interviews were scored by the same individuals who collected the interviews, or if they did not remove all indicators of the chronology of administration from the interviews. In the findings presented here a "double blind" coding scheme obliterated identity and chronology of the protocols. Data on scoring reliability are presented in Appendix B. Although no moral growth attributable to the Just Community programs could be found, stable differences were found for specific groups in the study. Correctional officers consistently scored higher than inmates, and administrators scored consistently higher than correctional officers (see Tables 15.4 and 15.5).

RECIDIVISM

A one-year follow-up of graduates of the Just Community programs and the graduates of the Response program indicates that participation in the

---

*Because Form B was used alternatively as the baseline and follow-up measurement of moral judgement, this error was an inherent part of the measurement.

TABLE 15.4

Mean Moral Maturity Scores (MMS) for Staff and Inmates

Group	Mean MMS
Nevada staff baseline	327.0
Nevada Inmates baseline	274.5
Nevada inmate follow-up[a]	296.0
Kentucky staff baseline	334.0
Kentucky juvenile girls baseline (all)	216.0
Kentucky Kennedy group home baseline	237.0
Kentucky Kennedy Group Home follow-up[a]	258.0
Mt. Pleasant, Iowa, staff baseline	313.0
Mt. Pleasant, Iowa, inmate baseline	294.0
Kirkland, S.C., T.C.[b] staff trained in Niantic baseline	397.0
Kirkland, S.C., Non-T.C. staff trained in Niantic baseline	296.0
Kirkland, S.C., all Niantic trained staff baseline	339.0
Kirkland, S.C., Therapeutic Community inmate baseline	294.0
Connecticut women's Just Community baseline	272.0
Connecticut women's response baseline	254.0
Connecticut men's Just Community (North Building I) baseline	245.0
Connecticut men's Just Community (North Building I) follow-up	262.0[c]
Connecticut men's Just Community (North Building II) baseline	Global 3(2)[d]
Connecticut men's Just Community (North Building II) follow-up	Global 2(3)/3(2)[d]
Connecticut Men's Just Community staff	398.0

[a] The follow-up data were for entirely different inmates in the unit.

[b] Therapeutic Community.

[c] The difference between baseline and follow-up here can be accounted for by one person who was high at the exit measurement, for whom there were no baseline data. The average individual difference between baseline measurement and exit measurement was a decline of 1.6 MMS points.

[d] Baseline data collected by Just Community recruiters at C.C.I., Cheshire, were often incomplete and only the Global Moral Maturity Score is meaningful. Global *medium* was 3(2).

Source: Compiled by author.

TABLE 15.5

Average Moral Maturity Scores of Unit Staff and Administrators

Group	Average MMS	Staff/ Administrator Difference in MMS Points
Nevada administrators	364	52 points
Nevada unit staff	312	
Kentucky administrators	370	69 points
Kentucky staff	301	
South Carolina T.C.[a] Unit staff [b]	397	NA[c]
South Carolina correctional officers	296	
Iowa administrators	350	47 points
Iowa unit staff	303	
North Building II staff[b]	398	NA[c]

[a] Therapeutic Community.
[b] Administrator data not presented because N = 1, and disclosure would violate the confidentiality given to these individuals with regard to their MMS scores.
[c] Not applicable.
Source: Compiled by the author.

Connecticut Just Communities did not appear to reduce recidivism. Recidivism was defined as reincarceration following discharge from the jurisdiction of the Connecticut Department of Correction or release to parole or a half-way house. Details of the definition of recidivism and the rationale for the computations are given in Appendix C. The reincarceration rate for the women's Just Community program is higher than that for the women's Response program, despite the finding that the primary offenses of women in the Just Community were less serious than the primary offenses of the women in the Response program. The Response program had a higher proportion of more serious (felony) offenders. The higher reincarceration rate for Just Community women is accounted for by the higher rate of reincarceration *without* a new sentence. There was no difference in rate of reincarceration *with* a new sentence. Of the women graduates of the Just Community program, 73 percent were reincarcerated in a Connecticut Department of Correction facility within 12 months of discharge or release from prison. The comparable figure for Response program graduates was 54 percent; for the men's Just Community (1975–76) the comparable reincarceration rate was 47 percent. For the six inmates expelled from this male Just Community, the comparable figure was 17 percent (see Tables 15.6 and 15.7).

TABLE 15.6

Analysis of Reincarceration Data for Program Graduates, Comparing Different Definitions of Program Graduate

Postrelease/Discharge Outcome	Initial Response Unit Data		Adjusted Response Unit Data Includes Those in Program Only 3 months		Women's Just Community Data for Inmates in Program 3 months		Men's Just Community Data for North Building I Program Graduates		Men's Just Community Data for Program Graduates in Unit between November 1975 and 1976		Inmates Expelled from Men's Just Community North Building I	
	$N=28$	Per-cent	$N=23$	Per-cent	$N='15$	Per-cent	$N=30$	Per-cent	$N=17$	Per-cent	$N=6$	Per-cent
R_1 Released and reincarcerated without a new sentence	7	25.0	6	26.0	7	47.0	4	13.0	4	23.0	0	0.0
R_2 Released and reincarcerated with a new sentence	4	14.3	3	13.0	4	26.5	9	30.0	3	18.0	0	0.0
R_3 Released and not reincarcerated for 12 months	7	25.0	6	26.0	3	20.0	14	47.0	10	59.0	2	33.0

D₁ Discharged and reincarcerated without a new sentence	0	0.0	0	0.0	0	0.0	2	7.0	0	0.0	0	0.0
D₂ Discharged and reincarcerated with a new sentence	4	14.3	3	13.0	0	0.0	0	0.0	0	0.0	1	17.0
D₃ Discharged and not reincarcerated for 12 months	6	21.4	5	22.0	1	6.5	1	3.0	0	0.0	3	50.0
R₁ and D₁	7	25.0	6	26.0	7	47.0	6	20.0	4	23.0	0	0.0
R₂ and D₂	8	29.0	6	26.0	4	26.5	9	30.0	3	18.0	1	17.0
R₃ and D₃	13	46.0	11	48.0	4	26.5	15	50.0	10	59.0	5	83.0
R₁ and R₂	11	39.0	9	39.0	11	73.0	13	43.0	7	41.0	0	0.0
R₁, R₂, D₁, and D₂	15	54.0	12	52.0	11	73.0	15	50.0	7	41.0	1	17.0

Note: Women's Response unit unadjusted data versus data adjusted to a "three month or more in program" definition. For men's Just Community unit, data analysis is for all men program graduates of North Building I for whom data were obtainable (N = 30), and for men in the North Building I unit during the time of the evaluators' observations (N = 17). Also included are the data for six inmates expelled from the men's Just Community unit and sent to C.C.I., Cheshire.

Source: Compiled by the author.

TABLE 15.7

Postrelease Outcome and Average Moral Maturity Scores (MMS)

	Women's Response Unit	Women's Just Community	Men's Just Community (North Building II)
Reincarcerated with no new sentence	262 N = 5	282 N = 5	262 N = 3
Reincarcerated with a new sentence	300 N = 3	259 N = 3	233 N = 3
No record of reincarceration for 12 months past release or discharge	258 N = 5	275 N = 2	254 N = 10
Reincarcerated with or without a sentence	276 N = 8	273 N = 8	248 N = 6

Source: Compiled by the author.

No relationship was found between reincarceration and level of moral judgment. Just Community women with no record of reincarceration for 12 months scored an average of 12 Moral Maturity Score (MMS) points higher than those reincarcerated with a new sentence. Just Community men with no record of reincarceration for 12 months scored an average of 21 MMS points higher than those reincarcerated with a new sentence. However, women in the Response program reincarcerated with a new sentence had the highest Moral Maturity Score of the groups in Table 15.7 (MMS = 300) and this was 42 MMS points higher than the score of those with no record of reincarceration for 12 months.* Response program inmates with the best postrelease outcome had the lowest Moral Maturity Score average. Because there is no reason to expect such a relationship in one unit and not in another, it cannot be concluded that there is any

---

*One might hypothesize that Stage 2 inmates in a Stage-2-oriented behavior modification program might have a higher probability of concluding that the crime is not worth the time (in prison) than higher stage inmates, and consequently have the lowest recidivism rate.

relationship between Moral Maturity Score and postrelease outcome. It is important that people interested in Just Community approaches to corrections understand the facts about claims that there will be a relationship between moral development (measured by Moral Maturity Score) and postrelease outcome: they are not supported by evidence available, are often believed to be true by administrators and staff trained to adopt Just Community methods,[47] seem to have been one reason for adopting a Just Community model by some of the administrators who decided to send staff for Just Community training, and are an implicit component of the mythology of Just Community units.*

Relationship between Postrelease Outcome and Selective Recruitment

The data were examined to see whether a relatively favorable outcome for any unit might be explained by "creaming," that is, the recruiting or attracting into a unit of inmates who were perceived to be better prospects for management within the unit or for a more favorable postrelease outcome because their prior record was more "favorable." Staff at the women's Response unit and the women's Just Community unit were occasionally heard to say that the other unit managed to get the better inmates for their unit. Examination of the categories of primary offense descriptions given in the files of the Department of Correction information system indicated that 50 percent of the inmates in the Response program, for whom there were postrelease data, were felony offenders. This was true for 31 percent of the comparable inmates in the women's Just Community program. Thus it does not appear that the Response program had selectively recruited better inmates.

The proportion of felony offenders found within the different postrelease outcome categories was also examined for each unit. For the Response program no relationship was found between prior offense category and postrelease outcome. Felony offenders were equally likely to be found in all postrelease outcome categories (see Table 15.8). In the women's Just Community unit, felony offenders had the highest probability of appearing as reincarcerated with no new sentence (75 percent) and zero probability of having no record of reincarceration. In the male Just Community unit (1975–76), felony offenders had the highest probability of being found in the postrelease category, no record of reincarceration (see Table 15.8).

---

*Interviews with Just Community female inmates elicited frequent statements that a benefit of moral development is that they will be less likely to be reincarcerated after graduating from the Just Community.

TABLE 15.8

Proportion of Felony Offenders in Different Postrelease Catagories (percent)

	Women's Response Program (N = 9)	Women's Just Community Program (N = 4)	Men's Just Community (North Building I) (N = 23)
Reincarcerated with no new sentence	33	75	13
Reincarcerated with a new sentence	33	25	35
No record of reincarceration	33	0	52

Source: Compiled by the author.

It is important to recognize that although populations are dealt with here and not samples, the total number of offenders for which data are available is small. Thus the data should be viewed with some caution.

NO CHECKS AGAINST A TYRANNY OF THE MAJORITY IN THE JUST COMMUNITY

One apparent structural flaw in the design of prison and school Just Communities was the absence of formal checks against tyranny of the majority. Structurally, this meant that legislative, executive, and judicial powers all resided in the plenary sessions of the communities.

The Just Communities plenary sessions retained virtually all constitutional power to make decisions governing their members, to enforce them, and to consider conflicting claims and appeals.[48] For example, they reserved to themselves, acting in plenary session, the right to specify with whom a community member could associate, the topics that could and could not be discussed with persons inside and outside the community, and the occasions when the community would demand self-disclosure of thought and affect. An individual's refusal to acquiesce in the legitimacy of the community's right to make these demands could result in expulsion from the community.

There were two potential checks against this tyranny and its inevitable partner, injustice. The first was unilateral staff decision making which preempted or overruled community decision making. This was a contradiction of the formal terms of the Just Community itself, which gave the community as a whole decision-making power in a specified domain. Such staff decisions violated the Just Community constitution, raised serious questions of integrity and good faith, and were demoralizing to the community.

The second potential check against the tyranny of the majority was unilateral action by the administration. Unilateral administration action against a Just Community majority occurred under two conditions. In some instances, administration decisions were exercised when a new constitution was being negotiated. This preserved the legitimacy of administration action because Just Community constitutions were promulgated for fixed periods, typically three months, and administration approval was acknowledged by all members of the community to be required for each new constitution. In some instances, unilateral administration action was taken during the three month duration of the constitution. This violated the constitution and was analogous to unilateral staff decision making in raising questions of good faith.

Unilateral decision making by staff has been observed in the Cambridge Cluster School Just Community,[49] and unilateral decision making by both staff and administration has been observed in prison Just Communities.[50] Ironically, these actions were rarely taken to deal with perceived injustices resulting from majority rule. Rather, unilateral action by staff and administration tended to be punitive and occurred in response to behaviors deemed socially or politically intolerable. Such actions involved expulsion of community members, suspension of the Just Community Program, or threatening to take unilateral punitive action unless the community made a specific decision.[51] The claim of an equal say by each member of the community[52] was justified only when the community decision was not in serious conflict with the opinions of staff and administration.

The operation of these Just Communities seems to involve an internal contradiction. If the ultimate objective of these programs is the promotion of justice, then both the means and the ends must be judged in terms of fairness. The naive equation of justice with democratic procedure, when that procedure does not include a system of checks against the tyranny of the majority, has produced a system that can tolerate unjust procedure in the name of just ends.

THE JUST COMMUNITY AS A MANAGEMENT TOOL OF SOCIAL CONTROL

It appears that to institutional administrators the pseudodemocratic means and procedures of Kohlberg's Just Communities are among the most important features of their operations. They are seen as effective means of social control. This does not mean that social control is the only reason institutional administrators have supported Just Communities. Some believe that the program does or might produce more justice than prior alternatives. Nevertheless, virtually all the senior administrators of Just Community programs interviewed by the author perceived that the Just Community, tempered by unilateral intervention by conventional authority, is a functional management technique of social control that utilizes peer pressure to urge conformity to middle-class values.

Not infrequently, staff publicly endorsed community decisions it considered unjust (but not intolerable) by equating democratic procedure, which was defined as one-person-one-vote, and fairness. A decision by a majority was typically equated with a just outcome so long as that outcome did not contradict the goals of building community cohesion and institutional maintenance.

Some administrators pointed to the efficacy of inmate peer pressure, which was promoted in the Just Community to reveal information on institutional violations and identify the perpetrators. Others pointed to the "carrots and sticks" of the Just Community: benefits used to induce verbal conformity with conventional middle-class values and the threat by staff and administration to withdraw privileges in order to coerce consensus.[53] One senior administrator in the Just Community School used the term blackmail to describe how staff had obtained community agreement on the politically sensitive topic of marijuana smoking at a school event.[54] It was often agreed that the benefits offered Just Community inmates were an effective incentive in inducing outward conformity to institutional regulations.

The cyclical nature of Just Community programs also seems to contribute to their efficacy as management tools.* In all cases a substantial period of

---

*More than half of the women in the Just Community prison unit had left the unit in less than three months. Women were almost constantly entering and leaving the program. The men's Just Community prison unit had a different cycle — beginning with a group of about 8 and adding to that group over the course of a year up to a group size of approximately 16, with men leaving the program after about nine months unless expelled earlier. The Just Community school followed the ten-month school year cycle with a new group entering each fall, and the annual departure of dropouts and graduates.

time is spent orienting new inmates or students to the program, discussing the governance of the program, and rewriting rules. The time required to discuss these matters is often a substantial portion of the nonworking hours of the day for inmates. The promise of an equal inmate say in rules and many disciplinary procedures is an important carrot in commanding an inmate's initial interest when entering a Just Community unit. Should disillusionment with the program's promises have a chance to set in, a substantial portion of the inmate's time in the program has usually passed, and for most it seems worth "going along" a bit longer. Those who challenged the integrity of the implementation of the program's ideals were often utilized by the staff to stimulate discussion of the program's goals and call for more effective implementation. The staff did not tend to see the Just Community program as a management tool. They were consistently dedicated to program goals of rehabilitation by treating inmates better, and virtually all Just Community staff articulated this objective. Nevertheless, the administrator's role necessarily has a managerial perspective and the efficacy of the Just Community prison programs justified their existence in Connecticut for about six years, although particular Just Community units were closed down by administrative fiat on numerous occasions, and reopened with new inmates and usually a selection of entirely or partially new staff. It is still too early to judge cyclical program effects on the Just Community school. At the most senior level, no administrators were found who took moral development claims of either prison or school Just Communities very seriously. Their objective was managerial effectiveness for system maintenance, and they viewed the Just Community programs in these terms.

DISCUSSION

This section suggests some answers to two questions: what managerial needs are these programs serving, and what have been the advantages of the pseudodemocratic model of governance implemented under Just Community auspices?

The Just Community school program appeared to respond to school administrators' concerns with school dropouts, with the distress of parents who sought an alternative to the regular high school and could not find a place for their children in the available alternatives, and with disruptive students. The program also provided a welcome opportunity to a small number of regular high school teachers who had their own ideological agendas and did not fit into the traditional operating mode of the school. The Just Community school appeared as an alternative school espousing democracy, increased freedom for students and teachers, and some departures from the traditional curriculum.

The Just Community prison programs followed managerial dissatisfaction with its control of prison conflict and a willingness to innovate on a small experimental scale in order to attempt to reduce internal pressure and conflict. Democracy used loosely is the most acceptable form of social control in U.S. society. To the extent that students and prisoners took part in a program that utilized some participatory mechanisms, the flow of information to the administration seemed likely to improve. Some program participants seemed likely to be coopted to take administrative goals as their own, and program ideology provided a rationale to deter sanctions against coopted community members because their behavior could be presented as being for the good of the group. Some traditional authority was diffused and delegated to community members, but it could be retracted at any time. Because this delegated authority was periodically taken away, the constantly implied threat to the existence of the program and its benefits was usually credible and coercive. The mechanism of control seemed to be the illusion of participatory democracy which increased information and surveillance via collective scrutiny while offering some tangible benefits to the inmates. It promoted convergence of judgments within the prison unit by the majority rule requirement for making community rules and decisions. Staff participation in the rule-making and decision-making processes facilitated communication and was good for morale. The most important device of control seemed to be the substitution of peer pressure for traditional authority until such time as a majority of the community differed from the opinions of the traditional authorities — that is, correctional officers, teachers, and administrators. When these limits were reached on an issue of serious consequences to the traditional authority, that authority was asserted. This could be done unilaterally or by the threat of a unilateral decision if the community did not offer an acceptable compromise or endorse the position of the traditional authority.

In a number of ways the Just Communities seemed even more coercive to the author than traditional programs. Although Just Community programs are generally voluntary, the term does not have its full meaning in prisons and schools. Few if any participants understand many of the implications of the Just Community programs they enter. In exchange for anticipated benefits Just Community members face strong coercion. There is the coercion to participate in the discussions of the group. There is coercion to tell about oneself, particularly about one's background, family, and history of deviant behavior. In this study the collective group pressure on an individual to confess to certain feelings or to violations of institutional regulations was occasionally brutal in terms of the emotional outbursts of anger observed. Demands that a person explain his or her opinion following the invariably open-ballot voting were often strong. The group occasionally imposed requirements that an individual not be allowed to speak with some other specified individual, and required secrecy of community discussions. The penalty of expulsion from the group could be imposed for violations of these requirements. Violations of the degree of freedom of association and freedom of speech available to individuals in comparable school and prison programs outside of the Just Communities struck civil-liberties-oriented observers as unduly intrusive, coercive, and inhumane. These infringements seemed particularly ironic in the context of a program designed to promote justice.

CONCLUSIONS

A critical examination of Just Community programs allegedly based on Kohlberg's theory of moral development has found that important claims about the operation and effects of the program in prison and school settings are not supported by most of the available evidence. The relationship between the programs promoted by Kohlberg and his associates and Kohlberg's theory is ambiguous. Evidence available indicates no significant moral growth and no rehabilitation of prison inmates in comparison with the alternative programs examined. Claims of participatory democracy are apparently illusory or false. The naive equation of one-person-one-vote with justice permits tyranny of the majority in the name of justice. Two major reasons for the appeal of Just Communities to institutional administrators responsible for their operation and maintenance seem to be a belief that they promote middle-class values and a perception of their efficacy as short-term techniques of social control.

APPENDIX A

Function and Schedule of Prison Just Community

Just Community programs have had four kinds of meetings: (1) community meetings which included all inmates, virtually all staff including the unit supervisor, at least one Just Community trainer (individuals thoroughly familiar with the handbook of the Just Community, called the "Just Community Manual," and designated by the director of the Connecticut Just Communities as teachers of the Just Community approach to corrections to correctional officers and supervisors), and occasionally the director of the Just Communities; (2) small group meetings which included half of the inmates, at least one staff member, frequently a trainer, and for periods of time, trainer/graduate students from Harvard University or Boston University; (3) marathon meetings which included all inmates, all staff including the unit supervisor, at least one trainer, and usually the director of the Just Community; (4) house meetings which included the inmates who happened to be in the building at the time the house meeting was called, the staff members, including the supervisor, who happened to be in the building at the time the meeting was called, and any trainer or other program affiliate who happened to be in the building at the time the meeting was called.*The Harvard evaluation team was present at virtually all community meetings. These occurred weekly at fixed times, from about 1:30 p.m. until it was decided they were over — usually between 4:00 p.m. and 6:00 p.m.; occasionally they continued after a break for supper. The assistant superintendent of the prison sometimes attended part of these community meetings. All community meetings attended by the Harvard evaluators were tape-recorded with the permission of all people present. An informed consent document was given to all inmates and to staff participants who took part in specific interviews, promising that they as individuals would not be able to be identified with any specific statements recorded; that the evaluators would not attribute confidential information to specific identifiable individuals to anyone outside of the research team. A copy of the informed consent form is in Appendix D. Federal Regulation 28CFR, Ch. I, Part 22 now makes the research data collected in this project immune from judicial process. Many of these community meetings were also tape-recorded and videotaped by the Just Community training staff for use in training both Connecticut and non-Connecticut corrections personnel in the Just Community program. Marathon meetings were tape-recorded by the Harvard evaluators and frequently also by the Just Community training staff. Small group meetings were usually tape-recorded by trainers or the Harvard or Boston University graduate student consultant/trainers. House meetings were tape-recorded by the Harvard evaluators whenever they were in the unit at the time a house meeting was called. Just Community trainers appeared to do the same if they had access to a tape-recorder.

Community meetings occurred faithfully on a weekly basis at each Connecticut Just Community unit. Community meetings dealt with issues in-

---

*Two other types of meetings occurred: staff meetings preceding virtually all community meetings, sometimes with a trainer, director, or assistant superintendent present; and staff meetings at the home of a staff member, sometimes lasting for half a day. The Response program had staff meetings that sometimes lasted all day.

volving the Just Community program, its rules and procedures, and community meeting procedures, with the citation of positively and negatively valued behaviors, and with a smaller number of other topics discussed and enumerated in the section of this chapter.

Small group meetings were designed to meet at least twice per week so that members of the inmate community met with their small group at least once per week. There were occasions when small groups met more frequently. There were periods of time when small groups did not meet. Small groups were designed to deal with personal problems of members of the Just Community, almost invariably with the personal problems of inmates rather than staff.

Marathon meetings, or "constitutional conventions" as they were sometimes called, occurred at most every 10 weeks, but usually at somewhat less frequent intervals. At these meetings, which lasted from 9 a.m. to the late afternoon and sometimes longer, the governing rules and regulations for the unit were proposed, debated, and adopted by majority vote of all members of the Just Community — inmates, supervisor and staff, trainers, and program director. Sometimes trainers and the director participated in the voting, sometimes they did not. They did participate in proposing rules, commenting on the discussion, and giving guidance to the community on which rules proposed were likely or unlikely to be acceptable to the superintendent of the institution. It was invariably made clear to the inmates by unit supervisors that rule changes made by the community that differed from the previous "constitution" had to be approved by the superintendent of the prison. The right of the director of the Just Community to veto a community decision was the subject of vigorous debate in the male Just Community on a number of occasions.

House meetings served to deal with almost any immediate problem that could not wait until the next community meeting. House meetings could be called by anyone in the community whenever inmates were in the unit, but not all inmates had to be in the unit. No fixed proportion of inmates was designated as required for a house meeting. House meetings were typically called during the lunch hour, after the inmates returned from their afternoon activities, or in the evening. On occasion there were house rules that specified that no house meeting could be called after 10:00 p.m.

Although the types and functions of Just Community meetings are mainly those that have been described, there was some flexibility in the functions served. Community meetings, marathons, and house meetings sometimes dealt with personal problems. Community meetings occasionally made de facto changes in the "constitution." Small group meetings sometimes dealt with hypothetical moral dilemmas.

The analysis of the processes of interactions reported here concerns primarily community meetings, and to a lesser extent house meetings and marathons. A major reason community meetings were chosen was that these were the most frequent and stable of the meeting types in terms of time of occurrence, which meant that the evaluators could almost always know when to be there with a tape-recorder and in theory could cover every one of these meetings. More important perhaps was the often heard assertion that the community meeting was the major vehicle for community self-governance and for the distribution of justice as fairness in the community, although these could also be functions of marathons and house meetings. Almost all marathons were tape-recorded and may be analyzed in a separate project. House meetings were irregular, and it was not possible to obtain a formal random sample of them, although the researchers have a selection of them. Small group meetings may well have been therapeutically important, but their occurrence was sometimes erratic, and they did not comprise the full community or have the power of community rule making or community decision making.

At the comparison unit, which was the Response program at the Connecticut prison, house meetings occurred on an irregular basis even when scheduled. Advancing the time of Response program house meetings certainly did no harm to the Response program, but it did mean that the evaluators missed some of these already most infrequent house meetings. Nevertheless, a small sample of house meetings was tape-recorded in this unit and comparisons were made between meeting processes here and at the Just Community programs.

APPENDIX B

Method of Analysis for Process and Content of Just Community Meetings

A probability sample was drawn from the tape-recordings of the three kinds of meetings that occurred in the Just Community. These were the weekly community meetings, the marathon meetings (held at approximately 10-week intervals) which proposed the basic rules for the Just Community, and house meetings which occurred when announced by any member of the community, but usually before 10 p.m. From the complete tape-recording of each meeting one of the following samples was drawn: a 15-minute sample from the beginning of the meeting, a 15-minute sample from the middle of the meeting, or a 15-minute sample from the end of the meeting. All such points of entry to the tape were made by estimating the location of the middle and end of the tape from the counter-indicator numbers noted for the beginning and ending of each taped session. This was done to insure against bias in the selection of material on the tapes. Thus, once a meeting was drawn in the random selection of meetings, the beginning of the session was clear, and the middle and ending selections could not be determined by the investigator's bias but rather by an automatic procedure. Ambiguity in the estimation of the middle 15-minute selection and the ending 15-minute selection had no effect on the random nature of the selection, for once a middle or ending 15-minute location was chosen, coding of the meeting always began at this point. The only material rejected was a tape-recording from the Response program which, although labeled "house meeting," was a lecture by the head of the laundry on how to sort, label, and tie up laundry. All other tape-recordings selected were analyzed from the predefined tape locations described. For each 15-minute selection of tape, the 15 minutes were extended for another 15 minutes (maximum), if necessary, to ascertain the nature of the decision on the issue being discussed (that is, decision by staff, residents, the community as a whole, no decision, ambiguous outcome, and so on). If no decision was reached during this 30-minute period, coding of interactions ceased and the tape was searched for the outcome of the issue at hand. The nature of the decision was then recorded on the code sheet (see Figure 15. B.1).

Three sets of random drawings were made for the Just Community programs: (1) 8 meetings were drawn from the male-unit (1975–76) tapes which were arranged in chronological order from November 1975 through May 17, 1976; (2) in the same manner, 9 meetings were drawn from the male-unit (1976–77) tapes which ranged from September 28, 1976 through July 11, 1977; (3) 18 meetings were drawn from the women's Just Community program tapes ranging from November 18, 1975, to July 1977. One of the major reasons for recording almost all the community meetings possible was to ensure that the random sample of taped sessions drawn would truly be representative of community meeting processes and topics covered. By attending virtually all the meetings the evaluators could insure that special meetings were not held for their benefit. (This cannot be guaranteed for the Response program.) Regular attendance at these meetings also helped give the evaluators excellent rapport with the inmates of the Just Communities because they had witnessed the same events. Evaluators did not participate in these meetings. They took notes, operated the tape recorders, and collected some data for a possible future sociometric analysis. Evaluators also monitored each other's behavior during their initial joint attendance at these meetings to be sure that they did not

FIGURE 15.B.1

Data Sheet for Content-Process Analysis Coding

						Issue Brought BY
						Statement BY
						Statement or Question BY
						Question BY
						Interrupt
						FAIRNESS
						TRUST
						RESPECT
						HSE. RULES OR CONSTI
						VIOLENCE
						SEXUAL BEHAVIOR
						DRUGS INCL ALCOHOL
						RACE
						CURFEW
						OTHER
						FURLOUGH
						HALF-WAY HOUSE
						PAROLE
						MEDICAL COMPLAINT
						OUTSIDE FAMILY PROBLEM
						DISCIPLINE CMTE. COMPLAINT
						STAFF LECT
						THREAT MADE BY
						SELF REVELATIONS REQ.
						INTERPRETS FEELINGS
						INTERPRETS SITUATION
						DECISION BY: S.I.A.Su.
						PRAISE (FROM TO)
						INMATES TALKING
						STAFF TALKING
						TOTAL TIME ELAPSED
						OTHER NOTES

A = Administrator   S = Staff   C = Community   Tr = Trainer
Su = Supervision   I = Inmate

Source: Constructed by the author.

unwittingly give positive or negative indicators of their feelings about community events. Inmates and staff accepted this noninterference stance of the evaluators quite readily (it did not really matter to them) and better than did the trainers, who often pressed the evaluators for recommendations and judgments. These were typically turned aside by asking the trainers how they thought the meeting had gone, or by saying that the meeting had been very interesting. A major concern of the senior evaluator was that he not compromise his independent observer position by having his recommendations implemented and then be required to evaluate his own recommendations in action. These requests could be viewed as an effort to coopt the evaluators or to compromise their independence. One request that the senior evaluator codirect the operation of the Just Community programs was viewed in this light, in spite of a fairly elaborate justification of how this might be done without compromising the independence of the evaluation. The evaluators refused this proposal because they did not believe that independence could be maintained under such conditions.

All unit meeting tape-recordings from the response program were analyzed in their entirety because the number was so small. Thus the analysis is for all unit meetings the evaluators tape-recorded.

The unit of speech recorded on the code sheets for this process analysis is designated a verbalization. A verbalization is a unit of speech that begins when an individual begins to speak in a selected unit meeting and ends when that individual ceases speaking and another individual begins to speak. The beginning of that second individual's speech is the beginning of the second verbalization. Interruptions by another speaker do not terminate a verbalization unless the original speaker stops speaking and another individual "has the floor." There occur instances on these tapes when so many individuals are speaking simultaneously in a unit meeting that no one can be understood. These selections of the tape cannot be coded and coding resumes when a single individual has "regained the floor." The code sheets for recording categories of verbalizations are given in Figure 15.B.1. Verbalizations were categorized as questions or statements by inmates, supervisor, other staff, trainer, or program director, and it was then recorded to whom the verbalization was directed (or whether it was directed to the community as a whole): to inmate, supervisor, other staff, trainer, or program director. Next, each verbalization was coded by topic.

The object here was to ascertain the relative proportions of inmate and staff verbalizations, not in terms of duration, but rather the global verbalization rate of inmates and staff.*

---

*A different analysis might actually use a stop watch to measure the duration of staff and inmate verbalizations. Here, however, the global ratio of inmate/staff participation is examined. One could, with considerable difficulty, look at the proportion of inmates in the unit who participate. The evaluators' subjective judgment is that a higher proportion of Just Community inmates participated in unit meetings than was true for the Response program.

APPENDIX C

Recidivism Definition

Recidivism for the purpose of this analysis is defined as reincarceration with a new sentence by an individual discharged or released from a Connecticut correctional facility. Computer-based records of the Connecticut Department of Correction were examined to analyze the cases of inmates released or discharged from Connecticut correctional facilities who were graduates* of the female Just Community unit (C.C.I.N., Fenwick South). A 12-month follow-up was conducted for each inmate released or discharged. It was not meaningful to analyze only the cases of those inmates who had been discharged from Connecticut Correctional facilities, because the vast majority of the inmates who were in these units from November 1975, through November 1976 had not yet been discharged.† A meaningful number had, however, been released (to parole or community release) and data are presented for both released and discharged inmates, and then aggregated (see Table 15.6).

---

*Inmates in Just Community units a minimum of three months were defined as program graduates. This was the female Just Community program's definition of the minimum time "required" for program participation and program effect. Inmates in the Response program were defined in two ways: identified by staff as in the program, and in the unit for a minimum of three months (see Table 15.6).

†November 1975 was the time when the evaluators began systematic observation of the units. The November 1976 cut-off point was required to allow 12 months follow-up through November 1977 when these data were assembled. The importance of continuing to follow up these units and the inmates released and discharged through summer 1978 is of critical importance in evaluating the results of North Building II.

APPENDIX D

Informed Consent Document

HARVARD UNIVERSITY

GRADUATE SCHOOL OF EDUCATION

Roy E. Larsen Hall, Appian Way
Cambridge, Massachusetts 02138

21 February, 1978

_____

(Name)

    You are being asked to consent to take part in a research project being conducted by Dr. Roy Feldman, Research Associate at Harvard University and his staff. The project is designed to evaluate the effects of various prison programs and to understand your attitudes toward life, particularly ideas of fairness, justice and power. We guarantee that we shall maintain the confidentiality of any information you give us within the limits of the law. No one outside the research project will be able to connect your name to any of the information you give us. Any tape recordings or television recordings made by us are solely for research purposes and may not be used for any other purpose without your prior written consent. Any information we receive during the course of this research about your background or previous record will be kept confidential.

    The only direct benefits to you for taking part in the project is our hope that it will be interesting to you. You should feel free to deny your consent to participate at any time. There are no penalties whatsoever if you refuse to participate at any time.

    If you have any questions about the nature of the project, Dr. Feldman or one of his staff will be happy to discuss them with you now or during the course of the project.

*   *   *   *   *   *

I agree to take part in this study.

February, 1978

_____   _____

(Signature)   (Date)

_____

(Signature of staff making request)

Please sign 3 copies of this form and keep the top copy for yourself.

RF:lb

APPENDIX E

Intercoder Reliability on the Moral Judgment Interview

The Annual Report for the first year of this evaluation indicated that the intercoder reliability of the most expert scorers at the Harvard Center for Moral Education was not high enough to be able to detect the relatively small amount of moral growth they anticipated as a good outcome for these Just Community programs — growth of one-third of a stage. Much additional material was scored for the analysis reported here, but the intercoder reliability remains disturbingly low. It appears that gross differences in Moral Maturity Scores are clearly detectable, — for example, the differences consistently reported between staff and inmates, or between staff and supervisors (see Tables 15.4 and 15.5) — but small differences of the kind sought in these Just Community programs are either absent or sufficiently small to be masked by the error demonstrated in the intercoder reliability indexes.

Reliability Results During the First Year of this Study

Two expert scorers of the Harvard University Center for Moral Education, A. Colby and C. Power, scored 20 protocols coded to disguise all identification of person and time. Ten protocols were randomly selected from the pool of Form A interviews from this project and ten Form B interviews from the same source. The mean intercoder difference in Moral Maturity Score (MMS) points was 14.5 for Form A, 20.4 for Form B, and 17.45 (S.D. = 13.7) for the two forms combined. This is 14 percent of the range covered by the sample of scores. Intercoder reliability for global stage score was computed by using Scott's pi (π)[55] which represents the extent to which the scorers are doing better than chance agreement, given the distribution of categories of the dimension. Pi (π) was computed to be 0.25 for total agreement on the Global Score and 0.63 for agreement plus or minus one-third of a stage. Intracoder reliability (score/rescore) was computed by having the scorer rescore a set of 15 protocols at an interval of two weeks. An average discrepancy of 23 MMS points was found between the original and rescore of the same protocol. Eight protocols showed an increase, six a decrease, and one was unchanged.

RELIABILITY RESULTS DURING THE SECOND YEAR OF THIS STUDY

Virtually all of the protocols scored during the second year of this evaluation were scored by John Gibbs, credited by his colleagues with writing the revised Scoring Manual for Form A (August 1977). Form B Scoring Manual was still incomplete in the winter of 1977–78. The method of scoring Form B, therefore, was to use the criterion judgments developed for Form B and then project or extrapolate to what the scorer thought the Form B Manual would likely show when completed. Expert scorers at the Center for Moral Education describe their scoring for Form B as "winging-it." Because no scorer is reputed to be better than Dr. Gibbs, the scoring is likely to be as valid as possible at the present time. Nevertheless, Dr. Gibbs's intercoder reliability with a second expert scorer at the Center was not better than reported for two other expert scorers during the·first year of the project. The reliability and validity of the scoring is apparently the best that the current state of the art can produce. Intercoder reliability, however, is not high enough to objectively detect changes of one-third of a stage with much confidence. Scott's pi (π) was again used to represent the extent to which the scorers did better than chance agreement, given the distribution of categories used. Pi (π) was computed to be -0.15 for total agreement on the Global Score and 0.67 for agreement plus or minus one-third of a stage. For Form A the average difference between scorers in MMS was 23 MMS points. For Form B the average difference between scorers was 31 MMS points. Average error covered 18 percent of the range of scores found in the set of protocols used in examining the intercoder reliability.

Because the scoring scheme had changed from 1976 to 1977, reliability was also computed for the scoring done by the 1976 most expert scorer and the 1977 most expert scorer. Pi (π) was computed to be 0.13 for total Global Score agreement and 0.56 for agreement plus or minus one-third of a stage.

NOTES

Collection of data on the Just Community prison units in Connecticut was supported, in part, by the Connecticut Department of Correction and the National Institute of Correction (N.I.C.) in conjunction with LEAA Grant No. 73ED-89-0021. The second year of data collection was supported by a grant from the N.I.C. to the State of Connecticut Department of Correction, which in turn contracted with Harvard University. The opinions, findings, and conclusions of this paper are those of the author and not necessarily those of the Connecticut Department of Correction. The data collection at Connecticut prisons was made possible through the very able and dedicated research assistance of Leonard Shrier, a law student at Boston College, and Deborah Ashton, then a doctoral candidate at Harvard University in Clinical Psychology and Public Practice. The author's sincere appreciation is extended to Estelle Brown, Judy Crotty, Martha Kneen, Peter Baumgartel, and their staffs and the residents of the Connecticut Correctional Institution (C.C.I.), Niantic. Throughout this research they extended to the author and his colleagues their full cooperation, full access to their units, helpful advice, and encouragement. Institution Superintendents Janet York, Elizabeth Durland, and Dwaine Nickeson have been extraordinarily helpful during the course of this project. Special thanks are also due to Ron Cormier and Art Thomas of C.C.I., Cheshire, without whose help much of the data could not have been collected. The Connecticut Department of Correction reserves a royalty-free, nonexclusive, and irrevocable license to reproduce, publish, and use these materials.

1. See Lawrence Kohlberg, Peter Scharf, and Joseph Hickey, "The Justice Structure of the Prison — A Theory and an Intervention," *Prison Journal* 51 (1972): 3-14; Roy E. Feldman, "Second Annual Report Evaluating the Just Community Moral Development Units at the Connecticut Correctional Institution, Niantic, and the Training of Staff from Nevada, Kentucky, Iowa, and South Carolina in the Establishment of Just Community Units." Unpublished report to State of Connecticut Department of Corrections, Harvard University Graduate School of Education, January 1978.

2. E. R. Wasserman, "The Development of an Alternative High School Based on Kohlberg's Just Community Approach to Education." Ed.D. dissertation, Boston University School of Education, 1977.

3. P. Scharf and J. Hickey, "The Prison and the Inmate's Conception of Legal Justice: An Experiment in Democratic Education," *Criminal Justice and Behavior* 3 (1976): 107–22. Lawrence Kohlberg, "The Cognitive Developmental Approach to Moral Education," *Phi Delta Kappan* 56 (June 1975): 676.

4. Lawrence Kohlberg et al., "The Just Community Approach to Corrections: A Manual, Parts I and II" typed and offset (Cambridge, Mass.: Moral Education Research Foundation, 1974); for promotion of Just Community Schools see Edwin Fenton, "Moral Education: The Research Findings," *Journal of Social Education* 40 (1976).

5. Kohlberg, Scharf, and Hickey, "Justice Structure"; Scharf and Hickey, "The Prison"; Kohlberg, "Cognitive Developmental Approach"; Kohlberg et al., "Just Community Approach."

6. Feldman, "Second Annual Report."

7. Wasserman, "Development of an Alternative High School"; Feldman, "Second Annual Report."

8. E. R. Wasserman, "Implementing Kohlberg's 'Just Community Concept' in an Alternative High School," *Social Education* 40 (1976):203–7; Wasserman, "Development of an Alternative High School"; Kohlberg et al., "Just Community Approach"; Fenton, "Moral Education"; also see Edwin Fenton, "A Response to Jack R. Fraenkel (on the Cognitive Developmental Approach to Education)", *Social Education* 41 (1977): 56–61; Feldman, "Second Annual Report."

9. For example, *Journal of Moral Education; Moral Education Forum;* C. Beck, B. Crittenden and E. V. Sullivan, eds., *Moral Education: Interdisciplinary Approaches* (Toronto: University of Toronto Press, 1971); T. Lickona, ed., *Moral Development and Behavior: Theory Research and Social Issues* (New York: Holt, Rinehart and Winston, 1976); E. V. Sullivan et al., *Moral Learning* (Paramus, N.J.: Paulist Press, 1975); E. V. Sullivan, *Kohlberg's Structuralism: A Critical Appraisal* (Toronto: Ontario Institute for Studies in Education,

Monograph Series No. 15, 1977); Lawrence Kohlberg, "The Child as Moral Philosopher," *Psychology Today* 7 (September 1968): 25–30; R. E. Galbraith and T. M. Jones, *Moral Reasoning* (Anoka, Minnesota: Greenhaven Press, 1976); and "Teaching Strategies for Moral Dilemmas, An Application of Kohlberg's Theory to the Social Studies Classroom," *Social Education* 39 (1975): 16–22.

10. Sullivan, *Kohlberg's Structuralism.* Cf., D. Ausubel and E. V. Sullivan, *Theory and Problems of Child Development,* 2d ed. (New York: Grune and Stratton, 1970).

11. Sullivan, *Kohlberg's Structuralism.*

12. Ibid., p. 1.

13. J. Gibbs, "Kohlberg's Stages of Moral Judgment: A Constructive Critique," *Harvard Educational Review* 47 (1977): 43–61.

14. W. Kurtines and E. G. Greif, "The Development of Moral Thought: Review and Evaluation of Kohlberg's Approach," *Psychological Bulletin* 81 (1974): 453–70.

15. See R. W. Brown and R. J. Herrnstein, "Moral Reasoning and Conduct," in R. W. Brown and R. J. Herrnstein, *Psychology* (Boston: Little, Brown, 1975).

16. See *Journal of Social Education* 40 (April 1976).

17. See Jack L. Nelson, "The Uncomfortable Relationship between Moral Education and Citizenship Instruction," this volume; *Journal of Social Education* 40 (April 1976); W. J. Bennett and E. J. Delattre, "Moral Education in the Schools," *Public Interest* 50 (1978): 81–99.

18. Lawrence Kohlberg et al., "Assessing Moral Stages: A Manual for Form A of the Moral Judgment Interview," mimeographed (Cambridge, Mass.: Harvard University, 1976). The Form B manual was still incomplete in November 1977; see Lawrence Kohlberg et al., "Assessing Moral Stages: A Manual (Part IV)," mimeographed (Cambridge, Mass.: Harvard University, 1977). Incomplete

19. Lawrence Kohlberg, "Indoctrination Versus Relativity in Value Education," *Zygon* 7 (1972): 785–810.

20. Ibid.; Lawrence Kohlberg, "From Is to Ought: How to Commit the Naturalistic Fallacy and Get Away With It," in *Cognitive Development and Epistemology,* ed. Theodore Mischel (New York: Academic Press, 1971), pp. 164–71.

21. Kohlberg, "From Is to Ought," p. 153.

22. M. M. Blatt and Lawrence Kohlberg, "The Effects of Class Discussion Upon Children's Level of Moral Judgment," *Journal of Moral Education* 4 (February 1975): 129–61.

23. Kohlberg, "From Is to Ought," p. 153.

24. Lawrence Kohlberg, "Stage and Sequence: The Cognitive Developmental Approach to Socialization," in *Handbook of Socialization Theory and Research,* ed. David A. Goslin (N.Y.: Rand McNally, 1969), p. 395.

25. Kohlberg, "Cognitive Developmental Approach," p. 672.

26. Kohlberg, Scharf, and Hickey, "Justice Structure," p. 8.

27. Ibid., p. 9.

28. Ibid., p. 11.

29. Scharf and Hickey, "The Prison," p. 118.

30. Ibid., p. 119.

31. B. K. Beyer, "Conducting Moral Discussions in the Classroom," *Social Education* 40 (1976): 194–202.

32. Edwin Fenton, "Moral Education," p. 143.

33. Beyer, "Conducting Moral Discussions," p. 194.

34. Kohlberg et al., "Just Community Approach," p. 27.

35. Ibid., p. 28.

36. Ibid., p. 31.

37. Fenton, "Moral Education," p. 191.

38. Lawrence Kohlberg, and J. Reimer, (funded) Proposal to Ford Foundation, "Proposal for Research Evaluation of a Just Community School," (Harvard Graduate School of Education, September 16, 1975), pp. 4–5. Basically the same material is found in Wasserman, "Implementing Kohlberg's 'Just Community Concept' "; cf. Wasserman, "Development of an Alternative High School."

39. Kohlberg and Reimer, "Proposal," p. 9.

40. Ibid.

41. Kohlberg et al., "Just Community Approach."

42. Ibid.

43. Wasserman, "Development of an Alternative High School."

44. Kohlberg et al., "Just Community Approach."

45. Ibid., p. 57.

46. Scharf and Hickey, "The Prison."

47. Feldman, "Second Annual Report."

48. The founding fathers of the United States and students of American government since that time have pointed to the compatibility of majoritarian democracy and tyranny unless there are adequate checks and balances in the exercise of governing power. See Alexander Hamilton, John Jay, and James Madison, *The Federalist* (New York: Random House, N.D. [1937], originally published 1787–88), No. 47.

49. Wasserman, "Development of an Alternative High School."

50. Feldman, "Second Annual Report."

51. Wasserman, "Development of an Alternative High School."

52. Kohlberg et al., "Just Community Approach."

53. Cf., Wasserman, "Development of an Alternative High School."

54. Ibid.

55. W. A. Scott, "Reliability of Content Analysis: The Case of Nominal Scale Coding," *Public Opinion Quarterly* 19 (1955): 321–25.

INDEX

329

ABOUT THE EDITORS AND CONTRIBUTORS

RICHARD W. WILSON is Professor of Political Science and Director of International Programs at Rutgers University. Dr. Wilson has published widely in the area of political socialization. In addition to numerous articles, he is author of *Learning to be Chinese* (1970) and *The Moral State* (1974), and is coeditor of *Deviance and Social Control in Chinese Society* (1977) and *Value Change in Chinese Society* (1979). Dr. Wilson received his A.B., M.A. and Ph.D. from Princeton University.

GORDON J. SCHOCHET is Professor of Political Science at Rutgers University where he teaches social and political philosophy. His main interests are contemporary problems of authority and seventeenth- and eighteenth-century Anglo-American political thought. Among other publications he is the author of *Patriarchalism in Political Thought* (1975) and editor of *Life, Liberty, and Property* (1971). He received his B.A. and M.A. from Johns Hopkins University and his Ph.D. from the University of Minnesota.

ELIZABETH LANE BEARDSLEY is Professor of Philosophy at Temple University, Philadelphia. She has also taught at Lincoln University (Pa.) and the University of Delaware. Dr. Beardsley has published in philosophical journals papers on moral philosophy, legal philosophy, and philosophy of language. She is coeditor (with M. C. Beardsley) of the *Foundations of Philosophy* series.

DANIEL CANDEE has been a Research Associate at Harvard University since 1973 at the Center for Moral Education. His major fields of specialization are social psychology and developmental psychology and he has published articles in a number of journals including the *Journal of Personality and Social Psychology,* and the *Journal of Social Issues.* Dr. Candee received his B.A. from Clark University and his Ph.D. from the University of Chicago.

ALAN M. COHEN is a judicial clerk with the U.S. District Court for the Southern District of New York, New York City. Until 1979 he taught courses on a part-time basis in Legal Reasoning and Law and Politics at University College and Livingston College of Rutgers University. Dr. Cohen's unpublished doctoral dissertation is entitled *A Critique of John Rawls' A Theory of Justice: The Use and Misuse of Moral Development Theories in Political Thought.* He holds a B.A. from Temple University and a Ph.D. and J.D. from Rutgers University, New Brunswick, New Jersey.

335

ROY E. FELDMAN is a Research Associate at the Harvard University Graduate School of Education and Senior Research Associate at the Boston University Regional Institute on Employment Policy. Between 1966 and 1975 he was a member of the political science faculty at M.I.T. His major concern is the interaction of social research and social policy. Dr. Feldman has published in the areas of cross-national social psychology, the education and employment of disadvantaged youth, and on ethical aspects of social experiments. His articles and reviews have appeared in the *Journal of Personality and Social Psychology, The Public Interest,* the *Journal of Interdisciplinary History,* and the *American Political Science Review.* Dr. Feldman holds a B.A. and M.A. from The Johns Hopkins University and a Ph.D. from Harvard University.

JAMES S. FISHKIN is Assistant Professor of Political Science at Yale University where he holds a joint appointment with the Institution for Social and Policy Studies. Dr. Fishkin is the coeditor (with Peter Laslett) of the fifth volume of *Philosophy, Politics and Society* (1979) and the author of *Tyranny and Legitimacy: A Critique of Political Theories* (1979). He holds a B.A. from Yale College, a Ph.D. in political science from Yale and a Ph.D. in philosophy from Cambridge, England.

IRVING LOUIS HOROWITZ holds the Hanna Arendt Chair of Sociology at Rutgers University. On the editorial boards of many journals and publishing houses, he is Editor-in-Chief of *Transaction/Society* Magazine. Dr. Horowitz has been Visiting Professor at a number of academic institutions, including the London School of Economics and Political Science, Stanford University, Hebrew University of Jerusalem, and Princeton University. He is the author of over 25 books of which his most recent publications include: *Dialogues on American Politics* (1978), *Science, Sin and Scholarship: The Politics of Reverend Moon and the Unification Church* (1978), and *Ideology and Utopia in the U.S.: 1956–1976* (1977). Dr. Horowitz received a B.S. in Social Science from City College of New York, an M.A. from Columbia University and a Ph.D. from Buenos Aires University.

LAWRENCE KOHLBERG is Professor of Education and Social Psychology at Harvard University. He has published widely in the area of psychosocial development and the growth of logical thinking, as well as moral development. Among his better known works are: "Stage and Sequence: The Cognitive-Developmental Approach to Socialization," in D. Goslin (Ed.), *Handbook of Socialization Theory and Research* (1969); "Education for Justice: A Modern Statement of the Platonic View," in T. Sizer (Ed.) *Moral Education* (1970); "From Is To Ought," in T. Mischel (Ed.) *Genetic Epistemology* (1970); "Development as the Aim of Education," *Harvard Educational Review* (1972); and "Moral Stages and Moralization: The Cognitive-Developmental Approach," in T. Lickona, (Ed.) *Moral Development and Behavior* (1976). Dr. Kohlberg obtained his Ph.D. in 1958 from the University of Chicago and in 1969 he received the Research Scientist Award from the National Institute of Mental Health. In 1974 he founded the Center for Moral Development and Moral Education at Harvard. This Center conducts moral development research and projects with persons and schools in the New England area.

JACK L. NELSON is Professor of Education at the Graduate School of Education, Rutgers University. He was an Assistant Professor of Education at California State University, Los Angeles, and Associate Professor at SUNY, Buffalo, in addition to being a visiting scholar at Colgate, Colorado University, Homerton College, Cambridge University, and University of California, Berkeley. Dr. Nelson has published eleven books on educational and social science subjects. His articles, papers, and reviews have appeared in *Theory and Research in Social Education, Educational Leadership, Social Science Record, AAUP Bulletin, Educational Studies, The Humanist, Social Education* and *The Annals of the American Academy of Political and Social Science,* among others. Dr. Nelson obtained his B.A. from the University of Denver, M.A. from California State University, Los Angeles, and Ed.D. from the University of Southern California.

ROBERT E. O'CONNOR is an Associate Professor of Political Science at the Pennsylvania State University. He is interested in mass politics and political psychology, and his articles have appeared in the *American Political Science Review, British Journal of Political Science, American Behavioral Scientist, Legislative Studies Quarterly, Administration and Society, Growth and Change,* and other journals and edited books. He is the coauthor of *Politics and Structure.* Professor O'Connor holds a B.A. from Johns Hopkins University and a Ph.D. from the University of North Carolina, Chapel Hill.

HERBERT G. REID is Associate Professor of Political Science at the University of Kentucky, Lexington, where he has taught since 1968. A member of the editorial board for the new journal *Human Studies,* he is interested particularly in social phenomenology, critical theory, cultural hermeneutics, and political education. Dr. Reid has published widely in the area of political and social theory. His articles have appeared in several journals including *Politics and Society, Cultural Hermeneutics,* the *Review of Politics, Theory and Society,* and the *Canadian Journal of Political and Social Theory.* He also has edited a volume on the problem of ideology in American politics and culture available from Longmans, Inc. Dr. Reid holds a B.A. from the University of Kansas, an M.A. from the University of Tennessee, and a Ph.D. from the University of North Carolina at Chapel Hill.

EDWARD SCHWARTZ is President of the Institute for the Study of Civic Values in Philadelphia, national coordinator of the Alliance for Citizen Education, and a board member of the National Association of Neighborhoods. He is currently writing a book about political education.

LARRY D. SPENCE is the author of *The Politics of Social Knowledge.* An Associate Professor of Political Science at The Pennsylvania State University, he teaches political theory and conducts research in the areas of bureaucracy and the politics of technology. He received his Ph.D. from the University of California at Berkeley.

ERNEST J. YANARELLA is Associate Professor of Political Science at the University of Kentucky, Lexington, Kentucky, where he has taught since 1970. The author of a recent book and over a dozen articles, Dr. Yanarella has published in the areas of contemporary political theory, critical peace research, and the philosophy of the social sciences. His book, *The Missile Defense Controversy: Strategy, Technology, and Politics, 1955–1972,* was published in 1977 by the University Press of Kentucky. His articles have appeared in a wide variety of scholarly journals, including *Polity, Theory & Society,* the *Review of Politics,* the *International Journal of Political Education, International Interactions,* the *Journal of Peace Research, Peace and Change,* and *Cultural Hermeneutics.* Dr. Yanarella holds a B.A. from Syracuse University and a Ph.D. from the University of North Carolina at Chapel Hill.

JULIE ZATZ is a Study Director with the Committee on Child Development Research and Public Policy of the National Academy of Sciences in Washington, D.C. She is directing research for the Panel on the Study of Public Policies Contributing to the Institutionalization and Deinstitutionalization of Children and Youth. Previously Ms. Zatz was an Assistant Professor of Political Science at Tulane University and a Research Fellow at the Brookings Institution. She holds a B.A. from American University, an M.A. from Arizona State University, and a Ph.D. from the University of Minnesota.